Doctors, Lawyers,
Indian Chiefs

Doctors, Lawyers, Indian Chiefs

Jim Thorpe & Pop Warner's Carlisle Indian School football immortals tackle socialites, bootleggers, students, moguls, prejudice, the government, ghouls, tooth decay and rum.

Tom Benjey

TUXEDO PRESS

Carlisle, Pennsylvania

© 2008 by Tom Benjey

Published by Tuxedo Press
Carlisle, PA 17015
Tuxedo-Press.com

17 16 15 14 13 12 11 10 09 08 5 4 3 2

ISBN 978-0-9774486-7-8

Cover illustration by Vic Lambdin, *The Syracuse Herald*, November 18, 1911;
Courtesy Onondaga Historical Association, Syracuse, NY

Frontispiece by Lone Star Dietz for *A Course in Football for
Players and Coaches* by Glenn S. Warner, 1912

Library of Congress Cataloging-in-Publication Data

Benjey, Tom.
    Doctors, Lawyers, Indian Chiefs: Jim Thorpe & Pop Warner's Carlisle Indian
        School football immortals tackle socialites, bootleggers, students, moguls,
        prejudice, the government, ghouls, tooth decay and rum / Tom Benjey.
    p. cm.
    Includes bibliographical references and index.
ISBN 978-0-9774486-7-8
1. United States Indian School (Carlisle, Pa.)—Football. 2. Football players—United
States—Biography. 3. Football coaches—United States—Biography. I. Title.
GV958.U33B46 2008
796.332'630974843—dc22
[B]
                                                                    2008010775
                                                                        CIP

This book is dedicated to the men
and women who attended Carlisle Indian School
and succeeded in spite of the numerous
obstacles placed in their paths.

Table of Contents

Foreword

I am honored and privileged to write this Foreword for Tom Benjey and his book, *Doctors, Lawyers, Indian Chiefs*. Tom has clearly become the foremost authority on the contribution of Native Americans to competitive athletics—most notably football and track and field—in America. His recent book, *Keep A goin': The Life of Lone Star Dietz,* is an excellent companion piece to two recently published best sellers regarding the Carlisle Indians, *The Real All-Americans* by Sally Jenkins and *Carlisle vs. Army* by Lars Anderson. Now—with *Doctors, Lawyers Indian Chiefs*, readers are introduced to the on and off the field accomplishments of great Native American athletes—not only the legendary Jim Thorpe but also notables like Frank Mount Pleasant, William Baine and Pete Hauser—whose stories are relatively unknown.

This book brings back wonderful personal memories for me. Memories of the Carlisle Indian School, Haskell Institute, my Alma Mater, Indiana University of Pennsylvania, and the College Football Hall of Fame.

I was a career military officer, serving in the US Army for over 29 years. In 1981, I attended the Army War College at Carlisle Barracks—the site of the Carlisle Indian School—in Carlisle, Pennsylvania. It was my privilege to play basketball in the same gymnasium and run laps on the same track as Thorpe, Lone Star, and Gus Welch. The biggest annual extra-curricular event at the War College is Jim Thorpe Sports Day. It is competition in ten sports among the military's senior service schools, the Army, Navy and Air Force War Colleges plus the National War College and the Industrial College of the Armed Forces. For two days, these future generals forget their military studies and compete for the honor of taking home the Jim Thorpe Sports Day Trophy. I was the Athletic Director for the 1982 Sports Day and in that capacity came to know Carl Thorpe, Jim's son, quite well. I still treasure the photo of Carl and me presenting the Sports Day awards.

The Great Haskell. This is the name given it by the proud students and graduates during its glory years—the decade of the 1920's. The Haskell Indian School—later called Haskell Institute—opened in Lawrence, Kansas—where I now reside—in 1884. From its beginnings, the young Indian boys loved to participate in sports: football, baseball and track and field.

In *Doctors, Lawyers, Indian Chiefs*, Tom cites thirteen Carlisle Indians who also attended, or in the cases of Lone Star Dietz and Gus Welch, coached Haskell. They represented the most noble tribes in our nation: Sioux, Chippewa, Sac and Fox, Cheyenne, Flathead, Cherokee and Oneida. Two of them, Thorpe and Joe Guyon, are enshrined in both the College and Pro Football Halls of Fame. William Baine earned football letters at Haskell, the University of Kansas and Carlisle—the only athlete known to do so. Pete Hauser is arguably the finest punter in the first half of the Twentieth Century. The list goes on and on and on. As the preeminent college football historian, Ray Schmidt, noted in his *Shaping College Football: The Transformation of an American Sport*, when Carlisle closed its doors in 1918, Haskell became the recipient of the best Indian athletes in America and emerged as a football powerhouse.

In 1991, I attended an American Indian Sports Hall of Fame Ceremony at Haskell. The undefeated 1926 Haskell Fightin' Indians football team was inducted into the Hall. Following dinner, I had an unforgettable conversation with two standout members of that team, Elijah Smith and Albert Hawley. Grace Thorpe—Jim's daughter—was also there. While I was talking with Smith and Hawley, she came up to me, introduced herself and said, "I understand you are doing research on Knute Rockne. You should know that he gave a very inspirational and pro-Indian speech to the entire Haskell student body in February of 1931—one month before his death in that airplane crash in the Flint Hills." Grace's words inspired me to become a Rockne Scholar, writing numerous articles and developing several presentations regarding the life and career of this special man.

One other personal connection for me in this book involves Frank Mount Pleasant. Frank was an outstanding quarterback and track man at Carlisle. He also was the head football and baseball coach at my Alma Mater—Indiana University of Pennsylvania (IUP)—then called Indiana Normal School—from 1911-1913. His 23-4-1 gridiron record is the finest registered by any coach in IUP football history. Mount Pleasant is a member of our school's Athletic Hall of Fame—the only Native American so honored—and, by a college whose nickname until two years ago was "The Big Indians."

Finally, while serving as Executive Director of the College Football Hall of Fame from 1995-2005, I took special pride in showcasing the contributions of Native Americans to college football. We had two special exhibits: one devoted to the Carlisle Indians and the other to the Fightin' Indians of Haskell. Both received high praise from our visitors.

So—Tom Benjey—I salute you for your latest effort in preserving the legacy of a group of forgotten American athletes and patriots. Don't stop now, as Lone Star said, "Keep A-Goin.'" There is much more yet to be told.

BERNIE KISH, Ph.D.

Lawrence, Kansas
July 23, 2008.

Preface and Acknowledgements

The journey to research the life of Lone Star Dietz had a definite start, but this trip was different. While delving into the beginnings of the single-wing offense, I had developed an interest in Frank Mt. Pleasant and had started looking into his life. Then Lynn Myers, who narrated *The Birth of Modern Football*, shared that William Gardner had been one of Eliot Ness's Untouchables. A casual conversation with Ann, my wife, about these two Carlislers evolved into a discussion of how interesting these men's later lives must have been. And there were surely others on these teams who did great or small things of note. Almost immediately, I was off researching and looking at Steckbeck to determine whom I should research. Roy Sye, a researcher with the Professional Football Researchers Association (PFRA), came to the rescue with a spreadsheet of all the Carlisle players of whom he was aware. Selecting people for inclusion was an arbitrary decision based largely on the amount of publicly available information that was found for the person. I probably left out someone or someones whose stories belong in the book. For that I apologize and promise to put them in the second edition if we are blessed with the need for one and if people come forward with information on them.

Organizing the stories was a challenge because I didn't want to write an encyclopedia of separate stories that seem unrelated. Arranging the men for whom enough information was available to devote entire chapters was relatively simple. The challenge for them was to place their stories in an order that makes sense to the reader. I made the arbitrary decision to include chapters for Jim Thorpe, Lone Star Dietz and Pop Warner, although book-length biographies are available for them because many readers may not be very familiar with them, and they played important roles in the Carlisle Indian School story. Fortunately, I stumbled across a few tidbits about these men that aren't widely known that should make those chapters a little more interesting to readers who are familiar with them. But what to do with those men for whom I couldn't find enough material to fill an entire chapter?

After a time, I noticed that several of them were brothers and that several of them were team captains. Later I realized that a number of them had played on all-Indian teams after leaving Carlisle. Finding a finish for the book took longer. Eventually it came to me that Stacy Matlock, whose football injury almost caused Carlisle to never field a team, was also a chief in later life and made the book come full circle. By this time I had a title but that's a story in itself.

I used a few different working titles while writing the beginning chapters but none of them seemed to fit perfectly. Kathy Aberman, my editor, and I were discussing the book one day when she asked what became of the players. I answered that they had become doctors, lawyers and Indian chiefs, literally. Immediately I knew I had my title.

Constructing histories of so many people requires the assistance of numerous people at numerous libraries and archives. Organizing their names into a meaningful order is impossible, so they are mentioned in no particular order at all. It's impossible to research people who have attended government boarding schools without looking at archives in Oklahoma because many were at Chilocco or lived parts of their lives in Oklahoma. Bill Welge and his staff at the Oklahoma State Historical Society helped immensely as usual. Milissa Burkart, Department of Special Collections, University of Tulsa ferreted out information related to the single-wing, Albert Exendine, and his bookend, William Gardner. Gladys Kitchen, Secretary of Pawnee County Historical Society, did her best to find information related to Stacy Matlock. Ken Crippen of PFRA provided hard-to-find information on the early days of professional football. Sara J. MacDonald of The University of the Arts in Philadelphia found a long-forgotten article about Lone Star Dietz in her archives to provide some new information about Dietz's theatric introduction to Philadelphia. Lawrence Stark of Washington State University provided his usual high level of excellence with information regarding Gus Welch and Albert Exendine as he previously had for Lone Star Dietz.

Researching William Baine was a challenge made easier by Tara Wenger, Reference Librarian, Kenneth Spencer Research Library, The University of Kansas and David Null, Director, University Archives, University of Wisconsin-Madison. Janet Dotterer, Special Collections & University Archives, Ganser Library, Millersville University, found and scanned a photo found in an article in an obscure 19th century publication.

William Gardner's granddaughter, Diane E. Garrard, interviewed her mother and provided a scan of her grandparents' wedding. She also put the author in contact with her aunt and cousin. The information Diane provided could never have been found in public records and rounds out her grandfather's story. Others who provided information about Gardner's time at their institutions include: Kathryn Stallard, Head, Special Collections, Southwestern University; Mike McDaniel, Director of Alumni, duPont Manual High School, Louisville; D. Pratt Paterson, Sports Information Director, Sewanee: The University of the South; and Mark Podvia, Associate Law Librarian and Archivist, University Libraries, The Dickinson School of Law of the Pennsylvania State University. D. Pratt Paterson also photographed the Gardner house on the Sewanee campus.

Several archivists located information on Frank Cayou's career stops: Linda Stahnke of University of Illinois University Archives; Barbara Larsen of the National Archives – Central Plains Region; Christopher Mitchell, Director, Sports Information, Washington University in St. Louis; Miranda Rectenwald, Assistant - University Archives, Washington University Libraries; Jill Gage, Reference Librarian, The Newberry Library, Chicago; and John R. Woods, Athletic Director, Champaign Central High School.

Help was needed for several of Frank Mt. Pleasant's career stops. Rhonda Bennett & Carol Bowman of West Virginia Wesleyan College not only pulled out the college's documents and local newspapers containing information about Mt. Pleasant but brought us information related to William Garlow, Pete Calac and Joe Guyon. Michael R. Lear aided me immensely with Mt. Pleasant's time at Franklin and Marshall College. Mike Hoffman, Sports Information Director, Dr. Theresa McDevitt, Special Collections Librarian, as well as Amanda K. Piper and Jessica Oliver, student workers, all of Indiana University of Pennsylvania (IUP) provided information on Mt. Pleasant's time in western Pennsylvania. Patricia M. Virgil, Director of Library & Archives, Buffalo and Erie County Historical Society, located information on Frank's time in Buffalo. Ed Farnham, grandnephew of Frank Mt. Pleasant and grandson of Mamie Mt. Pleasant, provided family insight into this mostly forgotten man.

Hall-of-Famer Joe Guyon and his brother, Charlie Wahoo, each required much research. For Joe, Alan Donhoff of St. Xavier High School Alumni Association, Louisville; Steven L. Baker, Associate VP for Academic Resources & Library Director, Emma Waters Summar Library, Union University; and Dennis S. Taylor, University Archivist, Special Collections, Clemson University Libraries dug through their files. Charlie's was more difficult to find. Ward B. Crabill, Eastern High School class of '41, recalled Charlie from the time he was a student. Dr. Kay Varnado, Librarian, Eastern Sr. High School, rooted through old yearbooks from the 1940s. And Shannon Lee, Reference Librarian, Historical Society of Washington DC, identified books on Eastern High that included chapters on Wahoo.

Nancy F. Rubenstein, Head Reference Librarian, Beeghly Library, Heidelberg College in Tiffin, Ohio assisted with the author's pouring over documents relevant to Dr. Caleb Sickles. Jay Garvie shared photos that his grandfather, Leon Boutwell's roommate, received from his old roommate after he left Carlisle. Debbi Young, Mechanicsburg Public Library, Mechanicsburg, Ohio, found public records pertinent to Leon's time in her town. Donald Erlenkotter, Professor Emeritus of Management, University of California, Los Angeles, researched the Boutwell family's long and glorious history.

Several people contributed information regarding Albert Exendine, including: Lynn Conway, Georgetown University Archivist; Michael B. Carey, Sports Information Director, Georgetown University; Kathleen Mazza, Recruiting Coordinator, Otterbein College Athletic Department; Stephen D. Grinch, Archivist, Otterbein College; Jeremy Liles, Northeastern State College; and Tom Cantrell, Superintendent, Anadarko High School.

Ann M. Kenne, Head of Special Collections Department / University Archivist, University of St. Thomas, St. Paul exhumed data and photos of Albert Exendine's stint at University of St. Thomas. Mary Caldera, Archivist, Yale University Library confirmed that Thomas St. Germain had indeed graduated from that institution's law school. Yale also had an obituary for him.

Marty Fuller, Sports Information Director at Kenyon College, provided information regarding Bemus Pierce's time in Gambier, Ohio, where he coached the Lords. Three people aided in the research of Bemus's brother, Hawley, particularly regarding his career as a railroad engineer. Sharon Turano, reporter for *The Jamestown Post-Journal*, did a piece on a 2008 calendar that features Hawley Pierce. Sue Grey of the Seneca-Iroquois National Museum located Hawley's obituary. Shawn B. Riley, volunteer with the Salamanca Rail Museum Association provided scans of a P B & R Railroad employee magazine.

Several people assisted with locating information on Gus Welch as football took him from coast to coast. Susan McElrath, Team Leader for University Archives and Special Collections, American University; Michael Colley, Asst. Athletics Media Relations Director, University of Virginia; Chris Kilcoyne, Sports Info Director, Randolph-Macon College; and Dan Paro, Director of Athletics, Head Football Coach, Georgetown Prep; all searched their archives for materials pertaining to Welch's time at their institution.

Perhaps the most surprising research was that done for James Phillips as he moved from the mountains of North Carolina to the Pacific Ocean. John Hawkins, Museum Director, Collettsville Historical Society, Inc., located information on the North Carolina branch of the Philips family. James Brown recalled his grandfather as he knew him. His wife, Coleen, scanned photos of James Phillips and emailed them to the author. Martin W. Kay and Derek Cook aided by providing information about Phillips' relationship with Aberdeen public schools.

Kevin B. Leonard, University Archives, Northwestern University Library, dug out information, largely from yearbooks, about James Johnson, James Phillips and Charles Williams. Bryan McDaniel of Chicago History Museum Research Center located photos of Carlisle and Northwestern players. Cindy Jungenberg of the Stockbridge-Munsee Library/Museum in Bowler, WI located newspaper articles and a letter from James Johnson's sister. Joan Gosnell, University Archives, DeGolyer Library, Southern Methodist University, searched for materials about Victor Kelley when he coached that school. Elizabeth Nielsen, Senior Staff Archivist, Archives – Oregon State University Libraries, located information about Emil Hauser after he moved to Oregon.

Sampson Bird's grandchildren were invaluable aids by relating their experiences with their grandfather. Stan Juneau put the author in touch with two other grandchildren. Liane Johnson interviewed her mother, Sam's daughter, who related stories about her father that would likely have been lost. Dick Bird related some of his experiences with his grandfather and told about the annual rodeo that was named in Sam's honor.

Julia Stringfellow, Lawrence University Archives, Appleton, WI, shared information about the liberal arts college that Nicholas Bowen attended for a time. Information about Joel and Hugh Wheelock was provided by Frank Mols and Julia Harvey, Vernon and Doris Bishop Library, Lebanon Valley College, Annville, PA, and Karen Aurand, Executive Secretary, Mifflin County Historical Society. Bradley D. Cook, Curator of Photographs, Office of University Archives & Records Management, Indiana University, found a seldom-seen photo of Jim Thorpe in an Indiana football uniform.

Carol Nahrwold, Allen County Public Library, Ft. Wayne, IN, found some information about Dr. Louis Island's later days and put the author in contact with nephew Dick Boganwright and niece Iris Davis, who shared their memories of Dr. Island. Great-grandson Geoffrey Johnston provided missing information. Michael Flanagan, Archivist & Research Center Manager, Onondaga Historical Association, Syracuse, NY, located the original newspaper in which the cover art was originally printed.

Rusty Shunk, Executive Vice-President, Dickinson College, arranged for the author to use the college's inter-library loan facilities. Debbie Ege, College Archives, Dickinson College, assisted the author in researching Carlisle athletes who attended Dickinson College, the prep school or Dickinson School of Law. Richard Tritt, Photo Curator at Cumberland County Historical Society, located numerous photos and researched the identities of players on a team photo. Fred Wardecker, of Wardecker's Mens Wear, Carlisle, discussed those athletes he remembered coming into the store and shared his many documents and photographs. Jeff Wood, proprietor of Whistlestop Bookshop, Carlisle, provided needed advice concerning arcanity known to booksellers such as BISACs. Authors Bill Crawford and Bob Wheeler and publicist Anne Dozier gave me much-needed encouragement while working on the book. Ives Goddard, Senior Linguist, Emeritus, Smithsonian Institution, provided insight and opinions regarding the prevalence of swear words in Indian languages. By editing the book, Kathy Aberman made the book more readable by correcting the author's grammar and providing editorial support of various natures. Graphic designer Keevin Graham laid out the book to be pleasing to the eye of the reader and put the numerous photos into useful form, a task that required much patience. Rhonda Newton proofread the finished manuscript, finding things the rest of us missed. And last, but far from least, I thank Ann for her assistance and patience with what she must by now see as an endless project.

Introduction

The on-field accomplishments of the Carlisle Indian School football team have been written about several times and were remarkable. Moreover, the accomplishments, both on- and off-field, of these men after they left Carlisle, are equally impressive. Over a quarter century before Indians were granted citizenship and the right to vote, three-quarters of a century before the 1965 Civil Rights Bill, and almost a century before affirmative action, Carlisle Indian School football teams competed toe-to-toe with the best in the land and more than held their own. Some today may consider the Carlisle School to be affirmative action in its purest form because enrollment was limited to students of at least one-quarter Indian blood with tuition, room, board, clothing and health care being paid by the government. Others view Carlisle quite differently. They think Richard Henry Pratt's assimilation policy of full immersion into the dominant society stripped students of their heritage and alienated them from their families and tribes. Regardless of one's opinion of Pratt, an extraordinary number of the Carlisle football players overcame obstacles placed in their way by prejudice common at that time and accomplished much in life after leaving the school. This book is the story of their triumphs and failures. Unfortunately, only those whose activities were recorded at the time in newspapers or were saved in archives can be written about. There are surely many others whose lives are worthy of inclusion but for whom documentation has not been found.

John S. Steckbeck's 1951 seminal *Fabulous Redmen: the Carlisle Indians and their famous football teams* provided a year-by-year history of the legendary Carlisle Indian Industrial School (CIIS) football program, a variety of statistics about the team, and blurbs about coaches and individual players. Much has been written about mega-star Jim Thorpe and Coach of All Ages Pop Warner. The author recently completed the biography of Lone Star Dietz. These three were not the only Carlisle football stars by any means. They're not even the only Carlisle Indians in the College Football Hall of Fame. Besides Thorpe, five other players were inducted years ago, and Lone Star Dietz is on the 2008 ballot for induction as a coach. At least twelve others received All-America mention. Warner is in the Hall in good part due to the work he did coaching the Indians and developing formations that mitigated their weaknesses and exploited their strengths.

Some – many as it turns out – Carlisle players continued their football careers after leaving the school, some as coaches, some as players and some both as players and coaches. So many of them went into coaching that they helped make the Warner system the dominant offensive scheme during the first half of the 20th century. Some were present at the birth of professional football and wet-nursed the NFL when it was in its infancy. Carlisle Indian School footballers played important roles in the development of the sport from the late 1890s through the 20th century up to WWII. Some lived public lives outside of sports and made their mark in other fields after departing from Carlisle. Unfortunately, few people alive today are aware of the Indians' contributions and their names have been largely forgotten. This book attempts to correct that situation. Those who led private lives after leaving Carlisle left behind little documentation of the accomplishments which makes them difficult to cover. The information that can be found on them is interjected at appropriate places. Because there is no obvious thread among these individuals other than they played football at Carlisle, the book takes the form of a set of mini-biographies.

The first chapter of the book is a brief history of the Carlisle program, from birth to demise. It is intended that this chapter will provide the reader a framework from which to relate the individuals to the team and the phase of the program. The second chapter is a brief history of professional football in America, the early part of which overlaps closely with Carlisle's lifespan. This chapter is necessary because independent or professional football provided opportunities for Carlisle players after their schooling was completed. Indians also played major roles in developing the new game. Two of them, Jim Thorpe and Joe Guyon, are enshrined in the Professional Football Hall of Fame in Canton, Ohio. The third chapter covers Glenn S. "Pop" Warner, the coach for the glory days of the football program and a factor in these men's lives. Because Warner is referenced so frequently, it is clearer for the reader unfamiliar with him for his chapter to precede the players' chapters rather than follow them.

The remaining chapters cover Carlisle players to varying levels of detail, dependent largely on the amount of information that can be found about the person. Some require dedicated chapters, others grouped together either by association, time, or family relationship. Their stories will be arranged in chronological order according to when they left Carlisle – more or less. An exception includes the chapters covering Lone Star Dietz, Gus Welch and Al Exendine, which are placed in the order they coached Washington State to improve the flow of the narrative. Little further needs to be written about Jim Thorpe, Pop Warner or Lone Star Dietz, but some readers may not be familiar with their histories. Therefore, a chapter is dedicated to each to provide a background for the unfamiliar. It is my hope that a previously undiscovered nugget or two about each of them finds its way into the narrative. The amount of space devoted to the others is not intended to be a measure of the significance of their contributions. The amount of information available about them today is the limiting factor. Professional football received little press in its early days, leaving behind fewer contemporaneous accounts of games and meetings than we'd like. Some players and coaches received little press due to their personalities, and others toiled in out-of-the-way places. The author hopes that people familiar with persons included in this book will share enough tidbits previously unknown about those players to make a second edition necessary. Also hoped for is that enough information surfaces about players regarding whom little was known to make a second edition necessary. Little is included about the girls who attended Carlisle beyond those who married players and James Phillips's little talk about their importance to the team, not because their stories aren't interesting but because that would require an entire book of its own.

Col. Pratt raised the issue of how football players perform in later life at the 1902 football banquet in his talk titled, "By their fruits you shall know them." Pratt talked about how he came to discuss this topic and then talked about the methodology he used in his "study:"

> "I went to the old football pictures, called on the memories of oldest inhabitants and used my own, and succeeded in getting together the names of sixty who have played on our first teams and have gone out from the school. I have put down here and made a mark opposite each one from my memory and the memories of those who know most about it, and from the best information we have I find some very singular results.
>
> ...

"Of the list of sixty who played on the first teams (I may not have them all) I have written opposite the names of forty-nine the letters 'O. K.' You know what that means.

"There are only five of the sixty named that we need be ashamed of. There are four about whom I have been unable to get any information. That leaves two. We have been playing football more than twelve years and have sent out from the school at least sixty, as I have said, who played on our first teams, and only two of the sixty have passed away, and that shows that football is a healthy business."

This was the first known attempt to determine how or if football players succeeded after leaving school, but it wouldn't be the last. On at least two other occasions, in 1907 and 1910, and likely others, Superintendents Mercer and Friedman sent questionnaires to former athletes to gather data on their lives after Carlisle. Many of the quotes in this book that the athletes themselves wrote about Carlisle come from those questionnaires that can be found in former student files. It is likely that the superintendents were selective in determining to whom to send questionnaires, more selective in determining which results to keep in the files and even more selective in choosing responses to print in school publications. So, the results may well have been biased to make the school look good, but the responses that survive were freely given and accurately reflect the thinking of the person writing them.

While researching this book, the author perused a number of census forms and made some observations. Prior to and during their time at Carlisle, students were generally listed on special forms used specifically for populations likely to contain Indians. A section of the form listed the tribes of the person and the person's parents. It also included the fraction of white blood the student was thought to have. The data on these forms was often incorrect because the child did not know the correct information or because the census taker made assumptions and errors. After leaving Carlisle, those who assimilated into the larger society were often classified as white in future censuses, probably because census takers didn't bother to ask. Indians in the population may have been undercounted as a result.

Period illustrations, particularly cartoons, will be included where appropriate to show how the Carlisle team was treated, even by big city newspapers. Today many of these caricatures with oversized noses and other exaggerations would be considered racist. Others make fun of the patricians the Indians so often defeated.

Sit back and enjoy reading about the exploits of Frank Cayou, Bill Gardner, Pete Calac, Joe Guyon, Frank Mt. Pleasant, Gus Welch, the Pierce brothers, Al Exendine and all the rest. You will surely become acquainted with some interesting individuals you may have never heard of before. Surely some interesting people will be missed. It is the author's hopes that this book will cause information about them to surface to necessitate a second edition.

Min-ni-wa-ka!
Ka-wa-wi!
Woop her up!
Woop her up!
Who are we?
Carlisle!
Carlisle!!
Carlisle!!!

1

Carlisle's Football Trail of Glory

In 1875, Lt. Richard Henry Pratt, after many years of leading Buffalo Soldiers in battle against Kiowa, Cheyenne and Arapaho warriors, was assigned the task of transporting 72 Indian prisoners to St. Augustine, Florida for three years of incarceration at Ft. Marion. During the imprisonment, with the influence of Quaker reformers, Pratt evolved the belief that the only hope for Indians to survive in the modern world was to assimilate into the majority culture, much as European immigrants were assimilating. His view was in sharp contrast to that of those who believed that extermination was the only viable option. Gen. Philip Sheridan denied having said, "The only good Indians I ever saw were dead." If he believed it, he was far from alone as that was a very common belief held at the time.

Their confinement over, Lt. Pratt convinced 17 of his former prisoners to pursue further education at Hampton Institute (now Hampton University). The Hampton, Virginia school had been founded a decade earlier by Gen. Samuel Chapman Armstrong as a boarding school to educate recently freed slaves by training "the head, the hand, and the heart." Educating African-Americans and Indians in the same facility, albeit segregated from each other, was controversial to some in those times of racial segregation as many thought that blacks and Indians were not educable. However, the experiment was successful enough that Hampton Institute continued its Indian division until 1923.

Richard Pratt, also a missionary's son, summarized his philosophy as, "Kill the Indian, save the man." He formulated a model similar to that being used at Hampton and successfully lobbied the government to set up a school just for Indians at an unused Army post. On October 6, 1879, Lt. Pratt, considered by some to be "an honest lunatic," and the first contingent of students, largely sons of Lakota chiefs (boys had little economic value when confined to reservations because they could no longer hunt buffalo or make war, but families could still receive a bride price for girls), arrived at the Carlisle Indian Industrial School located in Carlisle Barracks, adjacent to Carlisle, Pennsylvania. America's second oldest military facility – the one that housed the Hessian troops captured at Trenton by Gen. George Washington after crossing the Delaware – was not being used and thus made available for the Indian boarding school.

Students divided their days between academic studies and vocational training. They dressed in military uniforms and lived regimented lives. Free-time activities included music, athletics and literary or debating societies. Although Carlisle Indian Industrial School was essentially a trade school coupled to elementary and high school academics, Pratt envisioned some of his students advancing to college and professional schools.

Richard Henry Pratt, Susan
& Mary Anna Longstreth,
Spotted Tail, Rebecca
Haines; *U. S. Army Military
History Institute*

Extracurricular activities, particularly the literary and debating societies, helped prepare higher level students for further academic work as well as to think more critically and to communicate more clearly, skills that would serve future leaders well. Although Pratt desired that his former students assimilate into the dominant culture, many returned to their tribes and used the skills learned at Carlisle to become effective tribal leaders.

By the early 1900s, the girls and boys each had two societies from which to select: the Susan Longstreth Literary Society, the Mercer Literary Society, the Standard Literary Society and the Invincible Debating Society, respectively. Susan Longstreth, a Quaker educator who operated a school in Philadelphia for young ladies for 50 years, was a long-time supporter of Pratt's experiment. Major Mercer was the superintendent of the school after Pratt departed. These societies were much more than what their names imply as some of them formed bands, played sports, held dances and put on plays. They also had their own colors and elected officers as did the Freshman, Sophomore, Junior and Senior classes. Besides the usual officers, all of these groups elected a Critic, whose function may not be obvious to modern readers. The author found a definition in the *1918 Quittapahilla*, Lebanon Valley College's yearbook: "Over each meeting presides the Critic and he, by mode of criticism, points out the strength and weakness of the respective numbers with special reference to errors in style, English grammar, elocution, logic, literary structure and the speakers' manner on the floor." While some of the details may vary between schools and organizations, the description will hold in the main.

Rather than return to their reservations during school breaks, students received practical experience in their off-campus "outing" periods to further acculturate them into the dominant culture. In order to "kill the Indian," Pratt kept his charges away from their families and tribes three, four or five years at a time, depending on their period of enrollment. In 1883, explaining his philosophy, he wrote, "In Indian civilization I am a Baptist, because I believe in immersing the Indians in our civilization and when we get them under holding them there until they are thoroughly soaked."

Part of Carlisle's curriculum included off-campus work and/or study with white

1894 Carlisle Indians; *Cumberland County Historical Society, Carlisle, PA*

families in the East. The government saved money by not having to house and feed the children during the outings. Students had the opportunity to earn money of their own and were forced to save a significant portion of it. As the school's superintendent, Pratt constantly battled Congress for funding and did not fare very well. He was not shy about publicly criticizing the government's parsimony and other shortcomings, particularly those in the Bureau of Indian Affairs. The outing period was essential to keep costs within budget. However, some other funding sources would emerge.

One day in 1893, Superintendent Pratt was sitting in his office attending to administrative trivia when he heard a knock. He opened the door to see forty of the school's finest athletes standing outside with something on their minds. Pratt invited them into his office and the school's best orator stepped forward. The boy presented his case so eloquently that, although so personally opposed to football that he had banned its play because serious injuries had occurred in some games played in 1890, Pratt agreed to reinstate inter-school contests. However, he had two conditions:

1. You must never slug. Because if you slug another player, the people who are watching the game will say that you are just savages.
2. In two, three or four years, the Carlisle football team will whip the biggest team in the country.

Thus, inter-collegiate football was born in Carlisle. Actually the Carlisle Indian Industrial School was never a college, but its opponents included the most prestigious institutions of higher learning. Soon, the school newspaper would report on "football hair" sprouting on campus each September.

In keeping with Pratt's admonition, the Carlisle team scheduled Yale and Penn, two of the "Big Four," (Harvard, Yale, Princeton and Penn) in just their second full season of play and still posted a 4-4-0 record! The next year, 1896, Carlisle played and lost to all of the "Big Four" in successive weeks, but they won the rest of their games for their first of many winning seasons. The Harvard and Yale games were close enough that the Indians could have at least tied either of them. The father of American football, Walter Camp, said, "The team must have put up a capital game with Harvard, and their work this season certainly shows that they are in the first class." Frank Cayou scored the first points scored against Yale that season when he raced 75 yards for a touchdown. Several writers considered the calling back of Jake Jamison's touchdown in the same game to be a major officiating blunder that cost the Indians a tie with the Eli. *The New York Sun* was favorably impressed by their play against Yale. "Never was a team seen on the football field who fought harder, fairer and with so little unnecessary rough play." *The Sun* also thought the game should have been a tie were it not for an official's blunder. The *Rochester Advertiser* echoed that sentiment in a caustic tone: "Now, if we have a right to rob the Indian anywhere we certainly have a right to cheat him out of football games." Not only did the team survive the suicidal schedule, but they also convinced the experts that they were first rate.

Newspapers alternated between romanticizing the Indians, praising them for their stoicism or clean play, and belittling them, claiming that they could not rebound from adversity while ignoring the evidence to the contrary. Headline writers and cartoonists were often not very charitable. Indians were often said to ambush their opponents or massacre unwary teams. Players were often depicted as sneaky, skulking marauders or as caricatures with large noses and buck teeth. Scalping knives and tomahawks were often shown as being at the ready.

At the end of the 1896 season, Carlisle started what became near-traditions: Thanksgiving and post-season games. The Indians defeated Brown University 24-12 on Thanksgiving Day, and a post-season game against Wisconsin in Chicago was added. The Indians defeated the Champions of the West 18-8 indoors under the lights in the Chicago Coliseum. This was the Indians' first trip out of the East. Many more would follow.

The November issue of the Carlisle Indian Industrial School's newspaper, *The Red Man*, was subtitled "Games With The Big 4," and its eight pages contained reprints of articles from newspapers around the country. Typical was the editorial from the *Boston*

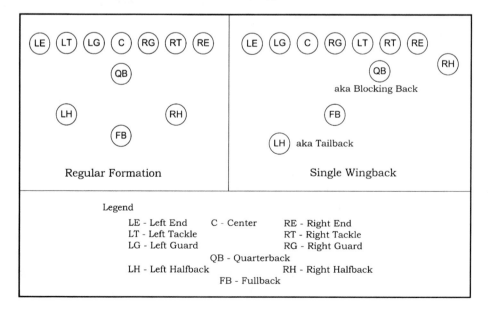

Regular Formation   Single Wingback

Legend

LE - Left End	C - Center	RE - Right End
LT - Left Tackle		RT - Right Tackle
LG - Left Guard		RG - Right Guard
	QB - Quarterback	
LH - Left Halfback		RH - Right Halfback
	FB - Fullback	

Herald, "The statement in our account of the football game on Saturday between the teams of the Carlisle school of Indians and Harvard, that, if the men making up the former had scientific training added to the strength, quickness and endurance which they now possess, no college team in the country could stand against them, is a conclusion endorsed by most of the college graduates and undergraduates who are experts in football and who witnessed the game." That scientific training wouldn't arrive for a few more years, but Carlisle competed while waiting.

The Indians sported a new look for 1897: uniforms in their school colors. A committee headed by former student then vocal teacher, Mary Bailey, researched the issue of school colors over the summer of 1896 and students voted to accept the committee's recommendation at the first Saturday evening meeting of the 1896-97 school year. Too late to obtain football uniforms in school colors for the season about to start, 1897 was the first year the Indian first team was clad in Red and Old Gold. Not too late for 1896 was "Carlisle Indian School March," composed by former student and then current bandmaster, Dennison Wheelock. It was played at football games and other events. Carlisle was also honored with another march that year. Celebrated pianist Robert Tempest of Philadelphia, who had recently visited the school, wrote "Roosters of Carlisle," borrowing an Indian melody that had been printed in the school paper for the refrain.

The football program was generating considerable revenue for the school by this time. *The Indian Helper* of April 17, 1896 reported on one use of the proceeds: "The 28 shower baths in the gymnasium are well patronized. These are not to take the place of the tub bath, but are in addition to the weekly scrub all hands are required to take."

Carlisle played, and lost, to three of the "Big Four" in 1897 by respectable scores, ending up at 6-4-0 again. Carlisle once again suffered four losses in 1898, coming up short against three of the "Big Four" for a 6-4-0 record. However, the team took another postseason road trip, beating Illinois, Cincinnati and The Ohio State University Medical College in seven days. In five short years, Carlisle had established itself as one of the better teams in the country just below the "Big Four." The Indians were very close to achieving what Pratt had directed them to do.

1899 was a pivotal year for Carlisle football because Pratt's first choice for head coach, Glenn S. "Pop" Warner, finally became available. Pratt, not knowledgeable about football himself, had asked Walter Camp, the country's foremost authority, to recommend a coach. Camp suggested a young, innovative coach by the name of Glenn Scobey

Skulking Indian, *New York Journal 10-24-1897*

Warner, better known as "Pop." However, Warner was not available until internal politics convinced him to leave his alma mater, Cornell. When Warner asked for $1,200 for the season plus expenses, Pratt didn't blink. After some minor negotiations, they shook hands and a new era started. The football world would be forever changed when "The Old Fox" took the coaching reins of this up-and-coming team of undersized footballers and embarked on a grueling schedule. Carlisle players gained their first victory over one of the "Big Four" when they defeated the Penn Quakers 16-5 in Philadelphia. *The Red Man* was so proud of that victory that it put "WON" in all capital letters by the score for that game. Carlisle students, led by their band, began a tradition of parading through town in their nightshirts after important victories.

They lost to two of the "Big Four" that year, Harvard and Princeton. The 22-10 loss to Harvard happened without the services of team captain and star player Martin Wheelock, who was too ill to play. The players were treated to a post-season rail trip to San Francisco (they always traveled first class) where they defeated the University of California 2-0 on Christmas Day. This road trip may have been the longest taken by a football team up to that time. The Warner era at Carlisle had begun with a 9-2-0 season, their best so far, a victory over one of the "Big Four" and capped with a win over previously unbeaten Cal. On the way back, Warner agreed to play an exhibition game with the Phoenix Indian School team that was coached by a Harvard alum. Because Harvard had switched to leather uniforms that year, so had the Phoenix coach. The players roasted in the leather suits and were soon exhausted. The Carlisle team stayed on for a few days and shared pigskin tricks with the locals. At season's end, Isaac Seneca was named to Walter Camp's All-America team, the first Indian to receive the honor and one of the few players outside the "Big Four" to be selected.

The 6-4-1 1900 season was a bit of a letdown for the Red and Old Gold with losses to the three of the "Big Four" they played and, for the first time since 1895, there was no post-season road trip. The undersized 1901 team lost a close one to Penn 16-14 and, crippled by injuries, was drubbed by Harvard 29-0. However, Carlisle did not have another losing season for over a decade.

Carlisle returned to winning ways in 1902 with an 8-3-0 season, splitting with the "Big Four" by losing to Harvard and beating Penn for the second time. The *Philadelphia Press* summed it up, "There was no doubt about the victory as the Red Man outplayed his palefaced foe at all points of the game and tied the second Red and Blue scalp firmly to his belt by the decisive score of 5-0." On defense much of the game, Carlisle scored a touchdown early in the second half, missed the extra point and played field position the rest of the way in an extremely hard-fought game with the improving Quakers.

The 1903 squad led by All-America quarterback James Johnson was probably the best Carlisle squad to date. The Indians lost to Princeton and Harvard but beat Penn again 16-6. The one-point 12-11 Harvard loss was a heartbreaker for the players, coming oh so close but still losing. It was also the game in which big Charles Dillon, a Carlisle guard, scored the touchdown using the famous "hidden ball" play. Mose Blumenthal has often been given credit for sewing a piece of elastic in the hem of Dillon's jersey to keep the ball from coming out, but Freddie Wardecker, proprietor of Blumenthal's former haberdashery, does not believes that Mose did the actual sewing. Although Blumenthal's store, also known as "The Capital," had sewing machines, the proprietor did not know how to operate them. He probably supervised the project. Quarterback James Johnson received the kickoff and placed the ball under Dillon's jersey while the team huddled. The Carlisle backs faked having the ball and then raced downfield to retrieve the ball from under the back of Dillon's jersey to touch the ball down for the score. Pop Warner later wrote that he was glad that Harvard outscored Carlisle that day because he didn't like to win on a fluke. The *Boston Sunday Post* had this to say about the game: "With a team outweighed nearly forty pounds to the man, crippled, bruised and battered from other contests, and on a foreign field, the Indians gave an exhibition of football that has no parallel in the annals of Harvard football."

After finishing the season 11-2-1, Pop Warner returned to his alma mater, Cornell, to coach the 1904-6 seasons. Richard Henry Pratt, then a general, was relieved of his command because of his most recent negative comments regarding the Bureau of Indian Affairs. Major William A. Mercer, a cavalry officer, was selected to replace him as superintendent of Carlisle. Former Carlisle stars Bemus Pierce and future hall-of-famer Edward Rogers were brought back to coach the 1904 Indian team. Their only losses in this 9-2-0 season were shutouts by two of the "Big Four," Harvard and Penn.

Likely because of the turmoil surrounding Pratt's departure, Carlisle did not participate in the St. Louis World's Fair. The band did play there, however, as part of the Pennsylvania exhibit. In the fall, the school got a second chance. Promoters were unable to get the Army-Navy game relocated to the Fair to coincide with President Roosevelt's visit, but they were able to arrange a Carlisle-Haskell Institute game on the Saturday after Thanksgiving. A Thanksgiving Day game previously arranged with Ohio State became a warm-up on the trip to St. Louis. The Indians' second team beat the Buckeyes 23-0 two short days and a few hundred miles away before overwhelming Haskell 38-4. President Roosevelt didn't see the game but a large crowd of the curious did. Nine Haskell players were so impressed with the Carlisle program that they later enrolled there.

1905 saw Carlisle coached by committee. George Woodruff, the renowned former Penn coach, was advisor to the coaching team of Bemus Pierce, Siceni Nori, Frank Hudson and Ralph Kinney. The Indians again lost to Penn and Harvard in back-to-back games but did beat a team that gave them much satisfaction, the "soldiers" at West Point.

THE ONON-DAGA INDIANS WILL SEE THE GAME.

KEEWIS WILL ENTERTAIN CARLISLE TEAM

In an 11-day period, with permission from the War Department the Indians beat Army 6-5, then demolished Cincinnati 34-5 and lost games to two semi-professional teams, Canton A. C. and Massillon A. C., 8-0 and 8-4, respectively. A decade later the Canton-Massillon rivalry would be the stuff of legends and would provide a place for Carlisle stars to continue their football careers and change football history.

The Carlisle Indians had gained a national reputation for excellence in football, and athletically-inclined boys on the reservation were becoming increasingly aware of it. Some boys aspired to attend Carlisle to play football with this heroic bunch. Other boys dreamed of playing in the Carlisle band. Still other boys, and some girls, too, wanted to attend Carlisle because of the educational opportunities. While no one would confuse the education that was provided at Carlisle Indian Industrial School with that of an Ivy League college, Carlisle provided opportunities that were not otherwise available to most boys and girls on the reservation. Students returning from Carlisle used their educations to move into leadership positions, a fact that did not go unnoticed by children on the reservation.

Before the 1906 season started, Pop Warner tutored Carlisle coaches, former stars Bemus Pierce and Frank Hudson, in the new rules instituted to keep President Roosevelt from banning the game. The neutral zone was established, the distance needed to make a first down was increased from five to ten yards, and the forward pass was legalized. The rule changes eliminated some of the disadvantages Carlisle teams had faced previously, including lack of size, and allowed them to capitalize on their strengths – speed, agility and conditioning. Warner developed a new offensive scheme to exploit Carlisle's strengths, speed and deception, and mitigate their weaknesses, size and depth. Warner's system, known to us as the single-wing, revolutionized football.

The two Indian coaches led their charges to a 24-6 victory over Penn but were outplayed by the Crimson in a 5-0 loss at Harvard. They unexpectedly lost to Penn State on a field goal, the only score in the game. Not reported by *The Arrow* (Carlisle's school paper changed its name in 1904) or Steckbeck was a Thanksgiving game hastily arranged with Vanderbilt while the team was on the road for games with Minnesota, Cincinnati and Virginia. The Champions of the South wanted a crack at the slayers of the Champions of the West and beat the Indians 4-0. Three victories against one defeat in 12 days isn't bad. Neither was a 9-3-0 season with a tough schedule.

On September 21, 1906, *The Arrow* reported, "Carlisle Indian football management decided to have its eleven directly coached by full-blooded redskins of intelligence. This was done largely because the Indian will work harder for an Indian coach than for the average college expert trainer. Coach Glenn S. Warner is undoubtedly the only white man who has ever been able to hold fast the attention of the redskinned footballist and teach him better things." At the end of the season, the *New York World* opined, "Bemus Pierce by skillful handling of the Indians has placed them in the front rank of the college world… Carlisle has done so well that the team is rated as one of the high class organizations of the year." The December 21 *Arrow* announced that Warner would return as athletic director in charge of coaching all sports. Bemus Pierce and Frank Hudson were praised but were not available year round. It was probably not coincidental that Mrs. Warner visited Superintendent and Mrs. Mercer over Thanksgiving.

1907 was Carlisle's strongest team to that time and, in Pop Warner's opinion, one of their best teams ever. The high points of the 10-1-0 season were another victory over "Big

Four" foe Penn and their first ever over Harvard. Frank Mt. Pleasant, whom Walter Camp later snubbed by naming him only to the Honorable Mention All-America team due to a perceived lack of ruggedness, led the Indians to victory with his passing and a 75-yard touchdown run in the 23-15 triumph. A parade of students in their nightshirts greeted the team upon their return to Carlisle. Hundreds of townspeople turned out with them to welcome the victors. Warner savored the 18-4 victory over Chicago and their coach, Amos Alonzo Stagg, considering it one of the high points of his career. The only loss in the otherwise perfect season was a 16-0 shutout in a downpour of rain by "Big Four" nemesis Princeton. Little Boy, one of Carlisle's best linemen, explained why the Indians usually did poorly in inclement weather, saying, "Football no good fun in mud and snow." Jim Thorpe sat frustrated on the bench his first year on the team as Mt. Pleasant threw 50-yard spirals, the first person known to do this.

Mt. Pleasant's snubbing by Walter Camp was not an isolated incident. Writers not infrequently found ways to disparage the Indians' successes by focusing on their infrequent losses. Detractors portrayed Carlisle's defeats as character flaws held by people of the Indian race. Reasons given included lack of discipline, disinterest in training, and being too close to their aboriginal state. These writers' theories conflicted with Warner's observations. Furthermore, they would soon have an Indian to both deify and denounce.

Jim Thorpe vaulted to the position of starting left halfback in 1908. In his first year as a starter, Carlisle lost only to Harvard and Minnesota and tied Penn. Carlisle won the other ten. The Indians either lost to or tied the national champions depending whether one thinks Harvard or Penn best that year. Jim Thorpe had a good year showing much promise, so much that Walter Camp ranked him a third team All-American. Thorpe then left school to play minor league baseball. Pennsylvania was the only "Big Four" team scheduled for 1909. That game accounted for one of Carlisle's losses, the first one in four years to the Quakers, in this 8-3-1 Thorpe-less season.

Moses Friedman, a civilian educator, replaced Major Mercer as Carlisle superintendent in 1908, but little changed with regard to the athletic program. Penn and Princeton were the "Big Four" teams Pop Warner scheduled for 1910. For reasons unknown, Harvard Law School replaced Harvard on the 15-game schedule. Western Maryland College mercifully canceled their game; otherwise the Indians would have had to play 3 games in seven days. A combination of injuries and bad luck resulted in a disappointing season with no "Big Four" victories and an 8-6-0 season.

Jim Thorpe, no longer a skinny kid, returned for the 1911 season. Pop Warner viewed this team as his greatest at Carlisle as it began the best three-year run in Carlisle's Football Trail of Glory. Gus Welch, Alex Arcasa and Lone Star Dietz all scored touchdowns in the win over Penn while Thorpe nursed an injury on the bench. Thorpe used his heavily bandaged leg to kick a field goal in each quarter for the victory over Harvard. This 11-1-0 season was their second and last two "Big Four" win campaign. The Indians picked up where they left off in 1912 but let up in their loss to Penn, the only member of the "Big Four" on that year's schedule. The scoreless tie was to a very good Washington and Jefferson team. However, it was not the one that was rewarded with the honor of being the Eastern representative in the New Year's Day game in Pasadena, California as has been reported elsewhere. It was in the much-written-about game against West Point that Pop used the double wingback offense to thwart the Soldiers 27-6. Trouncing Brown 32-0 on Thanksgiving Day was a fitting capstone to Thorpe's career at Carlisle and the 12-

INDIANS TREATED LIKE WHITE MEN UNTIL THEIR MONEY IS SPENT

FULL OF PERSONAL LIBERTY

1-1 season. Again in 1913, Penn was the only one of the "Big Four" on the schedule, but this time it was a 7-7 tie. The other blemish to their 10-1-1 record was a 12-6 upset by Pitt. Carlisle completed a three-year run of 33 wins, 3 losses and 2 ties against the toughest teams with only ten home games, and those were the warm-up games.

Carlisle Indian School teams were so well-known and respected that youth teams sometimes named themselves in their honor much as kids' teams are called the Yankees or White Sox today. For example, a Syracuse, New York YMCA league named their basketball teams Syracuse, Harvard, Rutgers and Carlisle.

Some think that the vaunted Carlisle Indian School football program ended in August 1918 when the school closed, because Carlisle Barracks, its home, was used as a hospital to treat soldiers wounded in The Great War. While it is true that the Red Peril of the East would take the field no more, Carlisle's competitive football ended before that. In his seminal work on Carlisle Indian School football, *Fabulous Redmen*, John S. Steckbeck places the end of Carlisle's football trail of glory at February 25, 1915, the date of Pop Warner's farewell dinner. I mark the end a year earlier. On February 6, 7, 8 and March 25, 1914, a joint commission of Congress under the direction of Inspector E. B. Linnen conducted an investigation of the Carlisle Indian School. The changes brought about by the commission led to the demise of the Carlisle football program. Although the U.S. Army technically brought the program to an end when it took back Carlisle Barracks in 1918, the football program was already dead, though still staggering from 1914 to its official demise.

Judge Cato Sells, new Commissioner of Indian Affairs, apparently at the urging of the Indian Rights Association and a student petition, began an investigation of Superintendent Moses Friedman's management of the Carlisle Indian Industrial School in January 1914. It seems that Cumberland County Judge Sadler (it is not clear whether it was Wilbur, the father, or Sylvester, the son, because the hereditary judgeship was transferred from father to son in that year) meted out a 60-day jail sentence, possibly at Friedman's urging, to an Indian girl and boy for an infraction punishable only by a fine under Pennsylvania law. The infraction was not stated but debauchery is a definite possibility. This did not sit well with the Philadelphia-based Indian Rights Association. There were also accounts of arrests of Indian boys found drinking alcohol in the town of Carlisle. According to Indian School staff and other students, "negro bootleggers" were to blame, not tavern owners. The timing could not have been worse for Carlisle as the walrus-mustachioed Judge Sells was on a rampage to stop the scourge of alcohol on his wards while trying to clean up the corrupt government agency.

On Friday, February 6, 1914, a joint commission of Congress arrived unannounced in Carlisle to interview staff and students at Carlisle in an attempt to get to the bottom of the situation. It was not a pretty sight. Superintendent Friedman made an unauthorized trip to Washington to plead his case, blaming Gen. Richard Pratt, founder of the Carlisle Indian School, with meddling but was told to get back to his post. Local newspapers ran editorials supportive of Friedman but several students and faculty members criticized his leadership. Meanwhile Inspector J. Linnen interviewed witnesses.

Rosa B. LaFlesch, outing manager, testified that discipline: "… is better now than when I first came here, although it is lax yet." She went on to say, "They [students] have no respect for him [Supt. Friedman]." Wallace Denny, assistant disciplinarian (and Pop Warner's long-time trainer) gave four reasons or causes for student dissatisfaction:

1. Superintendent Friedman reduced the number of receptions and sociables per month to one each.
2. Students were given more difficult [academic] work.
3. Food was of a poor quality.
4. Employees did not work in harmony with Superintendent Friedman.

John Whitwell, principal teacher, reported that Mr. David H. Dickey, outing agent, found Pop Warner drunk with Gus Welch. Whitwell also claimed that students wrote "the Jew" and other such things on a blackboard in reference to Moses Friedman. He accused Friedman of carrying almost 200 students who were no longer at the school on the roll. Angel DeCora, native art teacher, presented the commission with a list of twenty-eight girls who had been "ruined" and sent home. Band director Claude M. Stauffer was accused of beating a 17-year-old female student, Julia Hardin, at the insistence of Hannah H. Ridenour, a matron.

Pop Warner was accused of mishandling athletic funds. One of the charges was that the athletic association paid Hugh Miller, sports editor for the *Carlisle Sentinel*, and E. L. Martin to publicize the Carlisle team in the cities in which they played. The fact that hundreds paid out for PR resulted in thousands in gate receipts seemed to escape the commission. Or, it appeared unseemly to the senators and congressmen for the school to pay for publicity when they had franking privileges and reporters constantly asked them for stories. Warner was found to have kept scrupulous records but was criticized for how some of the money was spent. He argued that he was getting the best value for the school when he purchased canned goods from his family's Springfield Canning Company. The coach also mentioned disbursing some of the money to the players. "At the close of the season the boys are given a $25 suit of clothes and a $25 overcoat; that is, the first team. And the first team also gets a souvenir of some kind." This explains some of the $25 and $50 chits at Wardecker's Men's Wear (formerly Blumenthal's). Warner was also criticized for recruiting star athletes from reservations, something he adamantly denied. He countered that many of his best players had never seen a football before arriving at Carlisle.

Commissioner Sells dismissed Friedman and Stauffer, bringing charges against Friedman for theft of funds. Oscar Lipps was brought in as acting superintendent. During his trial, Friedman claimed it was Chief Clerk Siceni J. Nori who embezzled the money and destroyed the records. State charges against Friedman were then dropped and moved to federal court when it was learned that Nori needed the money to make support payments for his estranged wife and children. Friedman was acquitted, resigned, and took a job that paid $3,000 a year. A cook was suspended for taking an Indian boy into a saloon and buying him liquor. That infraction was worth a fine and imprisonment for the cook. Pop Warner was allowed to stay on as athletic director.

A result of the Congressional Investigation was a change in the curriculum and more stringent requirements for admission. A number of the faculty changed and many students did not return in the fall. The investigation brought out the fact that, although Angel DeCora and Lone Star Dietz had not been teaching native arts for about two years due to curriculum changes, Superintendent Friedman had kept them on because he thought they were assets to the school. Dietz was teaching mechanical drawing and DeCora had a sinecure. The commission apparently agreed with Friedman and did not recommend their dismissal. Complaints of students loitering in the former Native Art Department led to the Leupp Art Building being reassigned to the new alumni association. Students would no longer make or decorate things to be sold by the school. Resale items were to be purchased in NY.

At the beginning of the 1914 football season, an article, probably written by Hugh Miller or E. L. Martin, titled, "Carlisle Indian Stars Are Teaching the Palefaces How to Play Football Game," was printed in newspapers around the country. Bemus Pierce, Albert Exendine, Frank Mt. Pleasant, Frank Cayou, Wiliam Gardner, Wilson Charles, William Garlow, Emil Hauser (better known as Wauseka), Pete Hauser, Charles Guyon (also known as Wayoo), Fritz Hendricks, Ed Smith, Antonio Lubo, Joseph Shoulder and Thomas St. Germaine were or had been coaching football at colleges and high schools around the country. Jimmie Johnson, Gus Welch, Lone Star Dietz and several others had or were assisting in Carlisle by 1914.

After the great 1911-1913 run, things changed drastically football-wise in 1914 and not for the better. Pop Warner described the 5-9-1 1914 season as disastrous. Some excellent players, Gus Welch and Pete Calac for example, were back but the team lacked the depth of talent it had enjoyed in former years. The season started off with the usual victories in three warm-up games, but the margins of victory were smaller than the previous year. The next four games were played against tougher opponents. All four were lost. In 1913 the Indians went 2-1-1 against the same four teams: Lehigh, Cornell, Pitt and Penn. Next they were pummeled by Syracuse, a team they had beaten the previous year, by a score of 24-3. They then played a scoreless tie with Holy Cross, an opponent Carlisle defeated the only other time they played. The big game of the year was against the Fighting Irish of Notre Dame at White Sox Park in Chicago. Carlisle put up a good fight until Gus Welch was injured making a tackle. Notre Dame swamped Warner's charges 48-6 in the only time the teams from the two legendary programs met.

Carlisle easily handled cross-town rival Dickinson College 34-0 without Gus Welch, who stayed behind in Chicago's Mercy Hospital, but the annual Thanksgiving opponent, Brown, was a tougher match. Carlisle outplayed and outgained the Bears 3 to 1 but fumbled away a 20-14 loss. Three post-season games were arranged this year. The first was a charity game for the Children's Charitable Hospital of Marblehead, Massachusetts just two days after the Brown game. The opposition was an all-star team composed primarily of former Harvard players. The All-Stars prevailed 13-6. A week later the Indians were in Birmingham, Alabama where they beat the University of Alabama 20-3. *The Carlisle Arrow* mentioned that a third postseason game, a game against the University of Georgia, was to be played in Atlanta the following Wednesday but did not report on the game. However, contemporary newspaper accounts show that Carlisle played Auburn in Atlanta and lost

7-0. This game has not been forgotten by the Auburn faithful because it figures prominently in their folklore regarding the origins of the "War Eagle" battle cry.

Auburn supporters recalled the game this way:

> "The 1914 contest with the Carlisle Indians provides another story. The toughest
> player on the Indians' team was a tackle named Bald Eagle. Trying to tire the big man,
> Auburn began to run play after play at his position. Without even huddling, the
> Auburn quarterback would yell 'Bald Eagle,' letting the rest of the team know that
> the play would be run at the imposing defensive man. Spectators, however, thought
> the quarterback was saying 'War Eagle' and, in unison, they began to chant the
> resounding cry."

The only problem is that the Carlisle roster included neither a Bald Eagle nor a War
Eagle. However, it did include a Hawk Eagle – the star right guard. Given that Hawk
Eagle sounds more like War Eagle than does Bald Eagle and Hawk Eagle was a very good
player, the essence of the story may well be true. It's just the details that are muddled.

The National Archives' file for Charles Guyon contains a footnote to the Carlisle-
Auburn game. Apparently Wahoo underwrote that game and, due to Carlisle having an off
season and a short time to effectively promote it, lost $2,897.75. His lawyer requested that
Oscar Lipps return half of the loss. Lipps blamed the season's results on Carlisle having
an "off" year and predicted that, after all accounts were finalized, Carlisle would show a
small loss for the season. So, Guyon was out the money.

Even though the congressional investigator had wrested control of the athletic
funds from Warner, many things continued to operate pretty much as they had. But now
it was Superintendent Lipps sending chits to Blumenthal's to pay for the players' citizen
clothing.

The Auburn game was the last one Pop Warner and Lone Star Dietz coached for
Carlisle. After their game with the Indians, University of Pittsburgh officials began dis-
cussions with Pop Warner to head their football program. At season's end negotiations
concluded, Warner was feted at a farewell banquet attended by former Carlisle lettermen

The Providence Journal 11-28-1915

and friends. The death of Carlisle football formally honored, all that remained was for the corpse to die.

The University of Pittsburgh offered Warner, and he accepted, a salary of $4,500 which was very good money in 1915. However, one of the most ardent supporters of amateur athletics and outspoken critics of professionalism in sports, Amos Alonzo Stagg, was paid $6,000 by the University of Chicago in 1905, a full decade earlier. It is no wonder that Carlisle's 1907 thumping of Chicago was one of the victories Warner savored most.

Carlisle needed a new football coach. As soon as Warner's impending departure was made public, speculation ran rampant in newspapers across the country. First, Al Exendine was to take Warner's place if he could be released from his contract with Georgetown. Next it was Frank Mt. Pleasant, who chose the University of Buffalo instead. Pop's protégé, Lone Star Dietz, was an obvious choice, but he opted to leave the Indian Service and took his first head coaching job at Washington State College, establishing the Carlisle-Washington State connection. Gus Welch was at least one writer's choice if Dietz wasn't available. Several former players, including Charles Guyon, Bemis Pierce, Frank Hudson and Frank Cayou, applied for the job. But none of the Carlisle stars was chosen or would accept the job, probably the latter in most cases. In March, newspapers reported that well-known Indian lawyer and former Texas A & M quarterback, Victor M. "Choctaw" Kelley (often spelled Kelly) had been selected for the job. Before leaving for Pullman, Dietz predicted that Kelley would not be successful as the new Carlisle head coach. Gus Welch later charged that Kelley's hiring had been a political decision. The fact that Kelley's appointment was made by the Commissioner of Indian Affairs, Cato Sells, supports Welch's contention.

Leaving his former job at the University of Texas, Coach Kelley arrived in late August to take the reins of the Carlisle football team. Gus Welch, who had had a successful year of coaching at Conway Hall, a preparatory school in Carlisle, agreed to assist Kelley with the varsity. Although stars like Welch were gone, the season started encouragingly enough with a 21-6 defeat of Albright College. But the scoreless tie the next week with Lebanon Valley College, a team that had not scored on them in their 14 meetings, threw cold water on Carlisle's dreams of mediocrity. The following week at Lehigh the competition improved, and Carlisle doomed its fate by making errors, losing 14-0. Rousing speeches by "Choc" Kelley and former Carlisle great Al Exendine may have boosted the Indians' performance against Harvard but mistakes, such as penalties, destined their defeat, even though they outgained the Crimson 275 yards to 175. Harvard prevailed 29–7.

Next up was Pop Warner's new and undefeated team, the University of Pittsburgh. Pittsburgh, considered by some to be the best team in the country, pounded Carlisle to the tune of 45-0, their worst defeat of the year. The next week neither team played well when the Carlisle-Bucknell contest ended in a scoreless tie, Carlisle's second of the year. Unable to move the ball inside the opponent's 20 or defend the forward pass, Carlisle lost to a West Virginia Wesleyan team that it had hoped to beat. A week later, looking like the Carlisle of old, the Indians scored 23 points in the first half, but the breaks went Holy Cross's way in the second half. Carlisle had to hang on for a 2-point victory. Dickinson College was ready for the Indians this year and fought hard to the end. But the Indians fought back and pulled out a 20-14 triumph on Dickinson's home field. Two Carlisle fumbles spelled defeat in their 14-10 loss to Fordham. A fumbled punt on Fordham's 15 was returned 85 yards for a touchdown, and a fumble at Fordham's 3 near the end of the game sealed the Indians' fate. Last up on the schedule was the annual Thanksgiving game in Providence, Rhode Island against Brown.

What happened off the field was, perhaps, more interesting than what happened in the 39-3 shellacking at the hands of a strong Brown team featuring Fritz Pollard. One of Lone Star Dietz's friends at Carlisle informed him that, to get even with Dietz for the statement he had made about Victor Kelley, Kelley had given a copy of Carlisle's playbook to Brown. Brown had been invited to Pasadena, California to play an East vs. West game on New Year's Day against Dietz's team after the town's little floral parade was over. An editorial in *The Providence Journal* considered the statement to be absurd, saying that Brown coach Robinson had played Carlisle so often that he knew their plays better than Kelley and needed no assistance from him. Besides that, it asserted, when Brown played Carlisle it thought it was going to be playing against the University of Washington, not Washington State. Someone in Providence had confused the schools.

The Thanksgiving game was such a resounding defeat for Carlisle that *The Providence Journal* ran a cartoon depicting the then current state of Carlisle's program as having seen better days. A week later *The Journal* ran two articles about Carlisle on the same page. In one article, Gus Welch blamed Victor Kelley for the poor season, saying, "There was a meeting three weeks before Thanksgiving at which Superintendent Lipps, Manager Meyer, Kelley, Capt. Calac and myself were present. It was decided then that Kelley was to be dismissed as head coach. Now they want to make me the goat of the whole affair. I want the public to know the facts." This chaos was a far cry from Carlisle during its glory years. The other article reported a decision made in Washington, DC that would subordinate football at Carlisle to the point at which the team would not be competitive.

Rumors circulated in newspapers across the country that intercollegiate football at Carlisle was to end. Carlisle's team was not disbanded but came close. The 1916 schedule wasn't in place until late October because football wasn't allowed on campus for a month. When the schedule finally came out, it had only five games on it and those were not with top caliber teams. Victor Kelley resigned and physical education instructor M. L. Clevett took over the coaching duties. The first game was against Conway Hall with the Indians winning 26-0. Susquehanna University, a team for whom 24-0 was the closest they could get in eight previous tries, was the next opponent. The 12-0 loss to Susquehanna was a blow to the Indians' ego because they knew they had lost to a weak team. Carlisle then traveled to Conshohocken to play their Athletic Association. Tied at 6-6, Coach Clevett withdrew his team at halftime due to the brutal treatment his team was receiving. Clevett was thrown into jail for refusing to return half the guarantee money. Eventually the money was returned and Clevett was released, but the game was never finished. Two weeks later former Carlislians Joel Wheelock and William Winnishiek helped Lebanon Valley College defeat the dejected Indians 20-6 for the Dutchmen's first victory in the long series. Carlisle closed the 1-3-1 season with a 27-17 loss to Alfred University in New York City.

Leo F. "Deed" Harris, Carlisle High School alum and former Warner scout, took the coaching reins for the 1917 season. He tried to prepare the team for a nine-game schedule similar to those Carlisle was accustomed to playing. Unfortunately Carlisle's players were young and small. Also, a quarantine to prevent the spread of an epidemic on the school's grounds forced the team to relocate to one of the school's farms for much of the season, preventing organized practice. Carlisle started the season like Carlisle of old with 59-0 and 63-0 shellackings of Albright and Franklin and Marshall, respectively. Things went downhill quickly with seven successive losses, including the worst defeat in Carlisle's proud history at the hands of Joe Guyon's current team, Georgia Tech, in Atlanta, 98-0. Their last game both of the season and ever was a 26-0 loss to Penn, bringing the in-state rivalry and Carlisle Indian School football to a close.

When the United States entered the First World War in 1917, allowing or encouraging students to enlist became a topic of discussion among school superintendents. Hervey B. Peairs of Haskell Institute in Lawrence, Kansas and John Francis of Carlisle discussed the ways they were dealing with the issue in their correspondence in April, 1917 concerning Gus Welch's application for the athletic director position at Haskell. Peairs began the discussion with a question:

> "What policy are you adopting with reference to the enlistment of boys in the army? There is quite a demand here among the boys to be allowed to enlist, but at least 50% of the parents object. Probably about 50% are very willing to have their sons enlist and do their part. I have felt that I ought not to allow any of the boys or young men to leave the school and enlist in the army without the consent of the parents, even though the boys are of the age when they can lawfully enlist without such consent."

Francis responded:

> "With reference to the enlistment of boys here that are over 21, I have permitted them to go without the consent of the parents; under that age I required them to obtain the consent of their parents. I have also tried to avoid anything like a wave of wild excitement sweeping through the school, but on the other hand I have let them understand that where, after careful consideration, they felt they wished to enlist in the Army or Navy the school was proud to have them go and would do everything possible to help them go, and those of our boys who have enlisted have gone in this spirit."

Several former Carlisle football players were quick to join up. *The Carlisle Arrow and Red Man* issues of that time contained lists of former students and, if known, where they were stationed. Those who had attended college after leaving Carlisle were often commissioned as officers. Because of their athletic prowess, some were given the opportunity to represent their units in athletic competitions. *The Carlisle Arrow and Red Man* also included a former student's recollection of being treated as an oddity:

> "An Indian officer writes: "In the army one has splendid opportunities to make acquaintances, and being the only Redskin officer in camp, people want to meet me just for curiosity's sake."

The U.S. Army prevented further embarrassment to the once-proud school by taking the facility back to be used as a hospital to treat soldiers wounded in World War I. The mantle for Indian athletics was passed to Haskell Institute in Lawrence, Kansas, where football again flourished before Depression-era government funding cuts ended the Indian football trail of glory forever. In 1920 after the war was over, Society of American Indians passed a resolution demanding that the government reopen Carlisle or that another, comparable facility be established. Carlisle Barracks was instead used for the Medical Field Service School.

In 1931, Pop Warner planned a reunion of Carlisle Indian School football players at the 1932 Summer Olympics held in Los Angeles. He wanted to have a scrimmage with former stars, but it was necessary for Jim Thorpe and other Carlisle luminaries to attend for it to be successful. Jim Thorpe, then strapped for cash, did attend the Olympics courtesy of Vice-President Charles Carter and was seated in the Presidential box. He received a standing ovation from the 105,000 present for the opening ceremonies in the Los Angeles Coliseum when his name was announced. The Federation of American Indians also proposed that a reunion of former Carlisle students be held, presumably in Carlisle. It is not known if either of those reunions materialized, but the one proposed by former player Isaac Lyon did, at the New York State Fair in Syracuse in 1941. Pop Warner attended, along with a large number of former students. Attendance at the fair jumped largely due to interest in seeing the Carlisle Indians.

In early 1937, a newspaper article datelined Philadelphia discussed the unusual accents of many former Carlisle students: "American Indians with a Pennsylvania Dutch dialect may confuse visitors to western reservations, but William 'Lone Star' Dietz, assistant coach of the Temple University football team, can explain it.... 'For years hundreds of Indian boys and girls were brought from the reservations to Carlisle, and after they had become oriented to the institutional surroundings, they were sent to farms in Dauphin, Lancaster, Lebanon and other predominantly Dutch counties. There they were reared with the farmers' children, went to their schools and learned the topsy-turvey Pennsylvania Dutch dialect. They naturally acquired the accent and never lost it.'"

Thorpe and Warner died in the 1950s and were soon followed by many others. The last of the great football players died in the 1970s. The last surviving Carlisle student died a few years ago, but memories of the school linger on.

In 1910, Superintendent Friedman mailed a questionnaire to former football players no longer at Carlisle, as Pratt and Mercer had done before him, apparently to refute the widely held belief that athletes "never amount to much after leaving school" was a myth. Who received the questionnaires is unknown as is who returned them. What is known is some players returned them, and some of these responses still exist in student files. The results found comprise no scientific study but do represent the thinking of some individuals. Charles Guyon responded, "I owe my success to the training I have received in the two schools I have attended, and to make it short – I am working for something higher – to the highest goal." Caleb Sickles frankly stated, "From my own experience I think that the pupil who has attended Carlisle should never go back to the reservation to live. If he has holdings I would advise him to sell them, put the money in the bank and seek employment or attend a school and obtain a professional or technical education." Ed Rogers answered, "What little degree of success I have attained I attribute entirely to my early training at Carlisle" and offered, "I might add although the subject is not mentioned nor no opinion is requested that to abolish non-reservation schools is a mistake and would be a serious detriment to the progress and welfare of the future young Indians."

The next chapter discusses what several of the players did immediately after or, in a few cases, while attending Carlisle. Carlisle Indians played significant roles in the development of the early professional game. This book tells their stories along with numerous others.

"REVENGE!"

Celebrating an early Carlisle victory,
Pennsylvania Engraving Company

Although Carlisle generally played college teams, the Indians sometimes lined up against independent or professional teams.

2

Carlisle Indians Turn Pro

Professional football took a very different developmental path than did baseball. Football in America evolved much like rugby had in England in that both games were born at the elite schools in their respective home countries and grew to become inter-scholastic sports. American inter-scholastic sports began when Harvard and Yale, modeling themselves after what they viewed as their British counterparts, Oxford and Cambridge, competed in rowing. It was natural that the elite schools would be among the first to compete against each other in football (soccer and rugby) in this country. In the 1880s, Yale's Walter Camp, "Father of American Football," instituted the rule changes that differentiated American football from its English cousins when he was a student playing the game. Camp continued his involvement with football long after graduation and dominated the rules committee until 1905.

In the earliest days of American football, players were amateurs associated with the colleges they attended. Soon graduates played. It wasn't long before gypsy players matriculated at a school just long enough to play in an important game. Some were never students of the institutions they represented or, in at least one case, were students at other or both institutions. Ruling elites such as Theodore Roosevelt promoted sports to young men of his class as a means of preparing them for leadership. It was not for money that these amateur athletes were to compete, but for roles in leading the country. The brutal contests of strength, speed and wit helped determine who would later be making the major decisions for the nation. Requiring that college sports be amateur events for the most part restricted participation in them to the scions of the wealthy and powerful because few others could afford the luxury of paying college tuition while making no income.

Charges of professionalism started early on when players for other schools, of course, were paid outright or otherwise subsidized. Professional (paid) coaching was soundly criticized as well. William Rainey Harper, President of the fledgling University of Chicago, set a precedent in 1893 when he offered and Amos Alonzo Stagg accepted a tenured position as associate professor in charge of the Athletic Department for $2,500 per year. Stagg had a good salary and a job for life, or at least until mandatory retirement age. The often sainted Stagg was an ardent proponent of amateurism and constant critic of professionalism in athletics.

In those days college athletics were seldom under the control of college administrators. Student and athletic organizations generally raised the money to field a team and pay the coach. Football also generated profits that the associations could use to support other athletics at the school. Walter Camp, who also espoused the merits of amateurism, accumulated $100,000 for Yale's athletic fund over a ten-year period even while using some of the money to pay athletic tutors. Camp, however, was not paid for his efforts as he had a good-paying job as an executive of the New Haven Clock Company. But then, he was merely an advisor and not the coach.

Athletes were not to be paid, and this restriction was not just for playing football. Scholarships and part-time jobs were considered to be marks of professionalism. However, student-athletes from humble backgrounds, if they were good enough athletes and businessmen, sometimes found ways to afford playing college amateur sports. Some found paying jobs with alumni or supporters of the school's teams. Ace Clark, captain of the Washington State College 1916 Rose Bowl team, took entire years off to work at manual labor to save up enough to pay his way through school. In 1900 Penn State became one of the first colleges to officially authorize athletic scholarships to cover tuition, room and board. There were no set eligibility standards. It was not uncommon for the managements of two squads about to play a game to negotiate player eligibility in the week leading up to a game. There weren't even set rules regarding professionalism. Some schools allowed their athletes to play professional or semi-pro baseball over the summer. As a practical matter, it would have been difficult policing hundreds of baseball teams across the country, especially considering that players often played under assumed names.

Carlisle Indian School, being a government facility with students who were wards of the government, had an unusual situation. Neither its academics nor its economics resembled those of a prestigious university; nor were the views of its faculty and administration. Providing ways for students to earn money was an important issue for school administrators. Pratt instituted outings as a central part of his system, in part because they gave students the opportunity to make and save some money of their own. Later, the Native Art Department provided a venue to sell the objects that students created in the classroom. Even after Warner's departure, Superintendent Oscar Lipps signed chits for athletes to redeem for clothing at Blumenthal's Men's Wear. So, even though Carlisle's athletes were at least the equal of their counterparts at elite institutions, their financial status was definitely not. Few Carlisle students had affluent parents, whereas college students of the day largely came from the upper classes. While some, such as Jim Thorpe, received modest incomes from their allotments of tribal lands, many did not. Even if they had money in an account at the reservation, getting the Indian agent to release it was a challenge.

High schools also picked up the game and played according to college rules, but those students not wealthy enough or so inclined to attend college found their playing days ending at graduation. Soon town, neighborhood or company teams gave ordinary people with athletic ability an opportunity to play football as young adults, sometimes longer. Because they were not affiliated with schools, these teams were dubbed independents. For some reason, independents sprang up in the Great Lakes region in mill towns from New York to Wisconsin. Mill workers did not attend college and often worked at least part of Saturday, making it impossible for most to attend college games, assuming they had the money or interest in doing so. Sunday was when the working class could play or watch football, and that is when they did it. Cities often had blue laws that prevented games being played on Sundays, so the city teams that existed had to play mostly road games.

Independent games were often hard-fought with neighboring towns over bragging rights for the superiority of one locale over another. Partisans bet on their teams, often in large amounts. Team managers brought in ringers to ensure their teams' success and to protect their wagers. On November 12, 1892, the Allegheny Athletic Association of Pittsburgh (AAA) paid former Yale All-American William "Pudge" Hefflefinger $500 to play guard against Pittsburgh Athletic Club (PAC) in what is acknowledged as the game involving the first professional player. It is not unlikely that other players were paid prior to this, but AAA's financial records documented the fact that Hefflefinger had been paid to play. In 1895, David Berry, manager of the Latrobe YMCA team and editor of the *Latrobe Clipper*, paid John Braillier $10 more than expenses to play quarterback for his club. Braillier used the money to purchase a pair of pants that he wore proudly at Washington and Jefferson College, where the future dentist also played football. Braillier is the first known college player to also be playing on Sundays for pay. Independent football had become semi-pro as teams began paying a star or handful of stars to augment their local boys who played for the fun of it.

Complaints of professionalism of college players were widespread, but Carlisle probably had fewer instances, or at least reports, of its players playing on Sundays than did many football powers, due to logistics if nothing else. Because Carlisle played most of its games on the road, nearly all after the early season warm-ups, players were generally at distant cities on Saturdays, returning home late Saturday night or heading off to another city for a midweek game. This made travel from Carlisle to another city for a Sunday game difficult. Also, Carlisle players were under closer watch by their coaching staff and administration than were college students. Carlisle officials had tighter control and would not have been pleased to have their stars injured in a Sunday game and unable to play the next Saturday. However, under certain circumstances it appears to have happened. Keith McClellan, author of *The Sunday Game*, discovered that Frank Mt. Pleasant played for the Altoona Indians in 1905 and recruited some of his teammates. Warner wasn't at Carlisle in 1905. It seems unlikely that Pop would have allowed his players to risk injury playing for another team - at least during the season. Gus Welch related a story much later about having played for a professional team in Pottstown, Pennsylvania and having recruited some teammates to join him. However, a decade later Carlisle and Notre Dame were reputed to have more former or current players involved in the professional game than any other schools.

Western Pennsylvania was an early hotbed of independent football. Going into the 1900 season, the Duquesne Country and Athletic Club (DC&AC) was the dominant team but was burdened with a bloated (for its day) payroll. The Homestead Library Athletic Club (HLAC), supported by Carnegie Steel money, was on the ascendancy. HLAC hired Bill Church away from Georgetown University and loaded up on stars, including former Carlisle star Bemus Pierce and several DC&AC players. Historians disagree on the details of what happened in this time period. The NFL position is that William Chase Temple became the first owner of a professional team by taking over the DC&AC in 1900. Another historian believes that Temple left DC&AC between the 1899 and 1900 seasons and joined HLAC as its football chairman. Greensburg and Latrobe also expected to contend in 1900. The Greenies, financed by local stockholders, brought onboard Carlisle All-American Isaac Seneca and some other stars.

The 1900 season proved to be a financial disaster for the western Pennsylvania powers. The DC&AC and Greensburg teams folded. Latrobe returned to being a town team. HLAC was the only one of these teams to return the next year at full strength. That year it played several college teams and a few independents. Hawley Pierce, Bemus's brother, was on the roster of this undefeated team. Unfortunately, rain fell on almost all of its games, dampening enthusiasm and creating box office losses. William Temple had had enough of football. He later moved to Florida where he was credited with developing the Temple orange.

In 1902 baseball's upstart American League was plucking stars from the National League, creating a bidding war for players, with perhaps the most intense competition being found in Philadelphia between the Athletics and Phillies. Phillies owner Col. John I. Rogers responded to this threat by forming a football team. Athletics owner Ben Shibe followed suit and put his baseball manager, Connie Mack, in charge of the new football team. Rogers and Shibe felt that winning the football championship of Philadelphia would help their baseball teams. And if one of them beat Pittsburgh, that team could claim the world's championship. So, they contacted Dave Berry who agreed to reassemble the old Homestead team, thus forming the National Football League. The two Philadelphia owners so distrusted each other that they made Berry president of their new league. They contacted New York and Chicago about joining the league but were rebuffed.

David Berry recruited a number of the best players available for his team including Artie Miller, a former Carlisle star, who spent his summer working as a lumberjack in Wisconsin. Berry had recruited so many stars that he called his team the Pittsburgh Stars. The Philadelphia As roster included wacky lefthander Rube Waddell, who had just finished his first season with the club, going 24-7 after joining the club on July 1. Manager Connie Mack found it necessary to dispatch two Pinkerton agents to the West Coast to

Caught along the sidelines in Philadelphia-Homestead game, *Philadelphia Inquirer* *11-24-1901*

accompany the "sousepaw" to Philadelphia. He had been pitching quite well for the Los Angeles Loo Loos. Waddell was a great talent but his eccentric habits made it necessary for Mack to keep him close during the off-season. Connie did not risk injuring Waddell by playing him in a football game, but he might have been an asset to the team as he had played rugby in the off season for several years. Several excellent games were played by the new league's teams, but much money was lost in this inaugural year of the NFL. The league standings were so muddled that it was difficult to determine which, if any, had a legitimate claim to the championship. Enter Tom O'Rourke, manager of Madison Square Garden, in need of a New Year's event.

Needing to fill the Garden, O'Rouke came up with a grandiose idea about holding a World Series of Football. Unfortunately for him, the college teams weren't interested, so, he turned to the independents. The four best independents that year were the three NFL clubs and the Watertown, New York Red and Blacks. The Red and Blacks had already claimed the World Championship of football in spite of having lost to the Athletics, at home no less. O'Rourke invited three of the four teams, figuring that New York fans wouldn't be interested in watching a team from Pittsburgh. Watertown refused to risk its self-proclaimed championship and the Philadelphia teams weren't coming, at least not as the Phillies or Athletics.

The clever O'Rourke put together a five-team tournament: the New York team, an amalgam of the best of the Phillies and Athletics players; the New York Knickerbockers; the Orange, New Jersey Athletic Club; the Warlow Athletic Club; and the Syracuse Athletic Club, rechristened the All-Syracuse team, with the addition of the Pierce and Warner brothers plus the Watertown backfield. O'Rourke optimized the schedule to promote the greatest interest (read box office). New York was supposed to easily dispense with All-Syracuse in the first night's contest, but O'Rourke was unaware that Syracuse had loaded up his team. Pop Warner later wrote that his brother, Bill, talked him into playing this game, the only pro game he ever played. Warner's head injury probably caused him to miss an extra point and three field goals. Syracuse won anyway. Two nights later they defeated the Knickerbockers 36-0, without the elder Warner, to win the first World Series of Football.

The NFL disbanded after the season was over. In 1903 the Franklin team in Venango County, Pennsylvania loaded up with every talented player it could find and there was no real competition to test them. O'Rourke invited Franklin to the second World Series of Football at Madison Square Garden, and the team accepted. This time Watertown agreed to come but was pummeled by Franklin in a game most notable as the one in which the officials were in full evening dress, including top hats and white gloves. Some opined that they were officiating a funeral. In a way they were because this was football's last World Series. The Franklin team was disbanded after the game and other Pennsylvania teams didn't pick up their high-priced players.

As Western Pennsylvania football declined, Ohio football ascended in places like Canton, Akron, Shelby and Massillon. However, this ascendancy moved forward, and sometimes backwards, in fits and starts. Carlisle played the vast majority of its games against college teams but did occasionally play athletic clubs. Because athletic clubs and other independent teams did not have the opportunity to practice as often as college teams, they were viewed as being a notch below them. In 1905 for some strange reason – most likely for money – Carlisle scheduled both Canton and Massillon clubs as part of a

6-games-in-19-days suicidal road trip. The Indians beat the four college teams but lost to the much heavier Canton and Massillon contingencies by respectable scores. Playing, and beating, Carlisle improved the stature of these rivals.

In 1906, as interest and support in the game was increasing, an event happened that set the professional game back for almost a decade. The problem started to brew when Canton lured several players away from rival Massillon for higher pay. Rumblings about crooked work during the game erupted after the Massillon newspaper, *The Independent*, accused Canton coach and captain, Blondy Wallace, of having someone on his team throw the game. Wallace sued for libel but withdrew the suit, most likely because *The Independent* had enough evidence to prove its claim. Tensions ran high because a lot of money had been bet on the game. A brawl at the Courtland Hotel Bar erupted among Canton followers that put an end to pro football in Canton and Massillon – at least for a while. Ohio football descended into what historian Milt Roberts called the "Unglamorous Years." Football continued but without the high pay and fanfare of the preceding years.

As Carlisle Indian School football improved to a high level in 1907, critics complained of professionalism at the school. Pop Warner responded with a letter he circulated to newspapers and college football programs. He claimed that 52 of the 54 players on the 1907 roster were regularly enrolled students; the other two were employees. However, some students were enrolled at places like Conway Hall, Dickinson College or Dickinson School of Law. Warner accepted that allowing students to play on the varsity more than four years and allowing employees to play might not be cricket. So, he announced that, in the future, Carlisle would only allow students to play and for a maximum of four years.

Something neither Warner nor his critics mentioned is that Carlisle stars sometimes played for college teams after having played for Carlisle. Jim Thorpe did mention being approached by a number of schools who wanted him to play for them. James Johnson, Ed Rogers, Frank Cayou, Joe Guyon, Mike Balenti and Frank Mt. Pleasant, for instance, played for Northwestern, Minnesota, Illinois, Georgia Tech, Texas A & M and Dickinson College, respectively, after finishing their studies at Carlisle. Lehigh University raised concerns about the eligibility of these players in 1908 when that school refused to play Dickinson College if Mt. Pleasant was on the squad. No other complaints have been found for Carlisle Indians playing for more than four years, when the surplus was for a college or university. There were some complaints about players shifting to Haskell Institute, though. Some of these men were named to All-America teams at the schools where they played after leaving Carlisle.

Professionalism with regard to baseball had been an ongoing problem for Carlisle for a number of years when Pop Warner eliminated it as an intercollegiate sport in 1910. The Indians, of course, excelled at its replacement, lacrosse, and produced All-Americans in that sport, but providing Carlisle students the opportunity to compete in a truly American sport was not the reason for the shift. Star athletes, many of whom were football players or track stars, would leave school to play baseball for pay. Carlisle student files contain several entries for students leaving to play baseball. Some did not come back and others' eligibility to play intercollegiate sports became an issue. At that time hundreds, if not thousands, of minor league and semi-professional baseball teams needed players. Although the pay was low, it was attractive to young men who loved to play the game and who had little money. That former Carlisle student, Albert "Chief" Bender, had been a huge success in major league baseball surely encouraged others to aim for the big leagues even if they didn't have Bender's talent.

Jack Cusack considered 1912 the Renaissance year for professional football because so many teams began to blossom that interest in the game increased dramatically in a large part of Ohio. A Canton team was organized that year as the Professionals to distance itself from the 1906 Bulldogs scandal. Cusack, then 21, took the job as team secretary-treasurer as a favor to team captain Roscoe Oberlin. He did the job for free. The alternative was to take a share of the profits – should there be any. After some internal squabbling and tactical maneuvering on the part of Cusack, he took over as manager.

After a 6-3 season, Jack Cusack felt he needed to attract more former college players to compete, and to do that he needed to pay them. He switched his players from a profit-split basis to salaries. Cusack and Oberlin backed the team financially as partners. Even with several of the college men on the 1913 roster, Canton still lost to Akron, its then arch rival. Cusack believed that, if football were to become profitable, it had to live down the 1906 scandal and regain the public's trust. A major obstacle, Cusack thought, was the constant jumping from team to team by players wanting to make a little more money. He approached the owners and managers of the other Ohio teams who agreed verbally to treat players who had signed with another team as that team's property until the other team released him. This collusion resulted in increased respectability and lower player salaries. Even with that agreement, Canton still lacked something – a strong rival in neighboring Massillon.

Canton-Massillon contests had been quite popular earlier, but Massillon dropped its team after the 1906 scandal. In 1914 the Massillon Chamber of Commerce invited Cusack to a meeting, during which they proposed to start a team by enticing away the Akron Indians' best players. When Cusack refused to play the team if it were formed that way, the backers decided against it. Canton sorely needed a rival in Massillon to be financially stable. In 1915, a group of Massillon businessmen, led by Jack Whalen and Jack Donohue, formed a team. Knowing that he would have to upgrade his team to compete, Cusack contacted every All-American he could think of and landed some of them. However, many would only play under assumed names to protect their primary employment. Coaches in particular were in jeopardy of losing their jobs because colleges and sports-writers were generally opposed to professional football. One of his best catches was the former Carlisle star, Bill Gardner, who soon figured in an historic event.

Canton, then known as the Bulldogs again, opened the 1915 season with a 75-0 shellacking of the Wheeling Athletic Club, followed by a hard-fought 7-0 victory over the always tough Nesser brothers' Columbus Panhandles. A 9-3 road loss to the Detroit Heralds, a team they had beaten the previous two years, was followed by a 41-12 win over the Cincinnati Colts, a team that was better than the score indicated. The Bulldogs then easily dispensed with the "Champions of Pennsylvania," the Altoona Indians, that included Carlisle players Alex Arcasa, Joe Bender, Joe Bergie, H. Brennan, Furrier, Fritz Henderson, Hoffman, Ted Pratt, Stilwell Saunooke, Shipp, George Vetterneck, Hugh Wheelock, Joel Wheelock, Winnshick and Woodring. (First names of some of these players are unknown.) Several of these names never appeared in accounts of Carlisle games, so it is likely they never started for the varsity or got enough playing time to mention. Also, some may have been playing under assumed names. For instance, Stilwell Saunook had last played on the varsity in 1903, making it questionable that he could still play competitive football. Current players may have taken others' names to mask the fact that they were playing on Sundays.

Next up on the schedule were the newly reconstituted Massillon Tigers. Cusack didn't know exactly who was on that team because so many played under assumed names. One who played under his own name was Notre Dame star end, Knute Rockne. Notre Dame quarterback Gus Dorais was Rockne's passing partner on both teams. Through painstaking research, Keith McClellan has determined who were most of the players on the Massillon roster, and the team was loaded with talent. Cusack knew he was up against a very tough team and needed to do something. Anyone who read the papers knew that Jim Thorpe was assisting Indiana University that fall. Some may have even known that he was playing on Sundays for the Pine Village Athletic Club. Cusack dispatched Bill Gardner to Bloomington to talk with his old teammate. Gardner returned with a signed contract under which Thorpe would play for Canton for $250 a game.

Jack Cusack's financial advisors thought he would put the Bulldogs into receivership by committing to the unheard of sum of $250 a game. Sure, a few players had been paid even more than this for the odd game, but never had anyone made a commitment to pay this much game after game. Cusack estimated that attendance at his team's games had averaged about 1,200 people up to that point in the season. The peak was the game at Detroit which drew 2,900. Home games against Columbus and Altoona drew 2,500 and 2,400, respectively. 6,000 attended the Canton-Massillon game at Massillon, and 8,500 turned out for the standing-room-only rematch in Canton. Cusack's gamble paid off in spades. Thorpe's hiring was a watershed event for professional football. His ability to attract large, for that time, crowds made football an economically viable business, even if paying stars handsomely. And two Carlisle stars had played prominent roles in making this happen.

Canton and Massillon split with each other and tied for the Ohio championship in 1915, but Canton was a stronger team in 1916. Cusack added three more Carlisle Indians: Pete Calac, William Garlow and Gus Welch. Jack added additional All-Americans to his roster as the schedule toughened. Thorpe returned to captain the team when the baseball season ended. At times Canton had four or five All-Americans warming the bench; the team was that strong. In 1968 Cusack stated that he felt his 1916 Canton Bulldogs could stand up against any of the pro teams of the current era. The Bulldogs went 9-0-1, giving up a single score all season and that one on a blocked punt. Canton was "Champion of the World" again. 1917 was a similar story. With Thorpe and Calac leading the way, Canton finished 9-1, splitting with Massillon. By this time, the U.S. had entered WWI and professional football was stopped until after the Armistice.

Jack Cusack took a job in the Oklahoma oil fields during the war and wasn't around when it was time to restart the team. A friend of Cusack and Thorpe, Ralph Hay, offered to take over the Bulldogs and Cusack let him. Hay basically reassembled the 1916-17 Bulldogs for 1919 and signed former Carlisle Indian and Rambling Wreck, Joe Guyon, who some thought was better than Thorpe. Given the age difference, he may well have been at that time. However, when the chips were down, Big Jim carried the Bulldogs on his back to important victories. Canton won the championship again in 1919 but struggled financially. The Black Sox baseball scandal that year cast a pall on all sports, but professional football was hurt more than the others.

Red ink, team-jumping by players, skyrocketing salaries, fickle fans and the Black

Sox scandal haunted the professional teams. Something had to be done, and a regular league sounded just like the ticket. On the evening of August 20, 1920, Ralph Hay held a meeting of team owners and two players, Jim Thorpe and Stanley Cofall, in the office of his Hupmobile dealership in Canton. This meeting gave birth to the American Professional Football Conference (APFC). Membership rules that first year were so vague that no one is certain exactly which teams were in the league and which weren't. The league did have some rules, or at least understandings. Members voted not to recruit undergraduate college students, not to lure away other teams' players with offers of higher salaries, to cooperate in making up schedules and, most importantly, to put a cap on player salaries. Unfortunately, only four teams were represented at the meeting: Canton, Akron, Dayton and Cleveland. Three other teams had written to Hay before the meeting, most likely to arrange games with Canton. Hay chose to include these teams as league members. However, exactly which teams wrote him is murky.

On September 17 a second meeting was held. In addition to the four original members, six other teams were represented: Rochester Jeffersons, Hammond Pros, Decatur Staleys, Rock Island Independents, Muncie Flyers and Racine (Chicago) Cardinals. Due to the heat, the meeting was held in the showroom and then-illegal cold beer was distributed to the owners, who sat on running boards of new Hupmobiles. New members were accepted and the league name was changed to the American Professional Football Association (APFA). Jim Thorpe was named President, likely more for name recognition than any presumed executive skills. Missing was one key component: a viable Massillon team for a rivalry with Canton. Membership fees were set at $100, but there is no record of any team actually paying it. Rules were not discussed, so they defaulted to the college rules then in force. Three more teams joined the league in 1920: the Detroit Heralds, Columbus Panhandles, and Chicago Tigers, none of whom were required to pay the $100 fee.

Teams played warm-up games in September against non-league teams and began their league schedules, such as they were, in October. A *retired* Jim Thorpe played only when it was necessary for the Bulldogs to win or tie. The league finished its first season unable to name a champion or to keep all of its teams. A league meeting was held in Akron on April 30, 1921. By a vote, the undefeated Akron Pros were awarded the "World's Professional Football Championship." Joe Carr of the Columbus Panhandles was elected President, a move that turned out to be an inspired choice.

Twenty-one teams were listed as being in the APFA in September but only 13 were listed in the final standings, largely due to having played too few league opponents. Thorpe, Guyon and Calac were in Cleveland's backfield that year and, after playing two

Oorang Indians coming to town, *Baltimore News 12-6-1922*

games, the Decatur Staleys moved to Cubs Park in Chicago. At year's end both Chicago and Buffalo, who had a slightly better record, claimed the league championship. After George Halas and Dutch Sternaman were awarded the Chicago franchise – well, not the only Chicago franchise as the Cardinals also had one – Halas was given a seat on the league's executive council. A council meeting naturally awarded the 1921 championship to the Staleys. Halas wanted to name the team the Cubs because they were playing in what folks today call Wrigley Field, but cubs are cuddly creatures, not exactly the image of a ferocious football team. So, Halas picked the grown up version of the animal for the team we know as the Bears.

The day before the January 1922 league meeting, nine University of Illinois players were banned from college athletics for having played for Taylorville, Illinois in a game against Carlinville, whose management had hired Notre Dame ringers. Headlines demanded action by the pro teams to end the practice of enticing college players to play for pay. The pros needed a scapegoat but not one who would cost the other teams the loss of a large gate. The Green Bay Packers fit that bill perfectly and agreed to withdraw from the league and be refunded their $50 franchise fee. The moguls then discussed but did not pass a salary cap. Two days later the fledgling football association got the most publicity it had to date when the Chicago *Herald and Examiner* headline blared across eight columns, "Stagg Says Conference Will Break Professional Football Menace." Knute Rockne announced that Notre Dame would treat harshly any of its players who had played for Carlinville. The Associated Press said Rockne had "…long been known as a staunch enemy of professional football." That is, since he had last played for Massillon. Eventually eight players were dropped by the Irish, necessitating that four sophomores, Stuhldreher, Miller, Crowley and Layden, start in the backfield the next year.

At the June meeting, owners felt they needed a grander name to reflect their grandiose ideas and renamed themselves the National Football League, even though they had no team on the Atlantic seaboard and the westernmost team was on the east bank of the Mississippi. Among the teams that were added – teams came and went so fast in those days that the league had trouble keeping up with them – were teams from Green Bay, Wisconsin and LaRue, Ohio. The Green Bay Blues, coached by former Irish backup Earl "Curley" Lambeau, were soon redubbed the Packers by the press. The LaRue team, the Oorang Indians, featuring Thorpe, Guyon and Calac, is worthy of a chapter of its own.

In the off-season, league President Joe Carr borrowed the reserve clause from baseball. Players who played for a team one year were reserved for it for the next year. This kept players from jumping from team to team for better offers. Carr also had 15% of players' salaries withheld until the end of the season. That also caused players to stay put, especially later in the season.

After winning the 1922 championship, Canton Bulldogs' owner Ralph Hay, the man most responsible for establishing the NFL, wasn't selling enough Hupmobiles to offset the Bulldogs' financial losses and sold the team to a group of local businessmen. The Bulldogs continued their championship ways under the new ownership but would continue to hemorrhage money. After winning another championship while losing $13,000 in 1923, the new owners of the Bulldogs had had enough and sold the franchise, players and all, to Sam Deutsch, owner of the Cleveland Indians franchise. Had Deutsch decided to field both teams, the league would have had problems. Instead, he merged the two franchises into the Cleveland Bulldogs to represent both the team's location and its players. The Bulldogs won the 1924 championship, despite a 23-0 December loss to the Bears, because of a league rule sponsored by George Halas; the rule allowed only those games played between NFL teams before November 30 to count toward championship consideration. So, Halas's rule cost him a championship. The 1925 season was extended to December 20.

Chicago won the league championship in 1925 but this time it was the Cardinals, not the Bears. However, the Bears won something more important near the end of the season. On the Monday before Thanksgiving, Harold "Red" Grange signed a contract with the Bears two days after finishing his college career with the University of Illinois by gaining 192 yards against the Buckeyes of Ohio State. During his college career, Grange set records not yet equaled. The "Wheaton Iceman's" performance against the previously unbeaten Michigan Wolverines in 1924 is the stuff of legends. All he did was to return the opening kickoff 95 yards for a touchdown, then race through the Michigan defense for three more long touchdowns in the first twelve minutes of play. "The Galloping Ghost" returned briefly in the second half to run for one touchdown and throw for another.

A *Chicago News* reporter, apparently no fan of professional football, wrote, "He is a living legend now. Why sully it?" University of Michigan coach Fielding Yost said, "I'd be glad to see Grange do anything else except play professional football." Grange's college coach, Bob Zuppke, was opposed to professionalism and told him, "Football just isn't a game to be played for money." Recognizing the hypocrisy, Grange replied, "You get paid for coaching, Zup. Why should it be wrong for me to get paid for playing?"

Grange's business manager, C. C. ("Cash and Carry" to some) Pyle, arranged a 10-game-18-day exhibition tour for the Bears and their new star. The tour was to open on Thanksgiving Day as a home game against the cross-town rival Cardinals. 36,000 people, by far the largest crowd to attend a professional football game to that time, packed Wrigley Field in spite of a snowstorm that hit that day. It was still snowing on Sunday when 28,000 showed up to see Grange and the Bears host Columbus. Only 8,000 hearty souls turned out in St. Louis the following Wednesday, due to a continuing snowstorm and 12 degree temperature. The following Saturday a rainstorm didn't discourage 35,000 from attending a game in Philadelphia. The next day 65,000 paid plus an estimated 8,000 gate-crashers watched Grange and the Bears play the New York Giants at the Polo Grounds. That game turned around the Giants' season financially, turning a loser into a winner. This game was one of the most important games in the history of pro football, not because of what happened on the field but because so many fans were in the stands and because it was New York. Professional football was now important.

The next game was in Washington, DC, where President Calvin Coolidge, not a sports fan, when introduced to Grange and Halas of the Bears, said, "Glad to meet you young gentlemen. I always did like animal acts." 25,000 Bostonians watched the Bears play the Providence Steamrollers on Wednesday. The next day in Pittsburgh, Grange suffered a blood clot as a result of a torn muscle caused by being kicked in the arm. 20,000 Detroit fans requested refunds because he was unable to play and 18,000 cheered him in a token appearance in a home game against the Giants to end the tour. He was beaten up and worn out but $150,000 richer. They started a second tour of nine games on Christmas Day in Coral Gables, Florida, playing games in other Florida cities, New Orleans and up the West Coast from San Diego to Seattle, all to large crowds. Attendance and money had reached new levels in the NFL. Jim Thorpe raised semi-pro football to a professional level in 1915 and Red Grange took it a step higher in 1925.

When asked about his contributions to pro football in later life, Indian Joe Guyon responded:

> "Take like when I went to the New York Giants in '27. I must have been about thirty-five then. But I spearheaded the Giants to their first world championship. Spearheaded them, yeh. Did everything. I kicked kickoffs clear through the uprights. I could still outrun those pro ballplayers. That was my last year of pro football, because that baseball injury ruined everything, but gosh-darn, I enjoyed New York."

Thorpe, Calac and Guyon completed their professional playing careers before the end of the decade, but Carlisle's participation in the NFL was not over. Lone Star Dietz was hired to coach the Boston Braves in 1933. A controversy over the team's name change to the Redskins to honor Dietz continues long after his departure after the 1934 season. The importance of Carlisle players to the birth of professional football was not forgotten by Jack Cusack, one of the midwives. In a 1968 interview, he told Bob Curran, "Consider such giants of the game as Big Jim Thorpe, Doc Spears, Milton Ghee, Carp Julian, Bill Gardner, Pete Calac, Dr. Hube Wagner, Robert Butler, Howard (Cub) Buck, Greasy Neale, Fred Sefton, P. C. Crisp, Bill Garlowe, Costello, and Ernie Soucy; if they were not real 'professionals' – well, what were they?"

Glenn Scobey "Pop" Warner

3

Warner coaching; *U. S. Army Military History Institute*

Name: Glenn Scobey Warner	**Nickname:** Pop; The Old Fox
DOB: 4/5/1871	**Height:** 6' 0"
Weight: 205	**Age:** 28
Tribe: N/A	**Home:** Springville, NY
Parents: William H. Warner; Adaline Scobey Warner	
Early Schooling: Griffith Institute	
Later Schooling: Cornell University	
Honors: College Football Hall of Fame, Charter Member 1951; Helm's Athletic Foundation Hall of Fame, 1951; Stanford Athletic Hall of Fame; Greater Buffalo Hall of Fame, 2001	

Coach of All the Ages

Pop Warner, the Carlisle Indians' coach and athletic director in their glory years, was not an Indian and never claimed to be one. The closest Warner would ever get to being an Indian was when he was made an honorary Sac and Fox. It is necessary to know a little about Warner because he was an integral part of the team and of the players' lives in Carlisle and, in some cases, in later life. This chapter is intentionally short; readers wanting to know more about "the Old Fox" can read the biographies already written about him. The purpose of this chapter is to provide the reader unfamiliar with Warner a brief overview of his life with an emphasis on his time at Carlisle. It hopefully includes a few nuggets rescued from the dustbin of history unknown even to those knowledgeable about Warner.

Glenn Scobey Warner was born on April 5, 1871, on a farm near Springville, New York, the first-born son of William H. and Adaline Scobey Warner. The family moved into town when Glenn was 10, a relocation that made playing baseball on a daily basis more practical. He also played what passed for football at the time, but baseball was his game. He was a fireball pitcher and could hit the long ball. After he completed high school, he moved with his family to Wichita Falls, Texas, to work on their wheat farm and cattle ranch. After a year of working on the ranch, he spent two more years in Texas learning the tinsmith trade and making some money. However, his 1892 vacation in his old hometown changed the direction of his life.

At 21 years of age he returned to Springville just in time to play baseball for the town team in a series of games against the hated rival town's team. Both teams hired ringers and he established a friendship with one of his town's ringers, John McGraw, that paid off in later life. After some success betting on harness races, he convinced himself that he was an expert and followed the Grand Circuit the rest of the summer. He lost $150, all he had previously won plus everything else he had except his return trainfare, on the first day. Broke and not desiring to explain to his father what had happened to his money, Warner considered pursuing the course his father had wanted him to follow from the start. His father wired him the $100 necessary to enroll in law school at Cornell.

Money in hand, he caught the day train to Ithaca and, on the ride, made the acquaintance of football captain Carl Johanson who, upon seeing Warner's size (200 pounds), ordered him to attend football practice that afternoon. Despite having little experience, having missed the two previous weeks of practice, and having to play in a game the next day, Warner was made starting left guard. He did not relinquish that position during his playing career at Cornell. However, he was still more interested in baseball. On the first day of spring practice, Glenn tried to impress the coach even though he had been told to take it easy, and he developed a sore arm. The next day, in spite of the pain, he threw at full speed again, ruining his arm forever. His baseball career over, he dabbled a bit with boxing and track but found that his best opportunities were then in football.

Shortly after arriving at Cornell, he acquired the nickname "Pop" because he was three years older than his classmates. The name stuck to him like glue the rest of his life. Pop played football and studied law for two years, then graduated. He was elected captain for the following year but, since he had completed his law degree, he had to take some graduate level courses to be on the field. His father couldn't be expected to pay, so Warner solved that problem by selling watercolor landscapes he painted.

Some consider Glenn Warner to have been Cornell's greatest guard ever. However, after starring for three years, his playing days were essentially over. He passed the bar examination and was ready to litigate at season's end. After finding a law firm in Buffalo that was willing to accept him, he went to work in January 1895. Before his nascent body of clients could grow to provide him a decent income, an opportunity to supplement his income by coaching football appeared. While pondering the idea of making $25 a week in the fall, he got another offer for $35. Not wanting to let an opportunity escape, Warner negotiated with Iowa Agricultural College (today's Iowa State) to prepare its team for the season by working with it for five weeks at $25 a week. His assistant worked with the team the rest of the season while Warner coached the University of Georgia for $35 a week for the whole season. So, in Pop's first year as a head coach, he mentored two college teams, a feat that has seldom been duplicated. It should be noted that Warner lost the entire $125 salary from Iowa State in a wager on their first game. This two-team scheme worked well enough that Warner prepared the Iowa State team for five seasons running while coaching elsewhere during the season. After two successful years at Georgia, Warner's alma mater beckoned. He also had on-field success in his two years at Cornell, but internal politics made staying there unwise if not impossible.

The Carlisle Indian School football team had been described by pundits as a fine set of athletes sorely in need of first-class coaching. Superintendent Pratt took that to heart and looked for the best coach he could find. Walter Camp recommended Warner, thinking that this innovative young coach would be a good fit with the Indians. Warner asked for a salary of $1,200 plus expenses and Pratt didn't blink. So, when Pratt offered him the job, he jumped at it.

The 1899 Carlisle team, Warner's first at the Indian school, was loaded with fine players, several of whom may have already been first team All Americans had they played for one of the Big Four. Warner soon found that the methods he had used previously, and those under which he had played, would not work with the Indians. Pushing players hard and swearing at them was the norm for coaches at that time, but the Indians did not respond well to what they considered abuse. He recalled that a near mutiny resulted and several good players stopped coming to practice because of his tactics. Pop observed that they were not used to being sworn or cussed at and found the experience to be humiliating. Ives Goddard, a noted linguist, offers this opinion:

> "For one, Indian languages do not have the equivalent of using the name of deities in legal or religious oaths and hence do not have the use of 'God' etc. in what is called profanity in the narrow sense, taking the name of God 'in vain.' Secondly, they typically do not have slang words for sexual and other intimate functions and body parts, so there can be no equivalent of using 'four-letter words' in English. (Some speakers of some languages may avoid some words or use jokey substitutes, though.) Probably all languages have offensive ways of talking about people or cussing people out, considered serious or even 'fighting words.' In general, however, there are unfortunately few details available about the specific usages in these areas in various languages.
>
> "My guess would be that the Carlisle students who objected to swearing did so because of Christian upbringing in Protestant churches whose missionaries condemned such language in English."

Warner called a team meeting for all the players, including the ones who had stopped coming to practice. He explained that his verbal outbursts were meant to emphasize points and were not intended to demean players. He promised to tone down his language and asked them to come back to practice. "The next day, the Indians returned to practice and I went on to coach without using a lot of profanity to motivate my team. I soon found out that I would get better results from them by this method. Once this problem was settled, the Carlisle team began to concentrate on football. And the results were impressive."

The 1899 team with Warner at the helm was Carlisle's best to date. It was the first Indian team to beat one of the Big Four, Penn. The only losses were to that year's national co-champions, Harvard and Princeton. The Indians also defeated that year's West Coast power, California, on Christmas Day. For the first time ever, Walter Camp named an Indian, Isaac Seneca, to his All America first team at halfback. He also named Martin Wheelock to his second team at tackle and Frank Hudson to the third team at quarterback. Hudson was also the preeminent kicker of his day and others on the team, including Wheelock, were pretty darn good. It was reported in the press that, "Warner, the Carlisle coach, attributes the skill of the redskins in kicking to the fact that the lower part of the leg is hung straight from the knee, instead of slightly curving, as is the case of Caucasians."

Major Pratt sanctioned the long football trips because he thought the travel was educational for the players. That the school usually made a good bit of money couldn't have hurt. It was upon the team's return from the California trip that Major Pratt made Warner an offer to be the school's athletic director. The $2,500 salary was an offer he couldn't refuse. Because he then had a full-time position at Carlisle, Pop closed out his nascent law practice. However, he occasionally used his knowledge of the law to draft a contract for a player who was turning pro. Because the athletic director was responsible for all sports, Warner had to bone up on track, something he had never coached. Gaining a rudimentary knowledge of coaching track from books and conversations with experts, Warner inaugurated Carlisle's first ever track team in 1900. The track on which the Carlisle teams raced still circumnavigates Indian Field, the site of the Indians' football battles on Carlisle Barracks, current home of the U. S. Army War College.

Glenn made an interesting observation regarding his athletes: "And it was a noticeable fact that the Indian football players were often the brightest students at Carlisle and their teachers frequently remarked on how much quicker they were to learn than the other students."

Warner's 1900 team went 6-4-1 against a tougher schedule than was played the previous year. The 1901 team was weak over all and was one of the few losing seasons Warner experienced at the Indian school. Wanting to rest his first-string halfbacks for the upcoming game with Penn, Warner left them home when the team went to Michigan to play Fielding Yost's point-a-minute team. The backups, Louis Leroy and Edward DeMarr, decided Detroit was close to home and ran away, leaving Carlisle without running backs for the game. Their absence didn't materially affect the outcome of a game Warner had little hope of winning.

A junior player on that year's squad was a young man by the name of Charles Albert Bender. He would likely have turned into a good football player if he had persisted, but Connie Mack, manager of the Philadelphia Athletics from 1901 to 1950, beckoned. The young Chippewa left Carlisle to play in the big leagues where the future Hall-of-Fame pitcher was often called "Chief."

Things improved football-wise in 1902 when, by beating Penn again and losing only to Bucknell, Harvard, and Virginia, the Indians again had a winning record. After the season, Pop's younger brother and sometime assistant, Bill, talked him into agreeing to take what turned out to be the princely sum of $23 to play for a professional team in the World Series of professional football held at Madison Square Garden over the New Year. The Warner brothers held up one side of the line at guard and tackle. Carlisle Indians Bemus and Hawley Pierce held up the other side of the same line. In the first game, Pop received a bad cut on his head but didn't leave the game. After the injury, he missed a kick after touchdown and three field goals in a winning effort. As he told it, "The next morning – following the game – I awoke feeling very stiff and could only move my tired body with great difficulty. I even had to call upon my brother, Bill, to help me get dressed that morning because of the tremendous pain that I was suffering. After that single game, I decided to retire from my career in professional football."

The team improved considerably in 1903, having its best team yet, beating Penn again and losing only to Princeton and Harvard. The single-point loss to Harvard featured the much-written-about hidden ball or hunchback play that gave the Indians a lead. Warner later wrote, "In a way, I'm glad that Harvard was able to come back to win because I never liked to win a game on a fluke, although the hidden ball play was within the rules at that time."

Cornell alumni were disgruntled over their football team's performance in the last four games of the 1903 season. The coach with whom they were dissatisfied was one William Warner, Pop's younger brother. After being approached by a Cornell faculty committee, the elder Warner agreed to return to coach his alma mater in 1904. Knowing that Superintendent Pratt would likely be forced out of his position at Carlisle due to public statements he had made which would make conditions at Carlisle uncertain surely made Pop's decision to leave easier. His results in 1904 and 1905 at Cornell were slightly better than his brother's had been, from a won-lost perspective. 1906 was much better but he was involved in a campus controversy.

In early 1907 after an 8-1-2 season, Warner resigned to make peace at the school. He had found it necessary to drop a star player from the squad. "But my disciplining of this player nearly caused a campus riot. The player was a hero among the school's student body, and naturally my action created an uproar with them and caused a lot of trouble and unrest.... I had felt in my heart and mind that I was right in regards to my handling of the matter, because I had done what any coach would have done if he has any *backbone* to him."

Pop Warner apparently didn't sever all his ties to Carlisle when he departed for Cornell. In 1906 Carlisle's new superintendent, Major Mercer, invited Warner to help prepare the Indians for the upcoming season. Radically new rules had been adopted after the outcry over the inordinate number of deaths of football players experienced in 1905. The new rules shifted the advantage from bulk to speed and deception as well as legalization of the forward pass. Warner spent a week coaching Carlisle's coaches with his new innovations. One of the things Warner imparted to Bemus Pierce and Frank Hudson, former players then coaching the Indians, was the earliest incarnation of his new formation. He later wrote to football historian Col. Alexander M. Weyand, "As to the single wing formation I started using this in 1906. That was the year the rules were radically changed making it necessary to have seven men on the line of scrimmage and making it illegal to help the ball carrier by pushing or pulling. Walter Camp in his writings often referred to it as the <u>Carlisle formation</u>. I do not remember what team it was first used against. I also originated the double wing formation but I believe I used it before the Dartmouth game of 1912 [Carlisle only played Dartmouth one time. That game was played in 1913]. Although it sure worked havoc on Dartmouth I think I used it two or three years before 1912."

Perhaps it was seeing Frank Mt. Pleasant throw 40-yard spiral passes or it was seeing how well the Indians ran his offense under the Indian coaches, but Warner agreed to come back to Carlisle for the 1907 season. He later recalled:

"Carlisle played good football from the first, but it was in 1907 that the Indians rounded into true championship form., downing Pennsylvania by a score of 26 to 5, Minnesota by 12 to 0, Harvard by 23 to 15 and Chicago by 18 to 4. With the exception of the unbeaten Pitt team of 1916, it was about as perfect a football machine as I ever sent on the field. Typically Indian, too, for among the first-string men were Little Old Man, Afraid of a Bear, Lubo the Wolf, Little Boy, Wauseka,

[Frank] Mount Pleasant and [Mike] Balenti. The boys clicked into shape early in the season, and the very first game convinced me that a big year was ahead.

…

"The Carlisle eleven of 1907 was nearly perfect. Jim Thorpe, by the way, made his first appearance that year, subbing now and then for [Fritz] Hendricks. The forward pass had just been permitted by the new rules and we were about the first to see its value and develop its possibilities to the limit. How the Indians did take to it! Light on their feet as professional dancers, and every one amazingly skillful with his hands, the redskins pirouetted in and out until the receiver was well down the field, and then they shot the ball like a bullet. Poor Pennsylvania, among the first to experience Carlisle's aerial attack, finally reached a point where the players ran in circles, emitting wild yawps. The one defeat of the 1907 season was handed to us by Princeton.

…

"Few things have ever given me greater satisfaction than that Chicago victory. Stagg's team up to then, was laying claim to the championship and sports writers refused to concede that poor Lo had a chance. The game, in fact, was to be a field day for the great [Chicago quarterback Wally] Steffen, famous for his twisting, dodging runs and educated toe … Steffen did kick one field goal but that was his only pretense to glory. [William] Gardner and [Albert] Exendine were on him every time he tried to run back a kick.… I remember that Carlisle's share of the gate was $17,000, an almost incredible sum in those days.

…

"Our ends that year were Gardner, a Sioux [sic], and Exendine [sic], an Arapahoe, and I still maintain that they have never been surpassed for sheer brilliance. Pete Hauser, who did the kicking for us, was a big Cheyenne with a powerful toe, his punts averaging 60 yards, and under instructions he always raised them sky high. Gardner and Exendine were off at the swing of his leg, and it was rarely that they failed to keep up with the ball. In the game with Chicago they made life miserable for Wally Steffen, invariably nailing him in his tracks, although [Chicago coach Amos Alonzo] Stagg finally assigned three men to block each end."

1907 was not the end of a team's great runs; it was just the continuation of what Warner started in 1899 and continued for some years. Warner observed that some of the tougher teams became reluctant to schedule Carlisle now that they were often beating Penn and had defeated Harvard. Never again would they be able to schedule three or four games against the Big Four; even scheduling two Big Four opponents became less common.

The undersized Indians and Warner's offenses that capitalized on speed and deception were a perfect match. The combination was so effective that other coaches copied it.

Wauseka, James Johnson, Al Exendine, Pop Warner, *Cumberland County Historical Society, Carlisle, PA*

Warner started marketing a correspondence course on the rudiments of football in 1908. Soon the Warner system dominated American football.

Carlisle peaked with three straight one-loss seasons in 1911, 1912 and 1913. Warner considered the 1911 team as the best, having defeated both Penn and Harvard. It should be noted that Jim Thorpe had departed before the 1913 season, so Carlisle wasn't a one-player team as some have suggested. The outcome of the government investigation into improprieties at the Indian school in early 1914 made it impossible to field a competitive team, so Warner left.

Much has been written about Warner's role in the stripping of Jim Thorpe's medals, so that needs no repeating. However, what may be new information is that student records from the Carlisle Indian School contain numerous mentions of students leaving to play summer baseball. Even the school newspaper mentioned individuals and their teams. No mention was made of pay, but it was common knowledge which teams were professionals. It is highly unlikely that Superintendent Friedman and Coach Warner were unaware of this. They probably knew Thorpe left to play minor league baseball but didn't expect to see him return and, if they did, they certainly did not expect him to become the physical specimen who did return.

The most famous football referee of the period, Mike Thompson, officiated many Carlisle games and said this about Warner:

> "I first saw the Indians in 1902, when I refereed their game against Cornell. Bill Warner, Pop's brother, was captain of the Cornell team that year, as Pop had been in 1894... Pop knew his Indians. He walked and acted like one, and came to be a man of few words, mostly grunt, until his boys really believed that he had Indian blood. He knew an Indian's strength and limitations, capitalized on the former and avoided the latter. Warner showed each man his job individually, demonstrating it, not talking it. Perhaps he gave his quarter a little theory, but for the most part he depended upon their native cunning, skill and love of the game to do the rest. The Indians loved trick plays. Pop gave them plenty and knew just when to pull his tricks. I doubt that any other coach could have approximated his success at Carlisle..."

Warner himself learned that coaching the Indians required a different approach than coaching white players. "While at Carlisle, I had developed a theory that the Indian boys had been trained by their forefathers to be keen observers. Often when the Indian boys were exposed to a new sport or game they would usually refuse to participate. Instead, they would stand and watch the older, more experienced Indian boys, who were participating in the new sport or game, demonstrate how it was to be played. Then after having studied the play or actions, or motions of their elders, they would attempt to mimic those same actions, or motions, and would usually be almost as accomplished as those who they had just observed."

Pop Warner Is Sportdom's Greatest Inventor; What Would He Do if Tackled Baseball?

G.S. Warner

Reno Gazette 12-9-1915

Warner shared some other insights into his Carlisle players in a 1933 interview. "Carlisle was a school where the Indian would come as a mere boy and stay there a number of years obtaining his education. I had a chance to develop him from the ground up and to use his ability during his best athletic years.... Some of my boys came to Carlisle entirely uneducated and it took them years to get through, meaning I had them on my teams when they were more mature." When asked what the optimum age for a football player was, Warner responded, "It is hard to lay down a general rule because one man may be at his best at 27 and another at 20. On the whole, however, I would say that 23 is a fine age for a football player. He is old enough to know some of the tricks of the trade and young enough to have plenty of speed and fire."

After leaving Carlisle, Warner went on to coach at Pitt, Stanford and Temple, to win national championships and to win the Rose Bowl but he always loved the Indians:

> "Great teams, those Carlisle elevens that I coached, and what was even finer, sportsmen all. There wasn't an Indian of the lot who didn't love to win and hate to lose, but to a man they were modest in victory and resolute in defeat. They never gloated, they never whined, and no matter how bitter the contest, they played cheerfully, squarely and cleanly.
>
> "Whenever I see one of those all-America teams, I cannot help but think what an eleven could have been selected from those *real* Americans who blazed such a trail of glory across the football fields of the country from 1899 to 1914. One might go a long way before he found a better line-up than this:

Exendine	right end
Wauseka	right tackle
Bemus Pierce	right guard
Lone Wolf Hunt	center
Martin Wheelock	left guard
Hawley Pierce	left tackle
Ed Rogers	left end
James Johnson	quarterback
James Thorpe	right halfback
Joe Guyon	left halfback
Pete Hauser	fullback

"And for substitutes, if substitutes were ever needed for these iron men, how about such players as Bill Gardner, Lone Star Dietz, [Antonio] Lubo, Afraid of a Bear, Little Boy, [Isaac] Seneca, [Jonas] Metoxen, [Pete] Calac, [Frank] Hudson, [Frank] Mount Pleasant and Gus Welch?"

As great a coach as Warner was, he was no better at predicting the future than anyone else. In an article for Baseball Magazine, Pop looked into his crystal ball and saw a limited future for football:

> *Football will never be a great national game, for a variety of reasons. The season is shorter, not so many games are possible as in baseball, for instance; and the game is not so open or spectacular. But, in my opinion, one of the main reasons why it will never be a popular sport, is the fact that it depends too much on careful coaching.*
>
> Glenn Warner

4

Frank Cayou

Frank Cayou (right), Athletic Director of Illinois
Athletic Club; *Chicago History Museum*

Name: Francis Mitchell Cayou	**Nickname:**
DOB: 3/7/1878	**Height:** 5' 8-1/2"
Weight: 140	**Age:** 17
Tribe: Omaha	**Home:** Omaha reservation north of Decatur, Nebraska

Parents: Fred Cayou, white, probably French; Me-umba-the (Moonbeam)

Early Schooling: Omaha Agency boarding school, possibly the Presbyterian Mission School

Later Schooling: Dickinson College prep school; Dickinson College; University of Illinois

Honors: Wabash College Athletic Hall of Fame, 1982

Strongheart

Francis Mitchell Cayou was one of the more colorful of the Carlisle Indians and that is saying something. Frank first came east to Chicago from the Omaha Reservation in Nebraska in the summer of 1893 to work as one of the hundreds of Columbian Guards at the World's Columbian Exposition. Seeing what white men had accomplished caused him to think his people were ignorant and degraded. Three years later he spoke about that experience:

> "Drunkenness and laziness is their curse. The white people keep the Indians on reservations. This degrades them. They are environed by civilization, but they are not of it. The government sends my people money, and they drink it up. It was almost as bad to give them rations so freely, for they would eat in a short time what they had and go hungry without a thought for tomorrow. I was that way, but I saw what the

white people had done, and the desire possessed me – the ambition, I should say, to raise myself up and help my race. Their only hope is to live among the whites, be educated and adopt their ways."

His arrival at Carlisle on October 8, 1893 nearly coincided with Superintendent Pratt's rescission of his ban on inter-scholastic football. His later career path suggests that he might have been the orator who presented the students' arguments so well, but his age, 15, and newness at the school argue against it. Regardless, he was soon immersed in the school's athletic programs. Although small at age 17, Frank starred on the football and track teams, due in part to being a very fast runner. He soon made a splash in the big city papers. 1894 was Carlisle's first full season of football but it was already producing stars – and Frank Cayou was one of them.

The Saturday before the 1895 season started, he won a competition that was not exactly of an athletic type, but he won it in a cake walk – literally. In its article on the Standard Debating Club's first sociable of the year, *The Indian Helper* reported, "In a cake walk, Mr. Frank Cayou and lady, Miss Julia Long, won the prize of a handsome cake for the most graceful marching." Cupid's bow may have misfired as Julia returned to nursing school in Philadelphia two days after the dance. But Cayou didn't sulk. Instead, he threw himself into school affairs. He was active as an orator both as an officer for the Standards and in giving talks to the entire student body.

Frank completed his studies at the Indian School and graduated in March 1896. A month after commencement, consumption (tuberculosis) struck close. Fellow class member Edward Spott died of consumption a month after graduation and Cayou served as a pallbearer. Both graduates were still in town because they were enrolled in the Dickinson College Preparatory School.

1896 was Carlisle's first winning football season. Although enrolled in the prep school, Frank continued to play for the Indians. The speedy left halfback stood out in the Yale game played in New York City. His 45-yard run around end was the play of the game for Carlisle. As a token of her esteem, the wife of financier Russell Sage and future philanthropist, Olivia Sage, who had watched the game with the Pratts, gave the Carlisle players bunches of mums and roses in their school colors. Mrs. Sage tied Frank's bunch with the ribbon she wore during the game because of his outstanding run.

The *New York World* had a lot to say about Cayou's performance against the previously unscored upon Yale team:

"It was a heaving, twisting, squirming mass of men. Suddenly men in blue began to fall. Bass, the famous, and Rogers, pride of Yale's rush line, went down like ninepins. Between them sprang an Indian. He had the ball in his arms and he was free. One after another of the Yale men sprang after him, only to be bowled over by the stocky Indians who protected him. It was the business of Chauncey, the New Haven halfback, to stop this handsome Indian. The Yale man made a dash for him. Cayou shook him off and never checked his pace. Cayou ran sixty yards and made a touchdown. The Indians had scored against Yale in the first ten minutes of play. The 'bleachers,' the 'bridges' and the 'deadheaders' were drunk with excitement. People in the covered grand-stand even awoke to fine enthusiasm. The Indians along the side lines danced around. Now and then one would give an ear-splitting yell. The Yale men looked at each other as if they were not sure what had happened."

Frank made an interesting acquaintance at that game. William C. DeMille, an undergrad at Columbia University at the time, became familiar with Frank and his background when they met after the game. Cayou's life story formed the basis for a major literary work by DeMille less than a decade later.

During the week after the Penn game, *The Indian Helper* reported on something that had previously been a secret: "Frank Cayou surprised everybody with a solo. But a very few knew that he possessed such a rich, true voice. In fine baritone, he rendered 'Yearnings,' by Rubenstein, in a manner that showed study and cultivation; the song was enthusiastically encored." This would not be his last vocal performance.

The 1896 football season included a post-season trip to Chicago for a night game in the Coliseum against Intercollegiate Conference of Faculty Representatives (today's Big Ten Conference) power Wisconsin. The Indians defeated the Champions of the West, of course. Note that the Big Ten was often called the Western Conference in those days. Ever wonder what "Champions of the West" referred to in *Hail to the Victors*? Well, the Indians beat them a few times.

Frank represented the Indian School in the spring as captain of the track team. His primary events were the short dashes and the mile relay. Perhaps the most exciting race was the relay run in a meet at Dickinson College, in which the normal schools also participated. When Frank, who ran the anchor leg, received the baton, he was 20 yards behind the leader. He rapidly made up the ground and won going away on the home stretch.

Frank left for Northfield Summer School for Bible Study in June 1897 as one of the contingent from the Indian School's YMCA. The Bible conference was held on the grounds of the Northfield Seminary for Young Ladies which was founded by evangelist Dwight Lyman Moody in 1879 in his hometown, Northfield, Massachusetts. Religion was a key theme throughout Cayou's life.

Frank played football for the Indians again in 1897 while studying at the Dickinson College Preparatory School. 1897 featured a three-games-in-eight-days road trip to the Midwest in which they played Illinois, Cincinnati and Ohio State Medical College. The first of the three was a night game in the Chicago Coliseum. It was in that game that John Steckbeck thought protective headgear was first worn in the West when some Carlisle players donned them.

The day after winning the game, Frank and David McFarland, who had been injured in the game the night before, headlined a meeting of the Hyde Park YMCA. The *Chicago Daily Tribune* reported, "Frank Cayou, the substitute left halfback, was the principal speaker. He showed the pale faces how the same skill in mass play and line bucking and the same dogged endurance which won the Carlisle boys their great victory at the Coliseum had scored many a touchdown in the contest with Indian superstition and inbred depravity." He talked at length about the situation at Carlisle and quoted scripture. He also talked about the uphill battle against popular conceptions they fought. "Many of the whites have queer conceptions of the Indian. 'The only good Indian is a dead Indian,' expresses the general sentiment, apparently. There were no dead Indians at the Coliseum last night, but I think they are pretty good boys." He also spoke out against the reservation system and said winning by tricks was not necessary.

Frank also did some speaking at the football banquet held in January at Dickinson College when he gave a talk entitled, "Past, Present and Future of the Carlisle Indian School Team." After summarizing Carlisle's very short history at playing the game, he prematurely predicted victory over one of the Big Four in the upcoming season.

1898 again found Frank Cayou at Dickinson College, not in the prep school but in the college proper as an unclassified student. However, he still played football for Carlisle and continued to shine both off and on the field. After the Williams College game in Albany, New York, the team visited public schools where Cayou gave a speech, toured the Capitol, where the players were introduced to the governor, and cruised the confluence of the Mohawk and Hudson Rivers on the *Yale*.

The Illinois game, Frank's last in a Carlisle football uniform, was a bittersweet experience. Sweet because it was a victory but frustrating in its ending as reported by the *Chicago Chronicle*:

> "There were twenty-five seconds of time left when the signal was given for the last assault of the day. Cayou caught the pass, hesitated the fraction of a second and then gave a leap. The impetus carried him off on top of the struggling pile of players and his body swayed over the line, but before he could reach the earth and call down the whistle had blown. The game was over with the ball on the Illinois six inch line, half a foot from another touchdown."

However, Frank wasn't done with football for the year because Dickinson College still had a game left to play and it was a big one against Penn State. *The Dickinsonian* justified his appearance:

> "Two new faces appeared on the home team, Rodgers [sic] at left-end and Cayou at left half-back, both of them star players for the Indians, but *bona fide* students of the College and as such entitled to a place on our eleven. They played in their usually brilliant style, Rodgers especially distinguishing himself by fine tackling."

In the spring, Cayou was competing for Dickinson College in track. He won a gold watch at the Penn Relays, repeating his success of the previous year when competing for Carlisle. That spring he also sang baritone solos accompanied by the renowned Carlisle Indian School band under the direction of Dennison Wheelock.

After spending the summer in Boston, perhaps playing baseball or working, Frank returned to Carlisle long enough to gather up his things and head west. He moved to Champaign, Illinois where he enrolled in an electrical engineering program at the University of Illinois, played football and ran track. In a meet between Illinois and Chicago, Cayou and his competitor finished in a dead heat with both tying the intercollegiate record for the 220-yard dash of 22 seconds. The April 29, 1900 *Chicago Daily Tribune* reported that, on the previous day in a local meet in Champaign, he had won both the 440-yard dash and the 220-yard dash. Someone by the name of Brundage came in second in the 220. This was not be the last time a Brundage would finish behind a Carlisle Indian. Frank starred in football, of course, and ran 85-yards for a touchdown against Purdue.

Cayou also spent some time in Arcola, Illinois the next summer, ostensibly to train the Arcola Volunteer Fire Department Hose and Hook and Ladder teams for the Illinois and national championship competitions, both of which they won. *The Daily News* reported, "Handsome, an athlete, a knobby dresser, he won his way into the best society of the city, and was a marked favorite of the young women of the city… A graduate of the Carlisle school, he presented a most pleasing appearance, was a splendid conversationalist and had hundreds of friends."

In 1901 he continued playing in Illinois' 18-0 victory thumping of Indiana in spite of breaking his nose shortly after entering the game. In July 1902 *The Red Man and Helper* quoted Frank as writing, "The musical training received at Carlisle has enabled me to hold a position as bass singer in a quartette choir in the largest church in Champaign. I have been captain of the track team this year and my time in running for the quarter mile race has been fifty seconds."

In the summer of 1902, Frank's days of competing for Illinois came to an end, most likely because he and three teammates raced for Arcola in the state firemen's tournament held in Blue Island in mid-August. The Central Illinois AAU disqualified Cayou, his teammates and a Taylorville athlete from college athletics. All were accused of accepting pay for competing, and all denied the charges, saying they could prove their innocence. It does not appear that Frank competed for Illinois after that. During the 1911 season, a New York sports writer who wrote under the Monty byline listed Frank Cayou among the best fullbacks who ever played the game. That was something considering he played halfback.

That fall found Frank Cayou coaching, still in Champaign but now coaching the Champaign Central High School football team. A 6-2-2 record for his first year of coaching wasn't too bad considering that the first loss, a 29-0 beating by Danville, was quickly avenged in a rematch 5-0 later in the season. The only other loss was by one point to Bloomington. Two ties were the only other blemishes on their record. The next fall, in 1903 still in Champaign, he was in charge of the University of Illinois freshmen. However, football did not take up all of his time; he had some left for other matters.

In mid-November, according to *The Daily Record*, "Monday he arrived in this city and said he desired to take Miss Anna Snyder to Champaign, where 'The County Chairman" was to be presented. No one objected to the arrangement, and he took the young lady to the hotel to dinner. Some friend managed to steal all the wearing apparel of Miss Snyder while the dinner was in progress, and the pair took the fast train north for Tuscola. Arriving at Tuscola, Cayou hunted up County Clerk Hawkins, where a marriage license was secured, and the marriage occurred at the Methodist parsonage, Rev. William Brandon officiating. Immediately after the ceremony the happy young people left on the late

Cayou elopes, *Sandusky Evening Star 12-28-1903*

train for Chicago." A later illustrated article distributed nationally identified the bride's age, 18, as the only objection her wealthy parents had to their socialite daughter marrying a penniless Indian. *The Daily Record* reporter was apparently quite enamored with the winsome Miss Snyder when he wrote, "His bride is regarded as one of the most hand-some young women of Douglas County, a county famous for fair women." He was quite supportive of the groom. "During the summer months Mr. Cayou spent in this city he conducted himself with great credit, and many think he will make a name and fortune for himself and bride."

Indications are that the newlyweds set up housekeeping in the bride's home town and Frank took a job "traveling for a Chicago mercantile house." It isn't known if Frank's influential father-in-law arranged the job or if he got it using his own contacts in the sporting world. Regardless of how he got the job, he seems not to have stayed with it for long.

On May 6, 1904, *The Decatur Review* announced that Frank Cayou would be taking the helm of the Wabash College football program that fall. Because Wabash's home, the town of Crawfordsville, Indiana, was not terribly far from Arcola, Illinois, it is likely that the young couple maintained their household in Arcola while he shuttled back and forth to the campus as his schedule dictated. Before football season started, several of the best track men in the country, including Frank, were permanently suspended by the Western Association of the AAU for participating in the firemen's hose reel games in World's Fair Stadium in St. Louis in August. Reasons for the suspensions were not provided. Frank was likely more concerned with fielding a winning football team than running races at this point in his life.

The Scarlet of little Wabash College faced a daunting schedule for 1904. Included in its opponents that year were Illinois, Purdue, Notre Dame and Indiana. Only 300 students attended what is one of the few remaining all-male institutions of higher learning today. Fewer attended during Cayou's time. While watching his undersized team, which averaged a little over 140 pounds per man, battle the much larger opponents, Cayou remarked that they fought like little giants. Reporters picked up on it and Wabash's teams have been known as the Little Giants ever since. So pleased was the College's administration with Frank's performance that they awarded him a three-year contract as physical director and football coach. He then had a full-time job as athletic director in charge of all sports at the Indiana school. As another reward for the 4-4 season in which he lost only to the four large schools on the schedule, Frank was presented with two more majors to play: Northwestern and Chicago. The Little Giants beat one of them, Notre Dame, which wouldn't lose another home game until 1928. For little Wabash to go 6-5-1 against this schedule was quite an accomplishment.

1906 was considerably lighter with only three majors to play: Indiana, Purdue and Illinois. Cayou's charges lost only to Indiana, holding Illinois to a scoreless tie and beating the Boilermakers, the derogative name given to the Purdue teams in 1891 by Wabash fans who believed ringers from the Monon Shops were brought in to play instead of students. Having a good year, an open date and perhaps a lot of confidence in his team, Cayou telegraphed Carlisle in hopes of setting up a Thanksgiving Day game. That was not to be, so the 5-1-1 record was Cayou's best at Wabash. Perhaps sensing that their "famous Indian" coach, as reporters liked to say, was a valuable commodity, in March of 1907, before his contract ran out in June, the Wabash Board of Trustees authorized an extension to his contract accompanied by a substantial raise. Immediately after completing a successful spring track season, Cayou set about preparing his men for the upcoming gridiron campaign with pre-season practices in mid-June. Getting and keeping his men in peak playing condition was a key to his success because his players suffered fewer injuries than average as a result.

In September, an advance man promoting a road tour of William C. DeMille's hit play, *Strongheart*, which was to be staged in Crawfordsville, let it be known that the title character was based on the life of local football coach and athletic director, Francis M. Cayou. The playwright and the athlete had kept in touch during the years since they met in New York City. Cayou's well-publicized romance, his experiences at Carlisle and Dickinson College, and his athletic achievements formed the basis for the plot. DeMille fabricated incidents for dramatic effect but maintained the essence of Cayou's life in the play. The Broadway smash got much press regarding the then controversial topic of interracial marriage. Strongheart was the son of a chief who, like Cayou, had been sent first to Carlisle and then to college. Where Cayou attended Dickinson College and the University of Illinois, his theatrical counterpart attended Columbia, the playwright's alma mater. While starring on the football team, Strongheart and the sister of a teammate fell in love. The life and art differ in that the play's hero returned to his tribe to give them the benefit of his education. Sports and art would mix soon in Crawfordsville.

After a grueling practice that sportswriter and former Chicago star, Walter Eckersall, came to town to observe, Frank treated his players to a production of *Strongheart*, very likely staged in the coach's honor. A movie version of *Strongheart* was filmed in 1914 and was remade as *Braveheart* in 1926. The name change was likely to avoid confusion with the famous dog, Strongheart, whose picture can still be found on dog food cans in the grocery store. William C. DeMille's younger brother, Cecil, directed the remake at his own studio.

In the country edition of that morning's Chicago *Tribune*, Eckersall wrote, "Under the tutelage of Frank Cayou, the famous Carlisle Indian and subsequent University of Illinois athlete, Wabash has developed in all branches of athletics, and every western university has been compelled to look upon them as contenders in every line of sport. Their practice shows grim determination and that aggressiveness which has won for them the place they hold as the foremost college, outside of the 'Big Nine,' in western athletics. On Oct. 19 Wabash will meet Michigan at Indianapolis. Great interest is being manifested in the game throughout the state, and Coach Cayou is confident a surprise is in store for the Wolverines. The famous Indian has innumerable plays of an intricate nature, which may prove bewildering to the Michiganders. Wabash seems rather light for Michigan, but the Wolverines will have to work for every point they get. The 'Little Giants' will play Purdue the Saturday previous to the Michigan game. This may prove a handicap, for some may not be in the best of shape for the big game. It should be understood that the Purdue game will be no criterion to what the Michigan game will be, as Cayou has new plays and different men for that contest."

The 1907 Little Giants beat Purdue again but lost to Michigan 22-0 and to Michigan Agricultural College (today's Michigan State) 15-6 on successive Saturdays. The Michigan game took a toll on the team, physically. Captain Gipe was treated by an Indianapolis specialist for an unnamed serious injury. Right guard Sunderland was "out of his head for several hours and it required the attention of a physician to bring him around." Hess's back was badly wrenched and Sohl's ankle was strained. *The Lake County Times* reported, "The whole team shows the effect of the great weight of Michigan, who outweighed, according to inside information, Wabash, almost thirty pounds to the man." In spite of these injuries, Wabash ended up a more than respectable 5-2-0. The Little Giants rose to the task but that would be Cayou's last football team at Crawfordsville.

While he was preparing the track team for its spring 1908 season, "Chief" Cayou, as reporters loved to call him, submitted his resignation effective the end of the school year. A reporter for the *Fort Wayne Daily News* was sympathetic to his position when he wrote, "The graduate system of managing athletic teams was installed at the local institution this college year. Upon adoption, Athletic Director Cayou in reality became practically nothing more than the coach of the team." He also opined that students would rally to convince the "wily coach" to stay. He didn't stay. Friction between coaches, students and alumni was not infrequent in those days due to the closer involvement of the student body with the management of the team. Coaches often left schools when the meddling became too great. "Chief" Cayou had worked wonders at the tiny school and was ready for new challenges.

In the summer Coach Cayou became "Umps" Cayou when he took a job umpiring Eastern Illinois League baseball games at locations such as Staunton and Mattoon. Also reported was that he had taken the head coaching position at Washington University in St. Louis starting in the fall. He was the first full-time football coach to be hired by that school in its relatively short history of fielding a team in that sport. When the school year arrived, he was off to the Mound City but his bride remained in her home town.

Prior to football season *The Indianapolis Star* opined, "Wabash is somewhat of a doubtful quantity this year. The 'Little Giants' have lost their football wizard Cayou. The wonderful Indian coach is gone. In his place Ralph Jones will handle the football candidates. Jones, while not a football player, has made a remarkable career as a basketball coach." The veteran team Frank left behind finished 2-6.

Pundits didn't expect much from the Washington U. Bears in 1908 because, in the opinion of *The Indianapolis Star*, "he has practically no good material to work with." That was likely the case, but Frank did his best and turned in a .500 season. After opening with a scoreless tie with Carleton College, Cayou's new charges lost to Kansas, Missouri, Vanderbilt and Tulane while beating the likes of Shurtleff College (today's Alton Campus of Southern Illinois University at Edwardsville), Knox College, Rose Poly (Rose-Hulman Institute of Technology) and Millikin University.

A fan from Decatur, Illinois at the Rose Poly game observed, "He [the quarterback] made some small mistake in the first half and when the final whistle sounded, Coach Cayou, the Indian, ran out on the field, threw his arm roughly about the little man's neck and fairly dragged him back to the training quarters. I heard Cayou say afterward that he read the riot act to that youngster until he shed tears. Needless to say, in the final half, the lad played great ball." Apparently he felt the need to resort to applied psychology to motivate his players.

Frank started off 1909 by playing in a charity game on New Year's Day between the Walter Eckersall's Chicago All-Stars and Rube Waddell's St. Louis All-Stars indoors in the Coliseum. Eckersall starred for Chicago, kicking three field goals in the first half. Cayou drop kicked a field goal in the second half for St. Louis. These were the only points scored by either team. The most erratic and talented lefthander and probably the most difficult player to manage regardless of position in baseball history, Rube Waddell, was then pitching for the St. Louis Browns, and surprisingly played a good game at guard. More surprising was that he was still on the field when the final whistle blew and had not run off to chase a fire engine.

For ten days in September, Frank Cayou assisted Pop Warner prepare Carlisle for the 1909 campaign. This may have been a more or less annual practice but has not been documented for other years. Frank surely put Warner's formations in his bag of tricks. The Decatur, Illinois *Daily Review* looked forward to its home team playing Washington U, conjecturing, "As St. Louis turns out monster crowds to see Coach Cayou's football machine in action, the J. M. U. [James Millikin University] should clear from $75 to $100 on that game."

Cayou had a lot of vacancies to fill on his 1909 team, the largest being the two tackle positions. A number of other veterans also did not return. Any hopes for a good season were squashed when West Point Cadet Eugene A. Byrne died as a result of injuries suffered in a mass play on tackle by Harvard. The parents of Washington U's best player reacted to this tragedy by refusing to let their son play football. The Decatur *Daily Review* reported, "[Alvin] Durr according to Coach Cayou of Washington, is the most valuable man on his team and he is despondent as a result of this notification." Injuries during the season added to the misery. Washington U beat Shurtleff, Millikin and Knox while losing to Kansas, Missouri, Vanderbilt and Arkansas. For the second year in a row, the Bears lost to Missouri and Kansas, the two Missouri Valley Conference foes they played, ending up 0-2 in conference.

Wabash experienced something unusual in football that year: a coaching loss in mid-season to another school. In late October, Coach Jones, Cayou's successor, left Wabash, quite likely for reasons similar to those that convinced Cayou to leave. Jesse Harper, who later gained fame at Notre Dame, took over the reins.

Just prior to the start of the 1910 season, Anna Snyder Cayou filed for divorce from her husband of almost seven years on the grounds of desertion. She is said to have told a *St. Louis Post-Dispatch* reporter that she had great admiration for him and wished him success, but their temperaments were so different that they couldn't hope to get along.

The 1910 season was almost a repeat of the previous year but with some minor details changed. Washington U lost to Shurtleff, Missouri, Arkansas and Iowa, defeating Westminster, Rose Poly and Drury. Once again they went 0-2 in conference. On Sundays the wily Indian coached the Staunton, Illinois town team with some success. Reporters attributed much of the success to the "crafty redskin's" coaching.

Minnie Weaver, whose family folklore led her to believe she was related to Pocahontas, became Frank's second wife in May 1911. They decided to marry in Louisville to avoid the publicity their wedding would receive in St. Louis, but they were thwarted because the bride was only 19 and the minimum age in Kentucky law was 21. So, they crossed the Ohio River and married in Indiana. They spent much of the summer in Michigan with Minnie's sick aunt. In September they returned to St. Louis for football season.

At 4-2-2, 1911 would be Cayou's best Myrtle and Maroon team, his only over .500 team with Washington U. The losses to Indiana and Arkansas were closer than usual, and conference foes Missouri and Drake were tied. He had improved the team but in following seasons it wasn't better than its competition.

1912 would be a near repeat of Frank's first season at Washington U. His team went 4-4 (0-2 in conference) defeating the lesser schools and losing to the larger ones. Frank turned in his resignation in the spring as he was unable to produce winning teams in any of the sports he coached at Washington U. The football team was 18-18-3, exactly .500 under his tutelage. He did leave St. Louis with something of value though. His son, Francis Jr. was born there, possibly in October 1911.

Before leaving town, Frank made his feelings known about the treatment of Jim Thorpe at the hands of the AAU and U. S. Olympic Committee. A St. Louis newspaper reported him as saying, "This entire rumpus about James Thorpe was started by a jealous bunch of pigs who wanted something sensational to snort about. If every athlete is to be ousted from the AAU who has played professional baseball, we will have no college or preparatory school baseball at all. In more than half the schools in the country men are admitted on various athletic teams when at least a dozen persons may know that they have received money for their services at some previous time. Jim is the greatest athlete the world has ever known. They'll all have to go a long way to find another who will accomplish what he has. The AAU is run in a slipshod manner. The officials know that nine-tenths of the supposed amateurs play ball in the summer and receive pay for it, yet nothing is said. Then comes the world's greatest athlete, who won so much glory for the United States at the Olympic games, and they put him out of amateur contests forever."

Rather than hitting the gridiron for another campaign in the fall of 1913, Frank, then 35, started to work with sporting goods giant A. G. Spalding & Bros. in Chicago. He was likely assigned college accounts because of his background and fame. That summer his daughter, Louisa, was born in Michigan, where Minnie may have been spending the summer. Frank made what appears to have been a first step toward an eventual career change when he directed 25 Objiway in a production of Longfellow's "Hiawatha" at the Fifth Annual United States Land Show from November 20 through December 7. President Wilson opened the Land Show by pressing a button connected to an electric wire. This was quite a production. A stage over 100 feet long was built in the balcony of the Chicago Coliseum to accommodate the actors and scenery used in this drama.

At the winter baseball conference in January 1914, probably as an offshoot of his job with Spalding, Frank designed new uniforms for the Indianapolis Indians minor league team that changed ownership at that meeting. The uniforms used Carlisle's colors, red and old gold, as stripes on a black band on the socks. The socks' background colors matched the pants and shirts – white for home and gray for road. "Indians" was emblazoned on the front of the shirt and copper-colored Indian heads were placed on each sleeve.

Immediately after hearing that Pop Warner had resigned from Carlisle, Cayou wrote Acting Superintendent Oscar Lipps a lengthy letter in which he applied for the athletic director's position that would soon be open. Included was an extensive list of references that included names like Walter Eckersall and Andy Smith. Lipps informed him that only a coach for the football season was going to be hired.

When not promoting Spalding's products directly, Cayou promoted the business indirectly by officiating track meets and football games. He sometimes opined on the merits of teams. In 1915 he was particularly impressed with the Ann Arbor, Michigan town club. In 1917 he shifted to the upstart Thomas E. Wilson Company for whom he worked a year. After the U. S. entered WWI, he offered to "...join any regiment organized at any of the Indian reservations for work on the border in case Mexico tries to take over Texas or New Mexico." He claimed that several other Indians from Chicago would follow suit. Nearing 40 years old he was not a candidate for the draft. However, his offer wasn't as frivolous as it might sound. Apparently German agents had been hard at work in Mexico.

Frank returned to coaching as the athletic director of the Illinois Athletic Club (IAC) in Chicago where he stayed until 1920. The IAC, located in the 18-story classical/ Beaux Artes skyscraper at 112 S. Michigan Avenue in Chicago's Loop, was built for the club and is still used for a similar purpose but under a new name. His next assignment was a similar position with Great Lakes Naval Training Center that he held through 1923.

In 1919 the Illinois State Legislature designated the fourth Friday of September as American Indian Day. That day was first celebrated in 1920, the same year that the Indian Fellowship League was founded. Frank Cayou was active in the IFL and was involved in the annual celebrations of American Indian Day. He even served a few terms as president. The 1922 IFL convention, at which he was re-elected president, passed a resolution calling on President Harding and Congress to grant full rights of citizenship to Indians. On "Indian Day," his photo in full regalia appeared in newspapers across the country.

By 1926 Frank Cayou was reported to have had embarked on a new career as a lecturer who talked about Indian religions and lore. Pop Warner interpreted his career change a little differently, "I understand he has since gone into vaudeville under another name with considerable success, doing an Indian skit. He was a very good singer, which was quite an unusual accomplishment for an Indian." At age 49 Cayou remarried again, this time to Pearl Murray Buffalo who was Osage. Both could have been widowed or divorced. The great influenza epidemic of 1918-19 could have taken their spouses or their marriages could have failed or one of each. That same year, 1927, Frank was named Head Chief of the Omaha Pow Wow. At some point he joined the Native American Church, a distinctively American religion that combines Christianity with the use of peyote. In 1935 he was president of the church and was living with Pearl in Hominy, Oklahoma where both were registered Republicans. Pop Warner thought he was in vaudeville but other accounts had him on the lecture circuit. Because he may have worked under a stage name, it is difficult finding out precisely what he was doing. Frank died on May 7, 1948 at the Claremore Indian hospital in Oklahoma. Apparently a widower in later life, he was living with a stepdaughter in Hominy, Oklahoma at the time of his demise.

5

Frank Hudson

Frank Hudson;
*U. S. Army Military
History Institute*

Name: Frank Hudson	**Nickname:** Cunning Toe
DOB: circa 1877	**Height:**
Weight: 138	**Age:** 22
Tribe: Pueblo	**Home:** Laguna Pueblo, NM
Parents: Yo-y-ta-tsua; Juana Yo-y-ta-tsua	
Early Schooling:	
Later Schooling:	
Honors: American Indian Athletic Hall of Fame, 1973	

Koro-sers

Frank Hudson, Koro-sers, arrived in Carlisle on October 3, 1886 at about nine years of age. He came from the Paguate village of the ancient Laguna Pueblo located about 45 miles west of Albuquerque. Not known is whether Frank chose or was assigned his citizen's name as his parents were listed on government censuses under their Pueblo names. His father, Yo-y-ta-tsua, does not appear to have ever taken a citizen's name and his brother went by the name of Edward Stokes, the name of an English sea captain who figured in California and New Mexico history. Both of his parents were living at the time of Frank's enrollment at Carlisle but, based on a letter from his brother, it appears they were unaware that Frank had gone east. Also, he may not have gone by that name prior to arriving at Carlisle.

Starting in the summer of 1889, Frank spent his outing periods working on farms, always in Bucks County north of Philadelphia. His first five outings were spent on different farms but he apparently established a friendship with Charles Smith on his fifth outing because he returned to Smith's farm for his next two, and final, outings. Hudson rekindled his friendship with Smith some years later.

Frank Hudson was no slouch in the classroom. By 1891, he was leading his class in the afternoon session in Room No. 11 (Carlisle students studied academics half days and trades the other half). His mornings were spent in the Printing Department where he was learning how to set type and print all sorts of things including the school newspaper, programs, menus, etc. His spiritual life was not ignored. An 1893 article in *The Indian Helper* by Robert Hamilton reported that Frank was one of 16 outing boys who attended the Edgewood church.

Frank graduated with the class of 1896. The commencement speaker was, ironically, Fitzhugh Lee, the Confederate general who had burned Carlisle Barracks, future home of the Indian school, during the invasion of Carlisle in the days immediately preceding the battle of Gettysburg. Hudson's contribution to the festivities, beyond completing his coursework, was to captain a nine-man basketball team who played an exhibition game for visitors. His team won 1-0 in a game that modern fans would probably not recognize. Frank stayed on at the school as an employee after graduation and continued playing football and baseball on the school teams, something he had begun doing a couple of years earlier.

Although slight of build, Frank Hudson started playing quarterback for the varsity football team in 1895 but got very little press until 1896; he did not receive much then, due to being overshadowed by the all-time greats on that team that included Bemus and Hawley Pierce, Martin Wheelock, Frank Cayou, Isaac Seneca and Jonas Metoxen. However, he received some mention in the coverage of the 24-12 loss to Brown University in the Thanksgiving Day game:

> "Hudson, the little Indian quarter back, in endeavoring to interfere for McFarland was thrown heavily to the ground by Murphy and injured his shoulder. He was replaced by Shelefo [sic]....Murphy and Shelafo were injured and had to be replaced. The Indians had no other quarter back, so Hudson was allowed to reenter the game."

Following graduation he captained the baseball team, played first base and pitched some times. As a junior employee of the Indian school, he was assigned a number of miscellaneous tasks, often clerical, and sometimes filled positions during absences caused by illness, vacation or business matters. In February 1899, he was assigned a particularly unpleasant task as reported by the school newspaper: "Mr. Frank Hudson, '96, who was out visiting boys in the country when the blizzard came, was shut in by snow for several days, and has now returned, saying it is impossible to get from place to place in the present condition of the roads in Bucks County."

That football season was Frank's breakout year. He played quarterback and kicked for the 1897 team, becoming so good at drop kicking that pundits soon considered him the best kicker active at that time. Reporters referred to Hudson's "cunning toe" when writing about Carlisle games.

Few athletes can point to a single play that took them from obscurity to media idol, but Hudson was one such person. On October 23, 1897, in a game against Yale played at the Polo Grounds in New York City, one kick launched his career:

> "When they lined up again, Cayou paid his respects to Cutten, and the ball was downed five yards nearer the Yale goal. The signals were shouted out again and Hudson dropped back. 'A goal from the field,' said everyone, and all watched breathlessly to see if the young Indian would succeed. The ball was passed beautifully to him; then steadying himself for an instant the ball was dropped and with a delicate

touch from his foot was sent sailing straight as a die toward the Yale goal. The spectators held their breath and watched the ball as it sailed on just over the heads of the Yale players and finally dropped over the bar. Then they cheered and young Hudson was the hero of the day. The goal was one of the prettiest ever seen, and it made the score 18 to 5 in favor of Yale."

The New York Times

The Syracuse Herald published the following report:

"Hudson, the clever little quarterback, accomplished a feat not often seen on the gridiron, by kicking a goal from the field, from the 35-yard line. The prettiest part of it was the able manner in which the Indians blocked the college men from interfering with the kick."

A surprise was waiting for Hudson when the team returned from New York after the game. Carlisle jeweler John Steele, who also worked at the Indian school, presented him with a gold ring for kicking that goal. The following Monday the football team was drawn across the school's parade ground in a large herdic by a battalion of students. Frank Hudson, Bemus Pierce, Frank Cayou and Martin Wheelock led the parade in a small phaeton pulled by young boys. The band joined in and there was much celebration. But Frank was just starting. The following Saturday against Penn, he outdid himself. *The Syracuse Standard* reported:

"A noted football expert in a New York dispatch sums up the games of the big elevens yesterday as follows: The crack team of the University of Pennsylvania struck a snag today when the Carlisle Indians lined up on Franklin Field at Philadelphia. Instead of rolling up a big score and whitewashing the red men as many experts believed they would, the Quakers had a difficult task to score 20 points and the Indians covered themselves with never to be forgotten glory by scoring 10 points. The remarkable feat of kicking two goals from the field was accomplished by Hudson, the Indians' quarterback, who has been developed into a phenomenal player. The showing of the Indians was the best they have made this year, and their game with Brown University here next Saturday may result in their victory over a leading college eleven."

With those kicks Hudson scored half the points that would be scored against that year's eventual undefeated national championship team. In fact, he scored more points against Penn than did Harvard, the only other Big Four team the Quakers played that year, single-footed. When the pundit's hyperbole is put in context, it becomes less exaggerated. The upstart Indians, in just their first few seasons of playing the game, were playing tougher schedules than were the powerhouses and were recording successful seasons. While the Big Four teams each scheduled only one or two other Big Four teams each year, Carlisle scheduled three in 1897 and all four in 1896 and on successive Saturdays. While the Big Four rarely played road games, and those few were often unavoidable because both teams can't play a home game simultaneously and be on the same field, Carlisle played virtually all of its tough games on the road. Hudson was catapulted into the first ranks of football players by his feat, make that foot.

Demonstrating that these kicks were not flukes, Frank Hudson kicked another against Illinois in the night game played indoors under the lights in the Chicago Coliseum. For his efforts, he received national press for his work that year. One that was widely circulated included a sketch of his head:

"Frank Hudson, the quarter back of the Carlisle Indian school's football eleven, made himself famous by a single kick. In a recent game against Yale in New York the

Indian succeeded in scoring a somewhat remarkable performance. The game ended Yale 24, Carlisle 9.

"Hudson contributed even more than his share toward the success of the red men in scoring. He isn't much to look at, this little Pueblo from New Mexico, but his legs are of the sprinting kind. His soul knows no such thing as fear, and when it comes to head this quarter back, who does the thinking for the Indian football player, is so full of dash as a streak of lightning and as cunning as a fox.

"The game had gone against his eleven. The somber warriors were losing heart and hope. Somehow the ball went through the azure and landed in his hands. Before him, 30 yards away, stood those sentinels of victory, the goal posts, backed by a solid mass of enthralled and soon to be frenzied humanity. Thirty yards of space lay between, and he had to kick the ball between them. Between him and those pregnant posts the two contending armies waited. Couchant, ready to spring upon each other tooth and nail if the ball fell short. There was but a second for preparation, and not a living soul in all the 20,000 souls hanging spellbound on the play thought he could do it save alone the soul of Hudson.

"Ah, the precision of that kick! Not all the rifled guns that overcame the works of Krupp could put a ball more truly. Straight and true it sailed between the posts as near the center as if it had been shot by rule and line.

"An instant's gasp for breath, then frenzy. 'He's kicked a goal!' 10,000 throats were screaming. 'He's kicked a goal! Carlisle! Carlisle! Carlisle!'"

Frank's kicking ability not only made him famous but also changed the game itself. The Rules Committee made changes to encourage more drop kicking. Prior to the start of the 1898 season, changes were announced:

"The one radical change made by the committee was in the matter of scoring. Hereafter only one point will be allotted for a goal made from a touchdown instead of two, as before. The object of this change is to increase the value of a goal from the field by means of the drop kick. This is a feature of the game that hitherto has been very much neglected. It is a very pretty play and especially useful to a light team bucking against a heavier one. This was exemplified last season by Quarter Back Hudson of the Carlisle Indian school and by the work of Young of Cornell. The drop kick from the field opens up the play and is a very welcome change from the close formations and line bucking now so general, especially from the point of view of the lookers on. Now that a goal obtained in this manner will have just as much value as one from a touchdown we may expect to see more open play this fall."

It is unusual for one player's abilities to cause rules to be changed but Frank's did. Rule makers were also astute enough to see how a size advantage could be mediated a bit with a strong kicking game, thus making the game more competitive. Some might argue that this was a significant step toward breaking the Big Four's stranglehold on championships. It should be noted that Carlisle's victories over the Big Four came after this rule was enacted.

In some ways 1898 was a repeat of 1897 with Harvard replacing Princeton as one of the three Big Four teams the Indians faced. Something different was that Frank Hudson was elected captain, a position held by Bemus Pierce the three preceding years. Still the premier drop kicker in all of college football, Frank again provided a weapon few teams possessed, at least not with his range and accuracy. This year he kicked goals against two of the three Big Four teams Carlisle faced. Martin Wheelock kicked one against the other. Field goal kicking had very quickly become a major part of the Carlisle attack thanks, in large part, to Frank Hudson.

Expectations were high for the 1899 team. Some critics had said that all the Indians lacked was a first-class coach whereas others didn't think Indians had the intellectual capacity necessary for the game. Hiring Pop Warner eliminated those criticisms. Most of the 1898 team returned and pundits thought the three stars who were lost could be easily replaced from Carlisle's talent pool. Hudson and Wheelock, that year's captain, were described as "two of the best men who ever played back of the line on a football team."

Three weeks into the new season, Carlisle met the University of Pennsylvania in Philadelphia and outplayed the Quakers. James Johnson and Hawley Pierce each scored a touchdown (5 points each), Martin Wheelock kicked a goal after touchdown and had one blocked (1 point under the new rules) and Frank Hudson kicked a field goal (5 points) for a total of 16 points. All Penn could muster was a field goal by Truxton Hare (5 points) in this 16-5, the first ever, victory of the Carlisle Indians over one of the Big Four teams. Two days after this stunning upset, commentator Leo Etherington wrote in his column, "Little Hudson, the wonderful quarter back on the eleven of the Carlisle Indians, was probably the first to reduce the kicking of field goals to a science…" Two weeks later while nursing a sore leg injured in the game with Dickinson College, Hudson kicked one 45-yard field goal and missed another against Harvard. The following Saturday he sat out the Hamilton College game to recuperate for the upcoming game with Princeton. Likely because Frank's knee was wrenched in the shut-out loss to Princeton and other players were also on the injured list, the game with Maryland was canceled. A week after that game would have been played, Frank received praise from *The New York Times* for a different use of his legs, "In the first half Hudson made one of the most sensational runs ever seen on a football field in dragging himself, twisting and turning up successfully out of the grasp of nine Oberlin men, only to be downed by plucky Quarter Back Hobart."

He kicked another field goal against Columbia but missed some attempts against California before being removed from the game due to being injured again. Luckily for Frank, 1899 was the year in which Walter Camp belatedly started naming Carlisle players to his All-America teams. Hudson's name was listed as Camp's choice for quarterback on his All-America Third Team.

Pop Warner later stated that Frank's kicking success was no fluke for he had observed Hudson practicing in the gymnasium throughout the winter. Hudson practiced drop kicks with both feet until he was equally adept at kicking with either foot. Doing that required a lot of practice kicks. In his case, practice made perfect.

Upon returning to Carlisle after the long road trip to California, Frank Hudson spent his time working at various assignments, often clerical, at the school. One of his products that has been preserved for posterity is his recording of the census of those at the school in June 1900. His elegant handwriting and precise figures makes deciphering those documents much easier than most. A later newspaper article mentioned that his attempted transfer to Harvard around this time was thwarted by conference rules. (Harvard has no record of such an attempt.) Carlisle football players transferring to major colleges and universities continued to be a contentious issue for some time. In October 1900, Leo Etherington reported on Frank's new opportunity:

> "When a football team was started at the Carlisle Indian school, some years ago.
> it was said that the aborigines would never equal the whites at this game, in which
> quickness of thought and action is an essential. Nevertheless the red men have
> shown that, with good coaching they can put up a very formidable article of football

against the finest college elevens in this country. In spite of their good showing it is claimed that the Indians are still slow in learning tricks themselves and in grasping the secret of tricks played on them by opposing teams.

"This all may be and probably is true. Still young Frank Hudson, the noted Indian quarter back and drop kicker who was second to none in that position for several seasons, has shown that he is not dull when it comes to combining football with business to his own profit. He has recently secured a position in a Pittsburg [sic] bank and has signed a contract with a prominent club in that city, according to the terms of which he will give that organization the benefit of his skill at tackling dodging and dropping field goals, and in return will draw a fat salary."

Frank Hudson left Carlisle for a banking career in Pittsburgh in September. Siceni J. Nori, class of '94, replaced him in his clerical position at Carlisle. The "contract with a prominent club in that city" is believed to be to the Duquesne Country and Athletic Club (DCAC), an early professional football team in Pittsburgh. The previous year the DCAC had surrendered just two field goals and a single touchdown in an undefeated season. With competition as stiff as it was in western Pennsylvania at that time, even though loaded with stars, DCAC felt the need to improve its squad for the 1900 season. Bringing Frank Hudson on board was a natural move. Once again DCAC was very successful on the field but a financial disaster. Frank surely commanded a sizeable salary that may have pushed the club's fiscal woes over the tipping point. The DCAC's fine clubhouse was sold at sheriff's sale in 1901 to satisfy a $9,000 mortgage and the team was disbanded.

A December 1900 news report stated that Frank Hudson had been signed to coach the Haskell Institute football team. Based on later events, it appears that he was just signed to prepare the team for a big game. The Carlisle school paper reported that Hudson spent two weeks assisting Warner with his 1901 team and traveled with the team to games in Buffalo against Cornell and in Cambridge, Massachusetts against Harvard. His vacation over, he returned to his bank job in Pittsburgh. Later that school year he wrote to say that his bank duties kept him from attending commencement. (Pittsburg was a variant spelling of the steel city's name that was in use at the time.)

In the fall of 1902, *The Red Man and Helper* reported, "Frank Hudson, class '96, assistant bookkeeper, City Deposit Bank, Pittsburg, is here for a day or two. His friends are glad to see him looking so well, and gave him a warm welcome." He likely consulted with Coach Warner on that trip. The following year the school paper announced, "Mr. Frank Hudson, head bookkeeper in the City Deposit Bank, Pittsburg, Pa. is here to spend a two weeks' vacation in the home of Mr. Nori. He brought with him a little friend, James McCurdy who is manifesting great interest in Mr. Hudson's school home." Frank was included in a team photo taken while he was there, so it is likely that he did some work with the team again that year.

Pop Warner left Carlisle after the 1903 season, but Frank Hudson continued his practice of taking two weeks of vacation in the fall to assist Coaches Rogers and Pierce in 1904. Major Mercer replaced Gen. Pratt as superintendent in the summer of 1904 for reasons unrelated to athletics. Mercer supported sports more enthusiastically than had his predecessor. It appears that Frank Hudson became a full-time employee of the Indian school sometime in 1905 because he assisted with the coaching of the team for the entire 1905 and 1906 seasons. An internal investigation after the 1906 season brought an end to Frank's career at Carlisle and changed the direction of his life forever.

On December 30, 1906, Major Mercer received a report of an investigation conducted by U. S. Special Agent M. G. Oline:

"I have the honor of reporting to you that I have made a careful investigation of the accounts of Frank Hudson, your financial clerk and bookkeeper of the accounts of the pupils with the school, and who has at times small amounts of cash for the active banking privileges of the pupils at the school, and I discover that he is short in his accounts the sum of $1,410.62.

"I further certify that this shortage has resulted from small abstractions from the cash in his hands from time to time during the last year. I further say to you that in a personal conversation with Mr. Hudson he frankly acknowledged that he took these moneys from the actual cash which was in his possession as such financial clerk at the school; and that there was always a small cash balance in his hands for the active use in meeting the daily demands of pupils for spending money. Mr. Hudson further acknowledged that he knew when he was misappropriating this money that it would occasion a shortage in his accounts, and also that he did know that there was a shortage.

"I can say to you that from my most careful and exhaustive examination of his books that he has abstracted and appropriated to his own use unlawfully the sum of $1410.62."

No mention of this embezzlement has been found in the press, but U. S. Fidelity and Loan Co, the bonding agent that covered Hudson, was informed of the shortage the very next day and was demanded to make good on the shortage. It is not known what, if anything other than losing his job, happened to Frank Hudson but Major Mercer stepped down a little over a year later due to health stresses presented by the position. Angel DeCora wrote that rumors of Mercer's involvement were unfounded. Hudson's friend and successor as clerk, Siceni Nori, took notes.

Not surprisingly, Frank Hudson had no further association with the Carlisle football team. He next surfaced on the 1910 census as working on the Charles Smith farm, his old outing site, in Bucks County. The 1920 and 1930 censuses show that he continued working on that farm after Mr. and Mrs. Smith died and the farm passed to their daughters. A 1917 letter from the Chief Clerk at Carlisle to a request about Frank's whereabouts said that "About the year 1906 he left the school for Wycombe where he has been located since."

The embezzlement was not the last Carlisle would hear of or from Frank Hudson. In 1914 after Pop Warner resigned, he wrote Superintendent Lipps from Wycombe, Pennsylvania, requesting that he be considered for the open head coaching position. The response was essentially a form letter saying that he would be considered when the time came to select a new coach. Not surprisingly, he was not selected.

In 1918 Frank's brother, Edward Stokes, wrote the superintendent requesting assistance in locating him in order to get what must have been a very old debt repaid. Apparently Frank sold his brother a buckskin horse with the 3S brand on its left thigh that wasn't his to sell and still owed Stokes $45. It wasn't clear from the letter, but Frank may have also owed Martin Pasanio some money. Stokes advised the superintendent that his brother changed his name whenever he arrived in a new town. No evidence of Hudson using any other name was observed while he was at Carlisle or later.

Nothing further is known about Hudson beyond the 1930 census that placed him as a bachelor working on the Smith farm in Bucks County, Pennsylvania. However, family members were present for his induction into the American Indian Athletic Hall of Fame in 1973.

William Milton Baine

6

William Baine,
July 1896 *Stenographer*
journal; *Ganser Library,*
Millersville University

Name: William Milton Baine		**Nickname:**	
DOB: 9/10/1876		**Height:** 5' 11-1/2"	
Weight: 191		**Age:** 27	
Tribe: Sioux		**Home:** Fort Sisseton, SD	
Parents: William Bain, a white soldier at Ft. Sisseton; Susan, a full blooded Sioux			
Early Schooling: Haskell Institute; University of Kansas			
Later Schooling: Dickinson College preparatory school; University of Wisconsin			
Honors:			

Stenographer

William Baine and his older sister, Martha, were orphaned by 1889. He was born on September 10, 1876 at Fort Sisseton, South Dakota to a Scots-Irish father and a Sioux mother according to his enrollment papers for the University of Wisconsin. Exactly how young William came to attend Haskell Institute is not known; however, the facts that he was intelligent, athletic and orphaned must surely have been contributing factors. It was at Haskell that the sporting community first took notice of him.

Dr. A. R. "Burt" Kennedy, a future Lawrence, Kansas dentist who quarterbacked the 1896 Kansas University team, remembered how Baine came to be involved with the university across town:

> "We K. U. football enthusiasts noticed that the Indian boy had a definite knack for playing the game, so we went out to Haskell and got him to come in to K. U., where we enrolled him in the school of law to make him eligible to play. Despite the fact that he probably had no higher education than fourth grade, we saw to it that he kept eligible until the season was over."

Kennedy also recalled a minor historical event in which he and Baine played roles. Baine suffered a slight concussion of the brain – slight by Kennedy's estimation – in a practice session prior to the big game with Nebraska. So, Kennedy and a couple of co-conspirators fashioned a padded helmet out of canvas to provide some protection for the boy's throbbing head. Kennedy had clear memories of it:

> "That was the first football helmet I ever saw. We usually wore our hair so darned long that we never thought about helmets for protecting the head before. Baine made the first touchdown in the first half of the Nebraska game. Then in the second half, K. U. stalled against the big line of the Cornhuskers. We were crowded over to one side of the then new McCrook field and couldn't pick up a yard. I was quarterback and acting captain for the game, so I called Baine, still complaining of an aching head, in the huddle and told him he had to run the ball around Nebraska's right end and at least get it out to the center of the field so we could work on both ends of the Cornhusker line.
>
> "'No can do, no can do,' was Baine's response.
>
> "Anyway, I called a play that gave the ball to Baine for a right end run. He took the ball and ran around the end and down the field 60 yards for a touchdown so fast that not even a single Cornhusker had time to touch him."

After this experience with Kansas University football, it is likely that Baine stayed at Haskell for a few years. The July 1898 issue of *The Stenographer* tells a little more about his time in Kansas:

> "William Baine, a Sioux Indian, formerly a student of Haskell Institute, Lawrence, Kansas, is now employed by the government at Carson City, Nevada. Mr. Blaine is from the Fort Sisseton Agency, South Dakota, and has attended school about seven years altogether. He is a graduate of the Normal Department, also the Grammar School of the Haskell Institute. We have pleasure in presenting his photograph, together with shorthand notes written by him."

Apparently wanting to further his education, he transferred to Carlisle around 1899 when 23 years old but not to take courses there. He enrolled in the Dickinson College Preparatory School but played football for Carlisle. Most likely he spent the 1899 season on the scrubs, learning the system as the Indians had a strong team that year. Baine did play tackle in the 1900 Harvard game in which "he received a severe injury in the right side" but apparently recovered and was a regular after that. However, it wasn't always at the same position. Against Washington and Jefferson, he played left halfback. Against Columbia, he was back at tackle. Or was it his half-brother John Clarence Baine? Against Susquehanna early in the season, William played right tackle and John played left halfback. It's not always clear because first initials aren't always supplied and William generally played halfback at other schools.

Baine left Carlisle and Dickinson College at the end of the school year in 1901 and reenrolled at Haskell Institute. Some of the coursework from Haskell that was listed on his application for the University of Wisconsin may have been completed that year. He played on Haskell's team in 1901 and 1902, receiving some coaching from John Outland, after whom the trophy for the outstanding college football lineman is named. Haskell fielded strong elevens those years as Baine teamed with past and future Carlisle stars that included Redwater, Archiquette, Pete Hauser, Emil Hauser and Charles Guyon. They defeated such powers as Kansas, Kansas State, Missouri and Texas while losing to Illinois, Minnesota and Nebraska.

William shone as one of Haskell's stars as reported by *The Lincoln Evening News*: "The spectacular play of the [Haskell-Missouri] game was a getaway of Baine, the stalwart Indian half, near the beginning of play. He ran eighty yards to a touchdown but as in the Haskell-Nebraska game, stepped on the side line and was called back." Apparently he made a habit of stepping out of bounds at inopportune times. He also had a temper. In an article titled "Scalped" a reporter for *The Evening News* recounted a Nebraska score: "When [John R. 'Chief'] Bender had sifted through, he called 'down.' But before the Indians had ceased, they had pushed him back a foot over the chalk mark. Baine insisted that another effort be made before a touchdown should be counted. [Referee] Crawford ruled otherwise, and Baine, with a display of primitive temper threw the ball straight into the official's face. He was taken from the game for his unsportsmanlike conduct." Without William on the field, the Indians suffered their most one-sided loss of the 1902 season.

In 1903, William Baine, then living in Oneida, Wisconsin was admitted to the University of Wisconsin but, prior to being accepted, spent much of the summer working out with the football team and improving on his punting. Although he had good marks in his prep school work, he was admitted on probation. He was described as, "... a stocky fellow, weighs 184 pounds stripped, is fast on his feet, and is a promising man for the much-needed backfield." Wisconsin had an off year in 1902 and was rebuilding.

After a promising start, William Baine injured his leg but continued to play even though slowed down. When fluid accumulated on Baine's knee, the team physician benched him. He was considered healthy enough to play in the Minnesota game but missed two field goals he attempted barefoot. Although injured much of the season, he lettered anyway.

With the sponsorship of Governor LaFollette, Baine then worked as a stenographer across town in the state senate. Family papers include a recommendation signed by a dozen members of the senate. In 1905 Baine coached the South Dakota State College of Agricultural and Mechanic Arts (today's South Dakota State University) football team. Shortly after the end of the season, William's life came to an early end:

> "SISSETON. S. D., Dec. 2 – William Baine, the famous Indian football player, who played half-back on the University of Wisconsin football team, was to-night shot and fatally wounded by Night Watchman Mahoney. Baine, who it is said had been drinking, drew a revolver and began firing promiscuously. Mahoney appeared on the scene and ordered him to cease firing, whereupon the Indian turned his weapon on the officer. Before he could shoot again, however, Mahoney drew his revolver and fired, shooting Baine through the head."

William Jr., also a Haskell graduate, was a lawyer who worked as an accounting auditor for the Bureau of Indian Affairs, maintained that the watchman was a friend who shot his father accidentally. Great-granddaughter Rebecca Baine-Yates shared that William married Mary Jane (Jennie) Fitting and had two children with her, William Walter (or vice versa) and Paulina. He divorced Jennie and married Alice Powless, a fellow Carlisle student, with whom he had two children, William Milton, Jr. and Hope Winona. Rebecca's grandfather, William Walter, was born in Sisseton on January 28, 1894 and died in Hoquiam, WA on June 9, 1969. When young, he was quite a baseball star and is mentioned in George Olson's poem, "Lake City Baseball Team of the Twenties." He married Edna Locke and had one son, Leonard William Baine, who later played football for Washington State University. In WWII he served as a Navy fighter pilot. Afterward he married and had a son and two daughters, one of whom was Rebecca.

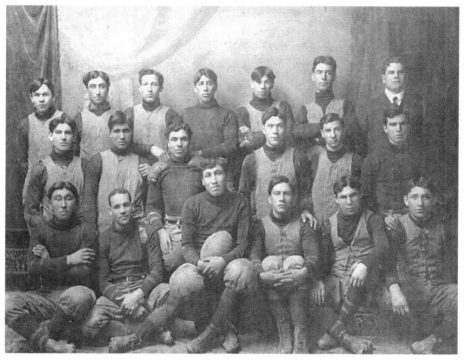

1902 Carlisle football team. James Phillips in back row third from left.;
Cumberland County Historical Society, Carlisle, PA
Front row (left to right): Nikifer Schouchuk, James Johnson, Charles Williams,
Frank Yarlott, Frank Beaver, unknown
Second row: Arthur Sheldon, Antonio Lubo, Joel Cornelius, Albert Exendine,
Walter Matthews, unknown
Back row: Wilson Charles, Charles Dillon, James Phillips, Joseph Sanooke(?),
Nicholas Bowen, William White, Coach Glenn Warner

James Marston Phillips

7

James Phillips (left) about to go hunting; *James Brown, grandson.*

Name: James Marston Phillips		**Nickname:**	The Fairest Man in Football
DOB: 5/8/1873		**Height:**	6' 0"
Weight: 190		**Age:**	27
Tribe: Cherokee		**Home:**	Burke County, NC
Parents: Theophelis Phillips; Katherine E. Phillips			
Early Schooling: Lincoln University			
Later Schooling: Dickinson School of Law; Northwestern University			
Honors:			

The fairest man in football

James Phillips' route to the Carlisle Indian School was the most unusual taken by any student, with the possible exceptions of Lone Star Dietz and William Baine. To make it more unusual, James never enrolled in a class at the Indian school but played on the football team for most of two seasons. But we're getting ahead of ourselves.

According to family accounts, Theophilis and Katherine E. Phillips emigrated to America from Ireland and eventually set up housekeeping in North Carolina some time in the mid-1800s. The 1880 census lists a Phillips family headed by Theophulus [sic], age 32, and Ida, age 28, on a farm in Upper Creek Township, Burke County, near the Caldwell County line. In addition to the parents are listed six children ranging in age from 2 to 17. It seems unlikely that Ida was the mother of the older children, as she would have given birth to Marcus, the oldest, when she was only 11 years old. And Theophilis, her husband, would also have been young to be starting a family at age 15. Perhaps the census taker had the wrong age for Marcus. It may be that Katherine had died and Theophilis married a

Brothers
Theo and James
Phillips; *James
Brown, grandson.*

younger woman. Caldwell County marriage records include a marriage between Theopholus [sic] and Ida Chambers in 1879. A second marriage to a person of mixed blood, if Ida was of mixed blood, might also explain why the census taker listed the entire family as mulatto regardless of the person's parentage. The possibilities include various combinations of ancestors who originated in or descended from people who did originate in Ireland, Africa and North America. However, the Phillips family believes the progenitors of their clan were Irish.

James was listed in the census as being 8 years old but was probably a bit younger as family records have his date of birth as May 8, 1873. He and his brother, also named Theophilis but listed as Theodore on the census, were later educated at Lincoln University in Chester County, Pennsylvania, the first educational institution in the world to provide a higher education in the arts and sciences for male youth of African descent. Their education was made possible by a wealthy aunt, Matilda Phillips, who owned a textile factory in London, England. Lost to history is the reason for the choice of educational institutions for the brothers. With their aunt's help, they could afford most colleges. The location of the school selected demonstrates that they did not have narrow geographic limitations. Photographs suggest that the young men could have passed for white had they chosen to do so if they weren't, in fact, white. The only reason that comes to mind is that, although the boys were highly intelligent, the schooling they received as children in a rural area may not have been of the same quality of that of college students of the day. Lincoln University faculty may have been better prepared to deal with educational deficiencies in incoming students than most colleges at that time.

After being awarded their Bachelor of Arts degrees at Lincoln University in 1900, the brothers followed very different tracks but both remained men of letters. Theophilis returned home to live, teach and preach in the Collettsville, North Carolina area. Shortly after graduation, he married Bessie Bell Walker Dula, his childhood sweetheart also classified as mulatto in the 1880 census, who had graduated from Palmer Institute near Oxford, North Carolina. Three of his descendents described Theophilis in *The Heritage of Caldwell County North Carolina, Volume I*:

> "As an educator, he was known as being strict, well-liked, and inspiring by his students.
>
> "In spite of his Irish heritage, Mr. Phillips was forced to register to vote as a black man, the first 'black' man in Caldwell County to register. Upon making his applica-

tion, he was asked to recite the preamble to the United States Constitution. His reaction to this request was, 'Which language would you prefer – English, French or Greek?'"

Brother James also cut a wide swath but in a different field and in different locales. The *Dickinson College Catalog for 1900-01* listed him as enrolled in the Dickinson School of Law as a member of the Junior Class who hailed from Collettsville, North Carolina. *The Dickinsonian* listed him as a new student coming from Lincoln University. Shortly after enrolling in the law school, he started playing on the Dickinson College football team. Being a very large man for his generation at 6 feet in height and weighing 190 pounds, he was very likely recruited to play on the line and he did. In the spring James competed in the shot put, hammer throw and high jump as a member of the Dickinson College track team. In the fall of 1901, then a member of the Middle Class at law school, he played on Dickinson's line, at least for a couple of games, including the one against the Indians.

James Phillips in Carlisle uniform; *James Brown, grandson.*

1901 was not a good year for Pop Warner and the Carlisle Indian School football team. Several of the old players did not return and, of those who did, few were experienced linemen and fewer yet were large enough to be effective against the teams on Carlisle's grueling schedule. Warner described his team's problems in a piece written for the *Philadelphia Press*: "The line fails to get the jump on their opponents, and, being much lighter than the team they compete with, this weakness in quick charging has been the cause of their poor defence [sic]. It is next to impossible to develop quick charging linemen in one season, and it is a noticeable fact that the material this year, besides being light is of very mediocre caliber." Soon, very soon, Pop would have another large lineman for his team.

How it came to be is lost to posterity, but James Phillips moved over to Carlisle Barracks and started wearing the red and old gold on Saturdays. Did he make the switch to play on a better football team, to be closer to a certain girl, or both? We'll likely never know the reason, but the important thing is that he did enroll at Carlisle Indian School. After the Navy game, Warner commented on his new lineman:

"Phillips, the new guard, has been improving very much, and his faults, high tackling and slow starting, are gradually being corrected. He is strong as a ground gainer and is used to carry the ball, but on the defense he is not aggressive enough and lets his opponents get the jump on him."

Warner was not happy with his new prospect's development as a player and pulled him out of his place at a practice. Pop told James that he was not playing nearly aggressively enough and said, "Now get down there and show me how it should be done." Warner lined up opposite Phillips as he did when trying to demonstrate a technique to a player. When the signal was given, Phillips charged so hard that he knocked Pop unconscious. When he came to and cleared his head, Warner just said, "Now, that's the way it's done!"

After the Pennsylvania game the *Philadelphia Ledger* commented on his play; "[Martin Wheelock] and Johnson were the mainstays of Carlisle, though Williams, Phillips, Beaver and Dillon all played well." James had become a starter on the Carlisle Indian School team but how had this come about?

According to school records, James Phillips, half-blood Cherokee, age 26, enrolled at Carlisle on October 27, 1901. His father, Theophelus [sic], was listed as living but his mother was already dead. Switching teams and schools in the middle of a term and football season was highly irregular. About a year later *The Red Man and Helper* explained what had happened: "Mr. James Phillips, of North Carolina, who is boarding at the school and attending Dickinson Law School, has returned." So, James was living at the Indian school but taking classes at the law school. There was nothing unusual in this except, in the past, students had completed a course of study at the Indian school before taking courses elsewhere. Unusual was that not a peep about it could be found in *The Dickinsonian*. The reason for this silence was not revealed, but one can make some educated guesses: 1) His play on the Dickinson football team was not so great that his departure was not considered a major loss, or 2) racist views held by many at the time may have convinced Dickinson students that his moving out of 27 E. C. and into the Indian school was better for all. The college students were probably perplexed because he looked white to them but had come from Lincoln University and departed for the Carlisle Indian Industrial School. Were his ancestors from Ireland, North America or Africa? All of the above? Two out of three? Although nothing was published, there was likely much discussion about the issue because the Cumberland Valley, in which Carlisle is centrally located as county seat, traditionally has been very insular and would have been very much so at the turn of the twentieth century.

At the annual football banquet held in January, James received an honor that had never before been extended to someone who had played on the varsity less than a year: he was one of the main speakers.

James Phillips in Dickinson
College uniform; *James
Brown, grandson.*

"Mr. Phillips, in his opening remarks told of an Irishman, who in a fierce battle had been pierced by bullets which had struck him in the side, in the front and back, in the region of the heart, but he had come out of the fight able to tell the tale. When questioned how a thing could be, he said it was because his heart was in his mouth, and just so the speaker felt on this occasion. He has played football two years only and could speak with the wisdom of those of longer experience. 'My Impressions of Football' was his theme, and he claimed that any man who played football did receive impressions. They sometimes came on top of the cranium, as well as in the cranium, and the ability to impart impressions rested with the individual. He referred to the game as played in England, and said that football in this country represented the spirit of the American people. If it is a rough game, players make it so. American young manhood don't want games that are too easy."

In the spring James competed in track as he had the previous year but this time in a Carlisle uniform. At the end of the school year, he left for Atlantic City, New Jersey, likely to work at a hotel or other resort business to earn money over the summer. He returned to Carlisle in September when school started.

That year, the 1902-03 school year, he was tried at left tackle in football but mostly played in his more familiar left guard position. He received kudos for his work in pre-season practice in the school newspaper, likely from Warner: "Of the old players, Captain Williams, Dillon and Phillips are showing improved form, and the latter is only just beginning to realize how strong he is and how much he can accomplish by combining determination and fierceness with his strength."

James was in the middle of a bizarre incident that occurred in the Penn game. He was making good yardage throughout the game, likely from the guards-back formation. As he attempted to carry the ball over the goal line for a touchdown, the crossbar from the goalpost fell, hitting him on the head. Fortunately, he was not injured. When the mass of players was untangled, the ball rested on the 1-foot line. Charles Williams carried the ball over on the next play.

At the annual football banquet held in December, Phillips, as one of the main speakers, was given a very delicate topic, "Our Football Girls," to speak about. After some introductory jokes about Wallace Denny and Tomahawk, he got to the meat of his talk:

"The football girls to whom fortune itself yields! That subject is too much for me. It would take the wit and eloquence of a Chauncey M. Depew to do the subject justice. Anyway the girls are here. By right divine they manage the football. They are monarchs of all they survey. It will be long before time will erase from our minds the eventful day when Pennsylvania was whipped and the football girls helped do it. 'Now then Pennsy we will scalp you,' the words of our song were too much for Pennsy."

During football season, James was also involved with religious activities. In October, he gave a Sunday night talk in which, "Bunyan and Milton were presented in forceful description as examples of cheerfulness amid diversity."

The 1903 Dickinson College yearbook included the following exchange between Dean Trickett of the law school and James as a student in his class:

Dean: Mr. Phillips, 106 Pa. 302.
Phillips: Doctor, I haven't that case. I got a stiff neck and can't study.
Dean: You don't study with your neck, do you?

The inclusion of this in the yearbook could have been a Dickinson student's way of making a negative comment about Phillips' playing football. It would not be unusual for Dickinson students to be less than happy about losing a starter from their team to their cross-town rivals who regularly pummeled them.

In the spring, he ran track again and, in a tie with Wilson Charles, set a new school high jump record. Although not the star of the track team, Phillips competed well, winning sometimes but, more often placing second or third in events with such competitors as Frank Mt. Pleasant, James Johnson, Al Exendine and Wilson Charles. Now that is saying something.

In mid-June *The Red Man and Helper* announced:

> "Mr. James Phillips is the Indian to graduate from the Dickinson College Law School this year. Mr. Phillips is a popular man both in his class and at our school. He boarded with us, but never attended the Indian School. He will be greatly missed on the athletic field and in all work for the good of the school and for the welfare of his fellow associates. He is large of stature and carries with him a great personality which makes friends and which, we predict will lend him to success in whatever he undertakes. He is contemplating practicing law in Chicago."

The next week Col. Pratt introduced James before he was to speak to the Saturday night meeting of the student body:

> "One who has been living with us and attending Dickinson School of Law for eighteen months is about to leave. Before another Saturday evening meeting he will have gone to other fields to put into practice the knowledge he has accumulated. I will ask Mr. Phillips to come to the platform."

After saying that he had little to say, James spoke at some length, sharing some of his personal philosophy which included:

> "It is one of the conditions of man to be looking forward to something better, and that continues through his life. That is one of the things that is responsible for his advancement all over the world. A man should never be satisfied with his present condition and not want to develop further; he ought not to believe that he has reached the zenith of his power. ... I am very thankful for what the school has done for me. ... I will remember you, I will remember the teachers and what I learned here; the songs and things that have impressed me, I will carry with me."

Pop Warner wrote in his autobiography, "Another of the Indian School's gifted athletes was James Phillips who was one of the best guards that ever graced the Carlisle football field. He later graduated from the Dickinson College School of Law and became a member of the State of Washington Legislature."

In September of that year, 1903, *The Redman and Helper* reported, "Mr. James M. Phillips stopped between trains to see his friends. He was on his way west in search of a good location for a law office. From Chicago he may proceed to Seattle. Mr. Phillips has been very helpful to our school and we feel assured that wherever he settles he will continue to exert an influence for good."

On Thanksgiving those Carlislians who were unaware got a bit of a surprise at the Northwestern game: rather than setting up a law office in Chicago, Phillips had enrolled at Northwestern University Law School and played on the University's football team. The Associated Press filed the following report:

"Chicago, Ill., Nov. 26 – Carlisle Indians in today's game with Northwestern University demonstrated the superiority of the football that has made the the the Redmen formidable gridiron warriors in the East by defeating the Purple 28 to 0. At times during the one sided contest snow fell in such blinding swirls that the gridiron and players were concealed from the 3,000 enthusiasts who gathered to root impartially for the Evanston eleven and the popular Indians. Coach McCormack's eleven was materially weakened by the absence of Guard Phillips from the line. The old Carlisle lineman refused to play against his former colleagues. Watching the contest from the stands, Phillips said that had the field been free from snow Carlisle's speedy back would have doubled the score."

For his efforts that season, "Big Jim," "Big Indian," "Big Chief" or "The Fairest Man in Football," as Phillips was called, was named to the All-Western team as a guard. He also won the hand of Earney (Ernestine) Wilber, half-blood Menominee, who he met at Carlisle. They married in a Catholic church near her home in Wisconsin on December 29, 1903 and headed west to make their fortune. In January, James informed Gen. Pratt who then informed the Indian school community of their marriage and future plans:

"Mr. James M. Phillips, with us last year as Dickinson Law student, since which he has been attending the Northwestern University, writes modestly: 'Earney and I have decided to take the trip to Seattle together.' Earney is our good Earney Wilber who graduated last year. Many congratulations to this bright and brave young couple just starting out in life."

James and Earney moved to Seattle with another couple but, due to a financial panic in Seattle at that time, he could only find work driving a delivery wagon, so they stayed just a month before going farther west. They went about as far west as could be done and stay in what was then the United States. Their next and last stop was in Aberdeen, the bustling port city for the very busy Grays Harbor. Aberdeen, Washington was a rough-and-tumble logging town, at that time sometimes called the "Gateway to the Olympic Peninsula" and now known to some as the "Birthplace of Grunge" due to being the birthplace of the founders of the rock group, Nirvana. Sailors then referred to Aberdeen as "Hellhole of the Pacific" or "Port of Missing Men" due to its high murder rate. Because immediate prospects for a legal career in Aberdeen were not promising, James took a position in the burgeoning construction industry.

Arriving in Aberdeen less than a year before the Phillips was one Billy Gohl. Billy Gohl, known locally as Goul, ran the conglomeration of saloons, whorehouses and gambling establishments in Aberdeen as his private fiefdom. Considered by some to be America's all-time champion serial-killer, hands down, Gohl is believed to have killed anywhere from 40 to 200 people, mostly sailors and lumberjacks, but was convicted for murdering two. Never shy about taking credit for his deeds, Gohl would regale listeners with tales of his exploits, unless he thought an honest law enforcement official, should any be found, would take his boasts seriously and prosecute him for the crime.

Billy Gohl, as agent for the Sailor's Union, operated out of the Spartan hall located in the second story of a building that housed a tavern. Sailors arriving in port with money in their pockets, some of which they intended on still possessing when they left port, climbed up the steps to what they thought was the security of the union hall to deposit their money for safekeeping. When a sailor bent over to deposit his money in the union's safe, Gohl dispatched him by whatever means seemed appropriate at the time (blunt instrument trauma was quiet and less expensive than gun shells). After taking everything of value out of the dead man's pockets, Billy disposed of the corpse by dumping it into the Wishkah (adapted from the Chelalis word for stinking river) by means of a trapdoor in the floor that connected to a chute or by taking the corpse out in a boat and dumping it; accounts vary. The corpses had a nasty habit of floating to the surface, so many in fact, that locals dubbed them the Floater Fleet with Billy Gohl as its admiral. Ten a month floated to the surface in one winter alone.

As one might suspect, the Aberdeen police force was not the most honest or efficient. One particular incident puts the integrity of the police department into sharp focus. A competing cigar store that had forced Gohl into temporary bankruptcy mysteriously burned to the ground, taking the hotel it was housed in with it. Of course the burned-out tobacconist blamed Billy for the fire and demanded that the police investigate the matter, as did a Sig Jacobsen. The latter's beef was not about the fire exactly; it was about money. Gohl hadn't paid Jacobsen for the use of the contraption he used to start the fire. The police investigator interviewed Billy and concluded that there was no substance to the charges. Although difficult, it was not impossible to get arrested in Aberdeen at that time. Mac DeLane, one of Gohl's enemies, was arrested for smoking a cigarette on the street.

Arguably less damaging to Aberdeen than Gohl's arrival in 1903 was "Black Friday," the October fire that that destroyed much of the commercial district, a likely reason for the building boom in which James Phillips found work as a hod carrier. One of his tasks was to lay the cornerstone of the Crowther Building, present day home of Billy's Bar & Grill, which was named in honor of Aberdeen's prolific serial killer. Carrying hod didn't provide Phillips with enough physical exercise, so he joined the Aberdeen Athletic Association. He soon made coach of the A. A. A. football team which was often referred to as the town team. He also played guard on the team. He coached and played for four years until, in 1908, it was announced that his "private affairs" required so much of his time that he would be unable to coach. *Aberdeen World* accounts indicate that his withdrawal from the coaching arena was far from total and he played in important games.

After three years of carrying bricks and mortar up ladders to bricklayers, he joined Robert Taggert in his law practice. Soon Taggert & Phillips were ensconced in the beautiful Finch Building. In a short time James became a police magistrate, mayor and, from 1928 to 1953, a Superior Court Justice, career choices that put him on a collision course with Billy Gohl.

James Phillips hunting; *James Brown, grandson.*

Present day Aberdeen attorney and grandson of James Phillips, Jim Brown, relates a story that indicates, as would be expected, Gohl and Phillips were not the best of friends. Gohl invited Phillips to go hunting and for reasons unknown to everyone, probably including himself, Phillips accepted the invitation. Phillips spent most of the day keeping himself positioned away from the business end of Gohl's gun while Gohl kept maneuvering for a clear shot. Phillips lived to tell the story.

After an unsuccessful run for the state legislature, he wrote Moses Friedman,

> "I am out of [political] office now and have been sticking pretty close to business getting back my practice. We are getting along well and will always keep alive our interest in Carlisle. William Hazlett and family are living here. He is in the real estate business and has an excellent family. William Paul married an Aberdeen girl of good family and they are living in Portland. Paul graduated from Whitworth College, Tacoma, after he left Carlisle. He is is working in a bank. There are many Carlisle graduates that are not so fortunate in the positions they hold but most of them that I have met give a very good account of themselves. And after all, it is far more important that the majority of us be satisfied and successful in the commoner walks of life. ... Remember us to inquiring friends and particularly to 'Pop'."

Phillips was elected mayor of Aberdeen in 1915. A headline in the *Tacoma Ledger* read, "Mayor of Aberdeen Part Cherokee Indian." The second sentence of the article said that he was 3/8 Cherokee. He would go on to become a Superior Court justice, but a war intervened before that finally happened. James Marston Phillips registered for the draft on September 12, 1918. At that time he was either out of office and practicing law, or mayor's pay did not support his family, so he continued his practice while serving in that office. The date of birth on his draft registration was May 8, 1874, which put him within a year of the age recorded for him at Carlisle but two years younger than his age on the 1880 census and a year younger than family records. He checked the box for 'White' under 'Race.' Given his age, 44, he was not likely to be drafted.

The census taken in January 1920 listed him as being 45 years old, white, married to Earney, now 37 and white, and father of three daughters: Virginia, Gladys and Richenda ranged in age from 12 to 2, all white. Richenda, the female form of Richard, was an unusual name but was also the name of Richard Henry Pratt's youngest daughter, who had died in 1915. James and Earney very well may have named their third daughter in honor of Superintendent Pratt or his daughter. James Phillips's parents were both listed as having been born in North Carolina. The 1930 census lists his wife as Ernestine, Earney's proper name, and a fourth daughter, Jeanette, then 6. His occupation was listed as Superior Court Judge. The other items were the same as on the previous census.

Possibly because of his work in the building trades, Phillips took an interest in the legal aspects that affected workers. He began his political career as a Republican – Aberdeen was a rock-ribbed Republican area at that time – but shifted to the Bullmoose party when he ran unsuccessfully for the state legislature. After the demise of the Bullmoose party, he drifted over to the Democratic party where he stayed for the rest of his life, as did the majority of people in Aberdeen.

His legal career often intersected with politics. One time he mediated a dispute between the AFL and the CIO before they merged, something that must have helped him become very good at bringing conflicts to peaceful ends. So good was he at resolving conflicts that his grandson named after him, Jim Brown, recalls a case that could easily have resulted in a feud. Phillips got a murderer off by using an insanity plea but became friends with the murder victim's family.

Phillips was adamant that his children would be well educated. His eldest daughter, Virginia, was to follow in his footsteps and become a lawyer but drowned in a tragic accident at age 16. Gladys then picked up the mantle, became a Latin scholar and graduated from the University of Washington Law School. Her father then swore her into the bar. She became one of the preeminent lawyers in the state of Washington, practicing for 60 years. Her nephew, James M. Brown, joined the firm and they practiced together for 20 years until she was elected to the state legislature. A scholarship for deserving students has been established in her name. Richenda toured as a model as "Indian Princess" and married sculptor John Rhoden. As of this writing, she still lives in the New York City warehouse her late husband converted into a studio home. Daughter Jeannette attended the University of Washington and trained at the Cornish School to be a concert violinist, but WWII intervened. She became a buyer for Lancaster's gift and hobby shop, married and waited for her husband to return from the war in the Pacific. He was captured by headhunters and thought dead for a year, but she didn't give up hope. Some time after his return she gave birth to a son named in honor of her father.

During WWII, although then a staunch Democrat, James Phillips opposed President Roosevelt's internment of Japanese citizens. He was not averse to bucking the party line. Principle was more important to him than politics.

James and Earney lived in Aberdeen's west end at 311 N. Washington Street on a large property. Behind their house ran a slough where they kept livestock for their own use. Earney kept a cupboard on their back porch stocked with foods she had canned. Having lived through the Great Depression, James and Earney were always conscious of having food on hand should hard times strike. In 1965 Richenda insisted that her mother throw out numerous mason jars filled with fruits and vegetables she had canned during the Depression. Earney resisted, considering such an act wasteful.

Always an advocate of education, Phillips kept his mind sharp by reading Greek and Latin classics such as *Anabasis* by Xenophon. In 1956 Hopkins Jr. High School was build on the land on which Phillips had run livestock. As of this writing the building has been repurposed as Hopkins Preschool. In 1963 a three-story modern school building housing math, science, home economics, business and language arts classes named in Phillips' honor opened as part of the expanded Aberdeen High School. That building also housed a lecture hall used for many group meetings and the school's administrative offices. The Phillips Building provided the space in which most classes were conducted after two students burned down the historic Weatherwax Building in 2002. A new building was constructed to replace both the Weatherwax and Phillips Buildings. The Phillips Building, maligned by architectural purists, was demolished during the writing of this book.

James lived a long, full life. In his later years his mind wasn't as sharp as it had been but he was still able to beat his grandson at checkers. He lived in his home on N. Washington Street until he died on August 12, 1959 at about 87 years of age. Earney was a very capable person active in community affairs until her death on October 13, 1972, at age 92. While researching his own heritage in western Virginia, North Carolina and Kentucky, the author learned of Melungeons, a mixed-race people of that region whose ancestors originally came from three continents: Europe, Africa and North America. It may be that James Phillips was Melungeon.

Edward Lowell Rogers

8

Coach Rogers;
*University of St.
Thomas*

Edward L. Rogers in his law office; *Benjey Collection*

Name:	Edward L. Rogers	**Nickname:**	
DOB:	4/14/1876	**Height:**	5' 10"
Weight:	163	**Age:**	18
Tribe:	Chippewa	**Home:**	Aitken, MN
Parents:	William D. Rogers, white, probably Scots-Irish; unknown Chippewa medicine woman		
Early Schooling:	Minneapolis area public grammar school		
Later Schooling:	Dickinson College preparatory school; Dickinson College; Dickinson School of Law; University of Minnesota		
Honors:	College Football Hall of Fame, 1968; American Indian Athletic Hall of Fame, 1973		

Enwu-ayie dung

Ed Rogers, a half-blood Chippewa born in a wigwam near Sandy Lake, Aitkin County, Minnesota, arrived at Carlisle in November of 1894 as an eighth-grader. His father was a Scots-Irish logger and his mother was a Chippewa medicine woman who was making maple sugar at the time of his birth. Around 1889, the family moved to Itasca County where his father operated lumber camps at Swan Lake, Bass Lake and down Splithand way where Ed, just a boy, sawed, drove and hauled logs. He became interested in attending Carlisle when an Indian agent showed him photographs of the school. At 5'10" tall and 163 pounds, Ed might not have been a prime size for a major college football lineman but was plenty big enough for Carlisle. By 1896 he was a substitute on the varsity team, but we're getting ahead of ourselves.

Rogers had reasons other than playing football to come to Carlisle. In fact, the program was so new that he very likely was unaware of its existence prior to talking with the Indian agent. He busied himself with school life and joined the Invincible Debating Society for which he was elected vice-president in April of 1896 and re-elected in two subsequent elections.

In October Ed rode a bicycle, an expensive piece of machinery at that time, up to the Doubling Gap resort on North Mountain as reported by *The Indian Helper*:

> "Thirty-one teachers, students and townspeople took an outing by wheel to Doubling Gap on Saturday. The day was apparently made to order. The ride as far as Newville was by [train or trolley] car wheels, but from that point the steeds of steel were mounted and the riders fairly flew to the mountains. At 1:30 a sumptuous feast in the shape of dinner was served and at three P.M. the ride back to the train was begun."

In the spring before making the football team, Ed Rogers was the starting center fielder for the school's varsity baseball team and received positive comments in the press for his play.

Graduating from Carlisle in the spring of 1897, Edward Rogers was one of the commencement speakers. His topic, football, was not much of a surprise. He discussed the benefits of athletic exercise for both boys and girls or the "new woman" as she was called in those days. He strongly supported intercollegiate football but denounced play for pay:

> "This desire on the part of some young men to become professionals has spoiled three of the best of college sports, namely boxing, base-ball and racing [track]. I hope football, which is one of the greatest of autumn games, will never be spoiled by any such desire, nor do I believe that it will, for the reason that nothing but a gentleman can ever play the game. A man with any of the brute instincts in him will always show them in a game and he will not be allowed to play. A gentleman will only play for the love of the sport and for the good results he may gain from it."

Rogers then touted the benefits of playing football: first the obvious physical benefits; then the mental discipline learned both from playing this team sport and preparing for the rigors of the games; and, lastly the moral training gained by setting a standard for other students to follow, developing temperance, self-control, attention to work and, above all, being a man even in defeat. He then waxed philosophical:

> "One who, while watching a game of football never felt the ambition to be strong, quick, alert and skillful is lacking in some manly qualities that he needs, and everybody else needs to be eminently successful in life. It is as Wellington said, that all the great men of England were made on the playgrounds of the public schools. ...
>
> "Class-mates and school-mates, here we stand lined up against civilization, with Capt. Pratt as centre and the Carlisle school and faculty as guards, and they are opening up the line for us to go through. Let us follow our interference well, and squirm and struggle and push and not give up until behind the goal posts of civilization, we have made our mighty touch-down."

For the 1897-98 school year, Ed Rogers enrolled in the Dickinson College Preparatory School. However, he continued to play football on the Carlisle Indian School team. Ed toiled at left end mostly anonymously that year due to the fine play of Bemus Pierce, Frank Hudson, Jonas Metoxen and Martin Wheelock, to name a few of the stars on that team. Carlisle finished its season early that year, making Ed available to Dickinson College for a Thanksgiving Day game. The logic in *The Dickinsonian*'s report about their big game against Penn State was curious, considering that Rogers appears to have been enrolled in the prep school at that time:

> "Two new faces appeared on the home team, Rogers at left-end and Cayou at left half-back, both of them star players for the Indians, but *bona fide* students of the College and as such entitled to a place on our eleven. They played in their usually brilliant style, Rogers especially distinguishing himself by fine tackling."

In spite of this brief shift of allegiance, Ed was given an opportunity to be a main speaker at Carlisle's annual football banquet, held that year in January. Again his talk was about football. After talking about the physical benefits gained by exercising, particularly when playing the game of football, Rogers touted the benefits to the athlete's academic career:

> "Football also promotes study, for a player must keep up to a certain standard in his studies if he wishes to play. The testimonials of doctors, lawyers and clergymen who were once stars on the gridiron goes to show that they had even greater standing during the football season than during any other time of the year, and I can humbly add my own testimony."

He went on to talk about the need to control one's temper and paraphrased the previous part of his talk that credited England's victories on the battlefield to games on public school playgrounds.

Ed participated in the basketball game played as part of the entertainment during the commencement week festivities. He made both goals for the white team that lost to the blue team 4-2. As a member of the Invincible Debating Society, Ed was automatically invited as a guest of the Susan Longstreth Literary Society at their end of school-year program. He also took the occasion to make a little speech that referred to the "Looking Backward" performance that was on the program. He used as an example Indian children being carried on their mothers' backs always looking backwards. He hoped that Indians would change old habits and start looking forward, away from the reservation and out into the light and life of the world.

The spring of 1899 found Ed Rogers on the diamond playing baseball for the Indians. That fall he enrolled as a freshman at Dickinson College proper, but he still played on the Indian School football team – even against Dickinson. Once again he played with some all-time greats. The fabulous 1899 team, Warner's first with Carlisle, was packed with talent, but Ed held his own. After the season ended his teammates elected him captain of the 1900 squad. Back-to-back-to-back games with Harvard, Yale and Penn wore down the Indians so badly that they rested and recuperated the week between the Harvard and Yale games at a resort near Pine Grove. Injuries to key players still resulted. Although he was part of a winning team, 6-4-1, against a brutal schedule, Ed was not satisfied as he had become accustomed to doing better.

Ed Rogers attended Dickinson School of Law for the 1900-01 school year returning home for the summer. In September 1901, he wrote Carlisle that he would not be returning because he was entering the University of Minnesota. Rogers later shared that while in New York, probably for the Columbia game, he had bought a Minneapolis newspaper which reported that the University of Minnesota won a football championship. That made him homesick so he decided to complete his studies at the University of Minnesota. He joined the football team, but his presence on the squad prompted a protest by the University of Nebraska. *The Nebraska State Journal* opined that, as a member of the Big Nine, Minnesota must abide by the conference's eligibility rules and thus would not be able to play Rogers against Wisconsin and Chicago. It went on to say, "Rodgers [sic] is a first year law student. He came direct from Carlyle[sic], having played on the team there last year. He is also a former captain of the team at that college. As a player, he undoubtedly has no equal at his position in the west. It is, therefore, unjust to ask the corn huskers to play against him if he is not strictly eligible." Nebraska apparently viewed playing for Carlisle one year and Minnesota the next without an intervening inactive year as being against the rules. Rogers played in the 19-0 thumping after which a Nebraska fan wrote a poem that ended:

> Trot out men of decent size,
> Minnesota,
> Not such great, ungainly guys,
> Minnesota.
> Average mortals can't compete
> In the game and hope to beat
> Freaks who run to neck and feet,
> Minnesota.

First Wisconsin, then Northwestern protested Minnesota's playing quarterback Gil Dobie, accusing him of having previously coached a team. His play against Wisconsin was subpar so Minnesota supporters didn't mind his being benched for the Northwestern game. Rogers was allowed to play because Carlisle was viewed as not being a college, which it wasn't. Therefore, he hadn't been attending and playing for another college immediately before attending Minnesota. No mention was made of the fact he had been attending Dickinson College. Perhaps that fact was not known in the Midwest. The *Cedar Rapids Republican* trumpeted that bets were being taken on and around the Iowa campus that Rogers would not return to Minnesota the following year.

The 1902 Commencement Issue of *The Red Man and Helper* ran an extract from Ed's letter in which he declined the invitation to attend commencement. He was unable to attend because he had a summer job in a law office in Minneapolis and would complete his program the upcoming school year:

> "Owing to studies I will be unable to attend your Commencement this year. Best wishes to the class of 1902 and to the alumni I extend greeting. My experiences since I left Carlisle have been smooth and pleasant. For my room rent I tend a furnace, and for the rest of my expenses I wait upon the table. I find plenty of time for play and study and am getting along well in both. University life is a great thing. Anybody can get through one and earn money besides. May more Carlisle alumni take advantage of this opportunity."

Rogers played left end for Minnesota that fall and received mention for his play by being named to all-conference and All-America teams by some writers but not by Walter Camp. *The Minnesota Daily Express* described his play against Wisconsin as "…a heady, brilliant game, which drew the comment from Wisconsin's coach: 'You might send forty men after that fellow and you couldn't tell whether or not they could get him.'" At season's end, he was elected captain of Minnesota's 1903 team.

Superintendent Pratt liked to report on the success of former students and never failed to miss an opportunity to preach his message. The April 3, 1903 issue of *The Red Man and Helper* contained such a piece:

> "We are pleased to see frequent allusions to Rogers – class 1897, now a student of the University of Minnesota in their *Daily*. The last item mentions Rogers and two others as having distinguished themselves on the diamond. With Rogers we feel sure it is not at the sacrifice of his studies."

He got in condition for football season by playing amateur, so they say, baseball over the summer. Captain Rogers again played left end on the 1903 Minnesota team that went 14-0-1, with the only blemish being the 6-6 tie with conference co-champions Michigan in the original Little Brown Jug game. Ed's teammate, Jim Kremer, told his version of how that tradition got started:

> "That was the year we had a large brown five-gallon jug of pure water on the field for game days. Michigan stole it that day and would not give it back until we had won a game. The (Fielding) Yost broke off relations and it was not until 1909 that games were resumed."

Ed was honored for his play that season by being placed on Walter Camp's All America third team. Pop Warner disagreed with Camp as he thought Rogers and Al Exendine were the best ends Carlisle ever fielded and belonged on the first team. In the spring Rogers graduated from law school and in June of that year he was admitted to the Minnesota bar; however, he had something more exciting to do before settling into a country law practice.

In March 1904, *The Red Man and Helper* announced, "Edward Rogers, known East

Ed Rogers in football uniform; *U. S. Army Military History Institute*

and West as one of the greatest end rushes that ever donned moleskins, will coach Carlisle next year. 'Ed' has been negotiating with the Carlisle management for several weeks and yesterday received a final offer with instructions to telegraph if he wished to accept, and after consulting [Minnesota coach] Dr. Williams and other friends, our late captain decided to accept the position and wired an answer to that effect." Warner had been enticed back to Cornell, making the opportunity with Carlisle available.

That fall an article titled, "Red Brains Matched Against White Brains," ran in the *Atlanta Constitution* and likely across the country. Its subtitle, "Carlisle Football Team Made up of Indians and Trained by Indian, To Meet Paleface Teams of United States." Accompanying the article were photographs of the team, Head Coach Rogers and assistants Frank Hudson and Bemus Pierce. Having all Indian coaches was a novel idea for the time and was the first time a major team had been coached entirely by Indians. The *Constitution* viewed Indian coaches as an experiment and was skeptical as to whether they had the intellect for such a demanding task. Such were the times that this was not an uncommon view.

Arriving at Carlisle almost simultaneously with the new football coaches was Captain William A. Mercer, the new school superintendent. The always controversial Pratt had been relieved of command or retired, depending on whose spin one believes, and replaced by another cavalry officer. Mercer, a major for most of his time at Carlisle, was an ardent football supporter and emphasized athletics more than had the school's founder.

The football season started with a 28-0 win over traditional warm-up foe Lebanon Valley College on a beastly hot day. Coach Rogers shuttled players in and out from the second, third and fourth teams after the starters built an early lead. Assistant coach Frank Hudson returned to his job in Pittsburgh after that game because he could only get off work for three weeks, leaving Rogers and Pierce to practice the team.

The next week's game with Franklin and Marshall College was cancelled, so Ed took his players across town to watch the Dickinson-Maryland game. He also started writing columns for the press. Whether he was paid for these columns or if he wrote them to ensure accuracy is unknown. There was a ready appetite for information about this colorful team.

Roger's Indians breezed through their first four games, winning by wide margins. Bucknell was tougher but succumbed 10-4. The closeness of the score in the 12-0 loss to Harvard on a soft field was a bit of a surprise, especially for Harvard, as so-called experts thought Carlisle to be a much weaker team that year. Harvard partisans accused Wallace Denny of carrying messages to players when he brought out the water bucket during time outs. He may well have been guilty. The Indians defeated the rest of their opponents except the eventual national champions, the Penn Quakers, who beat them, in part due to numerous fumbles. The season was to close out against the Buckeyes on Thanksgiving Day in Columbus, Ohio, but the 1904 St. Louis World's Fair officials had an idea.

Unable to get the military academies to relocate the Army-Navy game, they struck upon the idea of having the two most prominent government Indian schools play each other as part of World's Fair activities the Saturday after Thanksgiving. Ohio State fans were disappointed at not seeing Carlisle's best, but the Buckeyes were not yet a national football power and the second team handled them easily, 23-0. The first team rested for the first and only meeting between Carlisle Indian Industrial School and Haskell Institute. Word was out that Haskell had brought in some ringers for the game, but Carlisle had some of its own. Hawley Pierce made the trip west with his assistant coach brother. Rogers and both Pierce brothers all dressed for the game. As it turned out, they were not needed as Carlisle handled Haskell easily, 38-4, with Haskell's lone score coming from the toe of Pete Hauser, a name that would soon be associated with Carlisle.

Journalist Caspar Whitney, perhaps better known for collaborating with Walter Camp on selecting All-America teams, ranked the Indian-led Indians 14th in the country. Others might have ranked them a bit higher. At the football banquet shortly after season's end, Ed gave a philosophical talk titled, "The Scrimmages of Life," then returned to Minnesota. The Indians were coached largely by white men in 1905, but Ed wasn't benched.

He found a job in St. Paul, Minnesota, coaching the College of St. Thomas football team during the 1905, 1906, and 1907 seasons. Ed compiled a conference record of 13-2 with his teams winning the Intercollegiate Conference of the Northwest championships in 1906 and 1907. During the off season, he apparently did a lot more than practice law.

Ed married society belle Mayme Constance Ballton of Minneapolis in February 1906. After a honeymoon in New York and the South, the couple set up housekeeping upstate in Walker, Minnesota. Other than coaching in St. Paul in the falls of 1906 and 1907, the Rogers lived in Walker, where he had his law practice, the rest of their days together.

In the spring of 1908, *The Sheboygan Press* announced, "Ed Rogers famous the country over as a football player, formerly member of the Minnesota and Carlisle Indian, teams, is seeking the office of county judge at Walker, Minn. It is said that he has little opposition…. If Rogers is elected, he will make the third great western football player to go on the bench."

In January 1909, Ed responded to a request for information from then Carlisle Superintendent Moses Friedman:

> "I herewith take pleasure in submitting to you the report of my career since graduating from your school in 1897. You will note that I have been most fortunate in my endeavor to better myself and have had a comparatively easy road to travel. What little degree of success I have attained I attribute entirely to my early training at Carlisle.
>
> "I might add although the subject is not mentioned nor no opinion is requested that to abolish non-reservation schools is a mistake and would be a serious detriment to the progress and welfare of the future young Indian."

He responded to Friedman's request for photographs in March 1910 with:

> "My home is located on the shore of Leech Lake upon a 60 foot bank. It is in the best part of town. The house is not a very sightly looking affair but I have it well furnished with the best of everything, such as parquet floors, electric lights, mahogany furniture, oriental rugs and grand piano. My law library comprises about 300 volumes of law books. I am the Village Recorder, on the health board, Deputy County Attorney, Deputy County Coroner and have been appointed special census enumerator for the Leech Lake Indian reservation. I give you the above facts as they may be of some value to you and also to show in a slight way how an Indian may hold the confidence of the people amongst whom he lives. There are no Indians living in this town."

The 1910 census listed Ed and Mayme as the heads of a sizeable household consisting of their children, Constance, 3, and George, 14 months, as well as Ed's brother Charles, half-sisters Mabel and Sylvia, brother-in-law Harry and servant Anna Larson. By 1920, they had a son and four daughters. Their household expanded by 1930 to include daughter Vonda's husband Charles Herbison and their two daughters.

The Minnesota Chippewa tribe would have been wealthy had the government given them control of their many assets. Tribal leaders' yearly treks to Washington to argue their case to government officials had become junkets that accomplished nothing except creating rancor within the tribe. New leadership was needed, so a council of the ten tribes was formed. After many long meetings and much discussion around hearths and fires, Ed Rogers was chosen as Chief of the Chippewas. He was awarded a salary which he refused until the time that the new organization was on a stable footing. He was immediately called upon to settle differences between tribe members and with tribe members and the government. Sometimes these requests for arbitration were difficult to fulfill. Others were more mundane.

A member of the Nett Lake band requested that Chief Rogers administer the "Firewater Oath," apparently a pledge to swear off alcohol, to him. There were a couple of minor problems: Rogers knew little Chippewa and didn't know the Firewater Oath in any language, so, he winged it. He had the man raise his right hand and say, "May the Great Spirit make firewater as molten lead in my throat so that it will bubble up in my face till my Chief shall know me not." A year later the man had not yet let whiskey "melt" in his throat.

Ed had his detractors. In 1917, a voter filed charges of malfeasance against Rogers, demanding that he be removed from his position of County Attorney. The governor apparently took no action because Ed remained in office for decades.

In 1928, Ed used his skills as a negotiator to convince the Pillager band of Chippewas to give one of the tribe's most treasured possessions, a 70-year-old war drum, to the University of Minnesota to be used to "help the Gophers scalp Chicago." Rogers brought the drum, used 30 years prior in the Leech Lake Uprising that left six white men and 12 Chippewas dead, to Minneapolis for use in the homecoming game. The Associated Press reported, "Now that the drum is to become official property of the university, it will thump its defiance to invading gridiron hosts in the stadium."

In 1936 as Chippewa Chief, Ed placed a wreath at the base of the 26 foot tall statue carved by Carl Milles as part of the dedication ceremonies for a monument sculpted out of Mexican onyx to honor WWI dead. The statue, still located in St. Paul's City Hall, depicts a group of Indians smoking a peace pipe at the base; soaring above them is the majestic figure of an Indian god with a peace pipe in one hand and the other arm extended in a gesture of friendliness. When Roger spoke, he said, "It makes me proud Milles has seen fit to use an Indian subject to portray his conception of peace and I am glad as a representative of the Chippewas and as a citizen of Minnesota to join in the public presentation, both because of the nature of the statue and the fact that it is to be a memorial to the veterans."

In 1938, as Cass County Attorney, Rogers negotiated a truce between the Sheriff and Chippewa tribe members who were protesting a relocation of the government's consolidated Chippewa agency to Duluth. He successfully avoided bloodshed.

In 1943, Ed argued for the Chippewas in front of the Minnesota State Senate because they disliked the language of a proposed liquor bill. He reportedly said, "The Indians objected to language of a liquor law banning the sale of intoxicants to Indians. The present statute makes it a gross misdemeanor to sell liquor to any intoxicated person, to any person of Indian blood, or to any public prostitute." He asked that phrase, "any person of Indian blood" be eliminated. The second bill approved by the committee repealed a law which makes sales to Indians a felony. The alcohol issue was raised again when a bill was proposed that would make selling intoxicants to 95% of Minnesota Indians legal. Ed Rogers spoke in support of the bill.

He continued to work on Indian issues. In 1945, as a long-time leader of the Chippewa Council, Rogers read a position paper from the Council that he surely played a significant part in writing. *Minnesota Chats* reported that he wrote the following as part of a request for information:

> "The Council was outspoken on several important things.

> "The competency of Indians should be determined and those who are capable of looking after themselves should be given their share of tribal funds, taken off from the rolls and forgotten as Indians.

> "Those Indians who are incompetent should be looked after as in the past.

> "For those who are left there should be adequate school facilities and an insistence that all should learn some trade.

> "Indians should be given lands upon which a decent living might be made and these lands should be scattered among white communities so that the Indian may profit from the example of white neighbors.

> "All discriminating laws against Indians should be removed.

> "In discussing these vitally important policies, Mr. Rogers believes that to make any people wards of the government tends to diminish their industry and resourceful-ness. There are, as a matter of fact, few true Indians. Most of the people who are on the reservations are white people with some Indian blood. Most of them have no real claim to Indian property or protection of the government as Indians."

Ed expressed his personal opinions in a 1948 talk to the Lions Club when, in response to recent publicity regarding "starving Indians" he described their condition no better or worse than it had been 20 years prior. His remedy, which was not shared by the Indian Bureau, was that young boys should be required to attend school with whites to allow them to mix with the majority culture. He cited returning WWII veterans as support for his idea because few Indians who served in the army returned to the reservation as wards of the government. Most either stayed in the military or found civilian employment.

In 1962 at age 86, Ed Rogers was honored in Philadelphia as the outstanding county attorney in the United States by the National County Attorneys Association. He planned to retire the next year from the position as Cass County Attorney that he had held for 46 years. He stayed active in his private legal practice and continued to play a round of golf almost every day. He died in October 1971 at 95 years of age.

9

Bemus and Hawley Pierce

Bemus Pierce; *Cumberland County Historical Society, Carlisle, PA*

Hawley Pierce, the first Seneca engineer on the P B & R Railroad; *From the collections of the B&O Railroad Museum, Baltimore, MD.*

Name: Bemus Pierce		**Nickname:**	
DOB: 2/27/1875		**Height:** 6' 1/2"	
Weight: 199		**Age:** 18	
Tribe: Seneca		**Home:** Cattaraugus Reservation, NY	
Parents: Jacob Pierce; unknown			
Early Schooling: Cattaraugus Reservation School			
Later Schooling:			
Honors: American Indian Athletic Hall of Fame, 1971			

Name: Hawley Pierce		**Nickname:**	
DOB: circa 1877		**Height:** 6' 2"	
Weight:		**Age:**	
Tribe: Seneca		**Home:** Cattaraugus Reservation, NY	
Parents: Jacob Pierce; unknown			
Early Schooling: Cattaraugus Reservation School			
Later Schooling:			
Honors:			

Early Pro Stars

The November 7, 1890 edition of *The Indian Helper* announced, "Albert Bishop and Bemos [sic] Pierce, Senecas from New York have entered Carlisle as pupils. Albert enters class '92 while Bemos begins in third grade, NO. 6, but will work hard and be ahead of his class very soon and enter a higher grade. Both are gentlemanly and bright and will be acceptable additions to our school." Bemus's younger sister, Delia, was already at Carlisle and active in school life. She wrote an article about the Senecas living on the Cattaraugus and Allegheny reservations, which provided some background on how the eight Pierce children lived and were educated prior to coming to Carlisle. In her opinion, the Cattaraugus Reservation where she lived had better farmland and a better class of white neighbors than did the Allegheny Reservation, the other reservation with which she was familiar. Delia also stated that the Seneca language had no swear words, something that would seem to put Indian footballers at a disadvantage with their white opponents.

The next mention of Bemus was in March of 1892 when a physician examined his eyes in Philadelphia. The eye doctor found cataracts and removed them surgically in a procedure that, by all indications, was successful. His younger brother, Hawley, arrived at Carlisle in September of that year. Determining exact ages of the Pierce brothers is problematic due to conflicting records. Most likely they were born in the mid-1870s, as the 1885 census lists them as being 12 and 11, respectively. They grew up on the Seneca reservation near Irving, New York and attended day school on the reservation before coming to Carlisle. Bemus was listed as full-blood and Hawley at ¾, most likely due to a clerical error since both parents were listed as living on both boys' records. Bemus apparently liked school much better than did Hawley because he stayed. Hawley ran away and returned home after a year at Carlisle.

Bemus went through the seasons of Indian School life alternating between classroom and outing experiences until Captain Pratt lifted his ban and allowed his students to play inter-scholastic football games. Although Pratt had banned interscholastic football games shortly after Bemus arrived at Carlisle, he still allowed intramural teams to play - and get - positive press in the school newspaper. Bemus surely played on an intramural team because he was on the earliest inter-scholastic teams. In 1895, in just the second full season of fielding a team to represent the school, he was elected captain of the varsity football team. Bemus's five-year enrollment was terminated a few months early in August 1895 when he became an employee of the school. However, with eligibility rules being what they were, or rather weren't, in those days, he was allowed to remain on the team.

To the naked eye, the earliest Carlisle schedules looked easy. However, athletic clubs in those days were generally semi-pro teams with experienced older players, often with college experience. The Pittsburgh Athletic Club was one such team, as was the Duquesne Athletic Club that the Indians played in 1894 and 1895, respectively.

Football must have swayed Hawley's opinion of Carlisle because he returned in early 1895, joined the football team, and played regularly. Most Carlisle Indians were smaller and lighter than the opposition, but, weighing over 200 pounds each, the Pierce brothers were large muscular men, not just for Indians but for football players in general. As a result of their great size and strength, they almost always played interior line positions. Bemus played guard and Hawley tackle opposite some pretty good competition that in 1895 included Penn and Yale, two of the Big Four. Bemus gained some fame on

Sunday, November 17, 1895, when the *Philadelphia Press* published an article he wrote that was accompanied by a photograph of him in football togs. He gained more notoriety when *Yale Alumni Weekly* placed him as a substitute on its All-America team.

In spring 1896, Hawley played first base on Carlisle's school team. Because Bemus was then employed by the school, he had some disposable income. He must have saved a good bit of it because he was able to buy a Cleveland bicycle, an expensive item in that day. But everything wasn't fun and games for Carlisle students; there was also work to do. To the Pierce brothers fell the task of repairing the smokestack. Perhaps they were comfortable working at heights, as were their neighbors the Mohawks, or it may have been viewed as part of their work in the boiler room.

In the fall of 1896, Carlisle's first winning and, in Bemus's opinion, first real football season, he was again captain. That year he toiled opposite the best in the game by playing the Big Four – Princeton, Yale, Harvard and Penn – on successive Saturdays, and playing Wisconsin, that year's Champions of the West, all on the road. For his efforts, he was placed on the Walter Camp substitute All-American team at guard that year (there was only a first team and substitutes, no second or third team that year). His appearance also captured the attention of correspondent Owen Langdon who wrote, "One of their [Carlisle's] best men last year, Pierce, a fine guard and worthy of a great varsity team, has very pronounced Indian features."

It was the late Victorian period and clothing for the upper classes, although excessive by current standards, was much more practical than in earlier decades. Women, for the most part, were not knowledgeable about football, particularly if they had not gone to college. However, football games were becoming social events, particularly if the Carlisle Indians were playing. Capt. and his youngest daughter, Nana, Pratt were joined by Russell and Olivia Sage, wealthy industrialists and philanthropists, in New York City to watch the Yale game. Mrs. Sage, via Miss Nana, sent bunches of chrysanthemums and roses in Carlisle's colors to the players as mementos of the game and tokens of her appreciation. As team captain, Bemus received the largest bunch. After the Thanksgiving Day game against Brown, also played in New York City, Mrs. Sage sent the players "handsome neckties." Capt. Pierce was honored with the ribbon in school colors she wore at the game.

1896 marked the first year that Harvard and Carlisle played each other. In that game Bemus Pierce played opposite Crimson tackle Barkie Donald. Besides a 4-0 Harvard win, Donald came away from the game with a story to tell for years to come. Barkie was a rough player who knew how to use his arms against his opponent and, when rushing at his opposite number, to insert some extracurricular play with his elbows and open hand, both of which were allowed by the old rules. After being hit hard several times, Bemus had had enough and politely issued a warning, "Mr. Donald, you have been hitting me and if you do it again, I shall hit you." Barkie hit Pierce all the harder on the next play with no immediate reaction. Barkie later, much later, recalled, "But I thought I was hit by a sledge hammer in the next scrimmage. I remember charging, but that was all. I was down and out, but when I came to I somehow wobbled to my feet and went back against the Indian. I was so dazed I could just see the big fellow moving about and as we sparred off for the next play he said in a matter-of-fact tone: 'Mr. Donald, you hit me one, two, three times. I hit you only one. We're square.' And you bet we were square," Donald always added when he told the story.

During the off-season, in February 1897, Hawley orated to an assembly of the student body about the evils of intemperance. During baseball season, Hawley and the rest of the baseball team were the butts of good-natured puns and riddles printed in the school newspaper that were based on the positions they played. "Why should Hawley Pierce be able to get a good wife? Because he is big enough to catcher." Over the summer, he played on the nearby Mount Holly Springs town team. Bemus vacationed in New York State, on his farm most likely, as was his habit.

Bemus was elected captain of the football team for the third straight year. The 1897 team was another success, again winning six games and losing four. This year three of the losses were to three teams of the Big Four (Harvard wasn't on that year's schedule) and Brown University. The 18-14 loss to Brown came on a cold and windy day at the Polo Grounds in New York. A decade later, William "Big Bill" Edwards, a former Princeton player who in 1926 became commissioner of the short-lived upstart American Football League, retold a humorous story about the Pierce brothers and that game:

> "Brown University was playing the Carlisle Indians some ten years ago at the Polo Grounds at New York City. Bemus Pierce, the Indian captain, called time just as a play was about to be run off, and the Brown team continued in line, while Hawley Pierce, his brother, a tackle on the Indian team, complained, in an audible voice, that some one on the Brown team had been slugging him. Bemus walked over to the Brown line with his brother, saying to him:
>
> 'Pick out the man who did it.'
>
> Hawley Pierce looked the Brunonians over, but could not decide which player had been guilty of the rough work. By this time, the two minutes were up, and the officials ordered play resumed. Bemus shouted to Hawley:
>
> 'Now keep your eyes open and find out who it was. Show him to me, and after the game I'll take care of him properly.'
>
> It is interesting to note that Bemus only weighed 230 pounds and his little brother tipped the scale at 210 pounds."

Bemus had taken to heart Pratt's doctrine that Indians were just as capable as whites and, given proper training, could do anything whites could do. At the annual football banquet in January, he spoke his mind and said something that challenged the prevailing view of so-called football experts:

> "Now, I am glad to say we have a white man for a coach, but we have no white men on the team when we are on the gridiron. Therefore, I say if the Indian can do this, why can he not as well handle the team, and handle the financial part? If he can do so well in this game, I believe in time he can do most anything."

1898 was Bemus's last year as a Carlisle football player – until he was needed in a pinch. After Bemus's three years as team captain, the mantle of leadership was passed to Frank Hudson, the famous drop-kicker. Reporters still interviewed Bemus, possibly because they knew him from previous campaigns or more likely as the *Chicago Evening Post* put it: "Coupled with his shrewdness and prowess, Hudson has considerable of a retiring disposition, and cannot be drawn into an interview." Not so with Bemus, although he was sometimes misquoted. The *Philadelphia Call* reported that he attributed the clean play in the Harvard game to the fact that, "Harvard players made no attempt to violate the rules and indulged in only the fairest kind of play." The Philadelphia *North American* ran two stories that misquoted Pierce so badly that a response by a school official was required. The first quoted Bemus as predicting a victory over Penn. The second accused Yale of slugging. Carlisle said it would be an honor to defeat Penn if they ever did and that, "Not only did Mr. Pierce not say such a thing but, on the contrary, our boys had nothing but words of commendation for the clean work of Yale." Reporters hoped for controversy but had to create it.

Carlisle's 5-4 record included losses to three of the Big Four (Yale, Harvard and Penn) as well as to Cornell, a team that was coached by one of their alumni, Glenn S. "Pop" Warner. The Holyoke, Massachusetts *Globe* quoted Bemus as complimenting Cornell's captain, Allen Whiting, by saying that he "ought to be an Indian. He runs like one and never shows the white feather." Where the top Eastern teams were concerned that they had to play well to beat the Indians, others expected defeat, especially after seeing the Indians play. Illinois's supporters were no different. The *Chicago Times-Herald* feared the worst for the Illini. "Metoxen, Pierce and Hudson are names calculated to send cold shivers along the spine of the average knight of the pigskin and Illinois fully expected to have a large score made against its eleven." Their fears were not unfounded as the Illini lost to the Indians 11-0.

Bemus left Carlisle and returned to his farm on the Cattaraugus Reservation, but not before marrying Annie Gesis. Annie was Chippewa from the White Earth Reservation in Minnesota and had graduated from the Normal School curriculum where she prepared herself to teach young children. The ceremony took place in the Susan Longstreth Society Hall at the Indian School with Rev. Alexander McMillan, Rector of St. John's Episcopal Church, officiating. Due to the Indian School's facilities and the students' skills, Annie's wedding was surely more elegant than most Americans of modest financial means could afford at that time. She wore a white organdy gown and her attendants, Melinda Metoxen and Luzenia Tibbets, wore white dresses. The flower girls, little Grace Khy and Esanetuck, in white dresses with pink sashes, spread flower petals in front of the bridal procession as Miss Senseney played Mendelssohn's Wedding March on the piano. The groom and his groomsmen, Hawley Pierce and Artie Miller, all wore tailored dark suits. Major Pratt surely wore his dress uniform as he gave away the bride. The bride received high marks on her cake-cutting skill: "The bride's cake, which was a large and handsome one, was brought to the front, and the bride with a skill and coolness that was most becoming apportioned it to the guests, each of whom was eager to get a small piece to dream over." Hers was no small task, given that there were 75 guests to serve.

Even Superintendent of Printing Marianne Burgess, who referred to herself as the Man-on-the-band-stand, waxed poetic. "The Man-on-the-band-stand does not believe that the happy couple can ever forget the moment of departure from old Carlisle. The band was out in full force and playing stirring airs; the school swarmed about the Herdic coach, which had been secretly decorated with all sorts of curious things for 'luck,' and the old shoes and rice were sufficiently manifest to make the occasion memorable." The Pierces got quite a sendoff for their 9:00 p.m. train to their farm in Irving, New York.

The superintendent also shared his observations of the groom. "It was a trying moment for a man who has made himself conspicuous all through his school life for his retiring modesty, but as at times when on the football field his metal was the reserve power that made him equal to almost any emergency, so in this, one of the most trying moments of his life, this same metal proved sufficient to keep him, to all outward appearances, self-possessed and dignified, if a little pale."

Bemus may have coached the University of Buffalo team that fall. The *Carlisle Herald* was unclear which year, 1899 or 1900, was meant when, in December, it stated that he, "has been made coach of the eleven at the University of Buffalo."

Cayou, Metoxen and Bemus Pierce were gone from the 1898 Indian team, but some rising stars and a new coach, Glenn Scobey "Pop" Warner filled their shoes. Some old stars like Hawley Pierce returned and shone. 1899 was Carlisle's best season to date. Hawley and his teammates, under the tutelage of Coach Warner, went 9-2 for the season, losing only to Harvard and Princeton and beating Penn for Carlisle's first win ever over one of the Big Four. Coming out from under his older brother's shadow, Hawley was now considered one of the team leaders and, as such, was invited to important functions after games in the big cities. The trip to the West Coast for the Christmas game with California was surely a highlight of Hawley's time at Carlisle. Sightseeing in California, Arizona, and other points along the way must have been unforgettable for him.

1900 was a difficult year for Carlisle and Hawley Pierce because so few members of the starting team or substitutes returned. Needing an entirely new backfield, Warner even tried Hawley at fullback and also let him do some of the kicking. His brother also had a trying season but for different reasons.

No longer playing as an amateur, Bemus joined the Homestead Library and Athletic Club (HLAC), likely for substantial pay for the time. Homestead apparently stood for Homestead Works for Carnegie Steel. HLAC had not previously been much competition for other western Pennsylvania powers, but 1900 was a different year. Apparently some Carnegie steel money was made available for a winning football team. William Temple came over from Duquesne Country and Athletic Club to become the football chairman for HLAC. Bill Church was hired back from Georgetown to coach and play tackle. Church, with some Carnegie money to spend, set about hiring enough stars to bring home a championship. He hired Bemus Pierce to play one of the guard positions. HLAC had a good year on the field, undefeated in fact, but a poor year at the box office as did all the western Pennsylvania independent teams. The financial aspect was so bad, in fact, that all the other major independents in that area closed up shop. However, William Temple took over the ownership of HLAC in what may have been one of the first instances of an individual owning a professional football team.

Hawley Pierce finished his enrollment at Carlisle that spring by setting school records in the pole vault and discus, an odd combination of track and field events for a football lineman. In the fall, he joined his brother and former Indian teammate, Artie Miller, at Homestead. Church returned to Georgetown but virtually everyone else was back. Quarterback Willis Richardson handled the coaching duties. HLAC breezed through most of its schedule, but Hawley Pierce and P. D. Overfield, two important linemen, could not play the second game with the Philadelphia pro team and were needed. However, HLAC prevailed and closed out their second consecutive undefeated season. Tired of losing money as the owner of a pro football team, William Temple dumped it. He is best known for what he did after retiring to Florida: developing the orange that was named for him.

Bemus had established an annual cycle for his life: he played or coached football in the fall and farmed the rest of the year. Annie found the football season to be a convenient time to visit her family in Minnesota. After one such visit, she wrote a letter to Superintendent Pratt, part of which was printed in *The Red Man and Helper*:

> "Last fall I was out in Minnesota visiting my folks, I saw a great many of the Carlisle students. Quite a number of them were doing well, but would do still better if they were out of the reservation. Strong drink is doing its work with both the old and

young generation of the Indians. When I saw how much drinking was going on, while they were, or after they received their annuities, how I wished there were dozens of Carlisle Indian Schools, and every one of the young Indians was in it."

1902 found Bemus coaching at Sherman Institute in Riverside, California and getting praise for his work there. In early November Mrs. Jessie W. Cook, formerly a teacher at Carlisle but then at Riverside, wrote, "Bemus Pierce is giving great satisfaction as coach, the Indians having so far walked over every opposing team, and have not been scored against." Sherman Institute thumped the Reliance Athletic Association of San Francisco, an independent team of mostly Stanford and Cal graduates, 28-0, setting up a Thanksgiving Day game in Los Angeles between the University of California and Sherman Institute. The Cal eleven prevailed 29-12 but Pierce was still held in high esteem. Sherman supporter and Carlisle alum, Jessie Cox, wrote, "Bemus Pierce has won the highest praise on all sides for his coaching of the Indians."

Bill Warner, Pop's brother, assisted him in preparing the Carlisle team for the 1902 season and then departed for Ithaca to captain the Cornell team. The younger Warner was named second team All-American by Walter Camp for his work that season. Bill coached Cornell in 1903 and Sherman Institute in 1904.

Hawley Pierce played football for the Philadelphia Athletics of the first NFL in 1902. As discussed in an earlier chapter, the NFL teams did not compete, at least in their original forms, in the first football World Series held over New Year's in Madison Square Garden. Hawley was thus available to the teams that were competing. Since Bemus's season was over in California and he had returned to his farm near Irving, New York, he was also available. However, he arrived none too early as a newspaper blared, "Bemus Pierce, the Indian Player and Coach, Was Last to Arrive – Came yesterday on the Empire – Joined His team Mates in the Gymnasium and Went Into the Practice." The Pierce brothers played guard and tackle on one side of the center while the Warner brothers were their counterparts on the other for All-Syracuse. The other teams were no match for this assembly of stars, and they easily won professional football's first World Series.

Hawley unknowingly played a part in the development of the forward pass that year when he showed, or attempted to show, player-coach Howard R. "Bosey" Reiter how to throw a spiral underhand pass. However, due to having short arms, Reiter couldn't throw the ball much of a distance using this technique. Reiter then tried throwing the ball overhand in a manner similar to that of a catcher pegging the ball to second base. He was first able to use the technique in a game on October 8, 1906 when his Wesleyan team played Yale. His passer, Sammy Moore, threw an 18-yard strike to Irwin Van Tassel for what Reiter claimed was the first overhand spiral pass thrown in a football game. The genesis of the forward pass continues to be a disputed issue.

In September 1903, *The Red Man and Helper* announced, "The new assistant coach, Mr. Bemus Pierce, is on the grounds. The very sight of him rouses enthusiasm in the football men." Later that month he left for New York State to pick up Annie and head west to coach at Sherman Institute again, but he wasn't finished with the 1903 Carlisle team. Having lost only to Princeton and Harvard, Warner rewarded his players with an extended post-season trip to the West Coast where they played Reliance Athletic Association on Christmas Day and Sherman Institute on New Year's Day. Carlisle won both games easily, but Pierce had done such a good job that his team was considered to be Pacific champs and made a respectable showing against his mentor and superior players.

He also extended hospitality to the Carlisle team as they enjoyed their stay at Sherman Institute.

Hawley made his debut as a pitcher for Concord of the New England League in 1904. He was batted around, giving up five runs in the third inning of his first game, the season opener, on April 19. His name was not found in the box score for any game later in the season.

Warner announced that he would be returning to Cornell in early 1904. Carlisle, perhaps heeding Bemus's earlier request, announced that it was inaugurating the graduate coaching system then in vogue at many of the major schools. By hiring Ed Rogers as athletic director and head coach of all outdoor athletic teams and Bemus Pierce as assistant football coach, "...Carlisle will be entitled to all the glory for the victories our team achieves under the leadership and instruction of these former Carlisle students." Bemus may not have been selected as athletic director because off-season duties on his New York farm kept him from taking year-round positions. It is logical to think an experienced coach with a good track record would be selected over a former player who was still in school and had no coaching experience.

1904 was a successful year for Carlisle. The only losses were to Harvard and Penn, the only Big Four teams on the Indians' schedule that year. A special game against Haskell Institute at the St. Louis World's Fair was added for the Saturday after Thanksgiving. Because it was believed that Haskell would be using "ringers," Rogers, Bemus and Hawley suited up for the game. The *St. Louis Daily Globe Democrat* believed these suspicions to be true. "Quite a number of the Haskell players could hardly be distinguished from 'pale-faces,' but there was no doubt about every player on the Carlisle team being a genuine Indian." Using tactics Ed Rogers learned at the University of Minnesota, the Eastern team beat its Western counterpart 38-4. The season over, Rogers left Carlisle and returned to Minnesota to practice law and do a little coaching.

At the turn of the 20th century Jerry, Frank and Tommy Pierce, Bemus and Hawley's younger brothers, made names for themselves as distance runners. Frank competed in the 1904 Olympic marathon. Due to extreme heat, humidity and dust, Frank and several others dropped out of the race. He did not get a second chance in the 1908 games because he died of pneumonia earlier that year. It is not clear if he ever attended Carlisle.

Over the winter, the *Philadelphia Ledger* besmirched the reputations of both the school and the Pierces when it published a story saying that four former famous Indian School athletes, all Senecas, were incarcerated in Castle William, the old military prison on the northwest end of Governor's Island in New York City, for desertion. One of the men incarcerated was named Glen Pierce. *The Arrow* responded that Glen Pierce was not related to Bemus and Hawley and that Glen Pierce and Wallack Doxtator had been at Carlisle briefly before running away. The other two had never been at Carlisle and none of them had ever played on Carlisle's teams.

Legendary retired Penn coach George Woodruff agreed to be the advisory coach of the Indians for 1905. Bemus was his lead assistant. Under Woodruff, the Indians lost only to Harvard and Penn, with the loss to Penn attributed to fumbles. Woodruff left the team after the victory over Army at West Point. Pierce, Hudson and Kenney coached the team for its remaining five games, all of which were played on the road. The two losses were to the Ohio powerhouse independent teams, Canton and Massillon. Frank Hudson suited up for the Massillon but his nose was broken on the fourth play of the game. In 1906

Carlisle returned to a pure graduate coaching system – except for a visit by "the Old Fox."

At long last, Bemus Pierce was the official head coach of his beloved Carlisle Indians. Legendary drop-kicker Frank Hudson assisted him. Because of the revolutionary rule changes instituted for the 1906 season, Pop Warner spent a week in September with the Carlisle coaches showing them the earliest incarnations of his single-wingback formation. According to Warner, the single-wing was first run in 1906 and by the Carlisle Indians. That would make Bemus Pierce the first coach to use the Warner system in a game.

The Indians lost two regular season games: to Penn State 4-0 and Harvard 5-0. They notched a 24-6 victory over Penn along with wins over Pitt, Syracuse, Cincinnati, Virginia and Minnesota, the Champions of the West. A game against that year's Champions of the South, Vanderbilt, was the first time an Eastern power played in the South. The Commodores won 4-0.

Carl Flanders of Yale, considered by some to be one of the greatest offensive centers who ever played, assisted the Indian coaches the latter part of the 1906 season. Being 6'3 ¼" tall and weighing 202 pounds, he was a big factor in the Eli rush line. He later recalled the Indians developing a method of communicating secretly in full earshot of their opponents. "Wallace Denny and Bemus Pierce got up a code of signals, using an Indian word which designated a single play. Among the Indian words which designated these signals were Water-bucket, Watehnee, Coocoohee. I never could find out what it all meant, and following the Indian team by this code of signals was a task which was too much for me."

The September 21 edition of *The Arrow* made a major announcement:

"The Carlisle Indian football management has decided to have its eleven directly coached by full-blooded redskins of intelligence. This was done largely because the Indian will work harder for an Indian coach than for the average college expert trainer. Coach Glenn S. Warner is undoubtedly the only white man who has ever been able to hold fast the attention of the redskinned footballist and teach him better things."

On December 8, *The Arrow* announced that Warner was back in and the Indian coaches were out. So much for the graduate system of coaching at Carlisle.

While there are no further records of Hawley Pierce's athletic activities, records of his other activities exist. In 1907, he became a fireman on the Buffalo division of the Buffalo, Rochester & Pittsburgh Railway. The 1908 census included his wife, the former Lorenza Armstrong, and one-year-old daughter, Delma. The 1910 and later federal censuses refer to his first child as Sadie. The 1910 census and a letter to Superintendent Friedman both show him as living at 14 Broad Street in Salamanca, New York, where a railroad station was located on the Allegheny Reservation. He also had a house in Irving, presumably on the Cattaraugus Reservation, but did not live there because it was not situated conveniently for his work. Hawley was promoted to engineer on this coal-hauling railroad in 1913. At that time he was living at 79 Elm Street in Salamanca. The 1924 census listed the Pierces as living on the Allegheny reservation near the town of Great Valley. Their family had expanded to include sons Bernard and Paul and daughter Agnes.

Bemus stayed active in athletics, taking the head coaching job at Kenyon College in Gambier, Ohio in 1908. That year his Purple and White team went 7-1-1 and were crowned Ohio champions. The only defeat was by a respectable 19-9 margin to Ohio State. Pierce wanted to win this game so badly that he brought in Carlisle alums Caleb Sickles and Frank Mt. Pleasant to help him prepare the team for the Buckeyes. Things went progressively downhill after that to 6-4 and, finally, 1-6-1. In July 1911, he wrote Moses Friedman that he was engaged to coach at Lafayette High School in Buffalo, New York in the upcoming school year. A later letter indicated that the Kenyon College job ended due to "lack of funds." His 1911 letter included his thoughts on a different matter.

Apparently a rumor was circulating that Indians from New York State were no longer to be allowed to attend government schools, something that concerned Bemus greatly.

"...If a law should pass to that effect, the New York Indians would be one of the most backward tribes among the Indians ten years hence.

"Carlisle and Hampton have given the New York Indian his education and trade by which he can stand side by side with his white neighbors.

"I live on the Indian Reservation and from what I know, and see of the young Indians that have never been to Carlisle, or other Government schools, do not know of any trade by which he can support himself or family. The day schools do not teach him any trade and only an elementary academic instructions are given.

"Very few learn all that is being taught in day schools. The parents do not compel nor encourage their children to attend school regularly, and just as soon as the children attain the ages of fifteen and sixteen years the school is not thought of any more. What is the result? A youth with no trade – love to loaf around the saloons or street corners - The girls with practically no instruction on housekeeping. Of course there are a few ambitious youths who have advanced their day school education to higher institutions. Only a very few can furnish the means by which they can give their children such training as Carlisle or Hampton can give.

"Not only in trade and education would the New York Indian be deprived, should the Government institutions shut its doors against them, but in Christianity as well as a great many of the New York Indians are unchristian.

"If you wish, I can give you several names of returned Carlisle students that are holding successful positions in different parts of the United States at present. Had it not been for Carlisle, I would not have been known throughout the athletic world as I am to-day and these are some of the chances the Carlisle gives to her pupils."

Bemus wrote to Oscar Lipps in November 1914, immediately after Warner announced his resignation from Carlisle, to apply for the position that was open again. He again argued for an Indian coach. "I feel confident that I can do as good work as Warner for I have done it. I feel that Carlisle owe me the favor for I help her make her fame in the foot ball world." Charles Daganett, President of the Carlisle alumni association, wrote Lipps in support, "I think I am voicing the sentiment of the very large majority, if not all of the Carlisle alumni, when I say that they prefer to have the Carlisle team handled by Carlisle graduates." General Pratt wrote in support, "He has been coaching widely since leaving Carlisle and stands among the foremost of those who [were] at the school and since exerted wide influence for his race and Carlisle for clean manly living." But Pierce didn't get the job as Victor Kelley of Texas A & M fame was selected. According to Gus Welch, Texas politics determined the outcome of the decision.

The 1920 census listed Bemus, Anna, and their children, Lillian W., Heston B. and Dorothy W., as living in Brant Township of Erie County, New York. His son may have been named after Michigan great, Willie Heston. In 1922, Bemus donned his moleskins for another season – as a 47-year-old player. He was recruited to play alongside several younger Carlisle alums for an NFL team, the Oorang Indians. Although he was included in the 1922 team photograph, there is no record of him actually playing in a game that year. In 1923 he apparently joined the team late in the season and played one game, most likely to fill in for someone who was injured.

Bemus may have coached again at Sherman Institute. The 1930 census lists the Pierces as living on the Indian School in Riverside County, California. Heston and Dorothy were still listed as living at home but may have been away at college at that time. Bemus's occupation was listed as gardener, a job for which growing up on a farm would have prepared him. He died on February 15, 1957 in San Bernardino, California, at about 84 years old.

Hawley Pierce remained in New York working as an engineer on the railroad while staying connected to the community. A 1929 newspaper article declared that he was the only fully qualified and working full-blooded Indian railroad engineer. It also said that railroad officials considered him "to be an excellent engineer" who "pulls a through Buffalo, Rochester & Pittsburgh freight train from Salamanca to Rochester, N. Y." They had moved by this time to Killbuck, a suburb of Salamanca, where Lorenza served as president of the PTA. Their names were occasionally in the newspaper coverage of social events and funerals.

Every so often Hawley's Carlisle connection would come up in the news, such as the time in 1932 when Pop Warner invited him to see his current team, Stanford, play Pitt. Hawley, Lorenza, Jean and Bernard took the special train from Rochester to Pittsburgh to see the game and attend the banquet at which Warner was speaking. The following October Warner mentioned Hawley Pierce in a talk he gave to the Shriners in Philadelphia: "We fooled the Crimson in the Harvard stadium, and also tried it against Princeton in New York several years later but the player who was supposed to put the ball under Hawley Pierce's jersey couldn't catch up with him." In November of 1941, Jim Thorpe spoke at Killbuck High School to raise funds for the athletic program. Hawley and Thorpe reminisced for an hour before Thorpe had to leave for another speaking engagement in Cortland, New York. It is likely that Hawley attended the Carlisle reunion at the state fair in Syracuse the preceding summer because of its proximity.

The Pierces encouraged their children's education. In 1937 Sadie Jean won a scholarship for a "full Chautauqua course in vocal music" by the International Order of the King's Daughters and Sons. In March of the following year, they attended the capping ceremony at Buffalo General Hospital for daughter Vernice, who became a nurse. Son Paul followed in his father's footsteps and became a fireman on a railroad locomotive.

Hawley's influence spread beyond his immediate family as reported in the October 1952 edition of B&O Magazine. Hawley blazed the trail for Indian engineers so well that by 1952 eight Senecas were operating locomotives for the B&O. Others may have been working for the Erie Railroad, but the eight working for the B&O were the only ones thought to be operating the "modern" diesels at that time. The dean of the Seneca engineers was Hawley's cousin, Watson Pierce, as Hawley is believed to have retired in 1944 when he was 70 years young. The company was proud of the fact that none of their Seneca engineers had a black mark on his record.

Hawley Pierce died on December 6, 1969. According to his obituary, he was born on March 17, 1873 which would have made him 96 years old, an extremely long life for a man of any generation.

James E. Johnson

10

James Johnson demonstrating his unique punt-catching technique; *Chicago History Museum*

James Johnson's graduation photo; *Benjey collection*

Name: James Edward Johnson	**Nickname:** Whirlwind
DOB: 6/6/1879	**Height:** 5' 7"
Weight: 138	**Age:** 24
Tribe: Stockbridge	**Home:** Gresham, WI

Parents: James A. and Adis Johnson

Early Schooling: Reservation, possibly

Later Schooling: Dickinson College Preparatory School; Dickinson College; Northwestern University

Honors: College Football Hall of Fame, 1969

Whirlwind

Carlisle Indian School documents list James E. Johnson as a member of the class of 1901, which implies that he arrived in 1896 or before. Determining specifics about his enrollment is difficult because his file is void of these records. The 1900 census taken at Carlisle placed Jimmie's year of birth at 1878 and indicated he was full-blood Stockbridge with full-blood Stockbridge parents, all born in Wisconsin. From reading tribal rolls and federal censuses, it is reasonable to conclude that James Johnson's parents were James A. Johnson, mixed-blood originally from Tennessee, and Adis Tousey-Johnson, full-blood Stockbridge-Munsee. His father was a barber and his mother kept house and took care of the children. Difficulties in finding James A. Johnson on tribal rolls initially gave the impression that he may have died by the time James E. came to Carlisle. However, he shows up on the 1900 Federal Census. A September 5, 1902 article in *The Red Man and Helper* mentions James's brother, Adam, as helping his father at that time. This further supports that the Johnson children had a living father at that time. Later, James was listed as being from Gresham, Wisconsin, the town closest to the Stockbridge-Munsee Reservation. However, later records indicate that he was born in Edgerton, Wisconsin on June 6, 1879.

Records of Johnson's physical size at the time of his arrival do not exist, but later photographs and newspaper articles depicted him as being average height or shorter and thin. Mere words could not do justice to Johnson's hair as can be seen in his photo on the College Football Hall of Fame website.

Home for James was in central Wisconsin. The Stockbridge-Munsee Reservation, the relocation home for Jimmie's tribe, is located northwest of the Oneida Reservation immediately adjacent to the Menominee Reservation. The Dawes Act of 1887 and the Burke Act of 1906 caused much of the reservation to be sold off to white people during James Johnson's youth, and by 1910 the Stockbridge were no longer recognized as a tribe by the government. It is highly likely that James did not live on the reservation even if his father farmed his allotment. Thus, James had no on-reservation childhood, and attending Carlisle probably required less adjustment on his part than it would have required from many of his classmates.

James Johnson joined the Invincible Debating Society and, in December 1898, was elected reporter. In March 1899, James and Caleb Sickles teamed up to argue the negative in a debate about whether building the Panama Canal would be beneficial to the United States. They lost but put up a good fight as retold by *The Indian Helper*: "There were more members of the society present than usual, and a spirited debate occurred relative to points of order in which President Martin Wheelock maintained the dignity befitting his office, and rendered wise decisions." The next month Johnson was elected assistant critic. He would remain active in the Invincibles throughout his time at Carlisle.

October of 1899 found Pop Warner coaching the Carlisle Indian School football team for the first time. Jimmie Johnson received mention from *The Dickinsonian* as one of the new men "… who have the look of comers." Johnson had started his varsity career at Carlisle. At the end of the school year, Johnson enrolled in the Dickinson College Preparatory School but continued playing football for Carlisle. The College's yearbook described him as, "A renowned warrior of the Indian school. Flourishes black eyes, bandaged wrists and torn ears during the foot-ball season. Wants to be an angel."

The October 5, 1900 edition of *The Red Man and Indian Helper* opined on the upcoming football season, "Johnson, who was substitute for Miller, played in several of the games last season, and who is doing good work this year. He will probably fill the right half-back position …" James shone for Carlisle while attending Prep. He improved in 1901 and got more attention for his play, now at quarterback. Leading up to the Penn game, Pop Warner said, "… Johnson's playing at quarterback has been a feature of the team's play all the season." After the game the *Philadelphia Record* raved, "The star performer for the Carlisle team was Johnson. The speedy little quarterback ran his team with admirable judgment, played a strong game in the backfield on defense and on the trick quarterback run made more ground than any member of the team, with the possible exception of Wheelock." After the season, Walter Camp placed Martin Wheelock on his All-America Second Team and named James as his third team quarterback.

In the spring, Johnson played baseball, also for Carlisle, generally at second base. With his speed, he was a constant base-stealing threat. Surprisingly, he batted third or fourth in the order, places usually reserved for power hitters. So, Jimmie was not just a singles hitter; he must have had the ability to drive in runs.

Over the winter of 1902, James Johnston was made captain of the small boys' companies at Carlisle. It appears that he earned money for his education by working at the Indian school. His pay may have included room and board.

That spring in track season he gained renown as Carlisle's star hurdler. However, he and James Phillips were not allowed to participate in the meet against Dickinson College because Johnson was finishing his senior year at Dickinson's prep school and Phillips was a student at the law school. Eligibility rules were evidently evolving. Johnson's school record in the high hurdles was broken by Johnson Bradley in that meet as James watched while officiating.

Jimmie returned home for the summer and wrote back when he found work in Evanston, Illinois, a locale in which he would spend much time in the future. He returned to Carlisle in September as a freshman at Dickinson College proper, ready to star in football – at Carlisle. The Invincibles made him an advisory member of their society, likely because he was no longer studying at the Indian school and, thus, couldn't be a regular member.

James had no problem deciding for whom he would play in the annual Dickinson-Carlisle game because none was played. The teams were unable to agree on the lengths of halves to be played, a negotiable item in those days, and the game was canceled. *The Dickinsonian* placed the blame on Warner, who may not have wanted to play the game for reasons known only to himself. Carlisle had a pretty good team that year, going 8-3. Johnson starred but was overlooked by Walter Camp for All-America recognition. That oversight was rectified a little bit when President Roosevelt invited the team to visit him in the White House after the Georgetown game. A *New York Sun* article, possibly written by the Carlisle publicity office, gave the following account of James meeting the President:

> "'De-lighted,' exclaimed the President, grasping the hand of Johnson, 'you play quarter back. The mass play of your team was splendid. I am delighted.'
> "So was Johnson but he did not show it until he got outside.
> "'Mr. Johnson,' asked the President, 'how was it that Yale defeated my college, Harvard, while she played such a good game against you?'
> "The little quarterback replied, 'We did not play a very good game.'
> "'I do not know why Harvard took such a slump,' asked the President."

Walter Camp may have snubbed Johnson that year, but Nathan F. Stauffer, columnist for the Philadelphia *Inquirer*, didn't. Stauffer named Johnson quarterback of both his All-American and All-University teams, the distinction between the two being unclear to the modern reader. When naming Johnson, he wrote, "Johnson gave the Indians more life and ginger than any quarter they have ever had. He is a fine general in choosing successful tricks and clever executing such plays. However, he lacks ability in the kicking line." His teammates honored him by voting him captain of the 1903 team.

Although enrolled at Dickinson College, James did not abandon the non-sports aspects of Indian School life. In February, he gave an original oration titled "The Indian as an Individual" to a meeting of the Invincible Debating Society. The Man-on-the-band-stand was impressed by his "deep earnestness."

In March an indoor track meet was held for boys wanting to be on the team that spring. Jimmie won both high and low hurdle events. That spring he won a gold watch at the Pennsylvania Relay Carnival held at Franklin Field. He ran the third leg on what had to be Carlisle's fastest team ever. Wallace Denny led off, followed by Wilson Charles, then Johnson and anchored by Frank Mt. Pleasant. In June he was off for the Midwest, likely to Evanston to earn some money, over the summer.

1903 was an historic year for Carlisle football in many ways. James Johnson played a role in a play that continues to be talked about today. For the Harvard game, Pop Warner dusted off a trick play he had used at Cornell in 1897 against Penn State. Prior to the game, Warner had local haberdasher and Carlisle school tailor, Mose Blumenthal, install elastic cord in the hem of a player's jersey. The elastic cord would cause a football placed under the jersey, either front or back, to remain in place without being held there by the player. Warner saved the hidden ball or hunchback trick for the second half kickoff in the big game with Harvard. After kicking his first attempt out of bounds, the Harvard kicker arced the ball high and deep down the middle of the field to the waiting Jimmie Johnson. As he fielded the kick at the goal line, his teammates huddled around him facing outward. He slipped the ball under the back of Charles Dillon's jersey and shouted, "Go!" The team scattered and headed toward both sidelines, some for one and the rest for the other, each faking that he had the ball. The actual ball carrier, Big Dillon, ran straight for the Harvard goal line, arms swinging as if he were going to throw a block. Harvard's safety, Carl Marshall, not wanting to get blocked out of the play, sidestepped Dillon. While Dillon, a guard, was steadily making his way to the goal, several of his teammates raced to the end zone because someone had to remove the ball from Dillon's shirt in order for it to be touched down. Accounts vary as to who removed the ball. It may have been Al Exendine or it may have been Johnson or it may have been someone else. Regardless, the Boston crowd, always supportive of the Indians, loved the play, but the Harvard team was incensed at having been made to look like fools. The Crimson played with desperation and came back to win 12-11.

Walter Camp named the 5'7", 138-pound quarterback to his 1903 All-America First Team. The football team, Carlisle's best to that point, closed its regular season against Northwestern University in Chicago. Jimmie Johnson starred in that Thanksgiving Day game played in a snowstorm that was blinding at times in South Side Park, then home of the Chicago White Sox baseball team. The Indians defeated Northwestern, that year's Co-Champions of the West, 28-0 with Johnson responsible for 23 of those points. The *Inter-Ocean* praised his play: "Little Johnson was easily the most brilliant player on the field. He ran his team in a masterful way, carried the ball for good gains, and finally climaxed his performance by shooting the ball between the posts for a place kick." Northwestern was weakened a bit when guard James Phillips refused to play against his former teammates from Carlisle. *The Red Man and Helper* reported, "Watching the contest from the stands, Phillips said that had the field been free from snow Carlisle's speedy back would have doubled the score."

The Indians then made the longest trip to play a football game since the Indians' 1899 trip to San Francisco four years earlier. First stop on the trip was in Salt Lake City for a game against the University of Utah. Warner benched Johnson for an infraction of an unspecified team rule. The Indians still won handily, 22-0. An hour before the Reliance

Athletic Association game on Christmas Day in San Francisco, Johnson was still fuming over having been benched for the Utah game. While Warner was giving Johnson and his backup, Joe Baker, instructions, Johnson shouted, "Listen Pop. I don't care if I never play in one of your ball games!" Warner immediately informed Baker that he would be taking Johnson's place that day. Other players overheard the outburst and asked Pop to give Johnson a second chance. Warner cranked up the heat by saying, "Baker really did a fine job for us against Utah. And besides, I couldn't play a player whose heart would not be in the game." Johnson then spoke up, "Well, Coach. If the other boys want me to play, I will."

The Indians then handled the highly touted Reliance A. A. 23-0. San Francisco *Examiner* expert, C. M. Fickert, opined, "The team worked as one man, or rather Captain Johnson worked them as one man. He is the greatest quarterback that has ever played here. He exhibited great generalship in handling his team and in sizing up his opponents' play. He is very active, very aggressive, always on the ball, and he is continually urging on his men. With him off the team the score would have been different. And the crowd guessed right when they yelled that there was 'too much Johnson.'" On New Year's Day 1904, they defeated Bemus Pierce's Sherman Institute team 12-0 in Riverside, California near Los Angeles.

The June 3 issue of *The Red Man and Helper* announced that, after a visit with his family in Chicago and Wisconsin, Jimmie was to matriculate at Harvard University in the fall. Instead, he enrolled in Northwestern University's dental school and played on the university's football team. The Northwestern University football team experienced two of its better seasons when James was on the team, going 16-4-1. Two of the losses were games he missed due to injury. Even though 26 years old and banged up with injuries, Jimmie continued to score at will, leading Northwestern to wins over Marquette, Ohio Northern and Michigan Agricultural College (today's Michigan State). Because Northwestern had little depth, injuries were more costly and, very likely, more prevalent than for many of their opponents. Players had to play hurt more often and rest less often than they would with other teams who had deeper benches. Ten minutes into the game against the powerhouse Minnesota, James suffered a career-ending injury.

Johnson owns a bit of NU folklore in that he is the only person to have played against Northwestern in one game (NU's last game of 1903 against Carlisle) and to play for Northwestern in its next game (the 1904 opener against Fort Sheridan). He wrote a footnote to history in the last game of the season, scoring the last touchdown to be made on Sheppard Field, the game-winning touchdown over Illinois. He was elected co-captain with Harry Allen for 1905 but, over time, his name has been dropped from the captains' list. Perhaps his being late returning to school for pre-season football practice due to being on his honeymoon had something to do with it.

James married Florence C. Welch, an Oneida, also of Wisconsin, after she graduated from Carlisle as a member of the class of 1905. Florence may have put her Carlisle training to use by working in the Northwestern Dental School secretary's office, as she wrote to Major Mercer on the stationery from that office.

In response to all the deaths and serious injuries experienced in college football around the country, Northwestern terminated football as a varsity sport the following spring, making the 1905 season Johnson's last as a player. He continued his dental course, graduating in 1907. But he was not quite finished with football.

James assisted Pop Warner in coaching the Carlisle football teams in 1907 and 1908.

Warner may have selected him over others who had been involved during his three-year absence to put his mark on the team. Because Johnson and Warner were away from Carlisle at the same time, Pop may have been more comfortable working with him than with those who led the team in his absence. James also established a private practice at 5301 State Street in Chicago, but it may not have developed as quickly as he would have liked because he explored other opportunities.

In October, *The Carlisle Arrow* reported, "Antonio Rodriguez, Class '05, received a letter from James Johnson in which he said he will make a visit to Porto Rico [sic] in the first part of next December. I, like the other boys here at San Juan, P. R., who are Manuel Ruiz, Julio Hoheb, Antonio Rodriguez and the undersigned, were glad to hear that Carlisle's star quarter-back of the 1903 football team and all-American quarter-back for the same year, will soon land on our shores. We will do all we can to make his stay here as pleasant a time as he ever had."

The December 11 *Arrow* provided more detail: "Assistant Coach Johnson, together with Mrs. Johnson, left here last week for a two months' visit in Porto Rico. After their return from there they will go back to Chicago, where Dr. Johnson will continue his practice of dentistry." In May 1909, Enrique Urrutia, one of Carlisle's Puerto Rican students wrote that Johnson had opened a dental office on the island. That fall, the Johnsons wrote that he was "following his profession with profit to himself and relief to the natives." Florence had taken a job as a clerk with the Department of Education.

James Johnson responded to the requests for information from former athletes by Major Mercer in 1907 and Moses Friedman in 1909. Johnson provided the information that was requested but elaborated little. In September 1910, an issue of *The Carlisle Arrow* carried two articles about the James Johnsons. They had spent ten weeks vacationing in the United States. Dr. Johnson's business amounted to $4000 the past year and Mrs. Johnson earned $1200 a year as a stenographer and typist for the Bureau of Education. Mr. and Mrs. Siceni Nori hosted a surprise party for the Johnsons the evening before they left for their return trip to Puerto Rico, where they expected to remain for three years more. The income figures were included because they were so large. Florence Johnson was earning more than the average working man at that time. When the two incomes were added together, they were likely among the elite of their community, as were many of his patients.

In 1912, James Johnson wrote about his automobile tour of the U. S. The bulk of his writing dealt with the former Carlisle students he visited along the way and how well they were doing and how they had assimilated into white society. The May-June 1915 edition of *The Red Man* contained a photograph of the Johnsons' richly-appointed parlor and dining room in their home in Puerto Rico. The *Fund du Lac Commonwealth* reported on Johnson's purchase of the 70-acre Buskirk farm on Lake de Neveu Road just a half mile outside the city limits, referring to him as "a prominent dentist of San Juan, Porto Rico." He had vacationed in Wisconsin the previous summer and, while visiting with relatives in Wittenberg drove to Fond du Lac. Johnson planned on remaining in Puerto Rico for two more years, after which he planned on making the farm his home.

In 1916, James wrote the superintendent asking for a statement of credit for the biology and physics courses he had taken in 1900 and 1901. He was applying for admission for a medical course to prepare him to specialize, possibly in oral surgery. The principal, Mr. Blair, was directed to prepare the requested statement. Those plans may have been interrupted by America's entrance into the Great War in 1917.

A later census lists James Johnson as a veteran of the World War. Given his age, about 39 at America's entrance into the war, it seems likely that he did not see combat but was assigned to a hospital or clinic, possibly stateside. If he didn't enlist, he was likely drafted because of the Army's need for dentists during the war. When the war was over, he returned to civilian dentistry.

The 1930 census listed James Johnson, 51, as living at 559 East 63rd Street in Chicago with wife Teresa, 30, and daughter Jacqueline, 4 years 6 months. He was practicing general dentistry. Whether Florence died or they divorced is unclear, but census records make divorce appear more likely. This stint in Chicago must have been short-lived because, according to his obituary, he lived in Puerto Rico for 30 years, returning to the states when he became ill in the fall of 1941. James Johnson died on January 18, 1942 at about 63, at Kahler Hospital, part of the Mayo Clinic, in Rochester, Minnesota of stomach cancer. His sister, Ida, wrote their brother and sister in Wisconsin from Chicago that he had died and that his wife wanted him buried alongside his sister (presumably) Mary.

James Johnson's obituary in the The Chicago Defender, a weekly newspaper that served the African-American community, sheds some light on his background. Johnson's funeral was conducted in Metropolitan Funeral Home, a black-owned business, and he was buried in Lincoln Cemetery, a traditionally black burial ground. A further indication that The Defender considered Johnson to have been African-American was the sentence, "At Northwestern, he was referred to in the daily papers as an 'Indian.'" "Daily papers" may have been code for white-owned newspapers. In contrast, The Chicago Daily Tribune referred to him as a Stockbridge Indian and made no mention of his burial arrangements in its initial obituary on January 19, 1942. On January 25 it mentioned the address, but not the name, of the funeral parlor but did say that he was buried in Lincoln Cemetery.

If many white Chicagoans considered James Johnson to be black may explain why his dental practice there did not flourish as he hoped and would explain why he practiced for many years in Puerto Rico.

11

Caleb M. Sickles

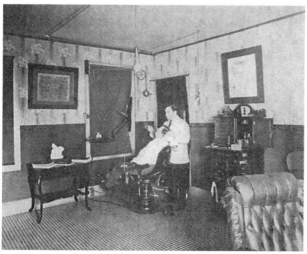

Dr. Sickles at work; *Benjey collection*

Caleb Sickles; *U. S. Army Military History Institute*

Name: Caleb Mathew Sickles		**Nickname:**	
DOB: 12/27/1880		**Height:** 4' 6"	
Weight: Unknown		**Age:** 12	
Tribe: Oneida		**Home:** Sagola Agency, WI	
Parents: Martin Sickles, Oneida; Semantha Sickles, white			
Early Schooling:			
Later Schooling: Dickinson College Preparatory School; Ohio Medical University			
Honors:			

Dentist

Caleb Mathew Sickles, a 12-year-old Oneida, arrived in Carlisle in August 1891 and enrolled for the standard-at-that-time five-year term. He was 4'6" tall then, but his weight was not recorded. At the end of the summer after graduation in 1898, he re-enrolled for an indeterminate period, listed then as age 21. The enrollment forms that were found included good information, including that his father's name was Martin, that he was half blood, and that he was from the Sagola Agency in Wisconsin; however, much information was missing or unclear. His mother was listed as living, but her name was left blank. Perusing census records and Carlisle Indian School publications leads one to conclude that Caleb, sometimes misprinted as Carl, was the son of Martin Sickles, a full-blood Oneida, and Smantha or Thimantha but likely Semantha (her name was spelled differently on each census), a white woman. Caleb was born in Munsey, Ontario as his father was from the English-speaking part of Canada. Semantha was born in Michigan, and their other children were born in Wisconsin. The 1910 census listed Semantha as the mother of 13 children, 12 living, one of whom was Raymond O., who was living with Caleb at that time.

Several other Sickles attended Carlisle but don't appear to have been Caleb's siblings. One newspaper article specifically mentioned that Martha, Florence and Arthur were siblings but omitted any mention of Caleb, something that would have been unlikely, given his notoriety, had he been their sibling. However, the August 26, 1898 issue of *The Indian Helper* casually mentioned Arthur as being Caleb's brother. Superintendent Friedman asked Caleb about Arthur's whereabouts in 1910. From his response, it is difficult to determine if they were brothers, cousins or no relation at all. The vagueness of his response may have been due to familiarity of the issue for both parties.

Home for the Sickles was in central Wisconsin. The Oneida Reservation extends from Green Bay to Outagamie County, the next county over. While some Oneidas lived within the Green Bay city limits, Martin Sickles was listed on the various censuses as being a farmer in Outagamie County. In 1898, Dickinson College listed Caleb's home as Little Rapids, Wisconsin. Later Caleb wrote, "I have never lived among the Indians to any extent." He may have meant that he had been at boarding schools since an early age as were many of his peers or that his family, although listed as Oneida, lived 5 miles from the reservation at Little Rapids. Thus, Caleb did not have an on-reservation childhood, and attending Carlisle probably required less adjustment on his part than it would have required from many of his classmates.

Caleb received his first newspaper coverage in the November 15, 1895 edition of *The Indian Helper* in an article that stated, "Misses Ely and Burgess, and Masters Johnnie Given, Caleb Stickles, George Conners and Ernest Peters went by wheel to Mechanicsburg late Saturday afternoon, returning in the deep shadow of the evening." Apparently he had taken up cycling, which was all the rage at that time. It's not clear whether the Misses, Carlisle faculty members, chaperoned the boys or whether the boys went along as protectors. On modern roads, assuming a time when there is little traffic, and on modern bicycles, that 10-mile ride would be a breeze. However, in pre-automobile times, Trindle Road, the most direct route between Carlisle and Mechanicsburg, would have been a rural dirt road with many hazards.

Caleb started to work in the print shop after the holidays, according to *The Indian Helper*. He continued there for some years and became a valuable worker. By April of that year, 1896, Caleb had joined the Invincible Debating Society. He was given high marks for what was likely his first major public speaking appearance, "Caleb Sickles made a happy hit in a recitation very naturally rendered …." A week later he, James Wheelock and Albert Nash participated in the entertainment given by the YMCA in town. Unfortunately, the nature of his participation was not mentioned.

By this time he was allowed to leave the school for the summer, but it is not known whether it was to work somewhere or to return home. Most likely it was to work somewhere because in later summers he earned money working at the New Jersey shore. After returning to school and the print shop, Caleb, now a Junior, was elected secretary of the Invincibles.

John S. Steckbeck, in *Fabulous Redmen*, lists Sickles as playing on the varsity football team in 1897 and 1898. Game reports make no mention of him and don't include his name in the lineups. He was most likely a substitute, no mean feat on teams that included the likes of Ed Rogers, Frank Cayou, the Pierce brothers, Frank Hudson, Metoxen (met the oxen) and Martin Wheelock in the starting lineup. This was the start, not the end, of his football career.

Caleb graduated from Carlisle in the spring of 1898 and enrolled in the Dickinson College Preparatory School at age 21. Dickinson College's first game of the season was on September 24 against Susquehanna University. Caleb's name was not in the line-up, but a Mr. Sickles of the Indian School umpired the game. In mid-October he got into a game. He played quarterback for the Dickinson College Prep School team in a game against Harrisburg High School and got press clippings for doing "the best work." The next game, a scoreless tie with nearby Shippensburg Normal School, found him at left end, the position he would play the rest of the year. He carried the ball a lot in Prep's offensive scheme and consistently made good yardage. He was a star at the prep school.

After football season ended, Caleb went out for Prep's basketball team and was a starter at one of the attack (known as forward today) positions. In the spring of 1899 he ran track in a meet with Mercersburg Academy and Franklin and Marshall College, coming in second in the 120 yard special event and third in the special open 120 yard dash. His best event that day was the relay race, the first and arguably most exciting event. *The Dickinsonian* gushed, "… But when the crowd saw young Sickles of Dickinson take his place at the line and wait on tiptoes to touch the hand of his panting colleague, and then dash off on the last lap with an astonishingly increasing speed, the chances for our Preps, because suddenly bright, but the distance was too great to be made up, and Mercersburg came in first, although their lead was quite perceptively decreased by Sickles who was heartily cheered."

In May, he played left field and pitched for the Indian School baseball team in a game against Dickinson College and lost 3-2. His relief pitching may have made the difference that day as he walked three batters and committed a balk. However, the reporter thought he had the potential to become a good left-handed pitcher.

In July *The Indian Helper* shared that Caleb had written them a "friendly letter." The article reported, "At the Beacon by the Sea [in Point Pleasant], New Jersey, a number of our boys are spending their summer waiting on table, and doing other work demanded of them. The other day they played a game of ball with the Trenton Military Academy and won by the score of 21 to 3. Siceni Nori, '94 who is living near Trenton, pitched for the Academy team."

October of 1899 found Pop Warner coaching the Carlisle Indian School football team for the first time. Caleb was still at the Dickinson College Preparatory School but played right end for Carlisle as a substitute for Joseph Scholder. His moment in the limelight came when he played the entire game at right end in Carlisle's win over Penn, their first against one of the Big Four.

Sickles completed his education at Prep in the spring and left for summer employment, first in Philadelphia, then on the Jersey Shore. In July 1900, *The Indian Helper* reprinted an article from a Point Pleasant, New Jersey newspaper, *The Beacon*, about the Independence Day races held as part of their festivities: "The running of Sickles, the Carlisle student, was the chief feature of the foot races. At the tape he won by a few inches. Sickles is such a clean, good fellow that he deserves all he won, and the crowd was with him, and the red man's praise became the 'white man's burden' at the end of each race."

A month later, *The Red Man and Helper* reported, "Caleb Sickles, '99, spent Sunday with us on his way to Columbus, Ohio, where he intends to work his way through

Medical College. Caleb has been spending a part of the summer working at the sea-shore. He looks in splendid condition, and has kept himself under athletic training. He intends that his athletics shall play no small part in getting him his M. D. diploma. The name of Dr. Sickles already runs through the ears of the Man-on-the-band-stand, and we desire him to realize his highest hopes." Pratt was not the only one pleased to see one of his students strive for professional education. Whether Caleb changed his mind or the newspaper got it wrong is unclear, an M. D. diploma was not in his future. Other opportunities awaited him instead.

At the end of the 1901 season, the *Ohio State Journal* had a large write-up titled, "Good for the Indian Captain," that celebrated Caleb's election as captain of the Ohio Medical University football team for 1902. He was described as being 21 years of age, likely wrong, and a junior in the Dental Department. Either he changed majors or Pratt had had it wrong earlier. When writing about Sickles' play, the *Journal* reporter wrote, "In his time he has gained the reputation of being one of the best, if not the very best end in Ohio. He is a hard and sure tackler, as well as very fast in the interference and a sure man when called upon to advance the ball." Dr. W. J. Means of the Athletic Board was quoted as saying, "The choice of Sickles for Captain is very satisfactory to me. We always like men who are well up in their classes as our athletic leaders, and Sickles, in addition to his football ability, is one of the best students in the university."

In April 1903, *The Red Man and Helper* reported, "Mr. Caleb Sickles '98, a student of the Ohio Medical College, Columbus, Ohio, is with us for a brief visit. He is taking a course in dentistry and hopes to finish in another year. This spring and summer he will earn some wherewithal on the New York State Baseball League, and is now on his way to Syracuse. Caleb had pneumonia a year ago and does not look as robust as before he was taken ill, but says he is feeling well now. He intends starting out in business for himself as soon as he finishes. Sickles, Sickles, Sickles! Rah! Rah! Rah!" Superintendent Pratt could hardly constrain his enthusiasm. In its next issue, *The Red Man and Helper* wrote, "Dr. Caleb Sickles has gone to Syracuse, where, as was stated last week, he will play ball on the N. Y. League, this season. He says dental Seniors in the Columbus University are called Doctors, and we wish to be one of the first to give him the well-earned title." A May 8 article shared some bad news: "… finding that his injured arm did not permit him to play ball as actively as the League requires. … He will get employment in Columbus for the summer and finish his Dental course next year." A week later he was negotiating with the Portsmouth, Ohio team. In June he was playing left field for the Lancaster, Ohio club.

Caleb Sickles ably captained the 1903 Ohio Medical University football team and, in October, was called on to help his former O. M. U. coach, John Eckstorm, prepare Kenyon College team for their big game with Ohio State. At the end of the school year, Sickles graduated from dental school. In late May or very early June 1904, Caleb wrote Miss Burgess, his supervisor when he worked in the Carlisle print shop:

"It has been some time since you have heard from me. I am through school now and am in the employ of the State. I have a position here at the State hospital.

"I have been here over three weeks. The day I graduated I was about "broke" but since, I have been getting a few dollars together, and am on my feet again, as it were.

"I am drawing pay here as an attendant on a good Ward, and doing the dental work-for the employees and some of the patients; combining the two I make quite a little sum.

"I have also had the good fortune to be selected to coach for Heidelberg University at Tiffin, Ohio. They have quite a school there. While the position does not pay so very much compared with salaries that some coaches get, yet it will be a great help to me this fall. I will get $275 and all expenses for my services for nine weeks. I can never make $275 any easier. They want me to be Athletic Director the year round at a salary of $700. The town is a good one and I have a chance to locate there permanently. I think it would be a good thing for me to accept, but I want to locate in the West and grow up with the town.

"One thing I am glad of, that is I have lost interest in playing baseball and football. I play here every Saturday for the Hospital, that's how I came to get my position. I have a good many privileges with it. Business has been rather brisk with me for the past few days. The other day I made $7.50, and yesterday I made four. Friday I'll make four more, besides my pay as an attendant goes on every day and I am getting all my expenses too. By the time fall comes around I'll have a little money."

His change of heart regarding playing the games must have been very recent as just a month earlier *The Newark Daily Advocate* published an article about his baseball playing:

"Caleb Sickles, the full-blooded Indian who played several time in Newark last season, is now covering center field for Manager James' Unions. The fleet-footed red man gave an exhibition of the speed that has made him famous on two occasions Sunday. In the sixth he dumped a slow one down the third base foul line which Snyder quickly gathered in and made a perfect throw to Francis, but Sickles had already crossed the bag. Again in the eighth, Sickles nearly beat out an infield hit, many believing he got to first ahead of Durch's beautiful throw, but Richards called him out."

Apparently, after acquiring gainful employment and a coaching job, he lost interest in getting bumps and bruises as a player. Or, knowing the disdain schools had for their coaches playing professionally, he may have spoken preemptorily.

The October 13, 1904 issue of *The Arrow* shared that Joel Cornelius was then in Tiffin, Ohio with Caleb Sickles. He was taking a business course at Heidelberg University and, of course, playing football. Like many others from Carlisle, Caleb gave his former schoolmates opportunities when he had the chance.

That October he got rave reviews for his work on the Heidelberg University sidelines from *The Advocate*: "Caleb Sickles, the Indian who is remembered by every Newark baseball fan, as a star center fielder, is coaching the Heidelberg team and has developed the best team the Tiffin institution has ever had." He later received accolades for keeping the Dennison game close when his players were outweighed by almost 40 pounds per man, and some of his best players were unable to play due to injuries sustained in the Ohio Medical College game.

Although he thought about heading west, Caleb set about rooting himself further in Seneca County, Ohio, for which Tiffin was the seat. A controversy rose in 1905 when he was elected delegate to the county convention, probably as a Republican. The issue was whether a non-citizen Indian who could not vote could hold an elected office. Indians as a group were not granted citizenship and the right to vote until 1924. Individual Indians had become citizens decades before that when they received allotments in many cases.

Caleb's dental practice flourished, due in part, surely, to his fame as an athlete and coach. In the fall of 1905 he coached the Heidelberg team again and in November supported his alma mater when the Indians played the Massillon Tigers. In December, Caleb plunged into matrimony by marrying Mabel Teachnor, a white girl from Manchester he met in Columbus. She was about the same age as Caleb and had been a seamstress. *The Newark Daily Advocate* reported, "'Sick' managed to keep the news of his wedding well concealed and escaped from Columbus before many of his numerous friends became aware of the fact that he had passed from the ranks of bachelordom. Dr. Sickles met his wife when attending O. M. U. She was connected then, it is said, with the Protestant Hospital." Caleb established himself quite well in the dominant society of the community and freely shared his experiences with Carlisle students.

The good people of Tiffin were also glad to have Caleb in their midst. The Heidelberg University school newspaper raved about his performance as their football coach:

"Heidel is proud of her teams and managers, but prouder of her loyal coach. Dr. Sickles needs no introduction to the athletic world, nor to the students of Hedelberg University. He is a perfect gentleman and a better football coach is nowhere to be found. He has the ability to work out new plays as well as to use old ones to a great advantage. He always has perfect control of his men, for they have confidence in him. The standard of athletics at Heidelberg has been raised fifty per cent since he has come to coach her teams. Three cheers for Coach Sickles!!"

In his history of the college, E. I. F. Williams gave Sickles credit for elevating Heidelberg's athletic program:

"The credit for this move should be given to Dr. C. M. Sickles, who had charge of coaching the athletic teams. No longer was the university janitor to be the football manager and students of penmanship the members of the teams. Heidelberg joined with other colleges in maintaining high standards of scholarship and sportsmanship in conducting the game as a prerequisite for a student['s] participation."

Caleb Sickles responded to the requests for information from former athletes by Major Mercer in 1907 and Moses Friedman in 1909. His responses went into detail and he began a correspondence with the school that lasted until its closing. From this correspondence, we learn much about the man and his experiences.

Dr. Sickles wrote a piece that was printed in the April 10, 1908, issue of *The Arrow* and is included in its entirety:

"Carlisle has done many things for me – good things. Entering when quite young my life was shaped there, it gave me an insight for higher things in life. When I left I strove four years to attain or rather fit myself for a useful life in the community in which I choose to live. I will advise every graduate of Carlisle to continue their studies. When you finish your course at Carlisle it is indeed a commencement – you are just beginning. Take up some special branch of work. A graduate of a technical school or of any special branch can always find employment and command a good salary. For my life work I chose a profession – that of dentistry. I put myself on a footing with the white man, struck out boldly in a small city of Ohio in competition with my white brothers, with nothing but my education and nerve. I am not eulogizing myself and do not want you to take it as such, I only want to set forth the facts that might help some one of my own race. I have so far succeeded in life although I have just begun. What I have done others of you can do. You may not all make a success in the 'tooth pulling' business but you can do something else equally as well. Since leaving school I have read considerably on the Indian question, which is no question at all. There may be no hope for the old Indians but the young men and women, there is plenty for them to do if they but would. The question is squarely up to you. The success you attain will depend upon yourself. Get away from the reservation and become a citizen of the United States. Work and your success is assured."

A month later an article titled, "Real Indian Joins Red Men" ran in *The Marion Daily Star*. Using more than a little irony, the reporter announced that Sickles, "… a former football star of national reputation, was among those initiated into the mysteries of the order [Improved Order of Red Men]." The very idea of an Indian joining a secret society of white men was newsworthy, let alone one that used Indian regalia in its ceremonies. Caleb was also a member of the Elks.

In 1909 he wrote again, this time about a different issue: "I am doing all I can to live up to the standards taught me while at Carlisle. It is very hard for the Indian to succeed among the white people on account of race prejudice. I find it no handicap because very few know I have the strain of Indian blood in my veins, but I heard on all sides about this being a white man's country. … God bless you and your co-workers in the good work they are doing."

The following year Caleb, at Friedman's invitation, had photos of his home and office taken to be published in Carlisle's *The Red Man* literary journal. Included in the exterior photo were, from the right, his brother, Raymond, who he was educating, Mabel and himself. Their servant is probably included in the unnamed people in the photo. Sickles went into great detail about the demographics of the town, his practice and his financial situation, which was very good. He was contemplating building a new house in two years. He stated with pride that "… I have no little back room, one 'horse-shack,' that a decrier of Indian education would imagine." Recalling some personal history he stated, "I came here without a cent – besides being in debt several hundred dollars – now I have over 1000.00 in cash in the banks here – This might seem as an object lesson to the other students there – 'that where there is a will, there is a way. … P.S. The photographer's bill is 3.00."

Caleb Sickles was doing very well indeed when one considers that he was one of 15 dentists practicing in a town of 1,700 people. He wrote at length describing his practice:

> "At present I have all I can do which means I do a business of from 250. to 300.00 per mo. Gross. I started in, in debt and have gradually paid out - all the time adding to my office – now I have over 1000.00 worth of furniture and instruments in my office – the accompanying photograph does not show all – as my laboratory does not show in the picture – among some of my instruments and machines – which are very expensive – I number – a Columbia electric engine with Dariot hand peice [sic] – (all cond) fountain cuspidor – Elgin casting machine, electric annealor – Columbia favorite chair – Sharp lamp – Electric lathe – gasoline blow pipe – just those articles represent an outlay of over 450.00. Then there are my countless smaller instruments aggregating over 500.00 more. My office is lighted by electricity. …"

Both dentists, Sickles and Johnson, were doing very well and were proud of their accomplishments. Pratt surely considered them shining examples of what top students could achieve and very likely used them to promote Carlisle's value as an educational institution.

Caleb's next letter to Carlisle was one of sadness to Wallace and Nellie Denny. It was to inform them that Mabel had died. After telling the details of her last days he wrote, "I know she is in heaven for she was a pure woman." He wrote Superintendent Friedman a year later to offer his regrets for not being able to attend commencement and to philosophize. "It would be a grand thing if all the members of the Class of 1912 could attend college, which would give them a wider range of thought and fit them to fight the battles of the world. … We all know there is room for the educated Indian – all we need is a chance. The proof is that today many Indians are holding responsible positions through-out our cities. Success to all of you."

Three years later he had better news. Caleb married Miss Nina M. Hankey on August 19, 1915, and visited Carlisle with his new bride on their honeymoon trip to Boston, New York and other points in the East. Sickles was rightly proud of what he had accomplished including owning his own automobile and farm. His July 15, 1916 letter to Acting Superintendent John D. DeHuff discussed a possible visit to the Indian school and also announced the birth of their son, an 8 ¼ pound boy, on the 13th. The visit took place and Caleb likely gave the talk on proper dental care that was discussed in the letter.

America's entrance into WWI changed many people's plans, and so it was with Sickles. An almost-40-year old Caleb Sickles served as a 1st Lieutenant in the U. S. Army 11th Battalion and was discharged on December 24, 1918 at Fort Oglethorpe, Georgia. It is not clear whether Caleb enlisted or was drafted. Regardless, he was inducted after the armistice was signed and served a very short time. After that, he was back to his dentistry practice.

The 1920 census listed Caleb (39) as living on Webster Street with his wife, Nina M. (32), Caleb M. Jr. (3 years 5 months), and Ralph M. (1 year 9 months). Caleb returned to his dental practice and did some coaching in the 1920s at the Tiffin Junior Home, an orphanage that was merged into the Tiffin State Hospital in 1944.

A newspaper from the seat of nearby Allen County, *The Lima News*, recalled Caleb's exploits in a 1954 article: "The 1921 team defeated Chicago East Lane Tech, then recog-nized as national champion although averaging only 138-lbs per man. Passing was their game. In fact, Dee Griffis threw one to John Starret for 80 yards and it still stands as a national record. Griffis is now a Tiffin policeman and Starret, later to become coach, is now head of a large boys' club at Nashville, Tenn. Dr. Caleb Sickles, a local dentist and former player with the Carlisle Indians, coached such a complicated offense that the officials had to be briefed before each game and the Tiffin captain had to notify the referee before each play. As a pre-game feature, Starret and Griffis would stand on the two 20-yard lines and heave passes back and forth, all of which had a rather demoralizing effect on the opposition."

Caleb must have maintained some ties with his family in Wisconsin as he owned land there until 1938. The local newspaper, the *Appleton Post-Crescent*, reported that Caleb Jr. sold a parcel in the town of Oneida that October. Now in his 60s, Caleb Sr. may have wanted to reduce his holdings to simplify his life. Caleb died of a heart attack in Tiffin on January 30, 1950 at about 70 years of age.

12

Frank Mt. Pleasant

Frank Mt. Pleasant competing before the 1908 Olympics;
Cumberland County Historical Society, Carlisle, PA

Name: Franklin Pierce Mt. Pleasant, Jr.	**Nickname:** Mounty
DOB: June 1883	**Height:** 5'8"
Weight: 135	**Age:** 21
Tribe: Tuscarora	**Home:** Tuscarora Nation, NY

Parents: Franklin P. Mt. Pleasant, Sr., Tuscarora;
Minerva Garlow Mt. Pleasant, Tuscarora

Early Schooling:

Later Schooling: Conway Hall; Dickinson College

Honors: American Indian Athletic Hall of Fame, 1971; Indiana
University of Pennsylvania Athletic Hall of Fame, 1998;
Dickinson College Sports Hall of Fame, 2003;
Frank Mt. Pleasant Library of Special Collections and
Archives, Chapman University, dedicated 2007

The Fastest Carlisle Indian

Franklin Pierce Mt. Pleasant, Jr. grew up on his family's homestead on the Tuscarora Reservation northeast of Niagara Falls and not terribly far from Buffalo, New York, with his parents, two brothers and one sister. The closest towns were Sanborn and Lewiston. Frank first arrived at Carlisle on August 25, 1896 for a five-year term of study when he was about 13 years old. Accompanying him from the family home in Sanborn was his older brother, William, who took a more traditional track than did his younger sibling. William completed his five-year commitment and graduated in February of 1902. He returned later that year and enrolled in the Commercial Course from which he graduated in 1907. After graduation, he departed for Lewiston, New York, where he farmed and preached occasionally. Their younger brother, Edison Perry Mt. Pleasant, age 12, arrived at Carlisle in September 1903 for a five-year term. At its completion, he enrolled for another three years and, after graduating, signed up again to attend Conway Hall, the Dickinson College Preparatory School. After a year he returned to Lewiston. Carlisle Indian School records indicate that he was a cabinet maker of some note. Their younger sister, Mamie G., arrived at Carlisle in September of 1908, less than a month before her 14th birthday, enrolling for 5 years. Mamie re-enrolled at Carlisle two more times, staying there until she graduated, and received a high school diploma for her work at the Indian school and at public schools attended during outing periods.

Rev. Franklin Mt. Pleasant, minister for the Tuscarora Baptist Church, and Minnie Garlow Mt. Pleasant were the parents of the aforementioned children. Mamie's records include a 1908 affidavit from her father stating that he and his late wife were both full-blood Tuscarora. That would, of course, make their children full blood as well. However, their school records indicate otherwise. Clerical errors and lack of knowledge on the part of the children probably are to blame for the inconsistencies. Census records indicate that Frank, Sr. and Minnie were both 3/4 blood Tuscarora. That would make their children 7/8 blood. Carlisle records indicate that the Mt. Pleasants were Presbyterian (likely in error), good students and well liked by their teachers and outing "parents." Nelson Mt. Pleasant, likely a cousin, also attended Carlisle Indian School. For reasons unknown, Frank's Carlisle file is tiny, consisting of just three cards.

Frank was only 4'8" tall and weighed just 71 pounds when he entered the Indian school gate. He was assigned to fourth grade. During his first enrollment Frank worked in the clothes room and for Mrs. J. C. Bucher of nearby Boiling Springs, Pennsylvania on his first country outing in 1900. The Buchers had extensive holdings and enterprises which makes determining exactly what he did difficult. Although a trolley line from Carlisle to Boiling Springs was completed that year, he stayed with the Buchers in the pre-Revolutionary War mansion that was their home because living with white families was part of the outing experience. (The Bucher mansion is now listed on the National Register of Historic Places). In August 1900, Mrs. Bucher visited the Indian school and gave Frank high marks. She also said that she wanted him to stay longer in Boiling Springs to attend school and take advantage of opportunities to improve his musical skills. In November, he returned to Carlisle with typhoid from which he recovered. Mt. Pleasant developed a reputation as an accomplished pianist while in Carlisle. He received notice in the school paper the next year for accompanying gymnastic drills on the piano.

By 1902 Frank had grown some and had become a fast runner. The Man-on-the-band-stand called him the hero of the day in the inter-class track and field meet for carrying off first prizes for the broad jump and 440-yard dash, second for the 220-yard hurdles and the banner of his class, which would graduate in 1903. A week later he competed in a dual meet against Dickinson College, winning the 440-yard dash. After the meet, thinking that year's track team would be Carlisle's best to date, Pop Warner combed the records of track meets in which the Indians had competed and compiled school records for the various events. Mt. Pleasant held the record for running the 440 in 54 seconds. *The Red Man and Helper* reported that Mt. Pleasant's performance in the annual dual meet with Penn State was not his best due to illness. However, he did mange to place second in the half-mile run and win the 440 while shaving a full second off his personal best and the school record.

Having completed tenth grade, Frank was discharged from Carlisle on July 4, 1902 because his 5-year term had expired, and he returned home. He re-enrolled on January 7, 1903 and began taking courses at Conway Hall, the new Dickinson College Preparatory School. Then 18 years old, he was 5'9" tall and weighed 140 pounds. Someone scribbled "weak heart" on the back of his enrollment card. His sister, Mamie, was convalescing from measles at the time of her initial enrollment and had a slight cough at that time. In a 1917 letter to the Commissioner of Indian Affairs, Superintendent Francis wrote, "She is not a rugged girl." Perhaps Frank and Mamie were a bit on the frail side, but there is too little information available to verify that.

The Carlisle Indian School relay team won their event at the 1903 Penn Relay Carnival held at Franklin Field in Philadelphia. *The Red Man and Helper* reported, "Wallace Denny was the first runner and he came in ahead by about five yards. Wilson Charles increased the lead materially, and James Johnson and Mt. Pleasant then 'took it easy' and finished about twenty yards ahead of their opponents. Besides winning a banner for the school, the boys each won a gold watch with the names of the contesting colleges engraved on the back. The team could have made much better time if it had been necessary to exert themselves in order to win."

At that year's class track meet, Frank won the 100, 220 and 440-yard dashes and came in second to Wilson Charles in the broad jump as he also did in points for the meet. He broke his own school record in the 440 with a time of 52.4 seconds. A couple of weeks later, Frank participated in the Dickinson College inter-scholastic track meet and won three events: 440-yard dash, broad jump and relay. He set a school record by jumping 20'8". He was the star of the Carlisle-Bucknell dual meet, scoring 18 points with a second in the 100-yard dash, first in the 220, first in the 440 and first in broad jump. He set school records in the 220, 440 and broad jump. Late that month he won four events in the Carlisle-Penn State dual meet, placing first in the same four events in which he competed against Bucknell. His performances in that year's meets resulted in his being elected captain for 1904.

Frank got a late start for the 1904 season, having only two weeks' practice before the Carlisle-Penn State meet. That lack of practice didn't hold him back as he won four events, setting a school record in the broad jump along the way. He nearly repeated that performance against Swarthmore, winning three events and coming in second in another. Although he was ill during the meet with Bucknell, Captain Mt. Pleasant managed two second place finishes and a first in the broad jump. Apparently feeling better, he got three firsts and a second against Penn State. After that meet, he headed home for the summer.

When he returned, he enrolled in the Dickinson College Preparatory School, but still lived on Carlisle Barracks and participated on Carlisle teams. The October 22, 1904 game against Harvard was the first time Frank was mentioned as being on the football team. He got into that game as substitute left end. Prior to that, he had received no mention as even being on the team. He was most likely on the junior varsity or played with the scrubs learning the game and preparing for the varsity. There is a good chance that Pop Warner would have discouraged his track star from risking injury playing football as he later did with Jim Thorpe, but Warner wasn't at Carlisle in 1904. He was back at Cornell at that time.

Mt. Pleasant was not included in the photograph of the varsity squad that was published early in the season. The next Saturday he played quarterback for the reserves or third team and scored a touchdown against Dickinson Seminary in Williamsport. The quality of his play was first mentioned in a November 5 article by Coach Ed Rogers: "Mt. Pleasant is another new man that is showing up well. He played a part of the Harvard game and will be given a try in the game against Pennsylvania. He is very light but has a lot of grit and sand." Frank got into the 18-0 loss to Penn substituting for Frank Jude, the future major league baseball player, at left end but received no mention for his play. A week later he played the entire game at left end against Susquehanna in Selin's Grove [sic] because Rogers rested his starters and let the second team play the weaker foe. Frank made the trip west for the big game against Haskell Institute on the Saturday after Thanksgiving at the St. Louis World's Fair but didn't play. However, he did start against Ohio State on the Thanksgiving Day warm up when the second team whipped the weaker Buckeyes. At the football banquet after season's end, Mt. Pleasant was awarded his first letter "C" for his play that year.

In the spring Frank won just two events in the inter-class track meet: the 100-yard dash and the broad jump, setting a new school record in the latter. The *Philadelphia Press* raved about his performance at the Penn Relay Carnival: "In the field events the most striking victory was that of Mt. Pleasant, a full-blooded Indian, from the Carlisle School, who cleared 23 feet 1½ inches, nearly a foot and a half better than his nearest white competitor. The work of Mt. Pleasant was a revelation and he was cheered to the echo for his performance." He also received a gold watch. Later that spring he placed first in the 100 and 440 as well as the broad jump in the dual meet with Dickinson College. He repeated that feat against Lafayette College and again in the Penn State meet held at Carlisle where he broke his own record in the 440. *The Arrow* conjectured that he would have broken the world's record had he not slowed up over the last 100 yards of the race. In June Mt. Pleasant had a field day against Penn State in State College when he won the 100-yard dash with a time of 10.4 seconds, the 440 in 50.8 seconds and the broad jump with the best American jump of the year at 23'9". The *Philadelphia North American* reported that he was going to enroll at Cornell, but *The Arrow* quickly denied that rumor and he was re-elected captain of the track team for the upcoming season. In July, the *Washington Post* ran an article describing him as possibly the greatest all-around athlete in the world. It also claimed that he would enter Cornell in the fall. That rumor may not have been too far-fetched, given that Pop Warner was Cornell's football coach.

In the beginning of the 1905-06 school year, *The Arrow* reported that Frank had returned from home and brought James Garlow with him. It also said that he intended to continue his studies at Conway Hall, the new Dickinson College preparatory school. He also found himself in the starting line-up as the quarterback of the football team in Warner's second year of absence. Filling the shoes of James Johnson, who had departed for Northwestern, was not an easy task. Bemus Pierce and Frank Hudson assisted George Woodruff, Advisory Head Coach. Woodruff departed after the Army game or rather, the team departed for five road games and he stayed behind. The Indians finished 10-4-0 with losses to college powers, Penn and Harvard, and major independents, Massillon Athletic Club and Canton Athletic Club, and impressive wins over most schools they played. Perhaps the 6-5 victory over the soldiers from West Point was the most satisfying. Frank lettered again and made Walter Camp's All-America Second Team. *The New York Evening Sun* selected Frank to its All-Eastern Eleven as quarterback, saying, "The best all round quarterback was Mount Pleasant of the Indians. Handling the ball cleanly and swiftly, he sent it to the runner in excellent form. In the backfield he was a deadly tackler and a dangerous player once a ball fell into his hands. In kicking he was not far behind Burr, Harvard; and Howard, Navy; and, all in all might be called the Eckersall of the East."

Keith McClellan, author of *The Sunday Game*, discovered that Frank Mt. Pleasant became the first Carlisle star to play for the Altoona Indians around this time and re-cruited a number of teammates to play for them as well. By 1915, so many Carlisle players worked for the Pennsylvania Railroad and played for the Altoona independent team that it was widely known as the ex-Carlisles. McClellan did not mention if Mt. Pleasant was paid but that was surely a distinct possibility.

After the holidays, Frank played forward on the Indian basketball team. When spring broke, he captained the track team again, this time with his eye on world records in the 440 and broad jump. Possibly out of fairness to the others, he didn't participate in the inter-class track meet that year. He did enter the Penn Relay Carnival, winning the broad jump but with a jump several inches off his personal best. He was not feeling well enough to participate in the annual home track meet against Penn State. Not yet back to full strength, Frank competed against Lafayette but didn't win any events. By Decoration Day he must have felt much better because he played shortstop for the second team in a game with Shippensburg Normal School. This was reported to be his first inter-scholas-tic baseball game. The June 1, 1906 edition of *The Arrow* also reported that Frank Mt. Pleasant had very recently become the first Carlisle Indian boy to graduate from the Conway Hall. He had a very busy spring.

Revolutionary new rules introduced for the 1906 football season created a new game. Bemus Pierce and Frank Hudson coached the team again that year, but Pop Warner spent a week with them in early September explaining his schemes for dealing with the new rules. Frank Mt. Pleasant was shifted from quarterback to left halfback, probably to take better advantage of his foot speed and passing arm. The new rules legalized the forward pass, and Mt. Pleasant was the first person Warner ever saw throw a football with a spiral. Warner went on to say, "The old end-over-end way didn't seem to work so well. It lacked direction, distance and control. We went to work on the spiral and Mount Pleasant picked it up quickly. I can still recall the startled looks on our opponents' faces when they first saw the spiral in action." Warner recalled seeing Frank throw the ball 50 yards downfield using a series of three photos of him to demonstrate the proper way of throwing a forward pass in his 1912 book, *A Course in Football for Players and Coaches*.

The Indians posted a 9-3-0 record, losing only to Penn State in the mud, to a strong Harvard team, and to Vanderbilt on Thanksgiving Day in the first game played between

Eastern and Southern powers. Several players were considered for post-season honors but, due to his Ivy League bias, Walter Camp named no Indians to his All-America team. Many coaches believed Exendine to be superior to Camp's choices at end. Warner favored Exendine and Libby for inclusion. The *New York Herald*, *Post* and *Washington Post* all supported Libby. The *New York Sun* supported Mt. Pleasant.

Just before Christmas, Warner announced that he had resigned his position at Cornell and had accepted the position of athletic director at Carlisle. Perhaps because Frank was not well enough to return to school after the Christmas break, newspapers including The *New York World* ran stories stating that he was leaving Carlisle for another school. One school prominently mentioned was Western University of Pennsylvania (today's University of Pittsburgh). His letter to Major Mercer about his recent illness was published in *The Arrow*.

In the spring after returning to Carlisle, Frank competed in the broad jump at the Penn Relay Carnival but only placed second, jumping 21'5" due to not being in top condition. He also placed first in the dual meet with Penn State with another short (for him) jump. Still crippled for the Navy meet, he only competed in the broad jump and did not place. He did win the broad jump in the Syracuse meet with a mediocre jump and placed second in the 220-yard hurdles, an event he normally did not enter. Perhaps this was a misprint. In the final meet of the season, Mt. Pleasant won the broad jump with a better jump than he had had in recent meets but far off his personal best. He also came in second in the 100-yard dash. 1907 had not started auspiciously for him, but football season was yet to come.

For reasons not recorded for posterity Warner shifted Mt. Pleasant back to quarterback. Likely reasons were that he was a better ball handler and tactician than anyone else on the squad and an adequate replacement could be found for him at left halfback in this very talented group. Warner considered the 1907 team his best to that time and one of the best Carlisle ever fielded. He considered some of these players among the all-time greats of the game.

After going 8-1 with the only blemish being a loss to Princeton in the rain, Carlisle headed west for a two-game road trip against Minnesota and Chicago on successive Saturdays. Minnesota fought hard and only yielded a victory to Carlisle at great cost to the Indians. Frank Mt. Pleasant's thumb was broken so badly he had to sit out the Chicago game. Bill Gardner was also dinged but was able to play against the Maroons. Pete Hauser rose to the occasion and led the Indians to victory to give Warner a most satisfying win over Amos Alonzo Stagg. When it was time to bestow All-America honors, even though he considered Frank's play "brilliant," Walter Camp demoted him to honorable mention because he deemed the Tuscarora not rugged enough. A skinny kid from Oklahoma who showed promise in track followed in Frank's footsteps to football and got some playing time as a back up halfback that year. Recently enacted eligibility rules ended Mt. Pleasant's football career at Carlisle, but not in college athletics. What might have been had his and Thorpe's ages or times at Carlisle overlapped more closely?

Newspapers speculated wildly as to where Frank would enroll next? A January 5, 1908 piece in *The Syracuse Herald* reported on the possibility of him entering Syracuse University:

> "The well-meant efforts of Antonio Lubo, captain of last year's Carlisle football team, to secure an athlete for the university have come to grief.

"Lubo, who to-morrow becomes a student in the engineering course had persuaded his friend Mount Pleasant, quarterback of the same team, to enter the university some time this month. A friend of Lubo's, however, states that some individual
connected with the institution took special pains to write to the football wonder and
tell him that while he was at perfect liberty to enter the university, he should remember that the question of his playing on the varsity team still hung fire and would not
be decided until certain gentlemen had plenty of leisure to discuss and decide the
matter. Lubo received a similar communication.

"The two men are very indignant, inasmuch as they had planned entering the
college to obtain a practical knowledge of engineering and not solely to play football.
Mount Pleasant has decided to enter some institution, probably Cornell, where he
will be received with at least courtesy. Lubo will stick to his original intention and
enter here not to play football but to take the engineering course. In fact, it is
extremely doubtful whether he can be persuaded to come out for the team after the
hint he has received."

In late January of 1908, the *Washington Post* reported, "Notwithstanding all reports to
the contrary, Frank Mount Pleasant, the famous Indian runner, has returned to Carlisle to
resume his work. The authorities, however, are much worried over the prospects of his
ultimate recovery from the illness which kept him home for some time."

Frank did not run track for Carlisle that spring; instead, he prepared for the Olympics. A reporter, falling for a joke, wrote that he would be representing the Irish American
Athletic Club. Frank's Celtic heritage was his affinity for Irish stew. He traveled to
London, England that July to compete in the broad jump and triple jump (hop, step and
jump). Unfortunately he injured a ligament in his left leg just prior to the games and, hurt,
placed sixth in both events. His Carlisle schoolmate, Lewis Tewanima, finished ninth in
the marathon in which the dazed Dorando Pietri of Italy was disqualified after two
officials guided him to the finish line. In early August at the special athletic games held in
Paris, a healthy Mt. Pleasant set French records when he defeated Frank C. Irons, the man
who had won the broad jump in London. On their return to the United States, he and his
teammates were welcomed in a parade in New York City. Afterwards he ran in some races
but was barred from a New York City meet due to residency requirements. After a few
competitions, he went home for a rest and to make a decision regarding his future education.

The September 30, 1908 edition of *The Dickinsonian* reported, "The arrival of Frank
Mt. Pleasant in Carlisle and the fact that he has decided to play with Dickinson this year
has been received with delight." Eligibility issues were also discussed, "Mt. Pleasant has
played with the Indians for several years notwithstanding his attendance at classes in
college, but owing to a new faculty ruling no student of the college is allowed to play on
another institution's athletic teams. He has been sought by almost every institution in the
land, and the presence of this popular athlete on our team will strengthen it wonderfully."
Apparently Dickinson College kept Frank's enrollment to themselves. In early October,
The Dickinsonian reported, "The appearance of Mt. Pleasant in the game at F. and M. on
Saturday was the first indication that the general public have had as to his whereabouts.
He was sought by every university and college in the East, and press agents were kept busy
chronicling his supposed intention to play with Syracuse, Dartmouth, Cornell, etc.
Mt. Pleasant is a full-fledged Junior and during his two years stay here he formed so many
friends that he could not leave the institution. Mounty is a good student and a popular
fellow and we are glad to have him with us. According to press reports, the Navy are

looking forward with anxiety to Saturday's game because of his presence." So were some other teams.

An Associated Press article reported that the game between Lehigh University and Dickinson College was cancelled because Lehigh refused to play if Mt. Pleasant were in the lineup. The article also reported that Frank was a faculty member, a claim that is more likely an error on the part of the reporter than an accusation by Lehigh. *The Dickinsonian* ran a series of letters between the schools which led up to the game's cancellation. Professor W. W. Landis summarized Dickinson's position: "I also endeavored to show that our playing Mt. Pleasant was not a violation of the four year rule as Mr. Mt. Pleasant, who is now a Junior in College, is playing for the first time on a college team. The fact that no members of the Carlisle Indian School team – with which Mr. Mt. Pleasant formerly played – were considered in the selection of the various All American elevens shows that that team was not classed by the leading writers on the game as a college team." A review of Walter Camp All-America teams for the four preceding years revealed the following selections of Carlisle players by Mr. Camp:

1906	center	L. Hunt, Carlisle, 3rd team
1907	end	A. A. Exendine, Carlisle, 2nd team
	halfback	P. Hauser, Carlisle, 3rd team
	quarterback,	F. Mt. Pleasant, Carlisle, honorable mention

Dickinson College provided neither the supporting cast nor the high visibility schedule of the Indian school, but Frank managed to excel as best he could. Immediately after the Lafayette game, he was elected captain of the 1909 team. Frank set school records for scoring, punting and field goal kicking.

At the end of the season, he assisted fellow Carlislian Bemus Pierce prepare his Kenyon College team for their big game with Ohio State – as an undergrad! Between football and track seasons, he played forward on the Junior Class basketball team. He scored 15 points from five field goals and five free throws in his team's 17-12 victory over the freshmen. Mt. Pleasant was an all-around athlete.

In track, he set a school record for the broad jump that held for nine decades. Later, Pop Warner criticized Mt. Pleasant and Dickinson College for less than full commitment to his training, implying that Frank would have achieved more athletically had he trained more diligently. It may have been a bit of sour grapes, because Warner may have wanted Mt. Pleasant to remain with him. Or, Warner's feelings may have been hurt because Frank chose to train under the renowned Michael C. "Mike" Murphy for the Olympics. As to the merits of Warner's charges, there are two things to consider: performance in events and ability to compete. Frank Mt. Pleasant's personal bests were as follows:

- 100-yard dash   10 seconds flat
- 220-yard dash   22.4 seconds
- 440-yard dash   50 seconds flat
- Broad jump   23'9" (24'4" in practice)

Would Frank's injury prior to the Olympics have been prevented had he been under Warner's wing? That is impossible to know, but he trained under one of the best known and respected trainers in the country and others on the Olympic team excelled under Murphy's tutelage.

Back at Dickinson College, he was one of the most popular people at the school. The *1910 Microcosm* described him as, "a frank, open-hearted gentleman, quiet and courteous. He is an artist on the piano and a great lover of music. He is exceedingly modest in regard to his athletic ability, and if you ask him in regard to it, you will experience the famed taciturnity of the American Indian." It also said, "To meet Frank Mt. Pleasant is to like him; to know him is to admire him; to live in the same little world with him is to appreciate his sterling qualities and his noble nature." Elsewhere in the yearbook, it said, "In the interval between studies and athletics Frank is busily engaged in making touchdowns and 100-yard dashes with a little girl from New York." This was the only known mention of a love interest in his life. In 1910 he graduated with a Ph. B. (Bachelor of Philosophy) degree and embarked on a coaching career, but not before playing some minor league baseball over the summer.

The head coaching job at Franklin and Marshall College in Lancaster, Pennsylvania unexpectedly opened up for Frank. Because J. C. "Jack" Hollenbach had had highly successful 1908 and 1909 seasons, he was considered to be one of the best coaches F&M ever had and had been extended an offer for 1910. However, before the season could start, Hollenbach accepted the head coaching job at Penn State and resigned from F&M. The September 15 issue of *The Franklin and Marshall Weekly* introduced Mt. Pleasant as the new football coach to the student body. Bill Crawford reported that Mt. Pleasant may have also taught French at the college level. He may have doubled as a French instructor that year because F&M needed one. The start of football practice was also announced with great expectations for a successful season, but no one associated with the Diplomats understood the impact the rule revisions would have on the veteran team.

A 4-3-2 record over a tougher schedule than previous F&M teams had played wasn't a fair indicator of the team's ability. Frank didn't have much time to worry about it because basketball season was starting and he was the coach. Going 5-5 wouldn't have been considered a bad year, but the yearbook, *Oriflamme*, criticized the team's flat performances against Washington and Lee and, to a lesser degree, Mercersburg Academy. Most coaches would be happy to go .500 with a green team. The end of basketball season brought spring training for baseball and hopes for a better season, but they weren't fulfilled. The 1911 baseball team went 6-7-1, but Frank wasn't done for the spring. He was also raising a team for track, a sport that had been dormant at F&M for five years. The school paper lauded him for organizing and fielding a team but chided students for not participating.

The June 8 issue of *The F. & M. Weekly* announced that Dr. Dexter W. Draper had been hired as chair of Professor of Hygiene and Physical Education and coach of all athletic teams. Mt. Pleasant was out but no announcement was made as to whether he quit or was fired. It may be that the college's administration wanted to make his position a faculty position and Frank had but a bachelor's degree. Regardless, he had little time to dwell on his misfortune, if it was a misfortune, because he had signed to play outfield for the Lancaster Red Rose minor league team in the Tri-State League that summer.

On August 7, 1911, Indiana Normal School (today's Indiana University of Pennsylvania) announced that Frank had been hired as athletic coach. Before football season started in earnest, Frank agreed to play for a hand-picked baseball team that represented Indiana (the town) against nearby Homer. His involvement in that rivalry probably helped endear him to the townspeople.

The Normalites as they were often called (the Indians' nickname didn't arrive until well after Mt. Pleasant departed) had had a highly successful season in 1910 but the head coach, Professor L. O. Kirberger, left to take a position at Carnegie Tech. At that time, Indiana Normal School (INS) played high schools, normal schools and small colleges, completing each season with a game against nemesis Kiski Prep. Francis "Bernie" Kish, former Executive Director of the College Football Hall of Fame and currently lecturer in sports management with the University of Kansas, clarified some confusion regarding The Kiski School when he wrote, "… the correct spelling is Kiskiminetas. It should be noted that eleven men who played at Kiski Prep went on to college careers and are now enshrined in the College Football Hall of Fame. They are – Harry Stuhldreher of Notre Dame, Frank Schwab of Lafayette, Cliff Montgomery of Columbia, Tom Davoes and Herb Stein of Pittsburgh, Gust Zarnas and Jim Daniell of Ohio State, James Moscrip and Bob Hamilton of Stanford, and Bill Edwards and Stan Keck of Princeton." The Normalites definitely had their work cut out for them when they played Kiski.

Although Normal supporters had high hopes for the season when Frank Mt. Pleasant was announced as coach, the results were less than spectacular with the team finishing 5-3-1, the tie being with Kiski. When spring broke, Frank switched from the gridiron to the diamond and coached the baseball team. Although his INS baseball team generally played well, they fell to the almost unbeatable Chinese University of Hawaii that lost just one game out of the 61 they played on their coast-to-coast tour. Making the Hawaiian team go 11 innings was a moral victory of sorts. Frank's summers were occupied by playing baseball for the Clearfield club or with Saginaw in the South Michigan League, as accounts vary.

That fall the Beaneaters, as some called INS teams, had arguably the best year in its over-100-year history by going 9-0 and becoming both the Pennsylvania Normal School Champions and Western Pennsylvania Interscholastic Champions. Grove City College was the only opponent to score against them. This result was almost duplicated in 1913 when the Normalites went 9-1, losing only to Kiski. Mt. Pleasant had built quite a reputation for himself in Indiana, Pennsylvania, but a small college in a neighboring state was upgrading its program.

West Virginia Wesleyan College (WVWC) in Buckhannon was a small school with ambitions for its athletic program. Its athletic director, football, basketball and track coach, John L. Felton (Dickinson College '12) had developed stars such as John Kellison and Alfred Earle "Greasy" Neale and had upgraded the teams' schedules. In mid-June, 1914, Felton resigned to take a similar job at Western Maryland College, leaving his position open. Seeing an opportunity to move up to the college level, Mt. Pleasant took the position. He arrived in Buckhannon in mid-September. His assistant, former Carlisle star center and possible relative, Bill Garlow, appeared a couple of days later, "…then work was started with a vim that has never been seen before on College Field."

First opponent on Wesleyan's schedule was none other than the Carlisle Indians. The teams had played for the first time in 1913, possibly due to the former coach's connections. This year Orange and Black supporters were hopeful of success because they felt they had a stronger team than at the same time the previous year. The 1914 Indians were not the team they had been and played a sloppy game. Many Methodist fans considered holding Carlisle to a single touchdown a victory of sorts. The local media gave the coaching staff high marks for the effort. WVWC lost two more games, the first to Al

Exendine's Georgetown team and the last to the Washington and Jefferson powerhouse. Winning all its other games, including two against in-state rivals Marshall and West Virginia University gave it bragging rights for the state championship. The 21-0 defeat of Dickinson College probably gave Mt. Pleasant and Garlow much satisfaction.

Frank's attention shifted immediately to basketball. The roundballers had a pretty good year, winning 16 and losing seven. By virtue of winning all 10 games played against in-state teams, Wesleyan claimed the West Virginia State Championship. However, something that happened on the basketball court on January 15, 1915 may have convinced Wesleyan athletic management either that Frank wasn't the man to direct their teams, in their view anyway, or demonstrated to him an insufficient level of support from the administration. *Washington Post* reporter Alfred L. Stern wrote, "Washington had its first look last night at a college basketball team in which 'a private in the ranks' controlled coach, manager, captain, et al!" An official tired of hearing "Greasy" Neale complain about calls ejected him from the game. When Neale refused to leave the floor in spite of entreaties from coach and manager to do so, the official, Jim Colliflower, declared the game a forfeit to Georgetown. Stern went on to say, "The manager was at a loss to say just what action would be taken, but it is a safe bet that the offending player will be severely disciplined." Three days later, newspapers across the country opined that, if Frank Mt. Pleasant were able to sever his current ties, he would be Carlisle's new football coach. If not, Lone Star Dietz would be their mentor. Bob Fulton attributed Frank's departure to needing to be with his ailing father. Neither of the predictions worked out as Frank's father lived decades longer, but Frank was not at Wesleyan in the fall. Whose choice it was is unknown; it may have been mutual. The June 1915 issue of *The Pharos* stated that a head coach for the football team had not been selected but reported that it was generally expected that Garlow would return in the fall as head coach. No mention was made of Mt. Pleasant, but Neale was hired as head football coach for the 1916 season. Now that was severe discipline.

Frank coached the 1915 University of Buffalo football team to a 3-3 record. In February 1916, Frank G. Menke reported in his syndicated column that Mt. Pleasant would not be back as Buffalo coach but would be retained by the school in some other capacity. Menke also gossiped about possible high profile replacements for Mt. Pleasant. In the summer, he played for the Clearfield, Pennsylvania baseball team. In the fall of 1916,

Mt. Pleasant throwing a spiral pass: *Football for Players and Coaches.*

Frank played quarterback for the Buffalo All-Stars, a team that went 5-2-1 but were hammered 77-0 by Jim Thorpe and the Canton Bulldogs and 15-0 by the Toledo Maroons, the only strong teams on their schedule. Despite this, team promoters made some outrageous claims about the team's goal line not being crossed all season. During the week he coached Buffalo's Hutchinson Central High School.

Frank's summer of 1917 was spent playing baseball with Clearfield again. That year's version was the first to have complete uniforms. In the fall, with the war raging in Europe, Frank joined the army. After attending Officers' Training School at Fort Niagara, he was commissioned as a 2nd Lieutenant. While at Niagara, he played on the student officers' football team alongside well-known college football stars. Promoted to 1st Lieutenant, he served at Fort Dix, New Jersey. In February 1918, *Washington Post* reporter W. H. Hottel announced that Frank would run on Ft. Dix relay team in games held at Johns Hopkins. On June 1, 1918, he competed as a member of the Ft. Dix relay team in the united services track meet held at Central H. S. in Washington, DC. He was then transferred to Camp Gordon, Georgia, where he served as a bayonet instructor. After that, he was transferred to Europe, where he was reputedly decorated for bravery.

Immediately before and after WWI, Frank worked as a stock clerk for the Pierce-Arrow Motor Car Company in Buffalo. While working there, he lived in a rooming house with people born in Canada, Sweden, Norway, Turkey, Greece, Italy, Connecticut and New York. It was a little United Nations under one roof. Pierce-Arrow manufactured luxury cars that are still held in high regard by collectors. During the Great Depression, sales plummeted for Pierce-Arrow as they did for many other car companies with bankruptcy being the result. A November 1920 company newsletter, *The Arrow*, included a short bio of Frank and indicated that he worked in Body Stock C. Because Pierce Arrow is no longer in business and the people who worked there are long gone, it has been impossible to determine exactly what Mt. Pleasant's function was at the motor car company.

Frank kept active in sports by coaching a semi-pro team as well as by officiating games and track meets. His name recognition was likely a plus in promoting big games. A syndicated newspaper column, "SportFolio," that asked what happened to Mt. Pleasant could have spurred some speculation or someone may have confused him with William Gardner and muddled the details, or there may be some other explanation. Regardless of the reason, a premature newspaper report of his death prompted a response on his part.

> "December 11, 1930. Frank Mount Pleasant, famed old time athlete of the Carlisle Indian School and Dickinson College, is not dead. Mount Pleasant wants that definitely understood. Recently, it was reported that he had died from a stomach ailment in a Minneapolis, Minn. hospital while engaged in secret service work. Many of his friends here were saddened at the news. The reports finally reached Buffalo, N. Y, where Mount Pleasant, hale and hearty, after the first gasp of amazement, sat down and wrote Gilbert Malcomb, Dickinson treasurer, that like Mark Twain, the report of his death had been 'greatly exaggerated.'"

In 1931 Frank wrote a letter to George H. Fraser of Wauwatosa, Wisconsin, regarding the meeting of his great grandfather, Nicholas Cusick, with Gen. Lafayette during the Revolutionary War. Cusick, a Tuscarora fighting alongside Washington's troops, shot and cooked a large squirrel and offered to share it with Lafayette. Lafayette enjoyed the roasted squirrel so well that he asked Cusick to dine together again, provided he roasted another squirrel. The letter also included a few details on the Cusick and Mt. Pleasant families. Frank was living at 350 Riley Street in Buffalo at that time.

Fresh reports of Mt. Pleasant's untimely death were not exaggerated this time. On April 12, 1937, Buffalo police officers found Frank lying on a sidewalk unconscious with a fractured skull, "possibly by violence." An Associated Press article headed, "One of Football's Immortals Dead," told of a police investigation that attributed the cause of the skull fracture to a fall. Later accounts attributed his demise to a hit-and-run motorist. According to the article, he was survived by two sisters and three brothers. Frank was working as a postal clerk at the time of his death. After the Pierce-Arrow collapse, a secure position in the post office would have been attractive to anyone in the depth of the Great Depression regardless of educational background.

Upon hearing of Frank Mt. Pleasant's death, Pop Warner was quoted as calling him, "the best football safety man I ever saw." In July, famed sports writer, Damon Runyon, asked politician and former football player, Hamilton Fish, who were the greatest football players. "He considered our question carefully. 'Well,' he said finally. 'I'll answer by naming the greatest players I have ever played against. They were Jim Thorpe, and Frank Mount Pleasant of the Carlisle Indians, Ted Coy, Johnnie Kilpatrick, and Steve Philbin of Yale, Tobin and Marks, of Dartmouth, and Mayhew, of Brown. They were all tremendous players.'"

Frank Mt. Pleasant has been inducted into several halls of fame. When will the Pennsylvania Sports Hall of Fame correct its oversight and induct him?

William J. Gardner

13

William Gardner and Alene French Gardner, 1919;
Diane Garrard, granddaughter

Name: William Jennings Gardner		**Nickname:** Birdie
DOB: 1/23/1883		**Height:** 6'0"
Weight: 172		**Age:** 21
Tribe: Chippewa		**Home:** Turtle Mountain Indian Reservation, ND
Parents: George Gardner, white; Anastasia Gardner Rolette or Mah-na-ki-vet (Foggy Cloud), Chippewa		
Early Schooling: Haskell Institute		
Later Schooling: Dickinson School of Law		
Honors:		

Untouchable

William Jennings Gardner's father is believed to have died when Bill was quite young. His mother then married Joseph Rolette and put him and his younger brother, George, on trains to boarding schools, first to Haskell Institute in Lawrence, Kansas. Bill arrived at Carlisle Indian Industrial School on September 4, 1904, a year of great change for Carlisle, administratively as well as athletically.

Brigadier General Richard Henry Pratt was relieved of his duties as Superintendent in July after having served in that position since 1879 when then Lieutenant Pratt founded the school. Football coach Glenn Scobie "Pop" Warner had resigned in February to return to coach his alma mater, Cornell, after five successful years of leading the Carlisle Indians. Future Hall-of-Famer James Johnson had departed for Northwestern

University Dental School and fullback Charles Williams was gone, but substantial material remained to field a competitive team. Alums Ed Rogers, another future Hall-of-Famer, and Bemus Pierce were tapped to coach the 1904 team. Another alum, the famous drop-kicker Frank Hudson, assisted them for three weeks in preparing the team for the season but had to return to his regular job in Pittsburgh. 1904 was also the year after Carlisle pulled the "hidden ball play" so successfully on Harvard. Gardner wouldn't see it run at Carlisle but surely became familiar with it and filed it away for future use.

At just under 6 feet tall and weighing 172 pounds, Bill Gardner was a perfect candidate for the football team. His first year was spent largely on the bench observing the more experienced players and learning what to do when it would be his turn. He did get some playing time at end, tackle and fullback as the coaches were figuring how and where he could help the most. He started some games, generally playing against weaker opponents or filling in for an injured first-stringer. He even scored a touchdown against Albright College. Bill received his first newspaper coverage for good play in a rare mid-season home game in which he substituted at fullback against Ursinus. Carlisle prevailed 28-0. A powerful University of Pennsylvania team that was vying for the national championship defeated the Indians 18-0 in front of a home crowd of 22,000 people, including 500 Indian School students who rode the special train to the big game. Gardner substituted at fullback in a game that would have been closer if Carlisle had had an accurate kicker that year. Bill started the 23-0 tromping of Ohio State at fullback and scored a touchdown. Carlisle rested its first team for the big game against Haskell that was played two days later at the St. Louis World's Fair. He didn't get into that game, but soon played alongside eight Haskell players, possibly old friends, who chose to transfer to Carlisle.

Spring of 1905 found William Gardner running the dashes in track. Although published accounts never had him finishing first or second in a meet, he set a school record for the half mile. It also found him playing baseball where he played outfield and batted clean-up or pitched. He may have been platooned because his name didn't appear in many box scores. He may also have left school for the summer shortly after commencement.

The 1905 football season brought coaching changes. George W. Woodruff, the Hall-of-Fame coach who originated the guards-back formation at Penn, closed out his coaching career by leading the Indians for a year. He enlisted the recently graduated Yale star Ralph Kinney to assist him. Bemus Pierce and Frank Hudson helped out once again. William Gardner got into the first two games of the season at fullback, backing up future Hall-of-Famer Albert Exendine. Gardner's name wouldn't get ink again until the University of Cincinnati game, when he started at right end, and that was probably because Carlisle was in the middle of a five-game, 14-day road trip. That was the last time his name would be in the lineup until the last game of the year when he backed up Frank Jude at right end in the 76-0 blowout of Georgetown. He wasn't too lonely on the bench because his brother, George, joined the team that year. Even though he had little playing time in 1905, Bill managed to letter in football.

January 1906 brought basketball, a newly organized team sport for Carlisle; Bill Gardner started the season jumping center but was platooned with J. Libby as the season progressed. When spring rolled around, he pitched a part of a baseball game for the varsity against Franklin and Marshall College. In early May he pitched against Bloomsburg State Normal and went 3 for 3 at the plate. His school records indicated that he spent the summer in Staunton, Virginia playing baseball. The *Washington Post* reported that "Indian"

Gardner pitched the Staunton professionals to a 10-0 win over Warrenton on July 3. It appears that he played under his own name or as close as the newspapers could get to it.

Between football and basketball seasons, revolutionary rule changes were instituted that created modern American football. Bill Gardner was one of those who was well-versed in both the old mass formations as well as the new open game. Pop Warner visited Carlisle in early September 1906 to instruct the current coaches, Bemus Pierce and Frank Hudson, in his new offensive scheme. C. L. Flanders, Yale '06 and center of note, joined the team as an assistant coach early in the season. The 1906 rule changes, among other things, legalized the forward pass. Tall William Gardner was ideally suited to play left end in the new passing scheme and played that position the rest of his time at Carlisle. Albert Exendine was assigned the right end position and Frank Mt. Pleasant, who could throw spiral passes over 40 yards, was shifted to left halfback, the primary passer in Warner's new single-wing offense.

At 3:00 p.m. Wednesday, September 26, 1906, Carlisle played Villanova in "the first important game under the new rules." The game was scheduled intentionally to allow officials, coaches and players from distant locations to attend. Publicist Hugh Miller promoted the game far and wide with the result that Carlisle's largest home crowd to that time was on hand to view the first modern football game at Indian Field. Bill Gardner wasn't watching the game from the sidelines. He was the first-string left end, a position he would not relinquish.

Carlisle defeated Villanova 6-0; then, within 10 days, it closed out its schedule of home games with drubbings of local small colleges, Albright College and Susquehanna University, 82-0 and 48-0, respectively. Carlisle's offense was hitting on all cylinders, particularly its forward passing attack. A wet Dickinson Seminary Field in Williamsport undid the Indians in their 4-0 loss to a heavier Pennsylvania State College (today's Penn State University). The Indians cruised through their next three opponents: University of Western Pennsylvania (today's University of Pittsburgh), Penn and Syracuse before losing 5-0 to Harvard on a wet field, always a problem for the undersized Indians. They then took on strong teams in other sections of the country. First they beat the co-champions of the West, Minnesota. Then they looked for the champions of the South. The Indians lost to Vanderbilt University 10-6 on Thanksgiving Day but bounced back two days later to defeat Cincinnati 18-0. Gardner played fullback in a lineup that included several second-stringers, likely due to injury or fatigue of many starters. A week later they just got by Virginia 18-17 before returning home at last. Gardner caught forward passes and onside punts and carried the ball on end-arounds and line plunges. Gardner and Exendine got high marks from sports writers for boxing out the opposing ends when their team was receiving punts as well as covering their own team's kicks. Caspar Whitney ranked the Indians fifth in the nation. Carlisle awarded Gardner another "C."

The Arrow reported that William Gardner had been appointed to West Point from his home state of South Dakota [sic]. He was discharged from Carlisle on December 5 as he was "preparing for West Point." All that stood in his way was the entrance examination. He apparently spent the winter and spring preparing for the exam and, possibly, studying law as there was no further mention of him in that year's *Arrow*. However, he and the rest of the Carlisle football team received an unexpected Christmas gift: Pop Warner was returning to Carlisle as athletic director in charge of all sports, including football.

September found Bill Gardner at Dickinson School of Law and at his familiar position of left end on the Indian football team, not at West Point. It was not uncommon for Carlisle students to study at other local institutions and continue playing on the football team. But it wouldn't have been possible for him to play for the Indians if he were at West Point. Whether he failed the entrance examination or just decided to finish his law degree is unknown. Regardless, he was better than ever anchoring one end of Carlisle's line. Newspaper accounts reflected that Bill was still a sure-handed tackler.

Carlisle faced a brutal schedule in 1907 that included three of The Big Four (only Yale was omitted), 1906 Co-Champions of the West, Minnesota, and 1907 champs, Chicago. The best team Carlisle had to that time and one of the best it would ever field chewed up their competition with but one exception. Over-confidence and wet field conditions teamed up and caused a loss to an inferior Princeton team, the only blemish on Carlisle's otherwise spotless record.

The 1907 team was not just a well-oiled machine; it had a number of individual stars. Pop Warner described the team as "nearly perfect." However, Walter Camp, always biased toward Big Four players when it came time to pick his All-American team, overlooked all of the Indian stars for the first team. Warner was displeased and later wrote, "In selecting his all-America that year, Walter Camp only put Exendine on the second eleven and Hauser on the third, not even mentioning Gardner, and also ignoring Mount Pleasant…" When Warner discussed Camp's selections with Wally Steffen, the great Chicago quarterback the Indians completely stifled in 1907, Steffen responded, "Well, I certainly would like to see the ends they think better than Gardner and Exendine. And as for Pete Hauser!" If Steffen had only known about Gardner's physical condition, as Pop Warner later related, "Gardner, a star end, had his leg wrenched and his jaw broken…and [yet he] played on the finish without telling me a word about it, afraid I would send in a substitute."

Twenty-four years later, Pop Warner, in an article to *Collier's Weekly* wrote, "Our ends that year [1907] were Gardner, a Sioux [sic], and Exendine, an Arapahoe [sic], and I still maintain that they have never been surpassed for sheer brilliance. Pete Hauser, who did the kicking for us, was a big Cheyenne with a powerful toe, his punts averaging 60 yards, and under instructions he always raised them sky high. Gardner and Exendine were off at the swing of his leg, and it was rarely that they failed to keep up with the ball. In the game with Chicago, they made life miserable for Wally Steffen, invariably nailing him in his tracks, although Stagg finally assigned three men to block each one."

The February 28, 1908 edition of *The Arrow* included a piece titled "Gardner's Good Job," a reprint from *The Sentinel*, the local Carlisle newspaper. William Gardner had landed the football coach's job at duPont Manual Training High School in Louisville, Kentucky and at record high pay. In late November, he wrote his Carlisle friends that his team was doing quite well. That was something considering that he had only four returning starters. While Gardner's tenure in Louisville didn't get off to an auspicious start – a loss to New Albany and a tie with the Kentucky University second team – he had a good first season, running off five straight wins coming into That Old Rivalry game with Louisville Male High School. The importance of this Thanksgiving Day game cannot be overstressed to those unfamiliar with rivalry games. Four straight losses created the opening for Gardner to fill.

In 1908 Manual had a small weight advantage over High School as it was commonly called (Male must have been assumed), something that was unusual in this series. High

School supporters were concerned about Gardner's making use of the trick plays famously employed by the Carlisle Indians, but they saw none of them. Roscoe Smith, High School's coach, was more concerned about Manual's passing game and spent much of his time developing a defense for it.

Fans of both teams expected the Indian Gardner to be stoic and meditate quietly on the bench alongside his substitutes. But that wasn't his way. He paced up and down the sidelines, nervously, taking in everything that was happening on the field. Under Gardner, Manual ran a new-style open offense but threw few passes, depending largely on what was called "straight football" at the time. Even though no trick plays were called, Manual prevailed 16-0. Some gave the new coach credit for normalizing relations between the rivals. Others thought that positioning a quarter of Louisville's police in the stadium had a greater effect. The previous year, excessive exuberance on the part of supporters marred the event.

What William Gardner did on Sundays during football season is unclear, but there is a good chance that he played on an independent or semi-pro team. There is also a good chance that he played under an assumed name as many other coaches did. Many schools did not want their employees playing professional football because it was deemed unseemly to accept money to play a game. In January 1909, his job was extended and expanded, making him the coach of all sports for $125 per month.

Originally a member of the Dickinson School of Law Class of 1907, Bill was admitted to the Class of 1908 because it was down three members. The precocious Van Scouten sailed through his bar examination a year early, Skinner entered a business enterprise and Hoover left to complete his legal education in New Jersey. The demands of athletics, both playing and coaching, took time away from Gardner's education and stretched out his program, so being moved back a year wasn't unexpected. Apparently well thought of by his classmates, his name was assigned the following mnemonic for Dean Trickett to use in later years should Gardner ever return to visit: Big man – big heart – true friend – fine partner – Gardner. He finally received his LL. B. degree on June 9, 1909. He was admitted to the Louisville bar in 1910 and likely practiced there when not coaching. The Carlisle Indian School newspaper indicated that Gardner would help prepare the team just prior to the start of their seasons. Doing this would have been an effective way of keeping up-to-date on the latest rule changes and Pop Warner's evolving wingback formations.

Manual's fortunes against High School declined after the great 1908 victory and, by 1911, Coach Gardner was ready to pull out all the stops for a win. This meant pulling some trick plays out of the bag he had kept tightly closed up to this time. By keeping his trick plays under wraps, he had lulled the previously alert, almost to the point of paranoia, opponents into a false sense of security. The timing was right for Manual's offense had been impotent, scoring just 28 points for the season. Gardner had learned lots of trick plays at Carlisle, so he had plenty of options from which to choose.

Putting a new twist on a then illegal play that his counterpart on the opposite end of the line at Carlisle, Albert Exendine, had run in 1907 against Chicago, Gardner had end Andrew Uhrig come to the game in street clothes. Only ten Manual players went out onto the field to begin the game, but High School apparently didn't notice that the opponents were a player short. Actually they weren't short a player. Uhrig was standing on the playing field, barely, blending in with a group of photographers standing along the sidelines. When the ball was snapped, he raced downfield – well not exactly because he wasn't very fleet afoot – and caught a pass from quarterback Thorne Crabbe. The play worked perfectly until it was obvious that the wrong person had been selected for the deception. The Male High School safety caught him after a 35-yard gain that was supposed to be a touchdown. The game, Gardner's last at Manual, ended in a 16-0 loss, the exact opposite of his first game against High School.

In 1911, Dr. Dudley A. Sargent, Director of Harvard's Hemingway Gymnasium, found W. J. Gardner to be the third strongest American, at least among those he measured. Sargent had developed a complicated formula for computing strength which involved several measurements and physical tests. Gardner beat out notables of the day including John L. Sullivan, Jack Johnson and James J. Jeffries. So, he was keeping in shape, but for what?

Professional, or independent as it was often called, football was in its early days at that time. Teams were often loosely organized without consistent rosters. Star players were often hired for just the toughest games, and newspaper coverage was sketchy. A complicating factor was that players often played under assumed names to hide that activity from their employers because many people did not view professional football positively at that time. It is quite possible that Gardner played football on Sundays, as records imply that he played for the Shelby (Ohio) Blues a couple of seasons. He very well could have played for other teams before, after, or during his stint with Shelby.

According to the December 20, 1912 edition of *The Carlisle Arrow*, the Carlisle Indian School weekly newspaper, William J. Gardner, star end on the great 1907 team, was athletic director at Oberlin College and was in charge of all athletics. A later newspaper article had him at Otterbein College. A letter in the Carlisle Indian School file in the National Archives provided the answer. On October 16, 1913, W. G. Clippinger, President of Otterbein University, wrote Carlisle requesting Gardner's current address and the name of his current employer. Clippinger verified that W. J. Gardner had been physical director at Otterbein the previous year. A letter from George Crocker, Manager of the Credit Department of P. F. Collier & Son, Publishers of Good Books, also trying to locate Gardner, arrived the next day. Both were advised that he might be with his brother who was then working at the Indian School in Keshena, Wisconsin.

Charles Guyon provided the answer in January 1914 when he visited Carlisle to arrange games to be played in the South during the upcoming season. He also told Moses Friedman that William Gardner was now working with the A. G. Spalding & Bros. in Atlanta as he was. During his brief stint with Spalding, Bill Gardner played left end on a local all-star team against the Seventeenth Infantry team from Fort McPherson. Both teams were loaded with former college stars primarily from the Southeast. The all-stars prevailed 22-7 over the Soldiers. Next, Gardner took the Physical Culture Director (Athletic Director) position at The University of the South in Sewanee, Tennessee for the 1914-15 school year. In 1914 he also served as trainer. The Gardner House in which he lived still exists on the Sewanee campus and is in beautiful condition. It is not known if he built the house, but it is believed that it is named after him. On August 27, Bill wrote Oscar H. Lipps, then Superintendent of Carlisle Indian School, inquiring about the possibility of obtaining a position as assistant football coach because the University of the South was "…in debt to the extent of four thousand dollars and are unable to pay me." Lipps responded that the two paid assistant positions had already been filled. So, Bill was a player instead of a coach that year.

1915 was a watershed year for professional football according to Canton Bulldogs manager Jack Cusack. In order to compete with the rival Massillon Tigers that was loaded with All-Americans, Cusack found it necessary to upgrade his squad. In a 1969 interview, he said, "I succeeded in strengthening the Bulldogs with some of the star players of that era, one of the best recruits being Bill Gardner, a great tackle or end from Carlisle, the government's famous Indian school in Pennsylvania." Gardner played left end on a powerhouse team consisting largely of former college stars including several All-Americans. But Gardner's greatest contribution may have been off the field. Jack Cusack made Gardner part of an important event in football history when he dispatched him to the next state to recruit an old teammate.

Indiana University head football coach Clarence C. Childs had recruited fellow Olympian Jim Thorpe to assist him with his backfield and kickers as soon as the major league baseball season ended. Thorpe was in Bloomington working with the Hoosier football team when his old friend raced over to meet with him. After Gardner told him he would be paid $250 a game, five times what most others received, to play for Canton, Thorpe happily became a professional football player on a regular basis. He had most likely played professionally on an informal basis prior to that as did many others. Gardner's recruitment of Thorpe changed professional football forever. Attendance at Canton's games jumped from a previous high for the season of 2,900 to 6,000 for the game at Massillon to 8,500 for the season-ending home game against the Tigers. The next year the lowest recorded attendance at a Canton Bulldogs game was 4,000; 10,000 attended the rivalry games with Massillon. The increased attendance that resulted from Bill Gardner's successful recruitment of Thorpe made professional football, at least for Canton (and its opponents on the days they played the Bulldogs), an economically viable business. The teaming of Thorpe and Gardner worked well for Cusack and Canton, but international events later broke up their partnership.

Apparently spending the off-season with his brother in Belcourt, North Dakota, William Gardner began corresponding with Oscar Lipps in August about "securing a position with the Ford Motor concern," a company with which Carlisle had a relationship. It is not known whether Gardner ever worked for Ford because Uncle Sam soon gave him a paycheck and a place to hang his hat.

World War I raged in Europe. The U. S. held back for a few years but joined the fray in early 1917. William Gardner signed up on May 15, 1917 and was reputed to be the only Indian to receive a captain's commission from Fort Sheridan. Assigned to Company H. 338th Infantry, N. A. at Camp Custer near Battle Creek, Michigan, Gardner became accustomed to being called captain both on and off the parade ground. (It was about this time that his nickname "Birdie" started showing up in the press.) Assisting University of Michigan head coach Fielding Yost, Capt. Gardner captained the Camp Custer football team. Because most of the college stars were then playing for service teams, Walter Camp selected an All-Service Team for 1917 rather than an All-America team. Showing that he had lost nothing in the decade since he played college ball, Bill Gardner was selected for this honor as an end. He contributed to the war effort in two uniforms.

In his military role, Capt. Gardner received an unusual assignment. He was given a large group of recent immigrants from Detroit, many of whom were from Poland and spoke no English. Training these men would be difficult assignment for most people, but

Gardner immediately tasked one of his lieutenants to learn some basic Polish. When Gardner trained his recruits to march, he issued a command, such as left face, and the lieutenant repeated the command in Polish. The recruits responded well to his initiative. The *Fort Wayne Sentinel* reported the captain as saying, "My company will not take a back seat for any company in the new army, even if they have to learn soldiering through an interpreter. They are the best drilled men in camp today, we think, just because they tried to work and show their appreciation of the work my lieutenants did with them."

Gardner's unit sailed to Europe and participated in the fighting. Family members believed that Bill's military pension was due to his being gassed in France. The Hun halted, Gardner sailed back to New York City with the rest of the 338 on the Leviathan, arriving on April 2, 1919. After helping process out the rest of his unit at Camp Custer, he returned to athletics and the law on October 1, 1919, but not without something to show for his time in the military.

William J. Gardner and Alene French Gardner's wedding photo portrays a dashing, handsome Army captain and his beautiful bride in her fashionable flapper dress. Alene, the daughter of the owner of French Paper Mill in Niles, Michigan, was no doubt charmed by this well-spoken hero of the gridiron and battlefield. Although ten years his junior, she married him in her home town on July 19, 1919, with Pastor Harold Hobb officiating.

With the war over and the world made safe for democracy, Capt. Gardner returned to civilian life. The 1920 census found the Gardners in Devils Lake, North Dakota where Bill had opened a law office. The census included a bit of information that might cast a speck of light on his paternity. He told the census taker, Gladys Ziebach, that his father was from New York. He told the 1910 enumerator that his father was from Vermont. What, if anything, he learned about his father's origin is unknown.

Gardner is reputed to have assisted with the coaching of the University of North Dakota football team in 1919. Bill definitely was hired as physical director and coach in all branches of athletics at St. Edwards College in Austin, Texas in 1920. A year later he started the position of athletics director at Southwestern University in Georgetown, Texas where he faced the task of rebuilding the football team. One can assume that this position was a step up salary-wise because he stayed with the school through 1925 and because he had two children: Frank, born in 1919, and Jacqueline, born in 1921. However, Bill's career was not always in education or coaching.

It was The Roaring Twenties, both for America and Bill's marriage. Bill and Alene divorced, remarried and had a third child, Alene Natalie, who was born in 1926 in Chevy Chase, Maryland. Having a law degree gave Bill Gardner many career options. Prohibition and the crime wave that followed its inception created a whole new area of law enforcement well-suited to someone as robust as William Gardner. In 1929 Eliot Ness was putting together a team of agents to combat the Capone breweries and distilleries in Chicago. Ness was looking for unmarried men who were accurate shots and could handle themselves in a fight. Team members also needed specific skills such as wiretapping, surveillance and tailing. He reviewed personnel files of prohibition agents across the country before finding Gardner in the Los Angeles office. Apparently Bill had omitted mentioning to the Bureau that he had a wife and three children. Family legend has it that one "Hellacious" fight ensued in the Gardner household that ended with Bill's catching a train for Chicago and a second divorce. Alene took the children to live in

Miami and Niles, Michigan, living off her late father's investments in French Paper Mill. William Gardner became the ninth, and last, man selected for the team that the media sensationalized as The Untouchables.

Then in his mid-40s, Bill was the old man of the operation but was still an imposing presence. Ness originally intended to keep him under wraps and use him in undercover operations; when he arrived in Chicago, Ness had him sign in to the Palmer House under an assumed name. Gardner complied and let Ness know that Henry Schlitz had arrived. Hearing that Gardner was in town, Ness's chief lieutenant Marty Lahart, a big sports fan, encouraged his boss to meet with Gardner immediately – and take him along. Lahart was so enthusiastic about meeting the big Indian because Knute Rockne had just named Gardner to his All-Time All-America Team recently published in Collier's magazine. Rockne would have known just how good Bill Gardner was because they had played opposite each other in the big Canton-Massillon rivalry games.

When Ness arrived at the hotel, he asked for Henry Pabst but no such person was registered there. Figuring that a six foot three inch tall Indian couldn't have checked in unnoticed by at least one of the desk clerks the Palmer House had stationed on each floor, Ness and Lahart took the elevator to the top floor and worked their way down, inquiring with the desk clerks as they went. A house detective couldn't help but notice and ushered them into his office. After Ness explained who they were, the house detective showed them a list of people registered in the hotel and pointed out their man's name to them. Seeing Henry Schlitz on the list solved the mystery and caused Ness to question his own abilities as a detective.

After seeing Gardner in person, Ness gave up the idea of using him undercover. He was just too imposing a presence to go unnoticed. So, Bill took part in the raids, openly chopping up breweries and distilleries and catching bootleggers as they tried to escape. His specialty became roof and ladder work as the crooks often tried to get away through roof exits and fire escapes. In the late 1950s, *The Untouchables*, a television program based loosely on Ness's team, was a sensation. Abel Fernandez was cast as Bill Youngfellow, a member of Ness's team based on Bill Gardner.

Bill Gardner's story after The Untouchables was not a happy one. Alcohol, gambling and women were his downfall. His tumultuous marriage to Alene French ended in divorce and others followed. His children were beautiful or handsome and charming, just like their father. A combination of a $150 monthly pension for having been gassed in the war and friends, relatives and wives supported him.

In 1954 he stayed with his youngest daughter, the one who hardly knew him, Alene Gardner Schnapf, for a short time when he was convalescing from hip replacement surgery. His first (and second) ex-wife, Alene French Gardner, was living in Henderson, Kentucky to be near her youngest daughter when she received a wire from a veterans' hospital in Arizona saying that he was gravely ill. She was contacted because Bill had listed her as next of kin. His daughter got his address from her mother and wrote, inviting him to visit when he had recovered. He took young Alene up on the offer and appeared a month later. The visit ended a month or so later when she felt he had begun to drink heavily and had become "ornery with the children." He became angry when Alene informed him that his behavior was unacceptable and left for a hotel in Evansville, Indiana. He later moved to The Brown Hotel on The Magic Corner in Louisville, Kentucky where he continued drinking heavily. The Brown called Alene Gardner Schnapf's husband, demanding that he pay $800 for damages done to the room. The Schnapfs did not pay. Bill went to Louisiana to stay with his son, Frank, for a while. At times he lived with his brother, George, who eventually moved to Arizona. He died at the Prescott Veterans Hospital on June 15, 1965 at age 81 and was buried in the adjoining Veterans Cemetery.

William Gardner, like many historical figures, is largely forgotten today, but was a significant part of three events that have become part of our folklore. How many others can claim to have starred on the legendary Carlisle Indian School football team, elevated the status of professional football by recruiting Jim Thorpe, and thwarted Al Capone as one of the Untouchables?

THE SIOUX RANCHER

Sampson George Bird

14

Sam Bird, captain, 1911;
Fred Wardecker

Sampson Bird playing end; *U. S.
Army Military History Institute*

Name: Sampson George Bird		**Nickname:**	
DOB: 8/14/1885		**Height:** 5'10"	
Weight: 177		**Age:** 22	
Tribe: Piegan Blackfeet		**Home:** Blackfeet Reservation, MT	

Parents: John Bird, white; Mattie Medicine Wolf, full-blood Piegan Blackfeet

Early Schooling: Fort Shaw boarding school

Later Schooling:

Honors: American Indian Athletic Hall of Fame, 1985

Blackfeet Rancher

"One time we found his ropes that he used to rope calves and cows for branding or treatment on the prairie. There were three of us and we took his ropes and climbed the cottonwood trees in the river bottom and tied them up so that we could play 'Tarzan,' who was the big hero of the time. When he discovered that we were swinging from tree to tree with his precious ropes, he quietly told us we had 15 minutes to get the ropes back to where we found them. Years later when we discussed this incident, my two boy cousins knew how much time it took to train a rope so that it would do what the roper wanted. We marveled that he said nothing other than to give us the short deadline to return them to their resting place. Many a cowboy would have probably used the rope to tan some little butts. Not him." – Liane Johnson, granddaughter

This patient, caring Indian cowboy grandfather was Sampson George Bird, the son of John Bird, a white man of English descent, and Mattie Medicine Wolf, full-blood Piegan. How Sam tamed horses provides some insight into why he treated his rogue grandchildren so gently: "We loved to sit on the corral and watch him work his horse that he was breaking. He was very patient and tender with the young colts. It was always special when he finally got them calmed and tamed and we could help curry them." The qualities Sam demonstrated with wild horses and untamed grandchildren were surely keys to his success as the captain of Carlisle's best football team.

As a boy, Sam, or Samuel as the censuses listed him, lived on the Blackfeet Reservation near Browning, Montana, just east of present-day Glacier National Park. His brother, Charles, came east before Sam, or Sampson as he was called at Carlisle, did. His last name also changed to Burd while at Carlisle, likely as the result of a clerical error. The clerk may have spelled his name the same way a local family spelled theirs. Sam was probably a better speller than the clerk because he made the Merit Roll, Carlisle's version of the Honor Roll, in February 1908.

Sam's career at Carlisle could have ended in March 1909 when he and four other football players ran away to avoid punishment for breaking unspecified rules. Newspapers across the country ran a story that Carlisle's administration tried to keep quiet: "The superintendent is out after the red-skins with warrant for their arrest, but according to Albert Payne, fullback, they are not likely to be found. Payne has also left for his home in Spokane." Sam did return or was allowed to return – it isn't clear which – and rejoined the team. It isn't clear what rule had been broken but some speculate that it had something to do with playing baseball for money, something that some of the runaways did, in fact, do.

Sampson Bird, age 24, started receiving notice in the school newspaper for his athletic ability in 1909 when he moved up from the second team to the starting eleven. Although light for a guard at 175 pounds, he had played well when he had gotten into games as a substitute in 1908, but now he was a regular. He didn't receive much mention in game reports because he toiled as a lineman. However, his name was in the starting lineup, something that made him a person to watch. And watch they did.

Sam and his partner, Margaret Blackwood, won dance prizes in competitions at no less than three receptions. His debates with the Invincibles were covered and his all-around work in track and field was acclaimed. He was also commissioned First Lieutenant of Company C. When the school year was over, he returned home but not by himself; he took his dance partner with him to be his partner in life.

At the start of the school year in September 1909, all associated with the school were stunned:

> "The members of the Carlisle Indian Press were shocked to learn of the death of Margaret Blackwood Burd [sic] this summer. She was a member of our office force all last term and was married to Sampson Burd, one of our students, in July. They were spending their honeymoon with Sampson's people in Montana when she was taken ill with spinal meningitis. She will be remembered by all of us for her pleasant, cheerful, accommodating disposition."

A couple of weeks later the school was surprised to hear that Sampson had returned to Carlisle to serve as an assistant football coach. However, *The Carlisle Arrow* reported that his contributions extended beyond coaching:

> "While most of the Indians played well, the work of Hauser, Dupuis and Burd [sic] stood out prominently because the two former did most of the ground gaining, while Burd was a power upon the defense."

At season's end it announced:

> "Sampson Burd [sic], who has played right guard upon the team for two years with great credit to himself and to the school, has been elected football captain for 1911. 'Sam' is one of the best players upon the team, a heady player, a natural leader, and very popular among the players and students, and he will undoubtedly make an able and successful leader for our next gridiron campaign."

Early in the 1911-12 school year, *The Carlisle Arrow* announced that Sam had returned from Montana with several new students in tow and that he would attend Conway Hall, Dickinson College Preparatory School. It also informed readers that Captain Bird's brother, Charles, a Carlisle alumnus who had left school a few years prior, was "…doing well as a farmer and ranchman; he has four hundred acres of wheat and a large number of fine cattle." Sam's name was found very frequently in the school paper that fall, due both to being the team captain and to his fine play.

Warner moved him from the guard position he had held down the previous two years to the right end position. That gave Sam more opportunity to be in the limelight, and he took advantage of it. Pop had added an end-around play to the playbook and Sam executed it perfectly against Georgetown. "Carlisle gained most of her points upon long gains by Powell, Thorpe and Newashe, while Captain Burd [sic] scored on a long run after a trick play." An end-around was considered to be a trick play at that time. Later *The Arrow* opined, "Captain Burd [sic] is proving to be another Exendine, and there will be very few ends in the country his equal this year." After the big 16-0 win over Penn, the *Philadelphia Ledger* reported, "The work of Burd [sic] was phenomenal and was the talk of the entire game. He was in nearly every play and was down the field like a hawk on punts, preventing the wearers of the Red and Blue from getting started when they caught the ball. Many times he crashed through the interference and brought down his man when a run was tried around his end." However, he wrenched his knee and had to sit out the Harvard game, something that probably pained him more than the injury.

Captain Bird led the Indians to arguably their most successful season because it included wins over two of the Big Four, Penn and Harvard. The only blemish was an 12-11 loss to a weaker Syracuse team, a game which the overconfident Indians played listlessly. After Carlisle's victory over Brown University, *Outing Magazine*'s annual poll of coaches listed Bird at right guard in its "Football Honor List for 1911." After the season ended, Jim Thorpe was elected captain for 1912 and *The Arrow* gave Sampson high marks for his leadership: "It is hoped and expected that Captain Thorpe will prove to be as able and popular a leader and set as good an example for his followers as has Ex-Captain Burd [sic], who has made an ideal record in this responsible position."

Sam wasn't just an athlete. He earned the reputation of being everyone's best man by standing up for friends at their weddings. He also participated in debates with the Invincibles and gave talks to other groups. In the spring, he competed in both track and field events, with his strength being the shot put and hammer throw. On May 27, 1912, he left for home, Browning, Montana, accompanied by Gus Welch.

Back in Montana, he was Sampson Bird again. He married another former Carlisle student, Margaret Burgess, Haida/Tlinget from Alaska, and soon had a growing family. He and his brothers supported their families by ranching on the reservation.

Liane Johnson, oldest living granddaughter of Sampson Bird's numerous grandchildren interviewed her mother, Sam's oldest daughter, Theo, and gained much insight into the adult Sam Bird. "Sam was quiet, loving and commanded respect. He never had to say much to his children to sway obedience. They all just listened to him." Theo could only remember two of the seven children ever getting a spanking from their father, and each of them only got spanked once.

Sam was considered the family patriarch by his parents and siblings. Although his father, John, was living, he was often absent, drunk or both. So, Sam ran the family ranch for his mother Mattie, whose Piegan name translated to Medicine Wolf Woman. He, Margaret and the children lived with his parents, siblings and their families on the ranch on the Cut Back Creek, which is located about a mile or so east of Lewis and Clark's Camp Disappointment. However, on returning home one day he found Margaret in tears. She was crying because his mother and sisters shunned her just because she was not Piegan. Sam immediately moved his wife and three children to the old Aubrey Ranch, never to return to live. He continued to work the family ranch, but would never live there again. He was a decisive man and held true to his decisions. He made a better life for his family at the new location. They later lived in Browning, Montana for better access to schooling for their children and later yet on the Two Medicine Ranch.

Theo recalled, "Sam was a very optimistic person. He always spoke positively about others. He loaned money to others with the assumption (not always correct) that they would pay him back when they were able. If time went by and the payment never came he would say, 'That was a cheap loan.' Because he knew his own stature in the community, he knew the person would not come back to try for a second 'loan.' Pleas for second 'loans' are very common on the reservation, but people knew not to bum him a second time. He would never ask for payment; he felt the borrower had the responsibility to remember his part of the bargain."

Theo also recalled that during the influenza pandemic, "Sam kept all the family isolated on the ranch. They supplied all their own food and he did not let people come to visit. If he saw someone coming, he would go out to a safe distance and let them know the family was staying in isolation to protect their health. Not one family member suffered from that epidemic."

Some hard financial times followed closely on the heels of the pandemic: "Sam's brother, Charlie, had obtained a loan to buy cattle from a company called the Portland Loan Company (PLC). Charlie bought the cows and then the winter of 1918 was horrifying winter weather that caused cattle losses all over the state of Montana. Charlie lost most of his cows. PLC approached Sam and made an offer. If Sam would run sheep and then ship and sell the wool and lambs for PLC until Charlie's debt was paid off, they would give him a ranch in their possession on the Two Medicine River. PLC sent seven bands of sheep (about 2,000 to 3,000 sheep per band). Sam applied for allotments in his name and all his living children's names and one yet-to-be-born child who he guessed to be a girl – and she was – and he pre-named her Lillian. She never used this name, preferring Marjorie, but it was on the Blackfeet rolls for years. He materially aided the grandchildren's education by providing them a place to live in town in the winter, by babysitting them, encouraging them and being a positive role model. The Sam Bird Memorial Rodeo (recently renamed to the Bird/Brown Family Memorial Rodeo) has been held on Memorial Day weekend for many years. People from all over Montana and Canada attend this event. Sam's athletic ability has been passed along to many of his offspring. A grandson, also named Sam Bird, is a champion roper and granddaughter Brittany Bird has been in barrel racing for some time. Several family members compete on the Indian rodeo circuit. Dustin Bird and Sami Jo Bird are 2007 champions in team roping and jr. barrel racing, respectively. Sam Bird's legacy will remain with us for a long time to come.

CATCHING WILD HORSES

15

Jim Thorpe

Jim Thorpe making a mighty punt; *U. S. Army Military History Institute*

Name: James Francis Thorpe	**Nickname:** Big Jim; Libbling
DOB: 5/22/1887 or 5/28/1888	**Height:** 6'0"
Weight: 178	**Age:** 22
Tribe: Sac and Fox	**Home:** Pottawatomie County, OK

Parents: Hiram P. Thorpe, Irish & Sac and Fox; Charlotte Vieux Thorpe, Potawatomie-Menominee-Kickapoo & French

Early Schooling: Sac and Fox Reservation Boarding School; Haskell Institute

Later Schooling:

Honors: Citizens Savings Athletic Foundation, 1950 College Football Hall of Fame, Charter Member, 1951; Professional Football Hall of Fame, Charter Member, 1963; American Indian Athletic Hall of Fame, Charter Member, 1971; Oklahoma Sports Hall of Fame, Charter Member, 1986; Athlete of the Century, 1999

Wa-tho-huck (Bright Path)

According to church records, James Francis (Jacobus Franciscus) and Charles Thorpe were born on May 22, 1887 near Konawa in Pottawatomie County, Oklahoma. Jim later claimed to have been born on May 28, 1888 south of Bellemont, Pottawatomie County, Oklahoma. As with many others in this book, the details of his birth are unclear; unlike anyone else, he became the world's greatest athlete. The purpose of this chapter is not to chronicle Thorpe's life – excellent biographies have already been written by Robert W. Wheeler (1975) and Bill Crawford (2005) – but to provide an overview for those unfamiliar with him and, hopefully, to provide a new tidbit or two of information to those who are familiar with Big Jim.

If there were a theme to Jim Thorpe's life, it was loss. The twin boys were born to an Irish-Sac and Fox father, Hiram P. Thorpe, and a Potawatomie-Menominee-Kickapoo-French mother, Charlotte Vieux Thorpe. He once told a reporter that his family background made him an "American Airedale." His mother was a devout Catholic. According to his daughter, Grace, "Grandpa was a horse breeder, a wife-beater and the strongest guy in the county. He was a polygamist and had two wives. My understanding was he kicked them out when he met Charlotte, my grandmother." Hiram loved horses and raised them, leaving the farm work to Charlotte. He enjoyed horse trading, racing, wrestling, betting and drinking. "He was a big, ornery guy. He liked to drink and fight. When Grandpa would come along in his wagon along Moccasin Trail, folks would turn off their lights, 'cause he liked to shoot them out as he came down the road." Such was the environment in which the boys grew up.

When away from their father, the twins spent idyllic youths – from a boy's perspective – hunting, fishing, trapping, berry-picking, swimming and wrestling on the family's 1,200-acre allotment. That all ended in early 1897 when a typhoid epidemic took Charlie before his tenth birthday. Jim was devastated and became a loner, taking up the habit of hunting raccoons all night with only a dog for a companion.

Hiram and Charlotte were both literate, a rarity in that time and place, and sent their children to be schooled at the government boarding school on the Sac and Fox Reservation. There has been some speculation that family strife, rather than the desire to see their children educated, prompted the Thorpes' decision. Jim hated it and ran away. A teacher considered him incorrigible. After a series of runaways and beatings from his father, young Jim was sent, "... so far you will never find your way back home." That would have worked with most boys, but not Jim. Haskell Institute in Lawrence, Kansas was not too far away for him to find his way home. He then spent some time in Texas breaking horses, a task that helped develop his strength and coordination. This was something he enjoyed.

Charlotte Thorpe died in November 1901, and Hiram quickly remarried. Jim lived at home and attended Garden School for awhile. He didn't run away from that school because, outside of school hours, he was free to hunt and fish – and he found it more bearable than being at home. Through a chain of events that will likely never be unraveled, Jim, now 17, enrolled at Carlisle on February 6, 1904, for a five-year enrollment. Hiram Thorpe died later that year of an infection that developed from a hunting accident. Jim was then an orphan.

Although a natural athlete, he was small at 5'5 ½ " tall and weighing 115 pounds, so he didn't immediately become involved in varsity sports but did play on shop teams. Also, he might not have felt comfortable competing for a position on the school team due to having had little previous exposure to organized athletics, especially those played with proper equipment and according to standardized rules. James, as did the other students, attended academic classes half day and worked in a trade the other half. He worked as a painter. Periodically, he went on outings to work on farms.

The story of the beginning of Jim Thorpe's involvement in Carlisle athletics is well known and can be found in Mike Bynum's autobiography of Pop Warner as well as in Thorpe biographies; that part of the story will be presented as briefly as possible here. In April 1907, wearing overalls and borrowed gym shoes, he broke the school record in the high jump. A track team member, believed to be Al Exendine, informed Warner of his feat. The coach then assigned Exendine the task of working with Thorpe. The result was that the lad soon broke all of Ex's records and some others. Jim was a rising star on the track team, but he wasn't satisfied; he wanted to play football, too. According to others' reports, he didn't see much point to running track because there was no money to be made in it. Warner did not want to risk his then skinny, up-and-coming track star to a career-ending injury in football; however, Thorpe insisted on a tryout. Pop accommodated him by having him give the varsity some tackling practice. That would surely change his mind, or so thought Warner. That plan blew up in the Old Fox's face when the upstart ran through the entire team. "Nobody going to tackle Jim."

The 1907 football season was a frustrating one for Jim because he spent most of the time on the bench learning from the first team. Being new to the game, he knew neither the rules nor the halfback position. Something else he didn't like was the training table at which, as a member of the varsity, he took his meals. Joe Guyon later related, "Jim hated the training table, because it never had enough on it to eat. He loved steaks. Pop Warner, our coach at Carlisle, would ration off steaks to us, and Jim would buy them off the other players. He could do that. Oklahoma Indians had money."

1908 was a better year football-wise for Jim. He became a starter at left halfback, which was the tailback in Warner's single-wingback formation. That position was ideally suited for a triple-threat player like Thorpe who could run, pass and kick with the best of them. Walter Camp rewarded the young back's efforts by placing Jim on his All-America Third Team. Not bad for a second year player.

In the winter, Jim Thorpe captained the Freshman Class basketball team and played on the varsity squad. He was also elected captain of the 1909 varsity track team. Open dates in a great track season gave Jim opportunities to pitch a couple of shutouts for the school's baseball team. That summer he joined some other Carlisle students to play summer baseball for the Rocky Mount Railroaders in the Eastern Carolina League. Thorpe had completed his five-year term, but school records listed him as a deserter. Superintendent Friedman may have been angry that he left to play baseball.

Thorpe, apparently feeling that he wasn't a deserter, spent Christmas at the school visiting old friends. He also brought some new students with him. However, he didn't stay or return for track season as The Arrow suggested he would. Carlisle heard little more from its prodigal son until Al Exendine encountered him, broke, on an Anadarko, Oklahoma street in the summer of 1911. Ex called Warner to inform him, among other things, that Thorpe was no longer a skinny kid but, at 24 years old, had grown to 5'11" tall and weighed 185 pounds. Warner wanted him back; Friedman didn't. Warner won out and Thorpe made history.

Pop Warner and Moses Friedman did not distinguish themselves in their handling of this situation. They surely were aware that Thorpe had played minor league baseball for pay, something that was clearly against the rules for college and Olympic athletes of that time. However, they were also surely aware that it was a widespread practice for college athletes to play summer baseball. The difference was that college boys were more sophisticated than Indian youths, who were in the difficult process of assimilating into white man's society, and, being better informed about such things as maintaining one's amateur status, played under assumed names. Discussing Thorpe's return to Carlisle presents an ethical challenge for the author because his conclusion is that Thorpe should have broken the rules. Had Thorpe not been allowed to play football and run track at Carlisle, he might not have been allowed on the Olympic team. Had he not played college sports or been an Olympic champion, he may lived a life of quiet obscurity or one very similar to that of his father. Playing at Carlisle created numerous opportunities for him that he would most likely have never had.

The football team of 1911 was arguably Carlisle's finest team, losing but a single game and beating two of the Big Four, Penn and Harvard. Jim was named to Walter Camp's All-America First Team. In a 1944 interview with John M. Flynn, Jim said his fondest memories of 23 years of playing football were from the November 11, 1911 game with Harvard in Cambridge. In spite of an injured right leg, Thorpe kicked four field goals to defeat the Crimson for only the second time in Carlisle history. He considered it the most fiercely played game in which he ever participated. Sportswriters of the day dubbed it "the most spectacular football battle ever seen in the East."

Jim was definitely the big man on campus at this time and against strong competition, except in the eyes of one fair maiden. Mamie Mt. Pleasant, younger sister of Frank Mt. Pleasant, told her grandchildren of the time he asked her out on a date. She said she turned him down because he was too ugly. Ugly to her may have extended beyond physical beauty because she was a refined young lady who may not have found Jim's less sophisticated ways attractive. Fortunately for Jim, there were plenty of other pretty girls on campus.

Thorpe's triumphs during the 1911-12 school year weren't limited to the gridiron. Jim was also spectacular in track in 1912 while he prepared for the Stockholm Olympic Games. Thorpe's performance in the 1912 Olympic Summer Games is legendary. He won gold medals in two grueling events, the pentathlon and decathlon, which are composed of five and ten separate events, respectively. He also competed in two other events but did not medal in either. Additionally, he participated in an exhibition baseball game. At the awards ceremony on the closing night of the game, King Gustav V of Sweden famously said, "You sir are the greatest athlete in the world." And Thorpe, just as famously, responded, "Thanks, King." Afterwards he had fun in other forms of competition while in Europe.

A reporter who covered the Olympics wrote about how Jim entertained himself in his free time:

> "We were in Paris and a lot of athletes and scribes were lolling in the hotel when Thorpe came in, and asked us to go with him. Said he had found a place where we could have more fun than any other place he ever saw. So we trotted along, and Thorpe led us to a joint under the shadow of Montmartre, a regular batcave, full of hard looking Apaches.

"'Where's the fun here, Jim?' I queried. Thorpe grinned a foot wide. 'Big lots fun,' said he. 'Here last night. Had to lick seven Frenchmen. Maybe so we get fine fight tonight. All we need do, just go in, act noisy, have elegant fight. Come along!'"

He was his father's son.

Thorpe was accompanied to the Olympics by Coach Warner and Louis Tewanima, the silver medalist in the 10,000 meters, a Hopi Indian and member of the Carlisle track team. Gus Welch qualified for the 1912 Olympics but did not compete due to injury. Upon their return, the Olympic team was treated to a New York City ticker tape parade which an estimated 1,000,000 people attended. Thorpe was the toast of the world.

Football season started soon after that, and Thorpe again showed that he was the best player by scoring 25 touchdowns. The team piled up a total of 504 points in this one-loss season. Their defeat of an Army team led by Dwight David Eisenhower is the topic of a recent book by Lars Anderson. Walter Camp again named Thorpe to his All-America First Team. In 1912 Jim had had the greatest year an athlete has ever had, but 1913 was different.

In mid-January, a story usually attributed to Roy Johnson of the *Worcester* [Massachusetts] *Telegram* broke saying that Thorpe had been paid for playing for the Winston-Salem minor league baseball team for two summers. Charles Clancy, manager of the team, was quoted making racial and personal attacks against Thorpe. Thorpe huddled with Warner to decide what to do. Although a lawyer, Warner failed to look at the rules regarding challenges, perhaps because he was preoccupied with saving his own skin. Thorpe was convinced that he had to admit playing for pay. There were even photographs of him in the team's uniform. It is unclear if he composed the letter in which he, a simple Indian boy ignorant of all the rules in the white man's world, admitted to having played for the Rocky Mount and Fayetteville teams, but he wrote it out and signed it. He also followed Warner's advice about returning the medals, and he regretted doing so the rest of his life. Now that Jim was no longer an amateur, he could not play on Carlisle teams nor could he tour with the AAU. Put another way, the days of his being exploited because he was an amateur were over. He was now a professional and would be paid to play – and paid very well at that.

There were plenty of teams – major league baseball teams, that is – ready to sign him up to big contracts. They knew he would be a big box office draw. Outside of New York, the press was rather supportive of Thorpe and critical of the AAU. Even the Brits favored Thorpe. The Fayetteville team claimed it had Thorpe under contract in an attempt to extort money from the major league team that would sign him, but that failed.

Possibly feeling a bit guilty over how Jim was treated, Warner stepped in as his agent to negotiate a contract for him. About the time Thorpe was ready to sign with Cincinnati, Warner's old fried John McGraw, manager of the New York Giants, called and doubled the highest offer. Being a lawyer, Warner was able to draw up a contract and he did – a very good one at that. The Giants were to pay Thorpe $6,000 a year for five years. That was more money than many people earned in their lifetimes, even professional players.

Shortly after the beginning of spring training, criticisms of Thorpe's baseball abilities started to surface. From Washington, DC came, "Jim Thorpe, the Indian, who was recently declared a professional by the A. A. U., is an inferior ball player, and if the New York Giants have signed him at a fancy salary somebody has been badly stung, in the opinion of five Washington boys who played in the Eastern Carolina League in 1909 and batted against Thorpe. They all state that the Indian was only a fair minor league pitcher, a poor hitter and a worse fielder, and that his only asset was speed on the bases, which availed him little, as he seldom got on the bags." Apparently John McGraw agreed with them.

On March 28, a report came out of New York that indicated Thorpe wasn't going to make the team:

> "Jim Thorpe will be released by the Giants after the first trip west has been finished, according to a private tip that comes indirectly from Manager McGraw. Thorpe, it is said, is a failure as a ball player and McGraw has not the time to develop him this season. The Indian signed a regular National League contract, in which the usual ten-day notice of release is included. His salary is said to have been set at $6,000 for the season, or $1,000 a month, beginning on April 10, 1913.

However, when the season started, Big Jim was in the Giants' dugout and McGraw was singing his praises. Could the critics have been wrong? A later article clears up the mystery:

> "He put his signature to a contract that couldn't be broken with one of the kaiser's forty-two centimeter guns. The parchment called for five years of service at a big salary, with the ten-day clause deleted, as the censors say. Under the terms of the parchment Thorpe can't be farmed out or even slapped on the wrist for violating any of McGraw's rules. The only power reserved by the Giants is to pay him his salary; otherwise they haven't a word to say.
>
> ...
>
> "The little Napoleon strove hard to pass this red elephant to another manager, including Pat Moran, but hasn't been able. Everybody is wise to the contract."

Warner apparently took care of Thorpe by leaving some standard clauses out of his contract. Jim would remain with the Giants. Not only would he stay in the big leagues through the season but, because the Giants finished in first place, he was with the team at the World Series. (Prior to expansion in the 1960s, the World Series was played between the winners of the National and American Leagues, each of which had eight teams, as God intended.) While sitting in the dugout, watching his teammates flail at fellow Carlisle alum Albert "Chief" Bender's pitches along the way to a 4 game to 1 game loss to the Philadelphia Athletics, Jim had plenty of time to plan his upcoming wedding. Tight planning was needed because the Giants and the White Sox were starting an around-the-world exhibition tour right after the World Series.

Margaret Iva Miller was the orphaned sister of Carlisle instructor Grace Miller. Being only 1/16th Cherokee, Iva did not qualify for admission to Carlisle, so her sister, knowing the requirements, filled out the enrollment forms in such a way as to make it appear that Iva was at least ¼ blood, and thus allowed to enter the government Indian school. Iva, Jim and Gus Welch were classmates. Thought by many to be the prettiest girl in school, she attracted the attentions of both of the young warriors. Iva picked Jim in spite of, or perhaps because of, disapproval by relatives and faculty members. Even Pop Warner counseled Ivy, as her friends called her, against the marriage but she was very strong-willed.

One of the things Jim did while watching the Giants get eliminated from the World Series was to negotiate the sale of movie rights for his wedding. To show how far ahead of the time that Hollywood types would sell the film rights to their wedding festivities, consider that a feature film had yet to be shot in Tinseltown. The World Series in which his team, the Giants, played was filmed that year. Perhaps he and the movie moguls (they were still in Fort Lee, New Jersey) thought Thorpe's marriage would make a perfect segue between the coverage of the World Series and the world tour. It might also attract more female patrons. The wedding, held at St. Patrick's in Carlisle, was quite an extravaganza with uncounted bridesmaids and other assorted attendants. Jim had plenty of money to spend on the wedding because a player's share on the losing team in that year's World Series was $2,361.16. Moses Friedman, the Jewish superintendent of the Indian School, gave away the bride at the high mass officiated by Father Mark Stock in what is called today the Shrine Church. After a reception at the superintendent's house attended by 200 of their closest friends, the couple dashed off to New York to join the Giants on their globe-trotting tour. Six to eight newlywed couples were on the tour. It wasn't possible to determine the exact number because some of the ballplayers were having difficulty convincing their brides to be to tie the knot on such short notice.

Whether John McGraw added players to his roster for the tour to rest injured ones or to take a look at some others is unclear. But the result was that he gave Jim much more playing time than he had during the season. McGraw being no fool, may have played Thorpe to increase the box office. Jim responded with some powerful hitting. The team worked its way west across the U. S. playing 35 games in 31 cities before setting sail from Seattle on November 19. They stopped to play games in Vancouver, British Columbia, baseball-mad Tokyo, Shanghai, indifferent Hong Kong, Manila, Brisbane, Sydney, Melbourne, Ceylon, Cairo, Rome, Monte-Carlo, Paris and London before returning home on the *Lusitania*. Jim and Iva Thorpe were the biggest celebrities in foreign countries with their photos often appearing on front pages of newspapers. She was as sought after as he was.

The tour ended in time for spring training - a little late actually, but these guys had played all winter. Jim didn't spend the season with the big league club as he was sent down to the minors to play in Toronto in April. 1915 wasn't much better baseball-wise but his first son, James Jr., was born that year.

That fall Jim took a job as assistant coach of the Indiana University football team. He, Iva and Jim Jr. arrived in Bloomington in October, after the end of baseball season. The *Indiana Daily Student* (*IDS*) gave their newly-arrived celebrities much coverage, but not all of the usual type. "The Fair Sex Forum," edited by Betty Carothers, '17, interviewed Iva whose responses probably weren't what the reporter expected: "It's just too bad I can't tell you more about Indians, as they draw pictures of them in books, with all the wildness there. I can't understand, you know, how some of my Indian friends can go back to the Indian reservation and wrap themselves in the same old blanket, and never make any use of the education they received at school. I have asked some of them how in the world they do it, and they tell me there is the only place their friends and relatives are and that they would be ostracized if they didn't." As the reporter started to leave, Iva said, "My! You are fortunate here in Indiana, to have gentlemen call on you so much – how many times a week is it? Four! Why, at Carlisle, Mr. Thorpe got to see me but once a week!"

That fall Jim changed history - again. Up to this time, professional football had been a marginal enterprise at best. Clubs were frequently insolvent and players had to have day jobs to survive. Jack Cusack, manager of the Canton, Ohio Bulldogs, heard that arch-rival

Massillon was loading up on former All-Americans for their upcoming games and felt that he needed to strengthen his team. So, he dispatched Thorpe's former teammate at Carlisle and Canton stalwart, William Gardner, to Bloomington to recruit Thorpe. Cusack, a pioneer of professional football, directed Gardner to offer Thorpe $250 per game to play for the Bulldogs – not just for a single game, but for every game. This was unheard of. Star players were sometimes paid large amounts to play as ringers in key games, but no one had ever been paid this much to play all the time. The best players were only getting $100 a game and the rest a lot less than that. Some thought Jack was going to bankrupt the team. Thorpe, no fool, accepted the offer.

Jim Thorpe's first known game as a professional football player was played on the second Sunday of November in Massillon. However, he didn't do much playing as Canton's then coach, Harry Hazlett, for reasons of his own, kept Thorpe on the bench for much of the game; when Jim got on the field, quarterback Don Hamilton seldom called his number. Canton lost the game, but Jack Cusack turned a tidy profit because 6,000 people paid to see the game. Hazlett was fired, Hamilton quit, and Thorpe was named captain. Also, a few more stars were signed. After all, Canton needed quality players to compete with the likes of Notre Dame and Massillon stars, Rockne and Dorais.

Cusack left the schedule for Thanksgiving week open to allow his players to rest and recuperate before the rematch with Massillon to be played in Canton on the fourth Sunday of November. This gave Thorpe the opportunity to pick up a $250 pay check from the Pine Village Indians. Pine Village, Indiana, a town of 300 people referred to by one

resident as "a half-horse town," was the home of an independent football team that hadn't lost a game to another town or college team in a decade. However, they did not play teams of the caliber of Canton and Massillon. Pine Village arranged a big Thanksgiving Day game to be played in Lafayette against a team of college stars and needed some help. Big Jim, conveniently located in Bloomington, was the right man for the job.

Assistant Coach Thorpe,
Indiana Daily Student.

To prepare for the contest, Jim scrimmaged against the Indiana University starting eleven. That's right: Thorpe, by himself, took on the entire starting line-up. But they played according to special rules he developed especially for the contest: the ball was kicked off from the 40-yard line and, if a player caught it, he could run five steps unmolested and punt the ball as far as he could or attempt a field goal. The *IDS* reported the outcome of the scrimmage: "Despite the efforts of the big eleven to kick the ball to all sides of the field, Thorpe's legs were able to get him under the ball and thereby gain a run of five steps. Of course he could punt the ball easily twice as far as his opponents and when he crossed the 40-yard line, the hearts of the eleven began to falter, because he was

'Dead-eye Dick' on a drop-kick anywhere within this distance. Thorpe won several games even with the wind against him, and all the sting was taken out of the minds of the men opposing him whenever one of those high balls went sailing over the goal posts, by that laugh which could be heard from one end of the field to the other."

Big Jim didn't collect splinters on Pine Village's bench; he was the star of the game and helped preserve the Indians' 108 game winning streak. His 81-yard punt wowed fans and sportswriters alike. He also played in the second Canton-Massillon game at which 8,000 fans turned out to see the big Indian in action. The game was a defensive struggle in which few first downs were made by either team. In spite of this, Jim had drop-kicked a field goal from the 18-yard line and place kicked another from the 45 to give his team a 6-0 lead into the fourth quarter. Jack Cusack recalled, "At this juncture I saw that something was wrong with [Earl] Abel, our new tackle. Our opponents were making far too much yardage through his position, and when Captain Thorpe made no move to replace him I took it upon myself to do so – in keeping with an agreement I had with Thorpe that it would be my right to substitute from the bench if I felt it necessary. (I might mention, too, that Jim was sometimes hesitant to substitute, especially as to replacing a player with All-American qualifications.) I found that Abel was ill with a heavy cold, and I replaced him with Charlie Smith, the Negro from the Michigan Aggies."

Canton eventually won the game and claimed the championship after a strongly disputed ending. As time ran out, a Massillon player, Maury "Windy" Briggs, caught a Gus Dorais pass at the two-yard line in the midst of a crowd of spectators who had flowed onto the field, but the ball bounded out of the crowd and Charlie Smith pounced on it to preserve the victory. Briggs was livid, stating that a policeman had knocked the ball out of his hands. However, it was common knowledge that Canton had no police force at that time and Canton prevailed. A decade later the man in the blue uniform with brass buttons, a streetcar conductor, acknowledged that he had done the deed because he had bet heavily on the game. Thorpe's appearance in a Canton uniform lifted professional football to a higher level, one of economic viability. Had Jim not played pro football, the game may have languished until Red Grange's arrival in 1925.

Thorpe and Canton were a perfect match and Jim was soon joined by some old friends. But before he could put on the moleskins again, Jim had another baseball season in front of him – after some time off for hunting, of course. After spring training, John McGraw sent him down to Milwaukee of the American Association to spend the 1916 season honing his skills. Jim definitely improved by leading the league in steals and hitting the longest ball hit in the Louisville Colonels' park to that time. In the fall, he was back in the majors again to play football, but he did take a little time off to help Pop Warner prepare his Pitt team for a big game with Syracuse.

The 1916 Canton Bulldogs were very likely the best pro team assembled to that time. Jim's old buddies Pete Calac, William Gardner, William Garlow and Gus Welch on the Canton roster were part of the reason the Bulldogs had an undefeated season. Some sports writers considered Jim to be playing the best football of his life at that time. He must have thought so, too when he said, "I am better than I ever was. A few more years hasn't hurt me in the least. Of course I have taken care of myself." Others might disagree with his last statement because of his reputation for drinking and carousing. Canton management might agree with Jim because 10,000 people bought tickets for each of the Canton-Massillon games.

In the 1917 baseball season, McGraw loaned Thorpe to Cincinnati after he played in 26 games. At Cincinnati, he played in 77 games, more big league games than he had played in the National League in 1913-15 combined. He also had 251 at bats, more than twice as many in those years combined. Pop Warner believed that Jim Thorpe would have had a much better baseball career had he been sent directly to the minors for some proper coaching prior to playing in the majors. Also, he and McGraw had a personality clash, and Little Napolean either didn't know how to deal with Thorpe or wouldn't allow himself to get Thorpe the coaching he needed. Perhaps he never got past Pop Warner putting one over on him with the missing clauses in Jim's contract.

Tragedy struck Thorpe again that year. James Jr. contracted infantile paralysis and died. Jim took it very hard and John McGraw showed him no sympathy. Joe Guyon remembered it well many years later: "Jim took some tough blows in his lifetime. Like the time they took away his Olympic medals because they found he had played some professional baseball. Oh, gosh, he took that hard. He said, 'Well, they can have the damn things but they can't take back the honor.' And then he lost his boy, just a youngster, and that really knocked him down."

At least 1917 was good football-wise for Thorpe and the Bulldogs as they went 9-1 again. Joe Guyon joined Jim and Pete Calac on the Bulldogs. The three would play together for many years more. The U. S. had entered WWI earlier that year, and teams were quickly becoming depleted of quality players. Jim played baseball for the Giants in 1918, riding the bench mostly, even though McGraw had many players go to war. Pro football was suspended for the duration and armistice came too late to get a season started that year. Jack Cusack left Canton and took a job in the oil fields of Oklahoma, leaving the management of the Bulldogs in the capable hands of Ralph Hay, a local automobile dealer.

Jim played his last, and best, year of major league baseball in 1919 when, in August, after having had but three at bats in two games for the Giants that season, he was sold to the Boston Braves. He hit .327 in his 60 games with the Braves. Not bad at all and he must have hit a few curve balls to accomplish that. Throughout his baseball career, he had the rap of not being able to hit a curve, but it appears that he had overcome that obstacle. All he did in the fall was to lead the Bulldogs to yet another football championship.

1920 marked Thorpe's permanent demotion into minor league baseball, where he stayed the rest of his career. However, he got a major promotion in football. In August, owners and managers of a few professional football teams met in Ralph Hay's Hupmobile dealership and, while seated on running boards and sipping beers, formed the American Professional Football Association (APFA) and named Jim Thorpe as the league's president. Thorpe was not picked because of his administrative skills, of which there were few, but because his name gave the league stature. Also, he was allowed to continue playing on one of the league's teams. After a so-so year with Canton, Jim's attention strayed.

He signed with the Cleveland Indians Football Team which was unfortunately owned by a large mercantile firm. During the season, Jack Cusack returned to Ohio to recuperate from malaria that he had contracted while building a refinery in Arkansas. Jim asked Jack to look after his interests because his contract included both a guaranteed amount per game plus a percentage of the gate. Jim was concerned that he was not receiving what was due him under the contract. After the last regular season game, the team's management got the players to play a game in New York for free but agreed to cover their travel expenses from the guarantee to be paid to the team. While in New York, the team's management reneged on the travel expenses. After enlisting the police and some burly football players, Cusack convinced Cleveland's management that it was not in their best interest to skip town without paying the players what had been agreed upon. Jack then took over the team and scheduled two more games. He and the players divvied up the proceeds from these games and the team disbanded, ending his involvement with professional football. Jack had much to say about his experience with Jim:

> "Many of the stories written about the great Jim Thorpe were pure fabrication. One such tale that went the rounds was that Jim's shoulder pads were made of sheet metal or cast iron. Maybe they felt like that to the men the big Indian tackled or knocked aside on his terrific plunges through the line, but the only metal involved was just enough interior ribbing to hold the layers of felt padding in place.
>
> "I had those pads made at Jim's suggestion. They were constructed of hard sole leather, riveted together, and their legality was never questioned while Thorpe played for me. The Indian and I planned to put them on the market and advertise them as 'The Jim Thorpe Shoulder Pad,' but the manufacturer we approached feared they might be classed as illegal, and we abandoned the project.
>
> "Another story current in those days was that Thorpe bet $2,200 on one of our games with Massillon. This was pure fiction, because to my certain knowledge Jim never carried more than $200 during an entire season. At his own request, I kept all of his earnings until the end of the season and then gave him a check for the full amount, which he banked when he went back to Oklahoma. There was not one iota of truth, either, in that preposterous story that Thorpe made a standing offer to pay $1,000 to any team that could keep him from gaining 10 yards in four downs. He simply wasn't the type to do a foolish thing like that."

Jim and his friend Walt Lingo hit on an idea: they would buy an NFL (the league name had already changed) franchise (heck, they only cost $100) and field an all-Indian team to promote Lingo's Oorang Airedales. He coached and played on the Oorang Indians for two years: 1922 and 1923. More about this team can be found in the chapter on all-Indian teams. Thorpe played for a few other NFL teams until he retired in 1928 when he was at least 40 years old.

Shortly before his tragic death in 1931, Knute Rockne, in his "Rockne Recalls" syndicated newspaper column, recalled,

> "In review of my playing career, one hard day stands out above all others – the day I tried to stop the greatest football player of all, the Indian Jim Thorpe.
>
> "My job was to tackle Thorpe, which I did. successfully and with much suffering, three times. After the third time Thorpe smiled genially at me.
>
> "'Be good boy,' he said. 'Let Jim run.'
>
> "He took the ball again and I went at him. Never before have I received such a shock. It was as if a locomotive had hit me and been followed by a ten-ton truck rambling ever the remains. I lay on the field of battle while Thorpe pounded out a forty-yard run for a touchdown.
>
> "He came back, helped me to my feet, patted me fraternally on the back and, smiling broadly, said:
>
> "'That's a good boy, Knute. You let Jim run.'"

That story was borrowed by a number of after-dinner speakers who replaced Rockne with themselves. They apparently considered it an honor to be run over by Jim Thorpe.

In a 1932 interview by *The Saturday Evening Post*, Red Grange reminisced: "I played against Thorpe only once – in a pro game in Florida in 1926. By then, Jim was old, fat and slow, yet he could still hit hard. He smacked me once and I still remember it!"

When Myron Cope interviewed Joe Guyon, he responded, "You've asked me, is it true that Jim Thorpe drank too much? Well, he participated pretty much after he got back from the Olympic games and everybody wanted to entertain him. But I can't tell you a lot about Jim's drinking because we didn't enjoy the same things. I never touched the stuff. Nightclubs didn't appeal to me. But I'll say this – if it was a big game coming up, Jim knew he had to take care of himself. Pop Warner put the theory of conditioning into him, and he knew the importance of it. But if it wasn't a big game coming up, then, yes, he'd go out and fill up."

After his playing career was over, he worked at a variety of jobs that included movie work, lecturing and physical labor. He even served in the Merchant Marines in WWII. He had children, divorces and remarriages but managed to weather them all. In 1949, Warner Brothers decided to produce his biopic, "Jim Thorpe – All-American." Although he no longer owned the rights to his life story, having sold them some time earlier, he was hired as a technical advisor for the film. The film, starring Burt Lancaster, was released in August 1951 and had two premieres: one in Oklahoma City, the other in Carlisle.

On March 28, 1953, Jim, then about 65, suffered his third heart attack, a massive one, and died in Lomita, California where he was living at the time. The good-hearted, easy-going Indian was gone but not forgotten.

For decades people attempted unsuccessfully to have his Olympic medals restored. Many blamed Avery Brundage, then head of the American Olympic Committee, who had finished well behind Thorpe in both the pentathlon and decathlon at Stockholm. In 1982, largely through the efforts of Florence Ridlon and her husband, Thorpe biographer Robert W. Wheeler, the International Olympic Committee reinstated Thorpe's medals and records.

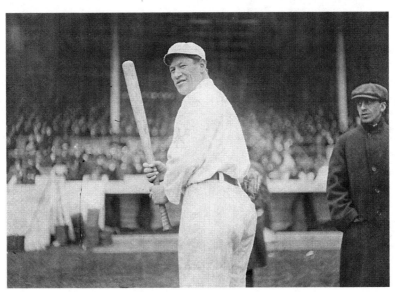

Jim Thorpe with Giants, 1913; *Library of Congress*

16 Charles and Joseph Guyon

Charles Mayo Guyon; *Memories of a Forty-Niner by Charles Hart*

Joe Guyon; *Cumberland County Historical Society, Carlisle, PA*

Name: Charles Mayo Guyon **Nickname:** Wahoo
DOB: **Height:**
Weight: **Age:**
Tribe: Chippewa **Home:** White Earth Reservation, MN
Parents: Joseph N. Guyon, white from French-speaking Canada; Mary Guyon, Chippewa
Early Schooling: Haskell Institute
Later Schooling:
Honors:

Name: Joseph Napoleon Guyon **Nickname:** Indian Joe
DOB: 7/26/1892 **Height:** 5'10"
Weight: 198 **Age:** 19
Tribe: Chippewa **Home:** White Earth Reservation, MN
Parents: Joseph N. Guyon, white from French-speaking Canada; Mary Guyon, Chippewa
Early Schooling: Haskell Institute
Later Schooling: Keewatin Academy; Georgia Tech
Honors: Professional Football Hall of Fame, 1966;
College Football Hall of Fame, 1971;
American Indian Athletic Hall of Fame, 1971;
Kentucky Athletic Hall of Fame, 1986

Wahoo and *O-gee-Chideah*

Charles Mayo Guyon often told how, at age 15, he ran away from home and joined Teddy Roosevelt's Rough Riders and fought in the Spanish-American War. The veracity of that claim has not been verified. He became intimately familiar with Carlisle at the St. Louis World's Fair in 1904 when he played left end for Haskell Institute in the game played the Saturday after Thanksgiving. Squaring off with Ed Rogers gave him first hand experience with the superiority of the eastern team. When his enrollment period at Haskell was up, Wahoo, as he called himself, headed east. Wahoo wasn't his Chippewa name; May-Mae-ta-gosche was the shortest form of his real name, and whites had difficulty pronouncing it. When a reporter asked Guyon his name at a team practice in Wahoo, Nebraska, he just gave them the name of the town he happened to be in at the time. The next September, 1905, he enrolled at Carlisle. Being 20 years of age, Charles didn't need permission from his parents; he probably negotiated with Carlisle officials a bit because his agreed-upon enrollment period was unusually short, just two years. Possibly it was short because Guyon was to attend the Commercial College in Carlisle.

Football practice was already underway when he arrived, so he didn't start in the early-season games. By the time Harvard rolled around, Wahoo was the starting left end, the position he held down the rest of the season. He received his letter at the annual football banquet and went home on leave in mid-January 1906, possibly for health reasons. When Guyon returned in late January, Dr. Shoemaker examined him and certified him to be physically sound. Physical examinations normally happened shortly after a student's initial arrival at the school; because Charlie didn't have one at that time something unusual must have happened.

Charlie was a natural with the media because he started being quoted nationally in the spring of 1906:

> "Wahoo, the Chippewa catcher of the Carlisle Indians, said the other day of form
> 'Form in athletics, as in everything else, counts for much. Form helps to do his stunts more easily. It also bluffs his opponents, making them think him better than he actually is.
> 'Yes, form in many ways gets us through at half the labor and. At half the cost.
> 'There was a man who dined regularly at a certain restaurant. He paid so much per week. One night at dinner he called the waiter over and said, frowning: 'Your portions are very small again this evening. As an old customer I generally have two pieces of beef, but tonight you have only brought me one.'
> 'By gum, sir you're right' exclaimed the waiter. 'The cook must have forgotten to cut it in two.'"

Wahoo left Carlisle in mid-May to play baseball in Washington, Pennsylvania. In June *The Evening Times* of Cumberland, Maryland reported on a game between Washington, Pennsylvania and the local team, "Charles Wahoo, the Indian catcher for Washington, would make a good model for an artist, but we do not want to look at 'faces.' so 'Big Chief' can cut it out." Apparently Guyon had been hamming it up. In September, after baseball season was over, he was discharged from the school because he was self-supporting.

In June of 1908 *The Charleroi* [Pennsylvania] *Mail* ran the article, "Catcher Wahoo Weds:"

"A dispatch from Canton, Ohio, announces the marriage at that city of Mrs. Ethel Rankin, of New York, and Catcher Charles Guyon, better known as Wahoo, playing with the Canton team in the 0. and P. league, who formerly caught for Washington in the P. O. M. league. The wedding occurred Tuesday evening. Both are very well known. Mrs. Guyon has made her home in Washington for several months, being employed as head milliner with the A. B. Caldwell company establishment."

Wahoo had a family immediately because he was the step-father of 5-year-old Valerie Rankin, Ethel's child from her first marriage. In July, Charles was released by Canton but was soon signed by another team. He was apparently able to support his growing family by playing minor league baseball.

On New Year's Day 1910 in New York City, Wahoo worked the big U. S. Navy North Atlantic Fleet championship game between the *USS Nebraska* and the *Missouri* as head linesman. This was convenient because the census taken in April listed him as living in Brooklyn and working as a sporting goods manager for A. G. Spalding & Brothers, the company that distributed the free tickets necessary for admission to the game. Officiating the game may have just been part of his job. Later it was reported that he had started with that company in 1908, in the off-season most likely. The census also listed his father, now divorced from his mother, as a member of the household. In September he wrote to renew his subscription to *The Arrow* from Atlanta:

"I have recently been transferred here from New York to take charge of the school and college trade of the South. The firm I am now working for has done well by me and have advanced me every opportunity, and I appreciate this change as it brings me in touch with the best class of people and I hope to do well by them in return. Give the boys my best wishes and the hope that they may win a championship this year."

The next month *The Arrow* ran an article about him: "Chas. Wahoo in Georgia: Charles M. Wahoo, a Chippewa Indian, former Carlisle student, and one of the greatest all-around athletes, in a talk before the boys of the Technical High School of Atlanta, Georgia, expressed his firm conviction that while athletics was a matter of great importance in school life, it should only be carried on with the understanding that it was only supplementing the work of the teachers in rounding out a boy's character. Wahoo is a good example of this theory, his educational attainments enabling him to hold a responsible position with a large business concern there."

In June 1911, Charles wrote Superintendent Friedman from a new location in Atlanta in response to his questionnaire:

"Manager of the College Dept – in A G Spalding & Bros – Covering six states.

"Had a beautiful Bungalow home at a fine residential section here, and Real estate being good – I sold it, to buy elsewhere. I still possess my land in Minn., and here I shall again hold property.

"Played professional ball and made coaching a specialty in all-round sports.

"Have had great success since leaving Carlisle. After playing professional baseball successfully for five years, I gave that up to enter a business career. Hence, with A G Spalding & Bros, since with the firm I have made a rapid stride, - advanced at every opportunity because of my good work. I am well tho't of – not only by the firm I represent, but the general public as well.

"My being an Indian and best of all, a Carlisle graduate, has given me the greatest prestige. I owe my success to the training I have received in the two schools I have attended, and to make it short – I am working for something higher – to the highest goal."

He closed the cover letter as follows:

> "I wish to extend you thanks for placing me upon the honor roll, and with news from the various ex-students of Carlisle I know it is going to be the most interesting piece of work ever gotten out.
> "I am anxious to receive the catalog.
>
> Yours truly,
> C. M. Wahoo

Wahoo's brother, Joseph Napoleon Guyon, arrived at Carlisle later that year, on December 7, 1911, at age 19. His medical examination was unusual. The physician found him "splendidly developed" at 5'10" tall and weighing 198 pounds with the "best heart I ever examined." His father had rheumatism, his mother was in good health, one of his two brothers had died of unknown causes and all four sisters were in good health. Joe's enrollment was for the usual five-year term. Prior to coming to Carlisle, he first attended school at White Earth Reservation, then Haskell Institute from 1904 to 1907, completing the 5th grade. Considering that Joe entered Carlisle still in 5th grade, he must not have furthered his education the intervening four years while living with his mother at White Earth.

Joe arrived after the close of football season and found studies and an outing awaiting him. In the months prior to going to the country, he joined the Invincible Debating Society, participated in the inter-class track meets and gained attention for his play on the lacrosse team. His first outing was in July 1912 to work for Mrs. Ella McCullough on her farm near Newville, Pennsylvania. He was paid $1.25 per day to work with the three McCullough boys and two other Indians. After visiting the McCullough farm, the Outing Agent wrote, "Joseph just went out as a farm hand and is doing excellently. He wishes to return to Carlisle in September." He probably wanted to return to be able to play football because boys on outing couldn't attend daily practices or attend most games.

Years later Joe described his early days at Carlisle:

> "In 1912, when I was about nineteen, I enrolled at the Carlisle Indian School, and that's where I first met Jim Thorpe. That was the year Jim went to Stockholm and won the pentathlon and decathlon in the Olympics. He was a Sac and Fox from Oklahoma, and I guess he was five years older than me, about twenty-four or twenty-five, and of course, he already was an All-American football star at Carlisle. I got to wrestling the boys there at the school, and Jim wanted to see who in the hell that damn Chippewa was that had come off the reservation and was flipping all these guys. So we wrestled. I couldn't throw him because he was quick and fast himself. We wrestled to a standoff and we became buddies right away. I was the best man at his wedding, and my first marriage was to a cousin of Jim's in Oklahoma."

That September found Joe Guyon putting his speed and strength to work as starting left tackle. Several starters from the powerhouse 1911 team had departed or were no longer playing on the team, making room for a few new players. It was highly unusual for a boy to make the varsity in his first year at the school, let alone start, but Joe was no ordinary athlete. Even more unusual is that the New York *Herald* and New York *Item* picked him for their All American teams. This was unknown for a first-year player. The *New York Evening Sun* columnist wrote:

> "In the tackle position there were two men who were unusually prominent, according to our point of view, and these men were Storer of Harvard and Guyon of

Carlisle. Both men were at the top of their form in the big games, and both had more range than any other tackles. Guyon, the Indian, easily outplayed the West Point star, Devore, and throughout the season has been a shade better than all the other men he has met. The Indian tackle also ran well with the ball from his position, and showed up as an all-round tackle that could not be matched in the colleges."

Walter Camp ignored Guyon and put Devore on his third team.

In the off-season, Joe visited his farm family and became quite active in the Invincible Debating Society. He also served as groomsman in a couple of weddings, including Jim Thorpe's. His brother, Charlie Wahoo, was also a busy fellow.

In February 1913, rumors about Wahoo taking a coaching position ran rampant. *The Constitution* attempted to quell the rumor:

> "The report spread over Atlanta yesterday that Alex Cunningham had resigned as coach of the Georgia team and. that Charlie Wahoo had been selected to take his place was denied late last night....
>
> "It is stated in Athens that in all probability the report was the result of the action of the directors some time ago in deciding to sign up Wahoo to act as assistant coach and to take charge of the business details of the teams. If asked to do this, however, it is understood that he would not take charge at Georgia until next fall.
>
> "A committee from Athens representing the University of Georgia, will come to Atlanta this afternoon to talk over the proposition with Mr. Guyon, and it seems certain that he will be tendered the place.
>
> "Wahoo says that he does not know just where the story came from, and he was sorry that it leaked out before the deal had been consummated.
>
> "'I have been, approached by the University of Georgia and I presume that a committee will call on me Wednesday to definitely close the deal,' said Guyon."

Articles speculating about Wahoo's status continued until February 21, when his signing of a one-year contract as an assistant coach and business manager was made public. He started his new job on March 1. Near the end of March, there was a rumor that Wahoo was wanted as a player for the LaGrange baseball team. But on March 31 he received a release from the university to manage the Waycross baseball team from April 17 through August 30. He was a player-manager because he caught and hit a homer in the 5-2 win over Thomasville on May 28. On June 16, Wahoo was replaced as manager of the 16-19 Waycross club.

On June 19 *The Constitution* reported:

> "Charlie Wahoo, who has been manager of the Waycross Empire League baseball team until recently, left Waycross tonight for New York, where he will make arrangements with a large sporting goods house for the establishment of an agency in the south. Wahoo has decided not to accept the offer of the position as umpire in the Empire and has turned down several other good offers in baseball."

On July 9, he asked the University of Georgia to release him from his contract to allow him to return to the athletic goods business. That fall Wahoo was back with A G Spalding & Bros. and often officiated football games.

With the departure of Thorpe and others, Coach Warner had three backfield positions to fill. He moved Joe Guyon from tackle to halfback, Thorpe's old position, with little difference in performance. After observing the game with Georgetown, the *Washington Star* compared him too the incomparable Thorpe:

"Guyon is a player of as much ability as has been seen on a field in this section in a long while. He is not far behind Thorpe, and it is probable that there would be slight difference in the value of the two men to the team if they could appear in the two half backs positions. Guyon played a better game than any man on Georgetown field yesterday. He is heavy, yet fast, and with it he can run in the open field or break his way through an opposing line with equal facility. His defensive play is all that could be desired, and is all the more capable because of his experience at tackle."

Some thought Carlisle could never replace a man with Thorpe's talent, but all Warner had to do was to look at his linemen. Joe also emerged as the team's best punter and occasional kicker. Even with all the personnel changes, the team racked up its third one-loss season in a row. Joe was mentioned by several publications for All America honors. This time Walter Camp couldn't ignore him and placed Guyon on his second team at halfback. His brother, Charles, traveled to Carlisle to visit with him and, no doubt, hobnob with Coach Warner and the rest of the team.

Joe filled his need for physical activity the rest of the school year by running track, and playing lacrosse and baseball. There were few sports he didn't play. Although articles in the press predicted great things for Guyon in the upcoming Olympics, nothing has been found to indicate that he even tried out. For his trade he studied carpentry and received notice for the millwork he made. At commencement, he received a certificate in carpentry. In June he was allowed to go home on leave even though he hadn't completed his 5-year term of enrollment. This was likely special treatment. It was this leave that triggered a major media controversy.

It all started on August 31, 1914, when Joe Guyon requested that Superintendent Oscar Lipps allow him to travel back to Carlisle at his own expense and later be reimbursed the amount Carlisle would have spent on a ticket for him to return directly from his home in Minnesota. Joe wanted to make a stop in Ashland, Wisconsin, on the way to Carlisle, something he couldn't do with a direct ticket. Joe discussed other things in his letter: "I suppose my brother Chas has written you in regard to my schooling so I guess I need not say any thing. I am busy right now repairing our home and what I've learned at Carlisle is helping me a lot."

Oscar Lipps responded quickly, indicating his pleasure that Guyon was returning

and approved his request. All Joe would have to do was to submit his receipts for tickets to be reimbursed. Neither Guyon or Lipps gave any hint as to what Wahoo wrote Lipps regarding Joe's future schooling. There were too many possibilities to speculate what he might have had in mind for his brother – and himself. But something happened that changed everything.

Joe either didn't make it to Ashland or went to Chicago after stopping there. In Chicago he met up with another former Carlisle football player named Peter Jordan. The two of them decided to attend Keewatin Academy in Prairie du Chien, Wisconsin. When Lipps got wind of that, he wrote Gus Beaulieu, an agitator at the White Earth Agency, requesting that he convince Guyon to reconsider his decision and return to Carlisle. Lipps tried to convince Beaulieu of his sincerity:

> "Of course, Joe has made quite a reputation here in athletics and the boys are very anxious to have him return. Aside from this, however, I am very much interested in Joe, perhaps largely for the reason that I knew him as a small boy. His first attendance at school was at White Earth while I was there about fourteen years ago. When I found him here I recognized him as one of my old pupils and naturally felt quite interested in him. He has made a splendid record here in every way, and I have felt that he had a great future ahead of him."

Beaulieu wasn't buying any of it and responded immediately,

> My dear Mr. Lipps:
>
> Last spring I arranged with Keewatin Academy to take Joe Guyon in that school so that he might obtain a higher education with which it consented to do. All arrangements were completed in Joe's behalf when Mr. Warner, coach of your school's foot ball team, commence[d] to take steps to get him back to Carlisle. Of course simply to have him on the team since he is considered one of the best athletes in the country.
>
> I do not know whether you are aware of this, and it is for this reason I write you to urge that in order to have one good foot ball player you should not permit Mr. Warner to destroy Joe's chances of obtaining a first class education, and, eventually, a professional one.
>
> You know as well as I do that at White Earth, while you were in charge of the school there, Joe was almost a regular boy tramp; he ate sometimes and sometimes he did not. I at first had some intention of bringing Joe here so that he could attend school, but I finally advised him to go to Carlisle. But now he has an opportunity of getting a higher education than he could hope to get at Carlisle, and for this reason I would ask you to help him get it.
>
> I am going to write the Commissioner of Indian Affairs today about this matter and this letter is to prepare you to think the matter over, and whether your school will be able to give the advantages Joe would receive at Keewatin.
>
> Yours truly,
> Gus H. Beaulieu

These letters and other information were made available to the press, which had a feeding frenzy. The press included the Pennsylvania News Association and the Associated Press as well as newspapers. Lipps accused Keewatin Academy of offering free tuition and other expenses as inducements to Guyon to attend Keewation. Both wire services demanded that the prep school respond to Lipps's accusation. Joe enrolled at the Keewatin Academy and played football for them that year. But his brother had something up his sleeve.

The September 14 issue of *The Carlisle Arrow* included a little piece about Wahoo:

"Mr. Charles M. Guyon, who played football at Carlisle in 1905 and was mentioned for all-American end for that year and who was also a famous baseball player, was a visitor at the school with Mr. St. Germaine on Thursday, June 11th. Mr. Guyon is now manager of a branch office in Atlanta, Ga., for the Spalding Sporting Goods Co. Mr. Guyon came up primarily to arrange a game for Carlisle at Atlanta, Ga."

The game Wahoo was setting up was the ill-fated Auburn game that played into the War Eagle legend.

The November 20 *Arrow* had a little news about Wahoo's younger brother:

"Joseph Guyon, a former Carlisle football star, and who is now attending the Keewatin Academy at Prairie du Chien, Wis., came to Chicago to see his former team mates and the game."

In December with Joe Guyon at halfback, Keewatin Academy claimed the Western Preparatory Championship. They annihilated not only high schools and prep schools but also St. Mary's College, Cornell College [of Iowa most likely] freshmen and the University of Southern Minnesota. The next month Carlisle received a card from Joe indicating that he'd "like to see the Alumni Association carry out their present plans." The card was sent from Keewatin's winter campus in St. Augustine, Florida, where, that winter, among other things they defeated a college all-star team from Jacksonville 41-0 even though outweighed by 20 pounds a man. Keewatin also played a team from Cuba. Keewatin got a head start on baseball season by spending the entire term in Florida. Joe, of course, played shortstop and batted cleanup.

Also in January 1915, Superintendent Lipps received a letter from Joe's older brother or, to be more specific, from Wahoo's attorney. Charles had paid Carlisle $3,000 as their guarantee for the Auburn game. Because ticket sales were low, Wahoo lost $2,897.75 and wanted Carlisle to make up at least half the loss. Lipps refused saying, "Carlisle had an 'off' year in football this last season and little, if any, more than expenses has been made. Final settlement of all accounts will probably show a small loss." One can only speculate as to what Wahoo's wife must have thought about this matter.

1915 wasn't a good year for him. In mid-June newspapers announced, "[Wahoo] has been selected to coach the Commercial high football squad of Brooklyn next fall. He has not yet signed a contract, but he has accepted terms and is expected to close the deal some time this week." He wrote Lipps to apply for the assistant football coach position at Carlisle for the upcoming season because, "War times have played havoc with the sporting goods end of it and in fact most every line of enterprise, as far as I have learned." Lipps responded, "I had you in mind while the matter was under consideration but in the conversation I had with you in Birmingham last fall you gave me to understand that a good offer had been made to you by a hotel man in Asheville. I did not wish to interfere by making you an additional offer and now Mr. Welch has finally been selected." Newspapers ran a piece saying that Wahoo was probably Carlisle's next coach.

He wrote Lipps again on September 9, again offering his services as a coach but this time with a twist. "I feel qualified to be of service to the team and perhaps too, my connection with the institution as coach, may influence brother Joe to return and help out wonderfully." Lipps painted a rosy picture for Carlisle's prospects that year and also that funds were tight, so he couldn't afford to hire Wahoo even if he wanted to. He went on to say that, had Joe returned to Carlisle, he would have been eligible for one of the jobs at Ford Motor Company that were paying $5 a day. It doesn't appear that Charles got the Brooklyn job either.

Joe enrolled at Keewatin again for the 1915-16 school year. A 13-7 upset by DePaul University on Thanksgiving Day in Chicago was Keewatin's first loss in four years. In the spring, the academy hired a former major league manager to coach their baseball team. This professional coaching may have helped Joe a good bit.

On September 29, 1916, K. G. Matheson, President of Georgia School of Technology (commonly called Georgia Tech), wrote Oscar Lipps regarding Joe Guyon's "eligibility to play football his first year." Immediately on receiving the letter, Lipps telegrammed:

> "Carlisle is not a college nor does it prepare for college. It is a vocational school giving academic work equivalent to ordinary high schools. For over twenty years our football team played only colleges and universities. In athletics Carlisle has had collegiate rank, but specific question raised by you has not been definitely settled so far as I know. Rogers played with university of Minnesota and Welch is this year playing with Dickinson. Both are former Captains [sic] Carlisle teams. Other Carlisle men have played on college teams after leaving us without serious protest."

Joe didn't play that year but not without a lot of posturing in the media on the part of the University of Georgia and Georgia Tech.

Professor S. V. Sanford, faculty director of athletics for the University of Georgia, wrote Professor H. W. Cox of the Southern Intercollegiate Athletic Association (SIAA) requesting a ruling on Guyon's eligibility. *The Atlanta Georgian* reported that Sanford:

> "… sent a copy of a letter from Charlie (Wahoo) Guyon, which he maintains is prima facie evidence which will prevent Joe Guyon's participation in any S. I. A. A. games and which will cause the blacklisting of Tech if the Indian is used in any of the Jacket battles. The letter is an application for a post as assistant coach at the University of Georgia, and was written several weeks before Charlie Guyon was named assistant coach at Tech. In this application Charlie makes the statement that his brother Joe, for two years an All-American halfback with the Carlisle Indian School, is willing to come to any Southern college where the elder Guyon is employed as a coach."

Sanford also said,

> "… Wahoo has been named assistant coach at Tech, and right on the heels of his appointment came the word that Guyon had registered as a student and had come out for football practice at the Atlanta institution. The inference is obvious. It seems peculiar to the Georgia people that Mr. [Head Coach John] Heisman should have so suddenly been converted to the cause of Wahoo. For several years he has refused to permit the Indian to act as an official in any of the Tech games. If he considered him incompetent as an official, it is strange that he should so suddenly find him competent to coach."

This Kabuchi resulted in Joe's not playing football for Georgia Tech that fall but didn't necessarily keep him off the gridiron. He got some playing time at West Virginia Wesleyan where his old Carlisle buddy, Pete Calac, was then enrolled.

In December 1916, after Georgia Tech's undefeated season ended, Charles Guyon wrote Carlisle, looking for a job yet again. "I have never been out of touch with the game since leaving Carlisle, and this year, and also last year, I had the pleasure of being one of the coaches at the Georgia School of Technology which won the undisputed championship of the Southern Inter-Collegiate Association for the past two seasons." This time he was informed that athletics were then playing a subordinate role at the Indian school and that, "… Mr. Warner has recommended a man for assistant to Mr. Clevitt during the football season, and in all probability the Athletic Committee will be inclined to follow Mr. Warner's recommendation." 1917 would be a very different story.

The U. S. entered the war in early 1917 and Joseph Napoleon Guyon, age 22, registered for the draft on May 25 at Georgia Tech. At that time he was a student but also requested deferments because he was both married and a farmer. His bride was apparently a cousin of Jim Thorpe whom he had surely met through his teammate. It is unclear how much, if any, involvement Joe had in the farming of his allotment in Minnesota.

To say that Georgia Tech was loaded with talent would be an understatement. Joe Guyon and his backfield mate, Everett Strupper, were considered to be the best pair of backs in the country. Strupper was placed on the Walter Camp consensus All America first team and Guyon on the second. Tech quarterback Albert Hill, third team All America, and Judy Harlan, freshman fullback, were arguably the best backfield in football that year and had few peers ever. The Golden Tornado rolled over its opponents, scoring 491 points and giving up but 17 in this 9-0-0 national championship season. Coach Heisman rated Joe one of the three or four greatest players of all time.

Joseph P. Byrd, III, a classmate of Joe Guyon at Georgia Tech, has fond memories. He described Guyon as "a wonderful fellow" who loved to tell stories and reminisce. In his younger days, he was "very wise, sharp and a good man." After leaving school, he visited Byrd at his home several times as Byrd thought the world of him. Byrd recalled that Guyon and Jim Thorpe were very close to each other.

Because WWI raged, most college players joined up, leaving football programs in shambles. Georgia Tech was no different as Guyon and Fincher were the only two starters to return. However, Guyon was commissioned as a second lieutenant but stayed at the S. A. T. C. at Tech where a number of other former college stars were assigned. They provided the missing pieces to make a good team. Tech fielded a more than competitive team, scoring 425 points while giving up none in its first five games. Pitt skunked them 21-0 but Joe played a good game, so good that the Pitt players dragged him back to their locker room afterwards. He was hitting them so hard they thought he had steel in his shoulder pads. Upon inspection, they saw that he was wearing the standard model. They weren't the only ones who were confused that day. Bum Day and Joe Guyon normally played as linebackers in Heisman's defensive scheme, but Day played in the line against Pitt leaving Joe as the only linebacker. Walter Camp was so impressed by the linebacker play that day that he named Bum Day to his All America first team, unaware that who he thought was Day was actually Guyon. That mistake wouldn't happen now that jerseys are numbered and often have players' names on them.

Tech bounced back against Auburn for a 6-1-0 season – successful but not undefeated. After the season was over, Warner stated that Pitt would not play Georgia Tech the next year if Guyon was in the lineup. Joe turned pro.

Young Atlanta attorney George Watkins got to watch "Indian Joe" in action when he officiated Georgia Tech games. Watkins was particularly impressed with the way Joe ran interference. "He blocked with his wrists, his elbows, his shoulders and his head. He resembled a windmill as he rolled down the field clearing a path for the ball carrier."

When asked about the differences between northern and southern football, Joe had an opinion. "I think they still play a little harder in the south. I've always thought it was the weather. You move a little faster when you're hot. Your reactions are quicker. You don't get hurt so easily when you're warm. We hit 'em hard at Carlisle. The order was to take 'em out and keep 'em out. That's how we blocked and tackled. They hit just as hard in the south – but they weren't so mad about it. In the north football's a serious business."

Ralph McGill, one-time sportswriter and later publisher of the Atlanta *Constitution* wrote, "There is really no argument about the identity of the greatest football player who ever performed in Dixie. There is a grand argument about second place, but for first place there is Joe Guyon, the Chippewa brave." One-time Georgia Tech line coach Bill Fincher observed that, "…tackling Guyon was like grabbing an airplane propeller." Joe was about to fly even higher.

In 1919, the Canton Bulldogs were the class of the pro game and Joe Guyon's old teammate, Jim Thorpe was their captain. He signed with the Bulldogs in August and played alongside former Carlisle teammate Pete Calac. The Bulldogs won the Ohio championship, but all the teams were in financial trouble. Although professional football paid the players well compared to most other occupations, it wasn't reliable work because the teams kept going broke. After the season was over, Joe headed for home.

It's not clear what the elder Guyon did during the war. Charles Wahoo Guyon, age 35, registered for the draft on September 12, 1918 in Washington DC, where he was the assistant manager for A G Spalding & Bros. operation on 14th Street NW. He may have enlisted in the Marine Corps and served as a sergeant, but that has not been confirmed.

The 1920 census taken in January found the Guyons living near or on the White Earth Reservation. Joe had quite a houseful at that time: his wife, Isabel, his son Joseph, daughter Geraldine, sisters-in-law Lola and Mary Bourboinase, and brother Charles, who had shed a wife and stepdaughter, was then single and unemployed. All lived under his roof, presumably on his farm. In February, Wahoo applied for a coaching job at Colorado University but didn't get it. In April he was hired as an umpire by the Virginia League. That summer, Eastern High School was in need of someone to teach physical education and coach its teams. The task of finding a person fell to Charles Hart, a business teacher who had been elevated to principal.

In his history of Eastern High School from 1896-1945, Hart, an alumnus as well as principal, told the story of Guyon's hiring:

> "I at once contacted my friend 'Cy' MacDonald, manager of A. G. Spalding's Washington Branch. He said that the only possibility he had in mind was an Indian named Guyon, who was associated with their Atlanta, Georgia, branch but who possibly would be glad to have an opportunity to establish a home in Washington. He made an appointment for me to meet Guyon in his office the following morning at ten o'clock. It was a never-to-be-forgotten interview…. He came to the conference smoking a big cigar and anticipating an interview similar to one he would have if he were about to sign up with a professional ball club. I briefly explained the possibilities of the position and said that it paid a salary of eighteen hundred dollars a year. He took a few quick puffs on his cigar and said, 'Did you say eighteen hundred dollars?' I nodded, and he said, 'Can't you make it two thousand?' I told him that if the poorest teacher in the world were given the position, he would receive eighteen hundred dollars and if the best teacher in the world were given the position, he would receive the same amount. The 'Chief' deliberated a few minutes and then said that he was obligated to help his family in Minnesota harvest the crops but that he would wire

me his decision within a few days. Evidently he found the farm work rather heavy, because three days later I received this telegram: 'Have decided to accept your terms. Stop. Wire transportation.' I immediately wired him that the position was still open if he decided he wanted it, but that he would have to pay his own traveling expenses. He wired back immediately that he would see me the following Monday. I did not realize at the time that his coming would usher in a new era in athletics for the Eastern High School…. The 'Chief' had a world of color and personality and at once captivated the interest and admiration of all Easternites and, indeed, of all interested in local high school athletics."

The next summer, 1921, when covering a game between Rome and Carrollton, *The* [Atlanta] *Constitution* reported, "Wahoo put up a good brand of umpiring which is unusual in this [the Georgia] league." Charles continued to work in the schools during the school year and umpire in the summer for several years. He also got frequent press for his antics.

A *Constitution* reporter who knew Wahoo well retold a story in 1921:

"For many years Charley was an institution in Atlanta. He had the best strutting form ever seen in a Peachtree parade and was highly efficient in both the Carlisle war whoop and the Ojibway college yell. Recently he has been fooling around Washington, D. C., where long coated and silk hatted gentlemen take liberties with the organic law of the nation and more recently closed an engagement with the Sally League as an umpire during which period he insists that he was called everything but 'Charlie.'

"He is in Atlanta primarily to visit his brother, Joe Guyon, a more or less well known member of Atlanta's baseball club. As usual Charlie comes in with a tale of woe, his particular narrative this time being to the effect that there is little reward for piety.

"According to his own unvarnished statement, Charlie after leaving the Sally, celebrated in due and ancient form last Saturday night at Spartanburg S. C. Waking up early Sunday morning, he felt in need of religious consolation.

"He sought out a church where the music would be inspiring and the sermon consolatory. He encountered a large and ornate edifice and the doors being closed, sat on the steps until the portals were thrown open in welcome.

"He had been seated for some few minutes when he was accosted by a gentleman wearing the blue and brass that represented the majesty of the Spartanburglan law. 'What are you doing here?' inquired the Spartanburgian law.

"'Waiting for church to open,' responded the Wahoopian piety.

"'The services are just beginning,' said the law. 'Come inside.'

"Mr. Wahoo acceded particularly as he was impelled thereto by the strong arm of the aforementioned law.

"'And do you know,' he said with emphasis, 'that all that churchly entrance was just the ornamentation of as strong a jail as I've ever been in, and before I got out I had put more in the collection box than I ever handed to an organized and orthodox church. After that I thought I'd better come to Atlanta.'"

About that time Joe had some legal problems of his own. A Benjamin R. Holton sued Guyon for $25,000 for alienation of affections of his wife, Gertrude Holton. The only thing Joe would tell the reporter was that he knew the woman. Mr. Holton claimed to have found a letter from Guyon to his wife that contained "startling revelations." He also claimed that she did not deny having been intimate with the ballplayer. He also alledged that she "mortgaged the furniture to get money to give to Guyon." Gertrude Holton sued her husband for divorce, alleging that he forced her to live a life of immorality because he refused to work. She was granted a restraining order.

Before the 1920 season, team owners organized the American Professional Football Association which later evolved into the National Football League (NFL). The Bulldogs were one of the charter teams and Joe Guyon, then 28, was a star. They had a winning team that year but didn't win the league championship. Joe was named to the All-Pro second team and kicked a 95-yard punt, establishing a record that held for fifty years. Thorpe, Calac and Guyon moved to the Cleveland Tigers, which were renamed Indians in their honor. Guyon starred as a runner, kicker, passer and, especially, blocker but Thorpe was injured early in the season. The team finished the season with a losing record. Guyon and Calac followed Jim Thorpe to the Oorang Indians for the 1922 season. Thorpe recruited many of the old Carlisle players to hang out with. The team played poorly but that wasn't the point. The point was to sell Airedales. The Oorang franchise folded after the 1923 season.

Thorpe and Guyon signed with the Rock Island Independents for the 1924 season. They finally parted ways late in the season when Joe moved over to the Kansas City Cowboys. He stayed with them for the 1925 season, too. He sat out the 1926 season but signed with the New York Giants in 1927. It was with the Giants that he would have a career highlight, a league championship made possible to a great extent by his fine play.

George Halas had a favorite story he liked to tell about Joe Guyon. One Sunday when the Bears were playing the Giants, Joe was ripping up the Bear defense for large gains and Papa Bear wasn't happy. So, he decided to do something about it. Seeing Guyon with his back turned toward him, Halas ran as fast as he could and threw himself toward the big Indian. Sensing something was coming, Guyon whirled raising a knee at just the right time to catch Halas in the chest. As the wounded Bear lay on the ground, the intended victim waved his finger at him and said, "George, let that be a lesson for you. Never try to sneak up on an Indian." The two broken ribs George sustained pained him as he was carried off but the 15-yard penalty for clipping pained him more.

In the summers, Joe played baseball in the high minor leagues all over the South. He played well enough to be one of the better players on whichever team he was on, but not quite good enough to make the jump to the majors. For several years he played for the Louisville Colonels and led them to championships. In the first half of the decade, he began coaching athletics at Union College (today's Union University) in Jackson, Tennessee. In October 1925, Louisville Colonels fans were unhappy that Joe couldn't make the trip to San Francisco with their team due to the start of the college football season. Before the 1928 baseball season, Irving "Speed" Wallace, world record holder for the 100-yard dash, claimed to have set the record for rounding the bases on a baseball diamond in 13 seconds. Joe claimed to have equaled that feat some five years prior. An injury sustained during the 1928 baseball season ended his careers in both baseball and football. So, he completed his shift to coaching and managing – more or less.

Joe related the details of the injury that ended his career:

> "I didn't go up to the big leagues because I got hurt. Kid let me run into a fence in Indianapolis when I was going like – oh, God, hitting around .400 my third year. Gee whiz. Yeh, a kid from the University of Kentucky did it. I call him a kid because he just came out of school. He thought he knew all about baseball. I played right field and he played center, so I told him, 'Now this is professional baseball. We play together. I'll take care of you, and you take care of me. I'll be over there to help you, and you help me.' But he let me run into a fence on a fly ball. I was always a high

stepper, you know, and goddarn it, I got stuck way up there on that old board fence. I had on new spikes, and I just embedded them into that wood and I got hung up there. Absolutely.

"Two boys come from the bench, gonna pull me off. Why, they couldn't move me! So two more come running out, and, oh, they pulled me out but they tore my knee, goddamn. That was just about the end of my athletics, baseball and pro football. I had been going like crazy. And *hit* a ball? Baseball is really my love."

With his career as a player cut short by that injury, Joe took a job as head baseball coach and assistant in football and basketball at Clemson University. However, newspaper articles stated that he lost the job before he started it when school officials learned he had played professionally. That issue was apparently resolved. In the summers he generally managed a minor league baseball team, sometimes as a player manager. In 1929, he took a team of Indians on a barnstorming tour around the country.

Wahoo continued his work at Eastern High School and umpiring baseball in his summers. Considerable praise came his way for turning around the Eastern Senior High School football program. He was soon considered one of the best high school football mentors in the area. In 1921 rumors that he was leaving the Ramblers circulated widely but he stayed put. Guyon cut a wide swath at Eastern, frequently providing the *Washington Post* with good material. He upgraded the football program by scheduling tougher opponents, including college freshman teams. While he improved the football program, it was in basketball and baseball that Wahoo had his greatest success. Where football championships were scarce for Eastern, basketball and baseball pennants were plentiful. Principal Hart recalled, "Since the 'Chief's' arrival, the school has won no less than thirty major championships and has placed second or third on many occasions."

Charlie continued his work at Eastern throughout the 1920s and 1930s. The 1930 census listed him as single, living with his father, Joseph N. Guyon, in Parklane Apartments in Washington, DC. Living in the nation's capital proved to be an advantage when it came to seeing old schoolmates who came to town on tribal business. A 1938 *Washington Post* photo shows Charlie getting together with Sam Bird and Stuart Hazlet at Gus Welch's home when Welch was coaching American University.

In May 1942, when he registered for the WWII draft at age 59, he was still working at Eastern High School in the Washington, DC school system but was then living in Prince George's County, Maryland, and married to Catherine L. Guyon. Dick Mentzer was hired to lead the football Ramblers in 1942. Alumnus Ward B. Crabill, '41, remembers "Chief Guyon" very well and even located a photo of "Old Charley Guyon" in *Punch and Judy*, Eastern's yearbook. Guyon continued to coach baseball.

Joe followed a path similar to his brother's, but generally he coached at colleges where his older brother coached high school and managed baseball teams in the summer while his brother umpired. In the 1930s, he even did some high school coaching at St. Xavier High School in Louisville, Kentucky, where he had settled his family and later at an Indian school in Arizona. During WWII, he coached in New Mexico.

Joe Guyon, Jr. played football at Catholic University in Washington, DC but graduated in time for WWII. He became the first Indian to become a Navy pilot and, after the war, became an M. D. He and his sister, Geraldine, who was a public health nurse, made their father very proud of them. They also produced 10 grandchildren, something that pleased him immensely. Joe Jr. led his Catholic University into the 1940 Sun Bowl for which he generated some good press when he packed his "tribal feathers" for the game:

"Only on rare occasions has 'Wahoo' Guyon danced the 'Dance of Victory' and then only when the game has been important enough. Joe says the Sun Bowl game calls for a special demonstration and if the Cardinals are fortunate enough to win on New Year's Day, the handsome Indian will strut his stuff with all the trimmings." It sounds like Joe Jr. had more of his uncle in him than just his nickname.

When WWII broke out, Joe was coaching in the Southwest. Too old to serve in the military, he moved to Oklahoma and worked at Tinker Air Force Base doing his part as an inspector in supply. When the war was over, he stayed in Oklahoma, having made his home in Harrah. He spent much of his free time teaching youngsters the finer points of baseball and football.

Charlie retired from teaching in July 1951 and moved to Harrah. He had spent the last 31 years at Eastern High School, first as a coach and physical education director and, at the end, was in charge of the school's infirmary and was teaching typing. In October his wife, Catherine, who was over 20 years his junior, filed for divorce on the grounds of desertion. Either she didn't want to move to Oklahoma or he left because he didn't want to remain married. His retirement was short-lived because, in February 1953, a car in which he was a passenger went over an embankment and landed in a stream near Tupa, Oklahoma. All four passengers were transported to a hospital in Tulsa. The other three in the car survived but Wahoo died. He was about 70 years of age.

In later life Joe was a pallbearer for his friend and long-time teammate, Jim Thorpe, but he didn't sit around waiting to die. At his induction at Canton in 1966, he lobbied for a coaching position, thinking he still had something to offer. But no one took him up on his offer. He requested that a former opponent, a West Point halfback by the name of Dwight David Eisenhower, give his induction speech, but the former President's physicians wouldn't allow him to do it. So, Dr. Joseph Napoleon Guyon, Jr. did the job.

Myron Cope interviewed Joe in his later years after he had suffered head injuries in an automobile accident. Indian Joe still had his wit:

> "I'll wager you can't guess my age. Take a guess. Try a double number. That's right, seventy-seven, but I'm the same damn weight as when I played ball. One-eighty-five. Indians are simply terrific, physically. The Indians who came off the reservations to play ball were agile and strong and quick. Wrestling is where they got their tricks. Even now, I can protect myself. You just run at me, and boy, I'll floor you. I mean *anybody*, see? I'll floor them before they can scat. They'll wonder what the hell hit 'em because I was drilled on the reservation."

Joe died in 1971, the day after his 79th birthday.

William Garlow

17

William Garlow, 1912; *Fred Wardecker*

William Garlow kicking a goal; *Cumberland County Historical Society, Carlisle, PA*

Name: William Garlow		**Nickname:** Spitball Artist	
DOB: 1/1/1888		**Height:** 5'7"	
Weight: 173		**Age:** 22	
Tribe: Onondaga		**Home:** Tuscarora Reservation near Lewiston, NY	

Parents: John Garlow, Onondaga; Martha Garlow, Onondaga

Early Schooling:

Later Schooling:

Honors:

Spitball Artist

The spitball has not always been illegal. However, as far back as the 1890s, rules forbade players from discoloring or "otherwise damaging" the ball. Whether the rule covered lubricating the ball with spit was a matter of opinion. Regardless, cutting or scuffing the ball with emery paper, a nail file or some other device was clearly illegal, but offenders were only fined $5 – when they were caught and prosecuted. The situation changed prior to the 1920 season when the spitball was banned by the major leagues. To put some teeth into the ban, penalties were stiffened. Offenders could be thrown out of the game and suspended for ten days, a lengthy period for hurlers of the day who pitched on much shorter rest than current day pitchers and who would miss several turns in the rotation. To ease the transition to spitfree pitching, teams were each allowed to grandfather in two pitchers who threw "shine balls." Seventeen identified spitballers, of whom Burleigh Grimes was the best known, were allowed to continue using the pitch for the rest of their careers. Minor leaguers were allowed to continue throwing spitters but could not throw them in the majors, should they make it. The Negro Leagues aren't believed to have ever outlawed the spitball. Long before William Garlow played a down for the Carlisle Indians, he was well known as an up-and-coming baseball player.

Bill was met by several familiar faces when he first arrived at Carlisle on September 19, 1905. His older brother, James, was already there and was in charge of the athletic training quarters. James also played outfield on the varsity baseball team and captained the lacrosse team one year. In addition to James were the Mount Pleasants, who were neighbors on the Tuscarora Reservation and cousins to the Garlows.

William's prior schooling is not known, but, based on his performance at Carlisle, there must have been more than an average amount. He started in Room 7 and proceeded right along, moving up room by room. His marks ranged from good to excellent with most being very good. His conduct was always excellent. Before he knew it, it was summer and time for baseball.

Well before they banned interscholastic baseball, Carlisle Indian School officials allowed Bill to go on leave for the summer and to play the sport, most likely for pay no less – and it is recorded on his official record to boot! But he did not leave before showing fellow students and staff his stuff. He pitched parts of the games against Franklin and Marshall College and George Washington University, both of which were victories for Carlisle. *The Washington Post* lamented, "George Washington's paleface baseball team was scalped 9 to 8 by the Carlisle School Indian braves yesterday at University Field." It also reported that Garlow pitched 3 innings, gave up 5 hits, walked one, struck out 6 and gave up 2 runs, including the tying run. White Crow relieved him in the bottom of the 9th, holding GWU scoreless after Carlisle scored the go-ahead run in the top of that inning. After a shaky spring, Bill honed his skills to a sharp edge while pitching for Sunbury that summer.

"Seybold," as his teammates called him, played baseball for Carlisle again the next spring, 1907, and continued to show improvement. In a game against Millersville Normal School, he struck out 17 batters, a personal best. After a spell in the hospital for an undisclosed ailment, Bill left on June 17 to play for the newly organized Hagerstown, Maryland Independent Team. Two days later according to *The Washington Post*, "Garlow, formerly of the Carlisle Indian School club ..." pitched the opening day shutout victory. Bill Newashe and Mike Balenti of Carlisle also played for Hagerstown, but only Newashe and Garlow lasted the entire season. All but two other players on the opening day roster were released during the season. Garlow and Newashe received considerable press that summer, both in *The Washington Post* and local papers of the teams they played. *The Daily News* of Frederick, Maryland hyped the upcoming game between the locals and Hagerstown for several days. Statements included: "Hagerstown's Indian pitcher is said to be a crackerjack, and an exciting contest is predicted by those who have arranged this game, and who expect it to be the star baseball event of the season in Frederick;" "The Hagerstown team will have an Indian for pitcher and an Indian for first baseman;" "See the great Indian battery of the Hagerstown team, when they play Frederick next Thursday at Athletic Park;" and "Barlow[sic], the great Indian pitcher, will pitch for Hagerstown on

Thursday, in the game with Frederick at Athletic Park. Barlow is a wonder." All three statements appeared at different places on the same page. Some of it was correct as Newashe did play first base and, although sometimes stationed in right field to keep his bat in the lineup, Garlow was the star pitcher. This hype was repeated several times before the game. Garlow lived up to his advance billing by pitching a 19-0 shutout. On the next to the last day of the season, Garlow pitched Hagerstown to a 4-3 victory over the Carlisle town team.

Oddly, official Carlisle records list Garlow's 1907 summer ball-playing stint as if it were a usual or positive thing for a student to do. Perhaps it wasn't too odd when one considers that *The Arrow* printed a piece by William Newashe in which he outlined Carlisle players' contributions to the Hagerstown team. Shortly after that, it printed a letter to Pop Warner from J. Frank Ridenour of the Hagerstown Athletic Association that included the following: "I feel that it would be remiss in me if I did not tell you that never in the history of baseball in Hagerstown were the three men connected with the team whose services were so uniformly satisfactory as were those three boys – Balenti, Garlow and Newashe- the past season. Not only did they do well their work as ball players, but their deportment both on and of the field, at home and away, was such as to make them respected and admired."

While waiting for baseball season to start at Carlisle, William was awarded his "C" at the Athletic Banquet in February that honored the athletes for their work in the previous calendar year. Right fielder J. W. T. wrote a piece of free-form verse titled "Our Base Ball Team of '07" in which he described each of the players. About Bill he wrote, "Garlow does the pitching and fans them out in style with every ball he pitches, always see a happy smile on 'Seybold.'"

William Garlow was no dumb jock. At the start of baseball season, he made the Final Merit Roll for Room 9. His brother, James led Room 8. Perhaps it was the blood the Garlow and Mt. Pleasant children shared that accounted for their academic achievements. Bill pitched again for the Indians that spring. One of the baseball team's trips in 1908 was to Elmira, New York, where Carlisle competed against Syracuse University in both track and baseball. Garlow wrote his first piece for *The Arrow* to describe the team's tour of an important site in Elmira, the reform school. After Carlisle's so-so season ended, he went on leave for the summer. That year he signed with the Shamokin, Pennsylvania team of the Atlantic League.

In November 1908, Bill Garlow received his first press coverage as a football player. Playing for the Hotshots, Carlisle's second team, he recovered a fumble against Gettysburg and returned it for a touchdown. But articles about the Hotshots were few and far between, so that's all that was printed about his football playing that year. However, his name became a regular feature in *The Arrow* for other reasons.

That year he began learning the tailoring trade. Most likely because he was a celebrity on campus due to his baseball pitching, *The Arrow* discussed the work involved in the officer's coat for Michael Balenti that Bill was making. The rest of the press, and there was lots of it, he got that school year was for his pitching.

In the spring of 1909, the pitching load was shared with Tarbell. Garlow had been overworked the year before due to a lack of additional pitching talent on the team. Bill generally pitched well, but his fielding support was spotty. On May 29, *The Carlisle Arrow* covered the game against crosstown rival Dickinson College: "'Old Reliable,' Bill Garlow, took his famous spitball with him and had the Dickinson players breaking their backs trying to connect with it." In the summer "the Indian spitball artist," as the *Tyrone Herald*, hometown paper for a rival team, called him, pitched for the Huntingdon, Pennsylvania team. His reputation was becoming widely known, at least while the spitball was legal.

1909 was the year he started making a name for himself in football as he burst into the varsity starting line up as a tackle. At 5'5" tall and weighing 176 pounds, the 20-year-old Garlow was built like a fireplug. He was very difficult for opposing offenses to move out of the way.

On October 6, William Garlow was elected President of the Freshman Class. Getting the opportunity to practice his public speaking skills more, he gave a declamation titled "Development" in the school auditorium. The talk was printed in its entirety in the following week's *Arrow*.

There was no interscholastic baseball played at Carlisle that spring or any spring after that. Because so many boys had been enticed away to play minor league baseball over the summers and Carlisle was being criticized for fielding football players who had played professional baseball, the school terminated its baseball team and replaced the spring sport with an Indian game, lacrosse. Bill Garlow was one of the Carlisle athletes mentioned prominently in the press as having played baseball for money and then playing football for Carlisle. In a bit of irony, his brother, James, who managed the athletic dorm, was named captain of Carlisle's first lacrosse team.

At commencement in April 1910, William received a certificate in tailoring but his formal education at Carlisle was not finished. Before that continued, however, he, Wauseka and Newashe spent the summer playing for the Harrisburg (Pennsylvania) League Team. The proximity of Harrisburg to Carlisle made it possible for the three to visit occasionally and to maintain ties with the school.

For the 1910 football season, Warner moved Bill Garlow to a guard position where he acquitted himself well: so well, in fact, that he was given the responsibility of calling signals. The Sophomore Class voted him an additional responsibility, that of being class Critic. Another responsibility he was given was that of repairing overcoats and making trousers for the new band boys.

During football's off-season, William Garlow remained involved in the sport and surely picked up some coaching pointers. He assisted Coach Warner with Carlisle's first ever spring football practice and played on the school's baseball team. After that, he and Bill Newashe played baseball. The summer of 1911 was spent with a South Michigan League team, the Jackson Convicts. *The Mansfield News* opined, "'Chief' Garlow, who stars for the Carlisle school on the gridiron, is one of the leading twirlers of the South Michigan league and is said to be ready for the majors." After baseball season was over, he returned to Carlisle as a member of the Junior Class and, having already received a certificate in tailoring, switched to telegraphy, a favorite of athletes.

The 1911 Carlisle football team was arguably the Indian school's best, and William Garlow was part of its foundation, a veritable rock of granite. Warner moved him from guard to center which was probably a better fit for his talents. Starting at three different positions in three years on those powerhouse Carlisle Indian School teams was no mean feat. He received praise for his play but worked in the shadows, both literally and figuratively, of his more famous teammates. He was doing well off the field, too. *The Arrow* reported, "William Garlow, the 'little center man' on the Varsity squad, is getting along finely in his telegraphy work." He was also active in the extra-curriculars, including the YMCA and the Invincible Debating Society. He was so active, in fact, that in Boston on the day after the Harvard game, he gave a speech at a special service at the Congregational Church at which a contingent of girls from Carlisle performed.

After a very busy school year, he headed off to Hamilton, Ontario to play baseball for their Canadian League team. At one point in the season, he pitched 12 straight wins.

When he returned to Carlisle, he immediately shifted from the diamond to the gridiron. *The Carlisle Arrow* summed up his 1912 season stating, "William Garlow, left guard, is 22 years old and had played on the team three years previous to this season. He is 5 ft. 7 in. tall and weighs 173 pounds. He has been a consistently strong player and was used as center in some of the games; in fact, he was an all-around man and could play quarterback or tackle as well as the positions he did play. 'Bill' was especially strong on defense."

In March, 1913 – U. S. Presidents took office later then than they do currently – Major William Garlow, commanding officer of Student Troop D, led part of the Carlisle Indian School contingent in the inauguration parade for President Woodrow Wilson. Carlisle students and especially the band often marched in inaugural parades. Earlier in the school year when still a captain, he and Mamie Richardson were awarded a prize for "best appearance" in the grand march held at the annual Officers' Reception. Bill Garlow had advanced to the top in several areas of endeavor at Carlisle. After commencement, it was time to head back to Canada to play baseball.

When William Garlow returned to Carlisle in September 1913, he enrolled at Conway Hall, Dickinson College Preparatory School, but still played football with the Indians. Several of the stars from the 1912 team did not return so a lot of green players were used, particularly early in the season. Arriving only a couple of days before the opener against Albright College, Garlow quarterbacked the Indians in that victory because Captain Welch did not return to campus in time to be ready to play in the game. *The Carlisle Arrow* explained how he was broadening his game in other directions: "Garlow kicked every goal from the touchdowns and is fast acquiring accuracy in this important department of the game." The *New York Times* applauded his play against Dartmouth: "… the chubby Garlow, who has been called the most versatile football player of the season, was a tower of strength." So good was his play that "Center Garlow was picked in mid-season by Glenn Warner as the greatest center the Indian school has ever had," according to *The Arrow*. Pundits apparently agreed with Warner because, at season's end, they selected him for honors. Frank Menke placed him at center on his first string All-Eastern team and second string on his All-America team. *Outing Magazine* considered him the second best center in the country that year. Tom Thorp placed Garlow on his All-America third team.

In January 1914, he negotiated for an assistant football coach's position with West Virginia Wesleyan, and in early February the Boston Red Sox signed him to a contract. A couple of weeks later, he headed south for spring training in Hot Springs, Arkansas with the Red Sox but was delayed for an entire day by snowbound trains. Bill must not have made a good enough impression with the Red Sox because they released him in early June to the Lewiston, Maine Cupids of the New England League. After a successful summer hurling for the winged imps, he headed for Buckhannon, West Virginia to help his cousin, Frank Mt. Pleasant.

Mt. Pleasant was the new head coach for the orange and black of West Virginia Wesleyan College (WVWC). In mid-September, William Garlow joined his first cousin as assistant coach and student at the college. WVWC was upgrading its athletic program and hired the famous Indians to achieve that end. Their first game was against the coaches' alma mater. Carlisle was on the decline as WVWC was ascending, with the result being a 6-0 win for the Indians. This game was a moral victory for WVWC after having lost to Carlisle 25-0 the previous year. In November, they were beaten badly by Al Exendine's Georgetown eleven. WVWC went 4-3 overall but, by beating in-state rivals Marshall and West Virginia, claimed the state championship. After WVWC's season was over, Bill played center on what was billed as the ex-Carlisle Indian team of Altoona in a late season game against the Monessen All Stars. The Monessen *Daily Independent* listed several of Bill's former teammates as "... form[ing] the nucleus of one of the best teams playing in amateur football today." However, 'amateur' was a nebulous term.

Murmurmonte, WVWC's yearbook, was optimistic in the spring: "With William Garlow, famous Indian athlete, as head coach at Wesleyan, prospects for track are looming up brightly for a most prosperous season in nineteen-fifteen." He also assisted Frank Mt. Pleasant with the baseball team. With regard to football for 1915, the yearbook said, "As to the coaching, nothing definite is known, but it is quite probable that Garlow will return. Garlow has proved himself an excellent coach, being admired by all and showing great knowledge of the game. His return will be greeted with joy."

In professional baseball's off-season, the Lewiston Cupids' owner put the team up for sale. So, Bill then signed with the Elmira, New York team. However, it is not clear if he ever pitched for them or anyone else after this point.

William Garlow served as Director of Physical Education for Men at West Virginia Wesleyan College and served as head coach of the football team in 1915. This was his first and only known season as head coach anywhere. After his 4-4-1 season, WVWC selected new grad Greasy Neale to lead his alma mater's team. Although many of his friends participated, it is not believed that Garlow played Sunday football in 1915 because it was so frowned upon by employers, especially academic ones. In the off season, he may have

1912 Carlisle line: Goesback, Calac, Busch, Bergie, Garlow, Guyon, Pratt,
Fred Wardecker

played hockey in Canada but that has not been verified. It is more likely that, as Director of Physical Education, he taught gym classes and coached basketball and baseball. In 1916, he was a free agent and could do whatever he pleased.

Pro football had taken a major step forward in 1915 when Jack Cusack hired Jim Thorpe for his Canton Bulldogs team. However, his opponents also saw the need to hire stars to be competitive. To keep up in this football "arms race," Cusack put together what he thought was the most powerful aggregation ever assembled in 1916. Bill Garlow was hired to play center on that team. The result was a legendary championship 9-1 team. The U. S. entered WWI in 1917, and many current and former Carlisle students signed up to fight. William Garlow was no exception, enlisting in the Marines on August 10, 1917. After surviving boot camp at Parris Island, North Carolina, he was transferred to the Philadelphia Navy Yard, possibly to play football. In December he was transferred to Pensacola, Florida where he and his brother, James, worked as firemen. In May 1918, he was back at the Philadelphia Navy Yard. (Could the brass have wanted him to pitch for their baseball team? Perhaps not because he was back in Pensacola with James in July.) In August, they were promoted to Private First Class. In October, William was back in Philadelphia. According to the press, he was to play center for the Fourth, or Philadelphia, Navy District football team. The team's quarterback was to be Hyman Goldstein, Garlow's old foe from Dickinson College. It's not clear if he actually played on that team because he was soon in Cuba working as Cook 2nd Class. In June 1919, he was transferred to the 2nd Machine Gun Battalion at Guantanamo Bay. Bill was sent briefly to Haiti for the end of November and the beginning of December. He may have taken ill in Haiti because he was returned to Charleston, South Carolina via the *U. S. S. Kittery* and hospitalized. He was discharged from the hospital on January 8 and from the Marines on January 16 with excellent conduct.

The 1920 Federal census was taken while Bill was at Charleston. He was listed as 32 years old and single. Tribal rolls recorded each year indicate little about him other than he was on the roll. The 1930 Federal census listed him as rooming with a white family in the city of Niagara Falls and working as a laborer at a paper mill. His marital status was widower. So, some time between 1920 and 1930 he married and his wife died. Very little is known about William Garlow after his discharge from the Marines, even after a notice of his death was circulated around the country by the UPI wire service. He died on April 14, 1959 at Ransomville General Hospital near the Tuscarora Reservation, where he had lived in recent years and was brother-in-law to the chief, Elton Greene.

18

Peter R. Calac

Pete Calac blocking for Joe Guyon; *Cumberland County Historical Society, Carlisle, PA*

Name: Peter R. Calac	**Nickname:** Indian Idol
DOB: 5/13/1893	**Height:** 5'7"
Weight: 130	**Age:** 19
Tribe: Mission	**Home:** Fallbrook, San Diego County, CA

Parents: Franscisco Calac, Mission; Felicida Molino, Rincon band Mission

Early Schooling: Rincon Day School; Fallbrook County District; Sherman Institute

Later Schooling: West Virginia Wesleyan College

Honors: American Indian Athletic Hall of Fame, 1971

Indian Idol

Pedro Calac entered Carlisle in November of 1908 for a three-year enrollment. From that time forward, he was known by the Anglicized version of his Christian name, Peter. This was not his first exposure to schooling; he began attending school in 1899 at the Rincon Day School near the Mission Tule River Reservation where he lived. He attended school more or less continuously until 1906, at which time he went to work, most likely on the family's farm. In addition to Rincon Day, he attended a school in the Fallbrook County District and Sherman Institute at Riverside, all in California. He was in fourth grade when he first arrived at Carlisle at 15 years of age.

Pete Calac, Philip Wellmas and two girls were selected from their reservation school to attend the Carlisle school. "We came East on the Union Pacific," Pete later recalled. "When we got to Carson City, Nevada, Philip said, 'Pete, I don't want to go East: let's run away!' I talked him out of that. At Chicago, people crowded around to look at us. I couldn't get out of there fast enough."

Pete spent a quiet three-year first enrollment completing grammar school and working on farms on outing periods. He received "good" to "very good" marks for his academic work and "very good" to "excellent" for behavior. His first vocational training was in the harness-making shop, but he was shifted to the general woodworking shop. In his last winter, he served as a night watch. His returned student report, completed on March 21, 1911 when he was about 18 years old, listed his health as excellent. He had grown to 5'10" tall and then weighed 197 pounds. The form described the instruction he had received: "Has spent most of his time on a farm under the Outing System. About 5 months in the carpenter shop." Also included was the curious comment, "Is not a musician."

The form described his character and disposition as "A boy of good character and good disposition." The types of employment for which he was deemed most suitable, in order, were: "Farmer, teamster, herder and laborer." It went on to say, "This young man is very strong and better fitted to do heavy manual labor. He is to be trusted." He left Carlisle on June 21, 1911, his enrollment completed.

The January 26, 1912 edition of *The Carlisle Arrow* contained its first mention of Peter: "Peter Calac, who is at his home in California, sends his best wishes to his friends at Carlisle." He later wrote the superintendent about his life on the farm: "I am living with my folks at present and I am enjoying the California life. But I thinking [sic] of going back to Carlisle next year. I will be very glad to get the catalog." He returned on September 22, 1912 for a second three-year enrollment. This time Pete would not be lost in the crowd.

He arrived just in time for football practice. The 1911 football team was arguably Carlisle's greatest, but some players had departed or had used up their eligibility. The line had some holes that needed to be filled, and Pete Calac was a strong, husky lad able to do the job. He toiled at right tackle, assistant coach Lone Star Dietz's former position, mostly in the shadows of Thorpe, Welch and the other, more experienced players. However, at season's end, Warner or, more likely, one of his press agents, wrote about Calac in *The Arrow*: "This was his first year at football, and for a player of such little experience, he has done remarkably well and should develop into one of the greatest tackles ever at the school." He wouldn't always toil anonymously in the trenches.

Although an excellent athlete, Pete involved himself in other extracurricular activities, too. He joined the Invincible Debating Society and participated with fellow footballers such as Henry Broker and William Garlow in debates with, and against, non-footballers. 1913 was Pete's breakout year at Carlisle – in more ways than one.

On July 15, Superintendent Lipps wrote to Calac's mother to inform her that Peter had deserted his outing home, which appears to have been the V. H. Griffiths farm in Ivyland, Pennsylvania. Lipps had no idea where Pete was and requested that she inform him if she became aware of the young man's whereabouts so he could discontinue the search. Apparently she didn't know because two weeks later Lipps informed her that "...he was apprehended and returned to this school on July the 23rd." No mention of his running away was mentioned in the school newspaper, nor was a reason provided in the school's records.

Jim Thorpe, Alex Arcasa and Stancil "Possum" Powell had departed, leaving huge voids behind the line. After the first game of the season, *The Carlisle Arrow* reported, "The new back field proved to be little less effective than last year's star aggregation, and Calac especially showed that he has the making of a great fullback." Three weeks later, after the Cornell game, *The Arrow* reporter wrote, "Captain Welch, Guyon, and Calac played their usual good game, and the latter especially showed lots of grit by playing the whole game with a very painfully bruised shoulder." It was fortunate this injury occurred when it did instead of during the previous game because, on the Tuesday before the Cornell game, Pete was a groomsman in Jim Thorpe's much celebrated wedding.

Fortunately Pete healed quickly and was ready for the big game with Penn. *The Carlisle Herald* reported on the ferocity of the Indians' play, "The Redskins played rings around George Brooks' men and only twice during the whole game did Penn gain first downs by straight football tactics, whereas the Indian backfield, especially Guyon, Calac, and Bracklin, tore through the Quakers' line at will." The next game was in Washington, DC against Georgetown University. After the 34-0 blowout was over, *The Arrow* reported, "Calac and Bracklin, while neither is as valuable as Guyon, are both clever performers. Calac is a good line-plunger and runs interference very well. He is a mighty good man to send out in front of a runner, and time after time yesterday he eliminated Georgetown ends and tackle with a precision seldom noted." After the season, the *Carlisle Herald* opined, "Fullback Calac, also new to the fullback position has made one of the country's best backfielders." Pete had arrived. He was also promoted to the Freshman Class – high school freshman, that is.

Calac had unfortunate timing: he was coming into his own as the Congressional Inquiry hit, the aftermath of which changed everything at Carlisle forever. The season started encouragingly enough but, when Captain Elmer Busch resigned, it did not portend good things for the team. According to *The Arrow*, "Peter Calac was elected captain of the football team last Saturday just before the Pitt game. That the boys have confidence in him and that he is a good leader was proven by the game the team put up against Pitt. Captain Calac has played two years on the team. He was a star tackle in 1912; and last year was one of the best plunging and defensive fullbacks in the country. Under his inspiring and cheerful leadership the team is bound to make steady improvement as the season progresses." The team didn't improve much, but Pete was elected Captain again for the 1915 season. After the season was over, a chit for an additional $25 in clothing for Calac was sent to Blumenthal's Mens Wear by the Supervisor in Charge of the Athletic Department. The practice of rewarding football players with clothing does not appear to have been discontinued with the 1914 regime changes both at the Indian school and in the Athletic Department.

Early in the new year *The Arrow* announced, "Mr. Lipps has selected six boys to go to Detroit, Mich., to work in Ford's Automobile Factory. They are Gus Looks, Peter Calac, Joseph Gilman, Norman Thompson, Everett Ranco, and Charles Pratt." The boys left promptly for Detroit to learn how to make cars and earn very high salaries for the day. Pete, as leader of the boys in Detroit, corresponded frequently with Oscar Lipps. Both Ford and Carlisle gained positive publicity from the venture. In June, more boys arrived to expand the size of the Carlisle contingent. Over the summer, Pete asked who would be coaching the team that fall and gave his opinions on some of the changes, including the loss of the athletic quarters and the training table which served special meals to the athletes. Pete stayed in Detroit learning to make Model Ts until it was time to play football again. He left Detroit in late August along with several other football players, arriving in Carlisle on September 1.

The Ford training program exposed a weakness in the education students received at Carlisle and recommended improvements. On January 5, in an attempt to recruit and retain the most qualified workers, Henry Ford increased wages he paid workers in his automobile manufacturing plants to the unheard of amount of $5 a day. Carlisle students in the Ford apprenticeship program demonstrated weaknesses in skills needed for the jobs at Ford, most likely in mathematics. Shortly after arriving back at Carlisle, the Ford boys, many of whom were football players, were informed that a new course had been added to the curriculum to better prepare them for careers in the automobile industry.

The football team looked like Carlisle of old in its opener against Albright College, and Captain Calac gave a talk entitled "Football Prospects" to the Invincibles at their first meeting that fall. He also wrote a column for the school newspaper reporting on the activities of the plumbers, which appears to have been the shop in which he worked.

The season went downhill quickly but Pete continued to play hard, even after getting his knee hurt in the Lehigh game. The next week he tore through the Harvard line, making five or ten yards at a clip in a losing effort. As the unfortunate season wore on, mention of Calac being considered for All American increased, at least in Carlisle. Taking a little break from football, Pete played in a basketball game between the vocational and non-vocational boys. He also kept active as a debater with the Invincibles during the season. The season closed with a humiliating defeat by Brown University on Thanksgiving Day. Pete did a yeoman's job of captaining the Indians through the most difficult period in their football history. He played on two of Carlisle's most glorious teams and then two years on teams that spiraled downward. Dealing with the coaching controversy that centered around Kelley and Welch had to be a difficult problem for him.

As soon as the season was over, Pete returned to Detroit. The Detroiters who were not football boys received pay raises after six months of work that put them at full pay. Having missed a few months' work during the football season, Pete and the other footballers had to work a while to be eligible for the raise.

The $5 a day rate was actually half salary and half bonus. The bonus came with character requirements that were enforced by Ford's Socialization Organization. This committee visited workers' homes to make sure they were doing things the American way. Ford workers were to avoid social ills such as gambling and drinking. If they didn't know English, they were to learn it, and recent immigrants were required to attend classes to become "Americanized." Only single women who were supporting a family were eligible for the bonus. Also, men lost their eligibility if their wives worked outside the home.

On September 22, 1916, G. W. Griswold of Ford Motor Company, Department of Education as part of a flurry of letters and wires between himself and Superindent Lipps, and possibly Calac, apprised Lipps of Pete's status, "… Peter Calac quit yesterday, stating that his mother was sick in California and that it was absolutely necessary that he return to her. This man has an excellent record in the shop; in fact, is considered the best man we have in the Motor Department. We have arranged to give him a three months' leave of absence and are writing our California Branch today to see if they can in any way make use of his services to enable him to be near his mother." On the 25th, Lipps sent Calac a check for $97.41, the balance of his account at Carlisle and encouraged him to eventually complete his apprenticeship.

The October 6 issue of the *New Castle* [Pennsylvania]*News* stated, "The celebrated Carlisle Indian players, Calac, a halfback, and Guyon, a line man will be in the visitors' lineup against the Red and Black. Wesleyan has no eligibility code and for this reason can play these Redskin stars, even though they played a number of seasons at the Carlisle school. Last Saturday against Muskingum [College of New Concord, Ohio] Calac was pretty much the entire works for Wesleyan, and at that time he had practiced with the team but one week." Pete's mother must have had a miraculous recovery as Pete was practicing football in Buckhannon, West Virginia, home of the Mountain State Methodists, the week leading up to the September 30 game with Muskingum, eliminating his need to return to California. He likely had little interest in returning to Carlisle because it hadn't scheduled any games at that point and didn't appear to be fielding a team that year. But why did he select West Virginia Westleyan College (WVWC)? A relationship between Carlisle and WVWC had been established a few years prior with the hiring of Frank Mt. Pleasant as head coach and William Garlow, first as assistant to Mt. Pleasant and a year later as his replacement.

In the middle of WVWC's season, Pete got a call or, more likely, a telegram from his old teammate, Jim Thorpe, who was then captain of the Canton Bulldogs professional team. Bulldogs manager Jack Cusack was loading up for the championship games with rival Massillon and brought Pete on board to beef up his backfield. It worked. The November 1 *Syracuse Herald* reported Calac as being the Bulldogs' starting fullback for a game to be played that Sunday against Cleveland. Why the game was being played at a neutral site wasn't explained. Pete contributed significantly on both sides of the ball, helping the Bulldogs win the professional championship. Some sportswriters called the Canton backfield the best ever collected. Cusack considered it the best professional team put together to that time.

Carlisle updated his file on November 11 to mark his status as discharged with "left Ford" as the reason. However, his three months' leave of absence from Ford had not quite expired. In January, Carlisle sent him a check for 63 cents to close out his account, implying that they were done with him or he with them, as the case may have been. The earnings report produced by Ford for the fiscal year ending June 30, 1917 showed that Pete only earned $289.40 for the entire 12 month period. He had to have worked between 58 and 115 full days to earn that amount. Because he was likely to have completed his apprenticeship by June 30, 1916, he was probably earning at the $5 per day rate at this time. The work reflected on Ford's report may have been performed between July 1, 1916 and the start of football season.

The literature of football history abounds with stories involving Pete Calac in the 1917 season. He returned to both WVWC and Canton teams that fall, so he was very busy on weekends. WVWC was coached that year by former stars Alfred "Greasy" Neale and John Kellison. On Sundays, Calac, Neale and Kellison played for the Canton Bulldogs as Anderson or Andrews, Foster or Fisher and Ketcham or Harris, respectively. That is the best anyone has been able to decipher the line-ups that were printed in the newspapers covering the games. (It wasn't unusual for the papers to have different fake names for the players.) They were usually joined by Bill Garlow, formerly of Carlisle and WVWC, and Frank Dunn of Dickinson College. Employers in those days, particularly colleges and universities, took a negative view of their coaches playing professional football, which explains all the fake names. One particular story stands out.

One Sunday the trio were taking a train from Bukhannon to a game in Canton when they were warned that WVWC administrators were on their way to that very game to check out rumors of the trio playing professionally. So, they got off the train in Pittsburgh and spent the day sightseeing and never made the game. Even with this, Canton won the 1917 championship.

Back at WVWC, Pete received some mention in the yearbook beyond his photo. Unfortunately many of the comments make little sense to those not familiar with the happenings on that campus. The day-by-day calendar for October 31 entry was "Miller takes Calac calling." In the *Can You Imagine This?* section is the item "Peter Calac at Sunday school?"

On April 6, 1917, the United States declared war on Germany and things wouldn't be the same in the sporting world for a few years. In June, Pete registered for the draft, giving his occupation as both student at WVWC and machinist in Detroit. He enlisted in the army, serving with the 91st Division, known in WWII as the "Wild West Division," and served in France and Belgium. He came through the war unscathed and later explained, "I guess I dug in too much." After the war was over, he returned to the U. S. and football as a member of the 1919 Canton Bulldogs and shortly after made Canton his residence. The 1919 Bulldogs, led by Thorpe, Guyon and Calac, were champs again.

Joe Guyon later related some memories of games in New York: "My roommate was Pete Calac, a great fullback who had been at Carlisle with me and could carry four men on his back. Pete didn't drink and, of course, neither did I. We'd take a ferry and go sight-seeing."

Between seasons, Canton became a charter member of what would become the National Football League (NFL). From this point forward Pete was playing in the NFL – when he was playing football that is. The 1920 incarnation of the Bulldogs didn't win the championship due to an early December loss to the Buffalo All Stars in the first important game played by the new league in the Big Apple. Jim Thorpe moved to the Cleveland Tigers for the 1921 season, taking Calac and Guyon with him. The team was immediately renamed from Tigers to Indians. The Indians had a losing season, suffered financially, and folded after that season.

Still staying in Ohio, Thorpe et al. then moved to LaRue where a dog breeder by the name of Lingo had bought an NFL franchise for much less than the cost of one of the Oorang Airedales he sold. The trio, plus a number of their old Carlisle teammates and assorted other, mostly over-the-hill, Indians played for the Oorang Indians in 1922. The team was far from a success on the field but that wasn't its point; it was a promotional tool to sell Oorang Airedales. After the season was over, Pete Calac, who was in Texas for some unknown reason, sent back a coyote to Nick Lassaw, also known as Long Time Sleep, a teammate who was staying in LaRue. The coyote was kept in a cage at Coon Paw Inn but got out somehow. A patron of the inn couldn't leave because the snarling coyote kept him from his car. Eventually Lassaw came and herded the bristling animal back into his cage.

1923 was also a bad year on the field for the Oorang team, but kept several aging Indian athletes employed for good wages. After two years of struggling with the financial burden the team presented, Lingo had enough and folded the franchise. Walter Lingo may have had his fill of football but not necessarily of sports.

Pete did not follow Thorpe and Guyon to the Rock Island, Illinois Independents, likely due to having recently been married. He signed on with the geographically closer-to-home Buffalo, New York, Bisons for the 1924 season. He also coached at nearby Canisius High School. Prior to the season, on June 12, he quietly married Ruth Croft of Marion, Ohio, in Kenyon, apparently in a successful attempt to avoid attention. Based on where the Calacs spent the rest of their lives, his bride probably preferred to stay close to home.

In 1925 he returned to Canton where he played his last two years for the Bulldogs. In January 1926, after his season was over, he joined up with Jim Thorpe's St. Petersburg Cardinals for an exhibition game played in Tampa, Florida against Red Grange's barnstormers. That would be the last football game the two played together. In the summer before his last football season, Pete was called upon to play on a baseball team sponsored by none other than Walter Lingo. It was rumored that Jim Thorpe also owned a piece of the Oorang Indians team on which he played alongside Calac. Oorang played exhibition games against independent and minor league clubs that summer. The roster included names familiar to those who had followed the football team of the same name as well as some younger players from places like Haskell Institute.

Pete played for Canton again that fall. After the 1926 football season was over, the Bulldogs played a post-season game against a semi-pro team in Brownsville, Fayette County, Pennsylvania. This may well have been Pete's last football game.

About that time, his new employer complained about him playing football. Pete had become a patrolman on the Canton, Ohio police force and city officials apparently didn't think playing football mixed well with police work. So, now a married man and past his prime in athletics, he made the practical choice and hung up his cleats. In 1929 he shot and killed a person in the line of duty and was found to have done nothing improper. He made police work his career for 25 years.

Peter and Ruth had two daughters, Marylan and Joan, and a son, Peter, Jr. Pete Jr. also made police work his career. Ruth died young, before their daughter, Joan, was married in 1946. Pete retired from police work in 1951, but the mantle was passed to Pete, Jr. who followed in his father's footsteps.

Living near Canton made it handy for Pete to participate in activities associated with the Professional Football Hall of Fame. He was one of those present for the 1962 groundbreaking ceremony. The next year he was selected to speak for the induction of his old teammate and friend as a charter member of the Hall of Fame. "I know that Jim, with that same old happy grin on his face, is looking down on all this from the happy hunting grounds and is very proud." Always a bridesmaid, Calac was often mentioned in the balloting but was never selected for induction himself. He died on January 13, 1968, after a long bout with cancer, leaving behind a son, 2 daughters and 7 grandchildren.

William Henry Dietz

19

W.S.C. Coach, "Lonestar" Dietz,
Dazzle's Portland's Dressy Avenue

Lone Star shows off new duds,
1915; *The Oregonian*

Lone Star Dietz;
University of Wyoming
Athletic Department

Name: William Henry Dietz	**Nickname:** Lone Star
DOB: 8/17/1884	**Height:** 5'11"
Weight: 175	**Age:** 24
Tribe: Sioux	**Home:** Rice Lake, WI

Parents: William Wallace Dietz, white; Julia One Star, Sioux
or Leanna Ginder Dietz, white

Early Schooling: Rice Lake Public Schools; Macalester College;
Chilocco Indian School (very briefly);
Friends University

Later Schooling:

Honors: Inland Northwest Sports Hall of Fame, 1963;
American Indian Athletic Hall of Fame, 1971;
Citizens Savings Athletic Foundation, 1976;
Washington State University Hall of Fame, 1983;
Pennsylvania Sports Hall of Fame, 1997;
Rice Lake Sports Hall of Fame, 2002;
Albright College Athletic Hall of Fame, 2008

Wicarphi Isnala (Lone Star)

Out of the darkness, a spotlight shone on the opening of a tipi placed in the center of the auditorium. A mystical Indian song emerged from the tipi and soon a young man, Lone Star, in Sioux attire complete with war bonnet, came forth. After demonstrating a war dance, Lone Star gave a talk about Indians with an emphasis on their scalping proclivities, which he claimed were taught to them by the white man. Such was the introduction pupils at the School of Industrial Art in Philadelphia heard from their new fellow student fresh from the Carlisle Indian School. A *Philadelphia Record* reporter thought Lone Star's talk nearly made one's hair stand on end.

William Lone Star Dietz, old for an entering student at 23, enrolled at Carlisle in September 1907, in time for the fall term and, just as importantly, only six months after Glenn S. "Pop" Warner returned and ready to start football practice. Although he played very little, if at all, he traveled with the varsity squad. His on-field time was most likely with the second team that played a schedule of games with other teams. At the end of football season, he went on outing to the School of Industrial Design where he studied illustration. Most students spent their outings working on farms or at their trade, but a few used this time to get additional schooling. Lone Star was likely accepted at this institution because of the recommendation of his instructor at Carlisle, Angel DeCora, the famous Winnebago artist. While he was still on outing, Angel and Lone Star eloped.

Lone Star is believed to have met Angel DeCora three and a half years earlier when he was doing artwork for the model government Indian school exhibit at the St. Louis World's Fair and she visited the exhibit, if for no other reason than to see the painting purchased from her on display. Angel was thirteen years older than Lone Star and well established in her career while he was still in school. Little is known about their courtship other than they were almost always in different places. However, just three and a half months after he arrived at Carlisle, they were married. But the school kept it quiet until commencement was over in a successful attempt to avoid a scandal. A department head marrying a student 13 years her junior, even though he was 23 years old, would not have been viewed positively, so Dietz was made an assistant art instructor before summer.

Angel and Lone Star soon started a literary magazine that generated much positive publicity for the school. Initially titled *The Indian Craftsman*, its name was changed within a year to *The Red Man* to avoid confusion with Gustav Stickley's *The Craftsman* magazine. Under Angel's tutelage and with the training he received in Philadelphia, Lone Star became a skillful illustrator and received much praise from critics for his work in Carlisle publications and ephemera.

Angel DeCora broadened Carlisle students' horizons by inviting luminaries from the art world to visit the school and give talks. School visitors reported very positively on what they observed happening in the Native Art Department that Angel headed and in which Lone Star taught. Angel and Lone Star teamed up on some outside projects as well. They illustrated two books together, *Yellow Star* and *The Little Buffalo Robe*, as well as a calendar that was printed in Germany. Articles were published about them and their work in magazines such as *Literary Digest*.

Both gave talks on Indian art with Angel doing more of that than Lone Star because of her greater reputation. In December 1913, they made the claim that Indians had invented Cubism 200 years prior to its being "discovered" by Europeans, citing square eagles that can be found on some Indian art.

Sometimes they mixed their art with other interests. One of Lone Star's illustrations included a dog in a canoe. That dog was a hint as to what else was going on in his life. In 1910, the Dietzes started raising Russian Wolfhounds (today known as Borzoi) in what they called Orloff Kennels behind their apartment on Carlisle Barracks, the old army post that served as the campus for the Indian school. Angel was always an animal lover, keeping a cat for a pet before her marriage, and the regal nature of these dogs probably appealed to Lone Star's theatrical side. He made quite a sight when he exercised these tall, long-legged dogs on local roads, racing along with them on his bicycle with his coattails flapping in the breeze. Before long, they were breeding pedigreed dogs and entering them in shows. The zenith of their success was in 1915 when their top dog, Khotni, won best of breed at Westminster and another of their dogs, Belvina, won a lesser prize. When they broke up their kennel that summer, one of their young dogs sold for $700, more than a year's wages for many people at the time. This dog may have been Nazitka, who later became an American Champion as had Khotni.

Lone Star continued playing football on the second team and riding the varsity bench in 1908. He broke into the starting lineup at right tackle and lettered in 1909. Dietz continued playing in the 1910 and 1911 seasons. Being a lineman, he didn't get the press backs often received, but he got enough to be known nationally. In those days, especially in the Warner system with all its tricks, tackles got to carry the ball occasionally, and he even scored a touchdown in the 1911 victory over Penn. That year's team was arguably Carlisle's best, losing but once while beating two of the Big Four. He then assisted Pop Warner for three seasons with good results, until changes made after the 1914 investigation made it difficult to field a competitive team.

Dietz and Warner became lifelong friends as they both loved football and art. They repainted a backdrop for the school theater together, and Dietz illustrated Warner's 1912 book on coaching football. Dietz did the illustrations for such things as the athletic banquet programs and football posters. One of the figures he developed was used widely both at Carlisle and at other Indian schools after it closed. A color version of this figure was used as the frontispiece for John Steckbeck's 1951 *Fabulous Redmen: the Carlisle Indians and their famous football teams*.

When Warner decided to leave Carlisle in 1915, Dietz had decisions to make. He could stay on as head coach at Carlisle or go to Pitt with Pop as an assistant. Instead, he chose to strike out on his own and lead another team. When Washington State College (WSC) contacted Pop Warner about a candidate who applied for their open head coaching position, he gave a lukewarm reference and informed them that Lone Star Dietz was the man they should consider. After an application process, reviewing references and negotiating a salary, WSC gave Dietz a one-year contract. Initially, he was to coach baseball as well but that didn't materialize, possibly due to cost.

When Dietz arrived in Pullman, Washington, he made quite a splash. No one in this wheat-farming community had seen an Indian dandy before, and there were lots of Nez Perce not far away. His landlady didn't have nearly enough room to store the trunks in which his more than ample wardrobe was transported, so they had to be stored in the gym. The press had a field day showing him shopping in Portland, Oregon, dressed to the nines in top hat, tails, spats and ivory-handled cane. The players weren't too sure, either. Team Captain Asa "Ace" Clark was used to scrimmaging very hard in practice. Dietz focused on conditioning and teaching the players the Warner system: single-wing with a little double-wing thrown in. Clark and the rest of the players were skeptical. A 3 to 2 practice game win over the alumni wasn't very convincing, far from it. Beating the heavy University of Oregon team 28 to 3 gave Clark reason to reconsider and, after thrashing the Oregon Aggies 29 to 0, he was convinced.

Dietz, never known for false modesty, claimed he knew the Warner system the best of anyone, and Warner once said Dietz ran the double-wing the best of any coach who tried it. Lone Star had his charges running these formations, mostly the single-wing, to perfection and rolled over their opponents, one after the other. In mid-November, sitting on a 5-0 record with a single, very winnable, game in front of them, Dietz got a surprise – one that would ultimately change history.

On January 1, 1902, the Tournament of Roses unsuccessfully experimented with playing a football game to round out the day after the parade in their mid-winter floral festival. Michigan was brought in as an eastern challenger, and Stanford was selected to defend the honor of the West. Fielding Yost, Michigan's head coach, had coached Stanford the previous year but was let go because of a rule change that required the coach to be a graduate of the institution he was coaching. He then took the job at Michigan, a school that had no such rule, and led the Wolverines to an undefeated season, scoring 501 points to their opponents' zero. West Coast football was not up to eastern standards at that time, so Michigan easily rolled over them. To make matters worse, early in the second half, Yost refused Stanford's offer to forfeit the game because they were being thrashed so badly. However, he did allow them to quit when Stanford no longer had eleven men without broken bones. The football experiment failed, so chariot racing became the after-parade entertainment. But good things don't last forever. By 1915 the chariot racing had become very dangerous and the professional drivers who were hired sometimes rigged the races. So, it was time to try something else, and the something was football again.

Coach Dietz received a telegram the day after the Whitman College game, offering his team the opportunity to play in Pasadena on New Year's Day. The opponent would be an eastern power. School officials quickly accepted the offer, but someone was trying to push them aside.

The University of Washington and Washington State did not play that year because a year earlier Washington's coach, "Gloomy" Gil Dobie, took WSC off his team's schedule because he considered them "too much like kindergarten." Also, Dobie rarely played road games and WSC expected UW to play in Pullman, or at least Spokane, occasionally, something Dobie abhorred. When Dobie got wind of the upcoming New Year's game, he tried to elbow his way into it. The only common opponents UW and WSC had that year were Whitman and Gonzaga. UW beat Whitman 27-0 but weather conditions held WSC down to a 17-0 victory. WSC's last game of the year was against Gonzaga, who UW beat 21-7. The WSC team had one last chance to bury Dobie's argument and they took it.

The Washington State players weren't about to let field conditions hold them back against Gonzaga as they wanted nothing to stand in their way of making the trip to Pasadena. Because comparative scores were taken seriously in those days, it was important to WSC, if for no other reason than to silence Dobie, to defeat Gonzaga by a greater margin than had UW. Also, tacking on another ten points to make up the difference in margins against Whitman wouldn't be a bad idea. Highly-motivated WSC showed Gonzaga no mercy, trouncing them 48-0. Ironically, a Providence, Rhode Island newspaper initially had Brown University playing Washington rather than Washington State. Dietz's sources in the East may have informed him of that.

Something Dietz's sources did tell him was that Carlisle's coach for 1915, Victor M. Kelley, out of spite for Dietz's saying that he wouldn't make good at Carlisle, gave Brown's coach a copy of Carlisle's play book. *The Providence Journal* claimed that Brown knew Carlisle's plays inside and out from having played the Indians so many times. Brown's head coach, Edward Robinson, responded by stating that he would develop new plays for the New Year's Day game. Dietz would spring some surprises of his own but they were largely off-field.

Lone Star packed two trunks of summer attire and led his team to Pasadena. The team stayed in the elegant Maryland Hotel, but the players didn't get much time to lollygag in the lobby: Dietz had negotiated a movie deal for them. The team played the football team in *Tom Brown at Harvard* and got $100 each for their efforts. Lone Star got a bit part for himself. Later, the players figured out that Dietz got the better of them on that deal because, for the $100, he got to hold two-a-day practices. In the movie business, there is a lot of hurry up and wait, so Dietz took advantage of the wait times by having his team run plays during those times. Always the master psychologist when it came to motivating teams, Lone Star found a way to get his team ready for Brown.

Fritz Pollard, the great African-American halfback now in both college and professional football halls of fame, was Brown's big threat. So, Dietz devised a scheme to stop him. He called each of his starters aside (they played both ways then) and told each of them in confidence that he was afraid of Pollard and wanted that player to make it his personal responsibility to stop the scatback. He then swore each confidante to secrecy because he purportedly didn't want the rest of the team to know he was concerned about Pollard. He also had tricks up his sleeve for the media. He told them it was a foregone conclusion that the heavier Brown team would win. He just hoped his team could make it look respectable. Then he went back to perfecting his strategy for victory.

The Tournament of Roses committee hoped to make a great deal of money off the game because the 1902 game, in spite of being a mismatch, was profitable. Promotional materials included blurbs about each team's head coach. The game program also featured two photographs – but both of them were of Dietz, one in formal wear, the other in full Sioux regalia. Dietz also gave the press great interviews. One of the best was the one in which he predicted that California boys would never amount to much as athletes because they relied on automobiles for even the shortest distances.

Two days before the game, it snowed in Pasadena and on the morning of the game it started raining. By game time, the field was muddy and the stands were half empty and Lone Star had no raingear. Taking no chances that the game would be delayed, Athletic Director and team trainer J. Fred "Doc" Bohler led the WSC team onto the field to warm up. It wasn't unknown in California at that time to postpone games in better weather than that, and Dietz had his team ready to play. But his high-powered offense with its razzle-dazzle plays was ill-suited for sloppy field conditions.

Brown had the best of the first half, threatening to score twice. But, on both occasions, the Dietzmen stiffened, stopping them well short of the goal line. Fritz Pollard later recalled that Lone Star's beautiful white suit was covered with mud early in the game and that, after being tackled, he feared he would be drowned in a mud puddle. At halftime,

Dietz made some adjustments.

He threw out all but the simplest plays and focused on line-bucking. Although Brown had a heavier line, particularly in the person of tackle Mark Farnum, Dietz felt his warriors could move them out. And they did. By hammering the line, they moved the ball forward and set a rushing yardage mark that held for decades. They also scored two touchdowns and made the kicks after touchdown while holding Brown scoreless. Fritz Pollard was held to less than 50 yards rushing in the 14-0 WSC landmark victory.

That historic game not only demonstrated that West Coast football was the equal of its eastern counterpart but also established what is now known as the Rose Bowl. As Rose Bowl historian Rube Samuelsen noted, this game was indeed the granddaddy of all them all, not just Rose Bowl games but all the New Year's Day games that followed. Recently a credible case has been made for naming the 1915 WSC team national champs. A 1915 Philadelphia newspaper predicted that they wouldn't receive the honor because of the press's eastern bias, even though they would deserve it if they beat Brown convincingly. As expected, the press was silent about it after the game was played. The team returned to Pullman to a hero's welcome; however, their coach wasn't with them.

Dietz had caught the movie bug and stayed behind in Hollywood to negotiate a movie deal. He didn't successfully negotiate a film contract he liked, claiming that the studios wanted him to portray Indians in a negative light. However, after rumors swirled around about Lone Star taking coaching jobs on both coasts and places in between, he negotiated a big raise for himself at WSC.

Expectations of what defined a successful season in Pullman had changed. In the several years prior to Lone Star's arrival, Washington State suffered through a series of losing seasons, but Pullmanites wanted no more of that. In fact, anything short of an undefeated season was considered subpar at this point. The 1916 team was accused of resting on its laurels, and Dietz was criticized for being distracted by Hollywood because his team had suffered two defeats, both at the hands of the Oregon schools. So in 1917, Lone Star set aside his fancy duds and got out his moleskins.

Some think that 1917 was Dietz's best coaching job because several key players were lost through graduation or enlistment, and he had a lot of green ones to teach the rudiments of Carlisle football. That team went undefeated, giving up just 3 points the entire year. They even beat UW. That was possible because Gloomy Gil had departed and his successor was willing to schedule a game. WSC players and fans were disappointed because they expected to make another post-season trip to Pasadena. However, the U. S. had entered WWI earlier that year and service teams were drawing large crowds. Two service teams were selected for the New Year's Day contest instead.

Like most colleges, WSC wasn't going to be fielding athletic teams in 1918 due to the war and didn't want to pay Dietz a coaching salary if he wasn't coaching the varsity. So, he was let go after three years which included two undefeated seasons, a post-season victory and only two losses. This was an excellent start to a coaching career, but Dietz wanted to consider other options.

Although Lone Star hadn't caught on in Hollywood, he still had the movie bug and a film career was brought to him. Tyrone Power Sr. blew into Spokane in August 1917, with visions of turning Minnehaha Park into a major motion picture studio. Dietz invested in the Washington Motion Picture Company and signed on to work on both sides of the camera. Funds were raised, a modern studio was built and a script was selected. A month into shooting, Power had a nervous breakdown and left town, never to return. Neither the cast nor the script was the strongest, which made the movie resemble its title, "Fool's Gold." The film made enough money to cover its expenses but contributed little return for the tremendous investment made for building the studio. Eventually the company went into receivership and was sold for pennies on the dollar.

However, another opportunity came knocking for Lone Star. Ten of his players left WSC and joined the Marines. Stationed at Vallejo, California, they joined the Mare Island Marines football team but lacked a coach. Dick Hanley was dispatched to Spokane to recruit their old mentor. Although a civilian, Dietz trained to become a Marine officer in the morning and practiced the team in the afternoon. Despite being quarantined during an influenza epidemic and a four-game, 3,500 mile bus trip, Dietz's charges went undefeated. Because a Mare Island team composed of different players had competed in and won the 1918 Tournament of Roses game (the Rose Bowl wasn't built until 1923), Dietz's team was required to undergo an arduous post-season playoff schedule. The Marines emerged victorious and were selected to defend the honor of the West on New Year's Day, 1919 against the Great Lakes Navy team.

The Mare Island Marines were beaten up and sick going into the game. Dick Hanley was in bed with pneumonia and unable to play at all. A combination of good play by the Great Lakes team that featured three future NFL hall-of-famers, including "Papa Bear" George Halas, and poor decisions on the part of the Marines' quarterback led to a defeat. That defeat was a harbinger of things to come for Lone Star that year.

For reasons that remain unclear, Angel DeCora had not come west with Lone Star when he first took the job with WSC and had not moved out in the intervening years, so he filed for divorce on the grounds of desertion. The divorce was granted in November 1918, but neither party was allowed to remarry for six months. Angel did not live that long. She was caught up in the influenza pandemic that raged around the world at that time and died in February 1919. Dietz considered himself a widower.

Shortly after the game, the head of the Spokane draft board announced that he was filing charges against Dietz for draft dodging. He and Dietz had previously had words over Dietz's using what he considered an excessive amount of sugar, a rationed item during WWI. A couple of years earlier a reporter, who was familiar with Dietz's background in the Midwest, wrote a column that claimed that Dietz had no Indian heritage. That column served as the basis for the charges. Dietz had claimed to be a non-citizen Indian on the draft forms he filled out in September 1918, with the advice of Marine officers, and the government disputed that claim. The WSC administration reacted by withdrawing its contract offer for Dietz. The trial, held in late June 1919 at the federal courthouse in Spokane, was quite sensational and received national coverage. According to the charges, William Henry Dietz was the natural-born son of William Wallace and Leanna Ginder Dietz, two white people. The Dietzes, since divorced, lived in Rice Lake, Wisconsin at the time of their son's birth and raised him in that community. The prosecutor brought in several witnesses, including neighbors and relatives, from Rice Lake where Dietz grew up. He also brought in Sally Eagle Horse from the Pine Ridge reservation because Dietz had claimed she was his sister.

The prosecution witnesses from Rice Lake testified that they had either seen the young Dietz shortly after his birth in 1884 or they had seen him grow up. They all supported the government's case that Lone Star was really the white child of W. W. and

Leanna Ginder Dietz and that he had no Indian blood. Through an interpreter, Sally Eagle Horse testified that her brother, James One Star, had gone to Carlisle Indian School decades before but she hadn't seen him since. Lone Star was too young to have been her brother and didn't have a scar she recalled her brother having as the result of a childhood accident.

Dietz also brought in witnesses from Rice Lake including the woman who raised him, her mother and two of his father's nephews. Two Marines from Mare Island testified about his activities with the Marines. Leanna Ginder Lewis, who had divorced Dietz's father almost two decades before, testified that her son was stillborn in August, 1884 and that W. W. Dietz took the corpse and disappeared. He returned no more than ten days later with a child that he had had with an Indian woman about the same time. Leanna testified that the baby had a clump of coal-black hair and grew up to be the defendant. She brought with her the red shawl the baby was wrapped in when she received it. Leanna's mother (also named Leanna) testified that she was present for the birth and supported her daughter's story. Two nephews of the elder Dietz and their mother, his brother's wife, testified that W. W. had shared with them that his son had Indian blood on his mother's side and to keep it a secret.

Lone Star also took the stand. He told of growing up thinking he was the son of W. W. and Leanna Dietz until, at about age 15, he overheard them fighting and learned part of the secret of his birth. He testified that his parents and grandparents were fair-haired and blue-eyed and that, unlike them, he was dark-haired and dark-eyed.

To say the trial was sensational would be an understatement. It was the O. J. trial of its day. News reports were wired to all parts of the country and created headlines daily for the duration of the trial. High school girls came to the courthouse hoping to meet the famous, handsome football coach. After several days of testimony, the jury was tasked to make a decision.

After considerable deliberation, the jury was unable to come to a unanimous decision. The jury deadlocked 8 to 4 in favor of dismissal. The judge declared the jury hung. The prosecutor immediately refiled charges, this time for filling out draft forms improperly. In January 1920, out of money and unable to defend himself further, Dietz plead *nolo contendre* to the revised charges and was sentenced to 30 days in the Spokane County jail. This sentence was very lenient for the time. People found guilty of lesser offenses were often given much longer sentences. The judge may have not been very enthusiastic about putting Dietz in jail.

Dietz's reputation and career were ruined. He never obtained a top-tier coaching position again. As Ray Schmidt, editor of the journal for the College Football Historical Society, sees it, Dietz then took on a series of "reconstruction projects." In spite of this, Lone Star persevered and compiled a hall-of-fame-worthy coaching career with

Lone Star Dietz's war
shirt and leggings

stops at Purdue, Louisiana Tech, Wyoming, Haskell Institute and Albright College. When he was between jobs, Pop Warner hired him to coach his freshman teams at Stanford and, later, at Temple. Wherever Dietz went, he immediately increased interest in the football program dramatically. Through it all he continued drawing and painting. He even illustrated Pop Warner's 1927 book on coaching football.

In 1922 he married Doris Ohm Pottlitzer of Lafayette, Indiana, whom he met while coaching at Purdue University. Their union lasted until his death. People who knew the Dietzes described her as a delightful person, very refined and a gourmet cook. She was the society page editor of the local paper when she met Lone Star. The author is dismayed over not finding a single photograph of Doris – Dietzee as the neighborhood cookie-munching children called her. Doris and Lone Star were not blessed with children of their own.

Lone Star's reputation as a strategist persisted, largely because he put out winning teams where others had failed. In 1929 he was called "Miracle Man" for turning around the Haskell Institute Fightin' Indians. Because of his brilliance, he was selected to submit a favorite play to "My Winning Play," a series run by the Associated Press in the early 1930s. Always a showman, Dietz selected the "Dead Indian Play" as one of his favorites. Pop Warner originated the play at Carlisle in 1910, and in 1911 quarterback Gus Welch used it to call his own number against Penn with a 65-yard touchdown run the result. Jim Thorpe was too injured to play in that game and Warner used the "Dead Indian Play" to offset this handicap. According to Dietz, "The play is most effectively used in a team's own territory, about the 40-yard line, where a kick formation is a constant threat, with the defensive backs playing rather deep and the defensive line somewhat scattered. The back behind center gets the ball on a 'lob' pass, drives into the line between left guard and tackle and is generally tackled by the defensive right halfback, who plays in front of the hole. Naturally, the other defensive backs are drawn up to this point in backing up the play. The offensive line then moves up to the point where the ball carrier is lying on the ground in a rather prone position. Another back, addressing the prone one, says, 'Are you hurt?' The ball carrier gets up slowly and responds, 'Oh, I'm all right,' and throws the ball to a third back who, with the aid of the flanking linemen and backs, circles around the opponent's end, usually for long gains which have resulted in many touchdowns." Dietz claimed to have abandoned the play but said there was nothing in the rules to prevent him from reviving it.

In 1933 Lone Star Dietz accepted the head coaching position for the Boston Braves NFL team. George Preston Marshall, owner of the team, moved the team to Fenway Park, necessitating a name change for the team. Marshall's granddaughter wrote an op-ed piece to the *The Washington Post* some years ago stating that her grandfather had renamed the team Redskins in Dietz's honor. Dietz has been embroiled in the Indian mascot controversy for many years due to his central role in the naming of the team.

Dietz's paid coaching career ended after the 1942 season when Albright College terminated its athletic programs for the duration of WWII. Lone Star put his skills as an artist to work to support himself during the war. After the war he operated an art school in Pittsburgh. When the Korean War siphoned off his students to the military or defense jobs, he used his life savings to pay off the school's debt.

In 1956, Lone Star stole the show at the Rose Bowl celebration honoring the 40th anniversary of his team's landmark victory. While on the West Coast, he visited Pullman at a time Washington State was looking for a new football coach. Although he did not formally apply for the job, it was clear he wanted it. However, those weren't the days of septuagenarian coaches. The school did give him a school blanket, a decades-overdue honor.

Dietz spent the last eight years of his life living in poverty in Reading, Pennsylvania where he assisted with youth football and remained involved in the Albright College community. He continued painting and several of his works can be found hanging at Albright. A former player whom Dietz visited frequently at his army surplus store remarked that, every time he saw him, Lone Star had some new idea. He was never defeated and didn't wallow in the past. Lone Star Dietz died of cancer in 1964 holding Pop Warner's inspirational poem, "Keep A-goin'," in his hand.

Since his death, he has had a number of honors bestowed on him but has not been inducted into the College Football Hall of Fame. In 2005 he may have come the closest. However, the selection committee chose to ignore the names of coaches on the ballots and selected two coaches for induction who were not eligible for induction at that time because they were still actively coaching. After Bobby Bowden and Joe Paterno were selected, the rules were changed to make others, should there ever be other coaches in their situation, eligible for placement on the ballot. Interestingly, both coaches accepted the honor and neither publicly questioned why they could be inducted when their names hadn't been on the ballot.

Lone Star Dietz was a fascinating man whose life deserved a book-length biography. Fortunately one has been written. Those interested in knowing more about Lone Star are directed to *Keep A-goin': the life of Lone Star Dietz* by the author who also wrote the book you are now reading. After writing that book while researching his own family background, the author learned of a man from whom he *might* be descended and who maintained two families, one white and one Cherokee, along the frontier in 1760. Apparently situations such as the one Leanna Lewis described may not be as far-fetched as they might appear at first blush. Also, while looking at census data for Gus Welch, the author stumbled across a Lonestar family in Washburn County, Wisconsin, the county immediately north of Barron County, the county in which W. W. Dietz lived. So, the facts of Lone Star Dietz's birth remain murky.

After completing this chapter, the author learned of Joel Platt's enormous collection of priceless sports artifacts. Included in this collection are objects that were surely in Dietz's possession at the time of his death. A 1974 *Sports Illustrated* article discussed his baby curls. Platt's Sports Immortals web site prominently displays the beautiful pair of gloves Jim Thorpe made at Carlisle and gave to Lone Star. Who knows what else is in that collection?

Gus Welch

20

Gus Welch punting; *U. S. Army Military History Institute*

Gus Welch, Captain, U. S. Army; *Cumberland County Historical Society, Carlisle, PA*

Name: Gustavus A. Welch		**Nickname:** Gus	
DOB: 12/23/1890		**Height:** 5'9"	
Weight: 162		**Age:** 19	
Tribe: Chippewa		**Home:** Spooner, WI	
Parents: James Welch, Irish; Mary Hart Welch, Chippewa			
Early Schooling: Tomah Indian Industrial School			
Later Schooling: Conway Hall; Dickinson School of Law			
Honors: American Indian Athletic Hall of Fame, 1971; College Football Hall of Fame, 1975			

Five-Time Brown Derby Winner

Gustavus A. Welch, Chippewa, arrived at Carlisle from Spooner, Wisconsin, on September 22, 1908, accompanied by his younger brother, James. The Welch children were orphans. A logging incident took their Irish-born father before the turn of the 20th century, leaving their mother, Mary Hart Welch, a widow with seven children. They lived in Washburn County, Wisconsin, according to the 1900 Federal Census. That census listed Susan, Lizzie, Robert and Gus as being "at school." James, Robert and Gus were on the roll of the Tomah Indian Industrial School in Monroe County, Wisconsin. In 1905, John and Robert, the two oldest boys, were living together on their own as tuberculosis had apparently consumed their mother as well as several siblings by this time. Brother John, being the oldest, signed the Carlisle enrollment papers for James and Gus. Gus's birthday varies widely across the several official papers that can be found. However, his short, handwritten autobiography puts his date of birth as December 23, 1890, near Spooner.

Before coming to Carlisle, Gus spent a lot of time with his maternal grandmother, Chemamanon, wife of the chief of the La Couriterielle band, Kewanzee. Washburn County is adjacent to Barron County, where Lone Star Dietz grew up. Both counties were heavily timbered and dotted with lakes. Towns were in early stages of development when the boys were growing up. Chippewas lived among and around the early white settlers. Living in the northwoods with fellow Chippewas, young Gus learned many of the traditional skills, including paddling a birch-bark canoe, harvesting wild rice, collecting maple syrup and trapping furs. He put the latter one to great use when he decided that he wanted to enroll at Carlisle in order to play on their sports teams in 1907.

Learning that the Carlisle Indians would play the University of Minnesota in mid-November, Gus trapped a wolf and used the proceeds from selling its pelt for trainfare to Minneapolis. After arriving in the Twin Cities, he located the practice field used by the Carlisle Indians' football team and watched the players prepare for the game. He positioned himself behind the goal post that kickers were attempting to split for field goals. Eventually Frank Mt. Pleasant made one. Gus outran all the other boys who were standing around, including two Carlisle substitutes, and retrieved the ball. Before anyone could take away what looked to him like a shiny new ball (mistaking a well-used practice ball for a new one is understandable because he had never seen a real football before; he had only played with homemade balls stuffed with leaves.), Gus kicked it back through the goal post over Mt. Pleasant's head. So impressed with the kick was the Carlisle star that he escorted Gus over to meet Pop Warner. The Old Fox invited Gus to apply for admission to Carlisle and let him watch the game from the bench dressed in a Carlisle uniform.

Shortly after arriving at Carlisle, James and Gus often gained mention in the school newspaper. James was at the head of his class, Room No. 4, in the October Merit Roll. He gave an impromptu talk to a meeting of the Dicksons in November in Room No. 4½. He had apparently been promoted. In December Gustavus participated in a debate for the Standard Debating Society, developing skills he would use in later life. He and David Robinson successfully argued for the negative for the proposition that business training is of more importance to the Indian than agriculture. In February 1909, Gus received positive mention in *The Arrow* for his recitation in the auditorium the previous week, "Men to be Honored." On the Final Merit Roll in April, James was first in his class, Room No. 5. Apparently he had been promoted a second time. The Welch boys definitely stood out academically.

Gus's first recognition for athletic prowess came for his victory in the July 4, 1909 school games. Gus and Joseph Trepania won the 100-yard three-legged race, winning new swimming suits for their efforts. Gus then went on outing to work on a farm where he earned $15 a month. Back at school in the fall, he studied blacksmithing, was elected President of the Sophomore Class, was ranked first in his class on the December Merit Roll, debated as a member of the Standards, was frequently called upon to make orations at school events, and was promoted to first chair in the cornet section of the famed Carlisle Indian School Band. *The Arrow* noted an immediate improvement in the band's sound. He also participated in athletics but not on the varsity level.

Gus continued to be in the first rank of students in all aspects of school life except, to the naked eye, athletics. He made the varsity football team in 1910 but did not start. In track the following spring, he made a small splash, placing in some meets and running one of the legs for the winning team at the Penn Relays. 1911 was Gus's breakout year in football. It was also the year his idol, Jim Thorpe, returned to Carlisle, and Welch was assigned to room with him in the athletic quarters. Gus thought Warner was joking when he told him to move in with Thorpe and had to be told again the next day before he believed it. Although Thorpe and Welch were opposites in many ways, they got along. Warner wasn't called the Old Fox for nothing. Where Thorpe was inclined to do wild, risky things, Welch was sensible; Thorpe was quiet while Welch was talkative; Welch was studious, but Thorpe would rather be playing or hunting outdoors. Both were orphans with American Indian mothers and Irish fathers. Jim had lost his twin early in life where Gus had lost several siblings. Perhaps this combination helped to bond them.

1911 was a special year for Gus as well as for Carlisle. Gus wore several hats and received numerous honors, including president of the Senior Class, orator, quarterback of the football team, president of the school's model republic, captain of the track team, sometime football scout, and subject of a limerick written by a classmate for publication in *The Arrow*.

Pop Warner considered the 1911 Carlisle eleven their best team ever with star players at every position. So strong was the team that it could defeat major opponents without the services of its left halfback, the incomparable Jim Thorpe. Although everyone else played in Thorpe's shadow, Gus got his share of media coverage and became known around the country as one of the best at his position. The quarterback in Warner's single-wingback formation is generally called the blocking back for good reason. Welch was a good blocker and led the way for Thorpe, the tailback. But the blocking back also called the signals, which in those days included selecting the plays to be called. Sometimes he even called his own because Warner developed plays in which the blocking back got the ball to keep the defense honest. Gus also ran back kicks and punts with the best of them. The game against Andy Smith's Penn Quakers provided a stage for Gus to display his talents. Both teams' stars, Thorpe and Mercer, were too injured to play, which made the contest all the more interesting. The Philadelphia *North American* described the contest in colorful terms: "The redskins scalped, raged, plundered and ravaged. The fleet Arcasa and the rapid-moving Welch skirted the Penn Ends as though the gentlemen set to guard these points were stakes driven into the skirts of tepees [sic] to foil the wind." Later in the game Gus made his big play as the *North American* reported, "…it was on the 15-yard line that Welch started for an end run. Coming sharply from midfield, he ran toward the north line. Running toward the south at a long angle, he finally formed the apex of a rapidly moving triangle. Only one man had a chance to catch him, but no player had the fleetness of foot of the Indian, and Welch, maintaining his burst of speed, pulled steadily away, and went over the line for a touchdown after a run of 95 yards."

The 1911 Indians lost but a single game, 12-11 to a weaker opponent, Syracuse, due to overconfidence. But the loss was not due to anything Gus Welch did or didn't do; he tried everything he could to salvage a victory. Because he was laid up with a bad back most of the week leading up to the game, he did not dress for it. When things didn't go well for Carlisle in the first half, Welch went to the locker room at half-time and suited up. His play and generalship nearly overcame the deficit that accumulated in the first half.

Gus also had a good track season in the spring of 1912, particularly in the 440-yard dash and 880-yard run. He made the U. S. Olympic track team but wasn't well enough when the time came to make the trip to Stockholm, Sweden. After graduation, he enrolled in Conway Hall, Dickinson College Preparatory School. At the end of May, he left for Browning, Montana, with Sampson Bird. *The Carlisle Arrow* didn't speculate about the reason for their trip. The always short-of-funds Welch was probably looking for an opportunity to make money. The following September, when reporting that he returned too late from roughing it in Montana to be ready to play in the first game, the *Arrow* commented on how fit he appeared. Elsewhere in the issue, the reporter mentioned that Welch had spent the summer in the harvest fields of North Dakota. Although playing baseball is always a possibility, he more likely worked on threshing crews those summers.

In the fall, Gus was back to studying at Conway Hall and playing football for Carlisle. The team was loaded with talent as most of the stars from the previous year's team returned. Once again, the Indians went through the schedule with one loss. An ankle injury kept Welch from performing at top form and was likely the cause of his not being named first team All-American. The *New York Evening Sun* chose him for its second team, stating, "Welsh [sic] of Carlisle had to handle probably the most versatile offense any team has shown this year, and he is therefore chosen as the second-best quarterback of the year."

Gus filled in as captain of the track team until Bruce Goesback was elected. After the 1912 Olympics, *The Carlisle Arrow* seldom mentioned Gus with regard to track, but he was still an integral part of the football team. Note of Gus's activity with organized religion began that fall when he gave a short talk to the Boys Catholic meeting on the good that can be accomplished by attending the meetings of the Holy Name Society. He even gave a talk about the Penn-Carlisle game to a Union meeting (presumed to be boys and girls together) of the Holy Name Society. Gus soon spent some more time at St. Patrick's for a major media event.

As soon as the World Series was over, Jim Thorpe returned to Carlisle to marry Iva Miller, a Carlisle student. Gus Welch, Thorpe's old roommate, was best man. This may have been Gus's first film appearance as Thorpe sold the movie rights to his wedding to two motion picture companies.

With Thorpe now gone, Gus had three new backfield mates in 1913; Pete Calac and Joe Guyon were moved from line positions to the backfield while Edward Bracklin was installed at right halfback (wingback). The team didn't miss a beat and had a one loss-one tie season. Gus led his team three years running to one-loss seasons and to three of Carlisle's greatest victories ever over Harvard (1911), Dartmouth (1913), and Army (1912). Several players, including Welch, were mentioned for All-America honors. So successful was the team that year that Gus and Superintendent Friedman were invited to speak at the Dickinson College football banquet.

Sadly, the Carlisle Indian School was in disarray at that time due to an incompetent administration. Teachers and students alike were at the point of mutiny. Impoverished, Gus wasn't happy that football players and band boys generated thousands of dollars in revenue for the school but were paid little for their efforts. He thought Warner to be profane and unprincipled. He also believed that Warner and Friedman had let Jim Thorpe take the fall for having played minor league baseball when they were likely aware of it well before the Olympics. Welch drafted a petition and got 214 students to sign it. He then delivered it to Rep. A. H. Rupley, who lived in Carlisle. When Gus's brother in Wisconsin fell ill in early January 1914, he wanted James to go help with the family. Perhaps sensing the upcoming investigation brought about in part by Welch's petition, Warner and Friedman insisted that Gus go and paid his expenses out of athletic funds. Although he was away for a month, he returned in time to testify. He felt that Warner exercised no moral authority over the boys and should be removed from his job. That didn't happen, but changes to the school and athletic program decreased Warner's power and the ability to field competitive teams.

In March, Gus, being the school's best orator, gave the welcoming address to Mother Catherine Drexel, the philanthropist nun who spent millions of her own dollars aiding Indians. He began the talk by saying, "We always welcome a friend of the Indian, especially a true and sincere friend such as Mother Catherine Drexel has shown herself." Earlier in the month he was informed by the acting supervisor that Washington would not pay his remaining tuition at Conway Hall. That was a severe and probably unexpected blow to a young man already living on the edge financially.

By summer's end, the superintendent started getting letters requesting that Gus repay some money he had borrowed, usually from former students. Edward Leo wrote from Atlantic City, almost frantic to get his $11 back in order to cover his travel expenses home. His letter was forwarded to Welch at Conway Hall, where he was apparently staying at that time. A few days earlier *The Carlisle Arrow* reported, "Gus Welch and Henry Broker, Carlisle '12 and '13, respectively, returned last week from a very enjoyable and profitable summer in Atlantic City." Apparently it was not profitable enough to cover his law school tuition, room and board. By that time, Gus was preparing for the start of football season.

Having finished his preparatory school courses in the spring, Gus was now a student at Dickinson School of Law and the coach of the Conway Hall football team. Although he had a year of varsity eligibility remaining, he had no intention of playing that year. The Carlisle Indian School was restructured after the investigation was completed, resulting in a student body with fewer boys of the age and size needed for a competitive football team. A few stars remained in 1914, but there weren't enough supporting cast members to generate the results Warner had been producing. Peter Calac was made team captain and Elmer Busch, who had been elected captain the previous spring, was relieved of that commission. November injuries had further depleted the team and the Notre Dame game was coming up soon. Left halfbacks Fred Broker and Jesse Wofford were both on the injured list, making it necessary to bring up Grant White from the reserves. James Crane showed promise at quarterback until he got hurt. The Indians were short a field general and faced a tough opponent. Exactly how it came to be is not known, but Gus Welch suited up as quarterback for the Notre Dame game.

With their old captain leading them, the Indians had a fighting chance against the Irish, going to the locker room down 17-6 at halftime. But the tide turned against them when Gus was seriously injured in a collision with Notre Dame fullback Ray "Iron Eich" Eichenlaub. The injury was so serious that Gus was taken to Chicago's Mercy Hospital. Without him on the field, things went downhill fast. What began as a beating by a superior opponent became a thrashing to the tune of 48-6, Carlisle's worst loss to that time. It was also Gus's worst injury. He was hurt so badly that he remained behind in the hospital when the team returned to Carlisle.

School administrators wrote Gus that his brother, James, would not be visiting him because James was in the hospital in Philadelphia. They were concerned that he had a tubercular knee. Fortunately, their fears were not realized and James made a full recovery, just not in time to visit Gus in Chicago.

On November 20 – the Notre Dame game was played on the 14th – Gus wrote to Oscar Lipps, the acting superintendent, telling him that he was feeling fine and expected to return soon. Dr. W. E. Morgan wrote Lipps on the 21st stating, "He not only sustained a fracture of the cheek-bone (which he feels) but he had also a fracture of the base of the skull in front (which he don't [sic] feel) but which requires absolute rest to insure a future without invalidism, such as epilepsy, paralysis, deafness or loss of sight, any one of which might develop in after years from recklessness or negligence at this time." On the 23rd Dr. Morgan wrote, "Mr. Gus Welch still continues with his gradual improvement and seems more contented than before. I believe he has decided to be good and mind the doctor. Has promised me to-day to do just as I say. He's a fine fellow and I can't take any chances with him." The next day the good doctor wrote, "I am sorry to say that our patient Gus Welch deliberately kicked over the traces to-day and in spite of all advice to the contrary, left his bed, and dressed himself, declaring that he would assume all responsibility." Gus's rashness came back to haunt him later.

Gus pulled into Carlisle on November 30th while the team was away on a four-game road trip to New England, Alabama and Georgia. The New England games were played before his return and newspaper accounts don't list Welch as having played in either the Alabama or the Auburn game. His playing days at Carlisle were finished.

Three weeks after Gus returned to Carlisle, the superintendent received a letter from Wesley Talchief demanding repayment of $10 loaned to Welch when he, Peter Jordan and Henry Broker were stranded in Buffalo, New York the previous August. Talchief sent another letter in January. On January 16, 1915, Welch wrote Superintendent Lipps that he had attended to the matter. Yet another letter from Talchief arrived in March.

Gus's inability to repay his debts apparently didn't influence Lipps's high regard for his indigent ward because, in June 1915, Oscar Lipps hired him as first assistant football coach. The job paid "$150 per month in cash for the months of September, October, and November" plus room and board for the entire school year. The contract contained clauses that required Welch to maintain high standards of conduct and "…see that our football players observe strictly the rules governing amateur athletics; and that they refrain from any conduct that would in any way reflect upon the school or affect their amateur standing as athletes." In other words, no pro football for Gus or his players, at least not this year.

Immediately after Pop Warner's departure in early 1915, several Carlisle alums applied for the vacant head coaching position, apparently viewing the job as a plum. Instead of one of the better known and more involved former players getting the job, it was awarded to Victor M. Kelley. Kelley had attended Carlisle for a year. Well, not exactly. He played for Carlisle in 1908 while attending Dickinson School of Law. Welch attributed Kelley's hiring to Texas politics. Influence from Texas politicians at the national level is probably more accurate.

The 1915 season was even more of a disaster than 1914 had been. The annual Thanksgiving game with Pasadena-bound Brown brought the 3-6-2 season to a merciful end. The 39-3 trouncing by the Bears was a fitting end to a season filled with dissension. A news piece out of Carlisle said that, as assistant coach, Welch did not want to take the blame for the disastrous season. It reported that, "Kelley asked him to assume charge of the squad after he found out that he could not develop it himself, and that three weeks before Thanksgiving Kelley was secretly deposed as coach by the school authorities, although allowed to remain at his own request on the campus until the season's end." *The Providence Journal* mocked Carlisle in a cartoon, depicting the team as a fat caricature of an Indian player long past his prime dreaming of better days. Gus returned to Carlisle with the team and continued his study of the law.

In April 1916, surely with mixed emotions, Gus received his inheritance from his mother. He could no doubt use the $149.35 for his portion of Wa-wi-ens's estate, but he had to sign over another check, this one for $85.00, to pay for the casket in which his brother, John, was buried. Now his oldest brother was gone.

There was much ink spilled speculating about whether Carlisle would field a football team in 1916, but it seems improbable that Gus wanted to be associated with it after what he had gone through the previous year. But he did accept a position as Indian Assistant at $20 per month plus room. The announcement in *The Carlisle Arrow* gave him the title of Assistant Disciplinarian at the Large Boys' Quarters. Also in *The Carlisle Arrow*, Superintendent Lipps provided reasons for Welch's history of financial problems when he wrote, "Unlike many of the Indian boys who attend higher schools after leaving the Indian school, Gus has not had the wherewithal to see him through college. He has had to work hard to meet expenses but by his push, willingness to do any hard work, by his stick-to-it-iveness and by his inimitable good nature, he has almost worked his way through college. It is good for the young Indian boys to have among them one of their own who has struggled as Gus has had to struggle for an education and all other things that tend to make a man."

While completing his last year of law school, Gus played football for Dickinson College. He threatened to quit, likely due to poor performance in the first game of the season, but agreed to stay after Dickinson College's student body prevailed on him to continue. Gus led the Red Devils in scoring for the year, which turned out to be a very successful one. After the college season was over, he and his coach, former Dickinson star Frank "Mother" Dunn, shored up the Canton, Ohio professional team. The Bulldogs were somewhat depleted by injuries over the tough season and needed some fresh players. Gus became part of an unofficial national championship team and part of what Bulldogs' manager Jack Cusack considered his best Canton team ever. After a quick scan of the team's roster, there can be little doubt as to how he became aware of that opportunity as his old roommate was starring for the Bulldogs. When not on the gridiron, he kept an eye on the future.

When Hervey B. Peairs, Superintendent of Haskell Institute, visited Carlisle for an unrelated purpose, Gus took the opportunity to approach him about the position of athletic director. Following protocol, Peairs made an offer of $1,000 per year for the position of Assistant Disciplinarian and Athletic Director through the new Carlisle superintendent, John Francis. In a letter to Peairs, Francis responded that he had discussed the matter and Welch would be available to start on July 1. However, a war intervened.

On June 7, John Francis informed Superintendent Peairs that Welch had enlisted and was at the Reserve Officers Training Camp at Fort Niagara where he was hoping to land an officer's commission. A week later he received his last pay check from Carlisle, along with a bill for unpaid board to the tune of $36.00. Second Lieutenant pay of $1,700 per year plus benefits, of which there were many, must have looked very enticing to an impoverished orphan.

Later in the month, Gus wrote Francis about his experiences, mostly good, at the army camp so far. But then he had to go to the rifle range. Gus was concerned about not qualifying for a commission because of his prior impatience:

> "I am somewhat worried over the result of the shooting. Three years ago I had my face injured, and this is the first effect I have experienced as a result of the injury. The shock received from the rifle fire causes me to have a severe head ache, while shooting the pain almost blinds me."

Because his scores were good, he said nothing to his officers about the pain and volunteered for the aviation corps at his first opportunity. He and Francis corresponded regularly throughout Gus's training. The superintendent suggested that he consider making a career out of the military, given its job security. Just before the end of the letter, Gus wrote, "I have done my best, keeping always in mind that I was a Carlisle man. I also had to remember that I was the only Redskin in camp, and of course my errors would naturally look larger than the other fellows'."

It being the army after all, Gus wasn't assigned to the air corps. Instead he was sent to Harvard – Harvard Reserve Officers' Training Corps, that is. The newly-minted 2nd Lieutenant spent his days attending lectures in Harvard Stadium, the site of some of his fiercest battles, listening to lectures given by six French officers, each of whom had been wounded multiple times. He found staying awake no problem, "About the time their [sic] think that the students are becoming weary, they spring one of these hair-raising experiences, and then you are ready to listen for another hour."

His next assignment was as an instructor at Camp Meade, Maryland. In his off-hours, he played halfback and captained the officers' football team and competed with teams from other military bases, sometimes at Penn's Franklin Field. On November 9, Jim Thorpe wired the Indian School from Canton, Ohio, inquiring about Gus's whereabouts. John Francis sent him the following response:

> Lieutenant Gus Welch with 14th Training Battalion
> Camp Meade, Maryland.
> Signed, Francis
> Western Union Collect

Thorpe was looking for Gus because his Canton Bulldogs had suffered some injuries in the Youngstown game and needed reinforcements, especially with two games against archrival Massillon coming up soon. Gus earned his pay in the home game against Youngstown with an 80 (89 in some accounts) yard touchdown run while Thorpe and Dunn nursed injuries on the bench and rested up for Massillon. Welch, Dunn and Thorpe started the first game against Massillon, and Pete Calac came in as a substitute. The game was played in a snowstorm but Canton prevailed. It's not clear if Gus made it to Detroit for the Thanksgiving game against the Heralds or the away game against Massillon because he, like most of the Canton team, played under an assumed name. Keith McClellan and PFRA Research deciphered game reports and determined that Welch generally played as "Wells" but might have been "Moore." Getting away and back in time for military duty may have been difficult at times. But he must have devoted adequate time to his military duties because before long he was attached to the depot brigade and promoted to 1st Lieutenant. A few months later he made captain. Gus argued long and hard to be sent overseas but was considered too valuable where he was. Finally he located a unit that was having difficulty finding officers to lead it and volunteered for the 808th Pioneer Infantry, which shipped out of Hoboken on August 28, 1918, and arrived in France in early September. The 808th was a regiment consisting of 2,721 black enlisted men and 81 white officers. For these purposes, the Army counted Indian officers as white.

Very shortly after landing in Europe, the 808th saw action in the St. Mihiel sector in the Argonne defensive initiative and, immediately after that, the Meuse-Argonne offensive that lasted until the armistice. The 808th Pioneer Infantry followed closely behind the assault troops and took over captured enemy engineer dumps. Many of these dumps were found well stocked with useable munitions and engineering materials which were quickly put to use against their former owners. After the armistice, Gus may have been able to enjoy the music performed by the 808th band which included former Carlisle student James Wheelock. With the war won, Gus was ready for gridiron battles.

After the war ended, colleges reinstituted their athletic programs. However, many of them needed coaches and players. Washington State College (WSC) supporters were excited and looked forward to the upcoming football season with great anticipation. Under Head Coach Lone Star Dietz, the team lost two regular season games in four years and split in two Tournament of Roses New Year's Day games in Pasadena. The fourth year the team was nominally called the Mare Island Marines, but Washington State considers it their team because ten players and the coach came from Pullman. The yearbook, *The Chinook*, even included a section on the Mare Island team!

Expectations were high because many of the pre-war players were returning. But Dietz was indicted for draft evasion and no longer coached WSC. *The Evergreen* exposed the school's strategy for hiring a new coach:

> "When the athletic council commenced casting around for a man to take the place vacated by 'Lonestar' Dietz, they agreed that it should be someone acquainted with the Warner system and able to teach it to his men. In considering applicants, they discovered that Exendine had made application and had an enviable record behind him. So out of a list of over a dozen candidates, he was chosen, and his salary was to have been between $2000 and $3000. That is the story given out by Graduate Manager Kruegel.
> "Coach Bohler stated, however, that Exendine had signed a contract with Georgetown for next year, so there was nothing to the 'rumor.' So then it goes to the student body just as I heard it – a confirmed and denied rumor."

WSC set about finding what they thought would be the next best thing. Gus Welch was located on a former battlefield in France after two months of searching and agreed to take the job. He promised to be in Pullman by September 10. After 10 months of overseas duty, the 808th returned to the U. S. Gus Welch separated from the army at Camp Lee, Virginia, in time to embark on a coaching career. Former standouts Carl "Red" Dietz and Clarence "Zim" Zimmerman were selected as varsity assistant and freshman coach, respectively. Now all Pullmanites had to do was to wait until September.

Coach Welch arrived in Pullman with much fanfare as local football fans expected him to repeat, or at least closely approach, the success Lone Star Dietz had had on the

Palouse. At Gus's first public appearance, Frank Corbett, Nez Perce, greeted him. Corbett had been behind Welch in the depth charts at Carlisle. After leaving Carlisle, he attended the University of Idaho but was now enrolled at Washington State. He told *The Evergreen* reporter, "Welch was unquestionably one of the best players turned out at Carlisle and was a popular favorite with players and students alike. I had heard a lot about the State College and followed the athletic programs of the college closely while Coach Dietz was here, but when I heard that Gus Welch was coming to coach this year I at once made up my mind that Washington State College was the place for me."

Not long after practice started in earnest, *The Evergreen* reported, "Captain Welch has also developed that disease so common to football coaches known as 'gloomia bearitis,' which particularly affects the vocal organs in such a way that he can only talk about the weak points of his team. The poor tackling of his men and the acute shortage of experienced players on his squad are coming in for their share of comment."

Welch spent his spare time on the rubber-chicken circuit. He told the Chamber of Commerce, "We are going to strive to give you the best team that ever represented the State College, but a winning team is not, by far, the sum total of the aspirations of the coaching staff. It is our desire to make Rogers Field a vast classroom for the development of real men. We want to teach them stamina, patience, aggressiveness and determination."

By October, *The Evergreen* bemoaned, "Football Prospects Not the Brightest." With the belated arrival of Walter "Fat" Herreid, WSC had but seven returning lettermen whereas several of her Pacific Coast Conference rivals boasted much larger numbers of experienced players. Hopes dimmed a bit more when the Marines would not release Walter V. "Boots" Brown in time for football season. Brown was quarterback Arthur "Bull" Durham's understudy in 1915 and 1916. He then played in the 1917 Mare Island Marines backfield that won the Tournament of Roses game on New Year's Day of 1918, the year before his former WSC teammates played in the Marines' uniforms. The Crimson and Gray opened the season encouragingly enough, crushing Multnomah Athletic Club of Portland 49-0, with the three Hanley brothers scoring five of the seven touchdowns. Lone Star Dietz gave the team a pep talk before the game "and encouraged the various members in his famous characteristic manner." Next up were Andy Smith's California Golden Bears, considered by many to be the class of the conference. Perhaps succumbing to a bit of grandiosity after WSC's unexpected 14-0 victory over Cal, *The Evergreen* opined, "No team in America could have held out against the crimson and gray on that memorable afternoon, for such fierce and constant onslaught as Welch's men displayed has never before been witnessed in the annals of coast football."

Wins against Idaho and Oregon brought the Cougars, as WSC's teams began to be called after a sportswriter dubbed their fighting spirit in the victory over Cal, to an unscored upon 4-0. Their once-beaten cross-state rival, Washington, invaded Pullman for WSC's homecoming. That Washington's sole loss was to Oregon, WSC's hopes for a Dietz-like season seemed to be materializing. Mother Nature intervened with the result that WSC was on the short end of a 13-7 score in a mud game. The Cougars may have been suffering a bit of a hangover from the Washington game when they played Oregon Agricultural College at Portland and lost 6-0. Welch's charges rebounded against outmanned Montana State, prevailing 42-14 on the road. 5-2-0 is normally a good start for a new head coach, but that record approximated Dietz's worst year, and the only year in which he lost any regular-season games at WSC. Although the Washington State faithful wanted a better outcome, they supported giving Welch another chance and the athletic council awarded him a second one-year contract. He left to practice law and returned for the start of football season.

Gus started the 1920 season with 13 lettermen and a new assistant coach, Hack Applequist, another player from the 1915 team who took time off from his job with the Anaconda Mining Company to help his alma mater. Carl Dietz was apparently unable to assist as he was battling tuberculosis, contracted when he was suffering from influenza in France during the war. The varsity started off the season by winning the annual game against the alumni. As one former player put it, "Bald heads and forward projections have no place in football." But they put up a valiant fight before succumbing to the younger men. Cougars' hopes of defending the honor of the West on New Year's Day in Pasadena ran high after defeating Gonzaga, Idaho and Montana, but they were dashed when California ran wild 49-0. *The Evergreen* put it this way: "A superior football team, with all the breaks in its favor, was the cause of the downfall of the Cougars." A win over Oregon Agricultural College and a come-from-behind victory over Nebraska gave Welch and WSC a 5-1 record for the season that, although the best in the Pacific Northwest, was not very satisfying without the New Year's Day trip. In early December, *The Evergreen* editorialized that, contrary to a common misunderstanding on the part of the student body, Gus Welch was not yet under contract for the 1921 football season. It also opined that other colleges were out to hire him and that WSC should sign him when he returned from Oklahoma for a short visit before Christmas. While away from Pullman he kept his hand in as a player so to speak by playing quarterback for Jim Thorpe's Canton Bulldogs in a big game against the Buffalo All-Americans in New York City.

At the end of spring practice, *The Evergreen* thought, with eleven lettermen and Gus Welch returning, that WSC should contend for the conference title in the fall. In the meantime, Gus would be busy managing the national Indian conference that summer. He may have rubbed shoulders with an earlier Carlislian who was involved in the event, Frank Cayou. Returning to Pullman in the fall, Gus was ready for a great season.

The Evening Star
2-4-1937

During training camp, Welch announced that he, Athletic Director J. Fred "Doc" Bohler, and Applequist would be conducting a couple of sessions for the public in the rules and formations used in football. These scrimmages did not turn out as expected. Gus was not pleased with the varsity's performance in a 31-7 pre-season warm up but hoped it would serve as a wake up call for complacent players. Decisive victories over Gonzaga and Idaho gave reason for optimism, but a loss to Cal once again dashed hopes for a New Year's Day game in Pasadena. But going through the remainder of the schedule with only a tie with Oregon gave Cougars a chance for an invitation to a December 26 game against Centre College in San Diego They needed to win a play-off game of sorts against Southern California at Pasadena to get the invitation. USC prevailed 28-7 in a game marred by fumbles. Gus's third season at 4-2-1 wasn't terribly satisfying. The editor of *The Evergreen*, tired of annual speculation as to who would coach the team the upcoming year, recommended that the administration sign Welch to a three to five year contract. Just before football season started, the Pacific Coast Conference announced it would enforce rules that disallow seasonal coaches for athletic teams effective immediately. Contracting coaches for a season at a time had been WSC's habit, so Gus was assigned "instruction in gymnasium work" to occupy him outside football season.

The 1922 Cougars went 2-5-0, winning the first two games and losing all the rest. Those five losses included a 61-0 shellacking by Cal and a 41-3 whipping by USC. It was not a happy time. Not surprisingly, Gus resigned on December 23. The factors affecting his decision were surely the losing season coupled with poor prospects for better results the next year, being forced by the conference to remain in Pullman the entire academic year, and his upcoming marriage. Whatever the reason for his resignation, Gus's coaching career was roughly parallel to that of Lone Star Dietz. WSC was the first college head coaching job for both as well as the last major college head coaching position either held in their long careers. Gus did not have the satisfaction of competing on New Year's Day or in the NFL or have a Hall-of-Fame-worthy coaching career, but he was making a name for himself with the trick plays he liked to run. WSC hadn't seen enough of the Carlisle System so searched for another Indian trained in the Warner system to replace him.

Gus married Julia Josephine Carter, daughter of long-time congressman Charles David Carter. The Carters were Cherokee-Chickasaws from Boggy Depot, Oklahoma, but had been in Washington, DC so long that it had become their home. That year, 1923, he also took the athletic director position at little Randolph-Macon College in Ashland, Virginia, near Richmond. Although only one of his football teams at that institution won two games during his six-year tenure and half won no games at all, he considered his time at Randolph-Macon as being among the happiest years of his life because of the caliber of the young men on that campus. But football wasn't the only sport Gus coached at R-MC.

In 1969 Welch wrote about introducing lacrosse to Randolph-Macon and the South:

> "We started Lacrosse, in the south, at R. M. C., and held our own with the best teams in the north. We had no money for our Lacrosse equipment but when I made it known to Mr. Lalle, who owned the only Lacrosse factory, at that time, that I was trying to start Lacrosse in the South, he very generously sent us sticks, and we made the rest of the equipment. Our student body at that time numbered around <u>225</u>. Some of my happiest days were the six years spent at R. M. C., and I never had finer men at <u>any</u> College where I coached."

In 1929, Gus's last year at Randolph-Macon and just before the start of the Great

Depression, he and Julia used their life savings to buy about 500 acres of land in the Blue Ridge Mountains in Bedford County, Virginia, on Apple Orchard Mountain near Natural Bridge. They set up a boys' camp named in honor of Gus's maternal grandfather, Kewanzee, and operated it for 30 years. They had no children but adopted their niece, Serena, and raised her as their own. Serena, the camp boys, and the boys Gus coached were their children.

Welch's next coaching stop was as an assistant football coach at the University of Virginia where he also coached lacrosse. Gus and Jim Thorpe both applied for the open Dickinson College coaching job in 1931, but neither got it. In 1933 the Athletic Director position at Haskell Institute opened up when Lone Star Dietz left to lead the Boston NFL team. Unfortunately for Gus, then 40, the problems that had plagued Dietz during his last year at Haskell remained. The country remained in the depression and government funding for the school's athletic program also remained low. His contract would have allowed him to stay longer, but reducing Haskell's status essentially to that of a high school created a situation in which the teams could not compete with their traditional opponents. The once-proud Haskell football program was no longer in existence by decade's end. After his stint in Lawrence, Kansas, Gus took a two-year hiatus from sports.

In 1937, Gus got a job closer to home when he accepted the position of director of physical education and athletics as well as head football coach at "victory-starved" American University in Washington, DC. Welch's signing ceremony attracted much media attention but little attention from football players. His AU teams were always playing shorthanded due to few people turning out to play the game. Injuries were catastrophic because he had almost no bench. By early November things got so bad that he threatened to use a co-ed to kick extra points, should the Eagles score any touchdowns against the Randolph-Macon Yellow Jackets. The season ended with an 0-7-1 record. Only four veterans returned for the 1938 season; the results were better, but only slightly, as the team finished 1-4-0. So few people turned out for the team that pundits accused Gus of dressing cheerleaders and other non-players in uniforms to trick the opposition into thinking he had a larger team. On December 3, Chancellor Gray wrote Welch to inform him that his contract would not be renewed because "…conditions in the University, financial and otherwise, will make impossible a renewal of your contract …" This wasn't the only bad news he got from Washington.

The National Park Service, in a government move only a little less egregious than the recent Supreme Court Kelo decision, planned to extend the Blue Ridge Parkway through Camp Kewanzee. Gus fought the taking of his land through the use of eminent domain in the courts and, after a long, hard fight, lost. The government offered him just $14 an acre for the land they were taking, far less than he paid for it. He did get one concession out of the government. The planned path for the roadway was through an ancient poplar tree. The government rerouted the road a bit to save the tree after Welch protested, but that was about the only concession it would make. When all legal means had been exhausted, Gus said, "The white man has been taking land from the Indian for so long that it has become a habit with him. There's nothing an Indian can do about changing the white man's habits."

From 1942 to 1945, Welch coached at Georgetown Prep School, the nation's oldest Jesuit school, where he went 10-21. The 4-3 1942 team was his best at Prep. During World War II, Gus also served as athletic director for the Alexandria Naval Torpedo Station and organized teams for the Torps in a variety of sports at the recreational level. He also trained soldiers in the Army's specialized training program conducted at Georgetown University during the war. After the war, he taught physical education at Lyndon Hill Junior High School in Prince Georges County, Maryland, adjacent to Washington, DC. In the early 1950s Gus and Julia bought an 80-acre farm near the Peaks of the Otter in the Blue Ridge Mountains and made it their home. Gus worked with young athletes and ran Camp Kewanzee until his head smashed into the windshield in a car wreck. His vision in later years was diminished by the detached retina which may have been caused by that accident. They sold the camp, which was used as a Methodist Boys Camp for a number of years. Ruins are still visible to hikers interested in seeing the route of the original Appalachian Trail which passed through the camp.

In 1962 Gus spoke at the groundbreaking ceremony for the Professional Football Hall of Fame in Canton, Ohio, as few old-time pros were still alive. Throughout his adult life he worked for the restoration of Jim Thorpe's Olympic medals, something that did not happen in his lifetime.

He lived to be a little over 76 years old, dying on January 29, 1970. Gus was inducted posthumously into the American Indian Athletic Hall of Fame and the College Football Hall of Fame. The honor he was best known for during his lifetime was the "Brown Derby" award given to the coach telling the tallest tale by the American Football Coaches Association. He won that "honor" five times. The yarn that won him the Brown Derby at the December 1930 meeting of the AFCA, as told by Associated Press Sports Writer Foster Hailey, follows:

> "Carlisle was playing Cornell and it was a tough game. Thorpe scored a touchdown against the big red earn and the Indians went to defensive play. There was one big guard, 220 pounds, who was laying down on the Job. All Gus's urging could not get him to wake up and stop the Cornell plays. Finally it was Cornell's ball on Carlisle's ten yard-line, goal to go.
>
> "'I was thinkin' hard.' said Gus, waving an unlighted cigar. 'And I had an idea. I was playin' safety but I called Jim back and went to the line. Then I went over to the referee and I told him 'if you see me slug somebody, it won't be a Cornell man. It will be one of these Indians.'
>
> "'The play came through this big guard. I ran up and there was a big pile up with this guard at the bottom and his face showing on one side. I reached down with my hand flat — like this — I slapped him.'
>
> "'The pile heaved and up he came, a nice rosy mark on his cheek. He rushed over and said to the referee: 'Did you see that Cornell slugged me.'
>
> "'The referee laughed and said, 'That's all right. I'll get them the next time.'
>
> "'On the next play this big bird went through and nailed them for a three-yard loss. On the next play he got a Cornell back for a two-yard loss. On the next play he nailed him three yards behind the line.'
>
> "'He and Thorpe worked on the guard for three years with those tactics,' Gus said, and won a lot of games. In a game with Pensylvania, Thorpe even bit the big guard in the side to make him play.'
>
> "'After a game with Brown and we were both quitting.' Gus continued, 'I was talking to this guy and I told him what we had done.'
>
> "'He looked at me for a minute and then he said:
> 'Why, I've said a lot of mean things to those referees. I must write them all a letter and apologize.'
>
> "'Here's the brown derby,' said Major Frank Cavanaugh, who was presiding."

Al Exendine

21

Albert Exendine;
Cumberland County
Historical Society,
Carlisle, PA

Al Exendine scoring touchdown against Chicago, 1907; *Chicago History Museum*

Name: Albert Andrew Exendine		**Nickname:** Ex	
DOB: 1/7/1884 or 1/27/1884		**Height:** 5'10"	
Weight: 174		**Age:** 22	
Tribe: Delaware		**Home:** Bartlesville, OK	

Parents: Jasper Exendine, half-blood Cherokee;
Amaline Exendine, Delaware

Early Schooling: Mautame Presbyterian Mission, Anadarko, OK

Later Schooling: Conway Hall; Dickinson School of Law

Honors: College Football Hall of Fame, 1970;
American Indian Athletic Hall of Fame, 1971;
American Indian Athletic Hall of Fame, 1971;
Oklahoma Athletic Hall of Fame, 1972

Ex

Albert Andrew Exendine arrived in Carlisle in 1899 at age 15. He was born in Cherokee Indian Territory near present day Bartlesville, Oklahoma, 10 to 12 miles from the closest neighbor. He was the son of Jasper Exendine, reputedly a half-blood Cherokee, and Amaline Exendine, a full-blood Delaware. Jasper must have been quite a character, serving for a time as a deputy marshal for "Hanging Judge" Isaac Charles Parker. He later became a prosperous merchant and rancher whose spread encompassed what is now the city of Bartlesville. The first oil finds in Oklahoma have been attributed to Jasper and George B. Keeler. Apparently, Jasper passed on an interest in the law to his son.

Prior to coming to Carlisle, Al had some formal education at the Presbyterian Mission School near Anadarko, Oklahoma, often referred to as Mautame, as the natives called it. Exendine described his early education to John L. Johnson in 1962: "We would plough, harrow and cut broom corn a few hours a day and attend classes the rest of the time. While attending Mautame, my friend, Joseph Tremp, and I read an ad in the Anadarko newspaper which stated: 'Students wanted for Carlisle Indian School.' Joseph Tremp turned to me and said, 'Albert, let's go to Carlisle.'" Tremp was able to get permission so he left almost immediately, but when Albert learned he had to commit to a five-year enrollment, he cooled on the idea. A few months after arriving in Carlisle, Tremp wrote his friend a letter extolling the school's virtues. Eventually, the letter prevailed.

Ex's first official recognition at Carlisle came in January of 1902. It did not come from his work on the football field or track. It came from his command of the language and his ability to frame his argument logically, skills that came in handy in later life. He debated successfully for the negative side against the question, "Resolved that Indian schools should be abolished." In May, he was acknowledged for his athletic ability: "Albert Exendine of the Freshman class was the best that took part in the sports for the Freshmen in a high jump, hammer throw, and shot putting." He wasn't able to win or even place against the upperclassmen yet, but he was ready to deliver an oration to a joint meeting of the freshmen and sophomore classes. His football work to this point was just to prepare him for bigger things. After all, he had never played the game before coming to the Cumberland Valley.

Making the football team wasn't a sure thing. He later related getting a cool reception from Warner: "He told me that I should have played football my first year there, and that it would be pretty tough for me to make the team because I had not. 'Pop' expected all the boys at Carlisle to play football, and conducted an excellent football program to attract them. He finally consented, and turned me over to an assistant coach on the field. He knocked me all over the field for an hour and a half before I learned to defend myself. By then I was wringing wet and so was he, but 'Pop' was convinced that I wanted to play football."

That fall, Pop Warner made Exendine a starter on the varsity football team, positioning him at right tackle, and he got some good press in *The Red Man and Helper* for the quality of his play. The day after the Thanksgiving Day victory over Georgetown, Al and the rest of the team visited President Theodore Roosevelt, who had invited them to the White House. Also that fall, Al was elected vice-president of the Invincible Debating Society and played a Roman counsel in "The Banishment of Catiline." He was becoming a big man on campus. In the spring of 1903, he did well in track meets but, like everyone else, performed in Frank Mt. Pleasant's shadow.

During the 1903-04 school year, Exendine played left tackle without much notice in the press and improved in track, getting press coverage but again not as much as Mt. Pleasant. Several students spent their summer vacation at Hotel Beacon-by-the-Sea in Point Pleasant, New Jersey, most likely earning money working at the resort. The *Philadelphia Press* reported on a charity benefit put on by the boys, in which Al's part was a war dance. That fall was Al's first year to play football under a coach other than Warner, because Pop had returned to his alma mater. Due to convalescing from an unspecified operation in the fall of 1904, he did not play in a game until the November 5th contest against Ursinus. Al made the trip to St. Louis to play in the game against Haskell Institute on the Saturday after Thanksgiving. Not only did he get to see the World's Fair, but he also scored a touchdown. After returning to Carlisle, Al left for Medico-Chi in Philadelphia for an unspecified operation. By the end of January, he was back at school giving extempore speeches for the Invincibles. His medical problems appear to have been behind him before the start of track season. In 1905, Exendine placed first many times in many meets but received mention only when he broke the school record for the shot put in a dual meet with Penn State. At season's end, he owned school records for the high jump and shot put, but Mt. Pleasant owned or shared records in four events. At the end of the school year, Al was elected to Critic for the Invincibles for the upcoming term, his senior year.

In the fall of 1905, Albert Exendine was active with the Invincible Debating Society and football, as usual. He played fullback in the early-season games but was shifted back to tackle for the rest of the season. As soon as football was over, Al was elected captain of the 1906 football team and, separately, captain of the Seniors' basketball team. Carlisle's graduation was generally held earlier in the spring than that of most schools, and few attended long enough to graduate. As a result, students participated in activities, such as baseball and track, after graduation but before departing for the summer. At his graduation, he spoke about blacksmithing, his specialty, as part of the ceremony. That spring, Ex again starred on the track team, although he was still in Mt. Pleasant's shadow. After spending the summer away, he returned to Carlisle to attend school again in the fall.

Al enrolled in Conway Hall, Dickinson College's preparatory school across town, and enjoyed his breakout season in football. Prior to 1906, he had been a starter for the Carlisle varsity, generally at tackle, but this year, the year that rules revolutionizing football were implemented, he was shifted to right end. Some combination of the new rules, Warner's new formations, the legalization of the forward pass, and available talent prompted this move. The reason for the position change is much less important than the outcome as Exendine became one of the all-time greats at end. The captain's 80-yard touchdown in the victory over Penn was perhaps the highlight of his season. The referee gave ends Exendine and Gardner high marks for boxing out Penn's ends, keeping them from covering the Indians' punt returns. The two covered Carlisle's punts as well as they prevented their opponents from covering theirs. Legend has it that Ex played a significant role in a transaction that shaped football history forever, and it is likely true.

Major Mercer, who became Carlisle Superintendent in 1904 with Pratt's ouster, surely wouldn't have missed the 1906 Army-Navy game that was played in Philadelphia, given its proximity and the fact that cavalry officers were seldom stationed so close to the all-important game's location. Also, Captain Exendine could have easily traveled from Norfolk, Virginia to Philadelphia in the two days since the Indians played the University of Virginia in their last game of the season. While sitting on the sidelines, Al received a powerful slap on his back. He turned, somewhat surprised, to see Pop Warner. After exchanging pleasantries, he asked Warner why he hadn't returned to Carlisle. Warner responded, "You have coaches." To which Exendine countered, "They're not coaches," and urged Warner to talk with Mercer. The stars were aligned perfectly as Warner was having problems at Cornell with students and alumni over disciplining a star player. After the game, Warner walked up to Exendine and extended his right hand, saying, "I want you to meet the new football coach." Mercer and Warner apparently met up and struck a deal.

In the spring, Al ran track again for Carlisle but also worked as an assistant coach. Warner, as athletic director, served as head coach for track as well as football. Pop assigned him to help a new, but highly talented, team member, Jim Thorpe. Later Exendine recalled that it took Thorpe just one day to break the records he had set in track and field over his career. Al now assisted in coaching the football team along with playing right end. Fortunately for him, Thorpe was a halfback.

One of Exendine's assignments was to teach Thorpe the rudiments of football. Al was pleased with his progress. "Thorpe was a good learner. He was quick at doing things the way you showed him. He wasn't afraid and I kept at him about being mean when he had the ball or was blocking or tackling." Six decades later, Ex told reporters, "I didn't know what a football was until I went to Carlisle, but I was a mean son-of-a-gun. Those were the days of push, drag and slug football. I would get the ball and just stand there pumping my knees while other fellows pushed me into the line." But that was all changing.

Warner devised new formations to capitalize on the 1906 rule changes and continued to tinker with them. The rule changes, particularly the one that legalized the forward pass, enhanced the roles of the ends and Carlisle had a crackerjack pair in Al Exendine and Bill Gardner. Carlisle also had great passers in Frank Mt. Pleasant and Pete Hauser. Warner always considered the 1907 team as one of his best. It was definitely his best one up to that time.

Exendine gained the respect of coaches, players and pundits for his contributions to the team's 10-1-0 record that included Carlisle's first ever victory over Harvard, a thrashing of Penn, and wins over Western powers Minnesota and Chicago. Exendine's skills as a pass receiver helped establish Carlisle as one of the better practitioners of the new weapon. It was no secret in the football world how good they were.

In order to stop the Indians' passing game, Chicago had put three defenders on each end. Al later described the strategy of Chicago's legendary coach, Amos Alonzo Stagg: "They just kept knocking me down and knocking me down. In those days you didn't have to wait until the receiver touched the ball to hit him. First the end would hit me, then the linebacker, then the halfback. They were doing the same thing to our other end." Al saw an opportunity when the ball was near the sideline. With Mt. Pleasant out of the game with a broken thumb, passing duties fell to Pete Hauser. Between plays he told Pete, "Hold that ball as long as you can, then throw it to me down by the goal line." When the ball was snapped, Ex stepped out of bounds and the defenders turned their attention to Hauser. But Al didn't stop moving; he ran behind the Chicago bench, down the sideline and reemerged downfield about 50 yards from where he started. Escaping several would-be tacklers, Hauser arched the ball to his teammate who scored an easy touchdown. Stagg was livid, Warner savored the victory more than almost any other, and the rulemakers made coming back onto the field after going out of bounds illegal.

Walter Camp, always biased heavily toward Ivy League players, only put Exendine on his All-America second team. Caspar Whitney and the *St. Louis Star-Chronicle* both named him as a first-team All-American. Years later Warner was still displeased with Camp's selections when he wrote, "... and I still maintain that they [Exendine and Gardner] have never been surpassed for sheer brilliance." Warner also related a conversation he had had with Chicago's star quarterback, Wally Steffens. When asked what he thought of

Camp's selections, Steffens replied, "Well, I certainly would like to see the ends they think better than Gardner and Exendine."

The spring 1908 track season was Exendine's last as a competitive athlete in any sport unless he played some pro football under another name, but there's no record of that. He had a good run by most measures, but Carlisle still had Mt. Pleasant and some young Turks were making their marks. In football, eligibility limits were evolving and Al's had been used up. From this point forward, Ex competed as a coach – in athletic events, that is. In the courtroom, he eventually competed as an attorney.

In the fall, Albert continued his studies at Conway Hall and assisted Pop Warner in coaching the Carlisle football team. His major assignment was the second team, commonly called the "Hot Shots." The September 11 issue of *The Carlisle Arrow* reported that the "Hot Shots" had changed their name to the "Hustlers" because they "… will make every team they meet hustle pretty lively to defeat them." The school paper gave Exendine high marks for making his undersized players compete well with much heavier teams. The Hustlers won as many games as they lost but by wider margins, ending up scoring a lot more points than they surrendered. It was with the Hustlers that Ex developed the passing game that was to become his trademark when he became a head coach. In the spring Al continued to participate in the Invincible Debating Society activities and hone his public speaking skills. He also officiated at track meets. After spending the summer in Oklahoma and Mexico, he was ready to strike out on his own.

Pop Warner received a call from Otterbein College in Westerville, Ohio. They needed a new head football coach and wanted some suggestions. Warner immediately recommended "Exie" for the job. Before he left for his first head coaching assignment, Warner admonished him, "Ex, you will become a good football coach if you remember that football is football, not basketball." Warner viewed the forward pass as football's bastard child and thought that Al was a bit too fond of it. Ex made an immediate splash in the Buckeye state as reported by *The Otterbein Review*:

> "The newspapers such as the [Columbus] *Dispatch, Cincinnati Enquirer* and other leading papers of the country, have discovered our team as one of the best in the State of Ohio. When we as students and alumni attempt to ferret out the source of this successful football season, we are confronted by this one question, 'What has made Otterbein's football team what it is to-day?' We can answer that question just as it is put by two words, "Albert Exendine," a coach respected by every man on the team, by every student and alumni of Otterbein. He is the man who has made a perfect football machine out of Otterbein's eleven, a machine which works out his marvellous [sic] plays to the letter. Coach Exendine is one of the best and cleanest coaches the Otterbein team has ever had. No man on the team can say that he has ever heard him use indecent language on the field. He is a gentleman, every inch of him. He knows every position on the team and he knows how to get the one great thing into the team-and that is 'ginger.' The newspapers of the country have recognized him as the best coach of the new game.
>
> "In this humble way, we as members of the team, students, alumni and faculty desire to show our appreciation for what Coach Exendine has done for us. We only hope that the college will do its part in securing him for next fall."

Admittedly the rhetoric was way over the top, but Ex had energized the school and with good reason. He led the Cardinals to a 15-7-3 record for the 1909-11 seasons. In the summer of 1911, Al did something that impacted Carlisle football as much, if not more, than had his playing. He ran into Jim Thorpe in Anadarko, Oklahoma, broke and out of a job. Ex suggested that Thorpe return to Carlisle. Warner, wanting to improve his team's lackluster 1910 record, welcomed the filled out and muscular Thorpe back to the team. Superintendent Moses Friedman wasn't exactly excited about allowing the runaway to return, but Warner prevailed and the rest, as they say, is history.

During this period, Ex also attended Dickinson School of Law, most likely in the off-seasons. Ex gained quite a reputation with his less worldly law school classmates. The *1912 Microcosm*, the school yearbook, described his view of education: "Ex. thinks there is nothing better in the world than a good Law education, unless it is free use of a million dollars, and we agree with him. We do not like to comment on this boy's character, for he once told us in class that he saw nothing unusual in stabbing a man." The Middler Class Census listed each class member's occupation, what he is, what he will be and what he knows. In their view, Exendine knew cussing, was husky, would be a leader, and knew the Theta Lambdas, his brothers in Theta Lambda Phi law fraternity. The *1913 Microcosm* listed him as a member of the Senior Class, but there is no record of his actually graduating. He may have passed the bar exam without having finished law school. Regardless, he practiced law in Oklahoma for many years. He also coached a local football team of mostly Indian players.

With only a week to practice inexperienced players, Attorney Exendine led the 1912 Anadarko, Oklahoma high school football team to a 4-2 record, which was good enough to be ranked in the top 13 in the state. The following year, he assisted Warner at Carlisle again. Not content to remain an assistant, he applied for the head coaching job at Cincinnati but didn't get it. Carlisle played Georgetown that year, and the powerhouse Indian team rolled over the Hilltoppers 34-0. "After the game Exendine remained in Washington at the request of Charley Cox, then graduate manager of athletics at the Hilltop, to help Eddie Bennis and Frank Gargan prepare the Hoyas for their final game of the year against Virginia. Exendine, the following Saturday, watched [quarterback Harry] Costello beat Virginia with three field goals in the last game played between the two old rivals," wrote Bob Considine of the *Washington Post*.

The head coaching job at Georgetown University opened up and he took it. Prior to the start of the 1914 season and several times during it, he visited Carlisle, no doubt to get advice from his mentor and former cohorts. His first game at Georgetown was a scoreless tie with Fordham. That was followed with three straight shutout losses. Ex's first victory with Georgetown was over Frank Mt. Pleasant's West Virginia Wesleyan team. The Hilltoppers finished the season at 2-4-2, not an auspicious start. After the season, newspaper reports incorrectly claimed that Ex had been signed to fill Warner's then vacant position at Carlisle. Beginning in 1915, he ran off a string of eight winning years at Georgetown, never going undefeated but never losing more than three games. A new rule was instituted at the school for the 1923 season that required coaches of athletic teams to be residents at Georgetown and members of the faculty. Exendine was neither.

The November 4, 1915 issue of *The Dickinsonian* reported that he had returned to McAlester, Oklahoma at the end of the season to practice law as a member of the law firm of Marianelli and Exendine to supplement his $2,000 income from the football season. Not known is if his law partner was Dickinson classmate Emilio Marianelli. Ex applied for the coaching job at Columbia University that was open, but that didn't materialize. He then heard the siren call of the Pacific Northwest.

With the resignation of Gus Welch in December 1922, Washington State College was in the market for a new head coach. Rumors were rampant. The day after Christmas, W. S. C. Athletic Director J. Fred "Doc" Bohler departed on an extended trip to interview candidates for the open head coaching position. He was able to interview 25 of the applicants for the job. On Valentine's Day, W. S. C. announced that Al Exendine had been selected as their next head coach. Strong references from Warner, Hugo Bezdek and Father Vincent L. McDonough may have been the deciding factor. Or familiarity in the Warner System, the one that helped them go undefeated in 1915 and 1917, not to mention their 1916 New Year's Day victory over Brown, may have been what W. S. C. wanted. The March 16 issue of *The Evergreen* announced that the new head coach would arrive on May 15 to start spring football practice and conduct a clinic for high school coaches over the summer. Accompanying Al to Pullman were his wife, Grace, whom he had married while at Georgetown, and their year-old son, Albert Jr.

Al was welcomed to Pullman at the first spring practice by a turnout of more than 50 players from the previous year's team. That evening the student body as a whole greeted him with a pep rally. When asked about the outlook for the team, he was optimistic. Whether his optimism was misplaced or whether he was motivating the players is unknown. The Cougars went 2-4-1 in 1923. The bright spots of the season were the win and tie over the Oregon schools. Things were not heading in the right direction if the objective was to return W. S. C. to its glory days under Lone Star Dietz. Things got worse in 1924 when the team did not win a single conference game. The only non-conference win was the season opener against the College of the Pacific. The overnight emergence of Eskimo passer Joe Koenig, who could throw accurately in inclement weather using the technique his grandfather taught him for throwing a harpoon, helped but was far from all was needed to turn the season around. 1925's upset of the University of Southern California led by the brilliant play of "Butch" Meeker wasn't enough to secure Exendine's job. Three straight losing seasons were enough for W. S. C. and Exendine. After eleven years, the Carlisle-W. S. C. coaching connection was broken.

About that time, Occidental College in Los Angeles fired head football coach Sid Nichols. His had sullied himself in the school's eyes by coaching the opposition team that played against Red Grange and the Chicago Bears when their barnstorming tour came to town. Ex took the job. Coaching Occidental at that time consisted primarily of providing fodder for Pacific Coast powers such as his mentor's Stanford Cardinal. His two-year contract expired after the 1927 season, and he was not retained. The reason given was that Occidental needed to have a coach present on campus more than three months out of the year. Because Ex's law practice occupied the bulk of his time and likely provided the bulk of his income, he wasn't interested in spending more time on campus. Al took his family home to Oklahoma to stay, but he wasn't finished with football.

Back in Oklahoma in 1929, Exendine practiced law and coached football at Northeastern State Teachers College in Tahlequah in 1929, where he went 2-6. From 1930 through 1933 he assisted Lynn O. "Pappy" Waldorf coach Oklahoma State in Stillwater. In 1934, when Waldorf left for another stop on a career that landed him in the Hall of Fame, Al was elevated to head coach. After two lackluster seasons at a school that had become accustomed to conference championships, his college coaching career ended. Ex's coaching record may qualify him for induction into the College Football Hall of Fame, but since he was inducted as a player, it makes little sense to promote him as the first Indian coach in the Hall. It seems unlikely that the Hall would select him when it chooses not to induct his old teammate Lone Star Dietz, who had a better coaching record.

After seemingly retiring from coaching, Albert Exendine continued practicing law and took a government position back in Anadarko as Organization Field Agent under the U. S. Indian Reorganization Act for the Bureau of Indian Affairs. While there, he coached an Indian high school team to an unbeaten season, scoring 300 points and giving up only 12. After the season, he told Bob Considine, "It took me until this late date to learn the secret of perfect seasons. I not only coached this team, but all the opponents asked me to be the referee of their games. It's a pity more coaches can't have this opportunity." After retiring from the government position in 1951, he and Grace moved to Tulsa where they remained until he died in 1973 less than a month before his 89th birthday.

Victor Murat Kelley

22

Victor Kelley (right), head coach, and Gus Welch, assistant, 1915; *Fred Wardecker*

Name: Victor Murat Kelley	**Nickname:** Choc or Choctaw
DOB: 10/31/1886	**Height:** 5'6"
Weight: 133	**Age:** 20
Tribe: Choctaw	**Home:** Wheelock, OK
Parents: J. J. Kelley, Scots-Irish; mother's name unknown, Choctaw	
Early Schooling: Presbyterian College; Texas A & M	
Later Schooling: Dickinson School of Law	
Honors:	

Choc or Choctaw

"But the longest run in football history is claimed by Texas A&M. Victor M. (Choc) Kelley, who played at A&M in 1905-6-7, at Carlisle in 1908 and back at A&M in 1909, made the great run against Louisiana State. He went back and forth across the field four times, then sprinted 65 yards for a touchdown. The entire run was set at 267 yards. It would have been 277 had not Kelley gone 10 yards back of the line of scrimmage to begin his maneuver."

Harold V. Ratcliff
Southwest Conference historian

Victor Kelley was born on October 31, 1886 near Wheelock, in Indian Territory that later became part of the state of Oklahoma. It is believed that he was the son of a Scots-Irish father, J. J. Kelley, and a mother of French-Indian descent, probably Choctaw. Little is known about Kelley's early schooling, and he was accused of having played football before 1904 when he was second string quarterback at Texas A & M. The most likely place was at Presbyterian College in Durant, Oklahoma where he was reputed to have played halfback and quarterback in successive seasons. In 1905, he became a starter for the Farmers and made the most of it over the next three years.

Choc may have also had ambitions as a newsman because the June 9, 1908 edition of *The San Antonio Light* carried a large piece under his byline on page 14. A front-page article reported that Texas A & M President Harrington had been charged with 13 offenses by the college's alumni association, and the school's board of trustees was to hear them that afternoon. Kelley's piece went into detail about the charges that covered, "… everything from using swear words to not being 'hep' to the games of the students, and one specification particularly sets forth that the president of the college permitted a quantity of the most commonly sold article that comes in bottles and barrels to be brought onto campus." Kelley went on to write, "… he denies the charges, saying that the kicks are registered by a bunch of knockers." Harrington was exonerated on June 24. It is not known if things in College Station had gotten too hot for Choc or if this tempest was unrelated to Kelley's personal situation. Regardless, Choc left town.

Victor, or Choc as he was better known, arrived in Carlisle on September 10, 1908. Also arriving about that time was Charlie Moran who served as "rubber" for the Indians that year. That they got to Carlisle just in time for football season was probably not a coincidence. Quarterback was Kelley's natural position, and being so small, both in height and weight, made playing out of position on a team as talented as Carlisle's an impossibility. You see, Mike Balenti was the starting quarterback in 1908 and, after playing behind Frank Mt. Pleasant for three years, he wasn't going to allow himself to be easily unseated. Kelley got significant playing time and generated positive press for himself, but he did not log enough playing time to letter. The year wasn't a complete bust, though, because he learned the Warner System, gained a national reputation, and honed his legal skills while also attending Dickinson School of Law.

Kelley returned to College Station the next fall, bringing Mike Balenti with him. Charlie Moran also returned to A & M, this time as head football coach. Perhaps bringing Kelley and Balenti with him had something to do with his getting the job. It had previously been insinuated that Carlisle and A & M were not the only places Kelley had played, and upon his return someone filed a formal complaint. Ratliff recalled: "In 1909 Baylor charged that Kelley had admitted that he had performed under an assumed name, thus should be ineligible. Baylor also contended that Mike Balenti, who joined the A & M team in 1909 with Kelley, had played professional baseball in the Western Association. Baylor showed an affidavit to prove it. However, Kelley and Balenti were never ruled out."

A combination of the return of Kelley, the addition of Balenti, and the selection of Charles Moran as head coach improved A & M's fortunes. The Farmers went 7-0-1 and defeated arch-rival Texas for the first time since 1902. It was a very good year, indeed.

It's not clear what Kelley did after completing his playing career at A & M. Carlisle records indicate that he was back at home in Durant, Oklahoma. In 1913, Carlisle records had him working as a clerk for the Union Agency, established in 1875 for the Five Civilized Tribes in Muskogee, Oklahoma. By the next year, he appears to have started working for the Great Southern Life Insurance Company out of Durant, Oklahoma. Carlisle publications had him practicing law and preparing teams across the Southwest for big games. Newspaper accounts also have him back in football in Durant in 1914 as head coach of the Northeastern Oklahoma Normal School eleven. How many years he coached in Durant is not known, but it is clear that he wasn't back there in 1915.

After what he considered a disastrous season and seeing little hope of improvement, given the prevailing policies regarding the Indian school, Pop Warner resigned his position of athletic director at Carlisle at the end of the 1914 football season. Major decisions regarding the athletic program were no longer being made at the school but, rather at the highest levels of the Department of Indian Affairs in Washington, DC. Angel DeCora, the head of the Native Art Department, was the only other person known to be hired directly by the commissioner prior to that. Several people applied for the open head coaching position, including some former players with solid coaching credentials. In April, the following appeared in newspapers across the country:

REDSKINS ARE PLEASED

"Appointment of Victor M. Kelley as football coach at Carlisle, as announced by Cato Sells, commissioner of Indian affairs, was a source of great delight to the lovers of' the game in Texas, where Kelley, familiarly called 'Choc.' matriculated in the Agricultural and Mechanical college after three years at Carlisle, and put that institution on the gridiron map.

"Glen Warner's successor holds a record as a quarterback. His work at Carlisle compares favorably with that of Thorpe, Welsh [sic], Mount Pleasant, Exendine, Calac and other stars. But Kelley thought more of his ambition to become a lawyer than a hero on the football field. Today he is said to be one of the best Indian lawyers in the state of Oklahoma and is a credit to the Cherokee [sic] tribe.

"However, he has in his spare moments devoted much of his time in the inner workings of football, and his friends are enthusiastic in the belief that he would make good at Carlisle."

The government's spin machine was apparently more interested in hyping its choice than in getting the details right. Gus Welch's contention that the choice of Kelley as coach was politically motivated was made more plausible by the government's actions.

On May 17, 1915, he wrote Carlisle asking when he should start his new job and for information about accommodations for his family, as he was then married and had a son. Superintendent Lipps responded and apologized for the delay in his response due to commencement responsibilities. Lipps informed him that, because his appointment was only for football season, he would not be required to report before September 1. Lipps also informed him that the house Warner formerly occupied was now the home of Harvey Meyer, the new director of athletics, but a room would be made available on campus for him and his family. Lipps also told him that he would be eligible to board at the Teachers' Club for a membership fee of $5 per person and a monthly fee of $13.50 to $15.00 each person. Oscar Lipps may not have been very pleased that Commissioner Sells had pulled rank in selecting the new football coach, something that would explain the cool reception Kelley received.

Victor Kelley wrote back on May 29 asking about the status of an assistant coach, as he had received letters from a number of people who wanted that position. Then as now, head coaches wanted to hire their own assistants, but that was not to be in this case. Lipps responded that he had hired a man named McGillis, formerly a player at Haskell Institute, who had helped out by taking care of the reserves the previous year at Carlisle. Lipps then informed Kelley that a second assistant was planned and that he would let Kelley know when a suitable man had been hired. That man would be Gus Welch.

Victor Kelley, wife, Fern, and son, Victor Jr., arrived in Carlisle in late August 1915. They were greeted by a beautiful football field made more luscious by the large amount of rain received that summer. They were most likely housed in a teacher's apartment rather than just a single room as had been implied by Oscar Lipps.

Kelley immediately went to work familiarizing himself with the school and the athletic department. Forty-five players turned out on the first day of practice, but the squad swelled to 75 as students dribbled in from their country outings. *The Arrow* announced that the training table would start on September 10. The school's reorganization after the 1914 congressional inquiry didn't eliminate that advantage for the athletes.

The season opened optimistically enough with a 21-0 win over Albright College. However, that score pales to the 54-point margin of victory Carlisle averaged in its previous games against that foe. Things looked considerably worse in their second game, a scoreless tie with Lebanon Valley College. Prior to 1914, 26-0 was the best the Dutchman had done against the Indians in 12 encounters. Any hope for a good season was lost in the next game, a 14-0 loss to Lehigh. The heart of the season arrived and it was dismal. Harvard thrashed the Indians 29-7, and Pitt followed with a 45-0 thumping. Then came a scoreless tie with pesky Bucknell. That was followed by a 14-0 loss to William Garlow's West Virginia Wesleyan College team in a must-win game. Sources conflict about what happened and precisely when it took place. Some say that Kelley resigned rather than being fired; others blame the problems on Welch. Regardless, Kelley's resignation wasn't made public, and his family was allowed to remain on campus for the rest of the season.

Looking like the Carlisle of old, the Indians beat Holy Cross 23-21, then hung on to beat a tough Dickinson College team. The season was mercifully over after losses to Fordham and Brown. The Brown game was particularly nasty in the press. Before the game, accusations were made that Kelley, out of spite for Lone Star Dietz's comment that he wouldn't make good at Carlisle, gave Carlisle's play book to Brown's coach. Brown supporters responded that Brown was already familiar with Carlisle's offense after having played them so many times. Also, at the time, Brown thought it was playing the University of Washington, not Washington State, the team Dietz coached. *The Providence Journal* ran a particularly nasty cartoon that ridiculed the Indians. That paper also ran an article in which Welch blamed the team's problems on Kelley and accused the school of trying to shift the blame to him.

There may have been something to Welch's charge of the school's making him the scapegoat, as a "Special to the Indianapolis Star. Carlisle, Pa., Nov. 29" ran in *The Indianapolis Star* in which Kelley was defended:

> "Those on the inside, however, do not hold Kelley responsible. It is said that friction between Kelley and his assistant, Gus Welch, resulted in the disintegration of the team. The majority of players sided with Welch until they saw that his advice was treasonable and was really wrecking the machine. Superintendent G. H. Lipps has taken a hand and this week will abolish the gridiron game at Carlisle. He is said to have been contemplating the action for a long time."

Such "specials" were generally provided by Carlisle's administration. However, in this case, it may have come from the Bureau of Indian Affairs because Gus Welch maintained a cordial relationship with the Carlisle administration after this blew over.

Kelley was done with Carlisle and likely had a bad taste in his mouth. He disappeared from public view for a period. In June 1917, when he registered for the WWI draft, he was living in Globe, Arizona with his wife, son and father, John J. Kelley. He was then engaged in farming and managing oil leases, perhaps on family property near Durant, Oklahoma. He probably didn't serve in the military in WWI because he coached the Hardin Military School football team in the 1918 season. In 1920, he was living in Abilene, Texas and operating a restaurant. His household had expanded to include a daughter, Betsy Ross Kelley. He didn't stay in that business much longer because in 1921, after head coach J. Burton Rix left in midseason, he and Bill Cunningham were named co-head coaches of the Southern Methodist University Mustangs. Cunningham later recalled that Choc suited up for the second half of the Arkansas game and scored the winning touchdown. The only problem with that story was that his touchdown would have been scored for Arkansas because they beat SMU 14-0. The SMU gig didn't last long. The 1-6-1 record probably had something to do with none of the three co-head coaches returning. 1922 found him coaching the Selma American Legion football team in Fresno County, California. Kelley appears to have emerged from the football desert, metaphorically speaking, in 1924 when he began coaching high school football in the Los Angeles, California school district. He did apply for the head coaching job at Texas A & M in 1929, but Matty Bell got the nod for that position.

During a 30-year stint working for the Los Angeles School District, a good chunk of which was spent coaching future college stars at Hollywood High School, Choc had the opportunity to dabble in another local industry. Kelley was technical director for the football sequences in the 1936 film, "Pigskin Parade." He later moved to Woodrow Wilson High School, also in the Los Angeles district, where he stayed until his mandatory retirement at age 65 in 1953. Because he was a fixture in Los Angeles football for decades, 300 people attended a banquet to celebrate his career. Over the years, Choc had opportunities to return to the college coaching ranks, including some at double his salary, but he chose to remain where he was. He probably made the right decision as he turned out dozens of players that went on to play for major colleges. The players he turned out were considered to be "polished gems."

Vic looked beyond sports; he remained involved with Indian issues, even serving as president of the National Congress of American Indians for three years. His son, Victor Jr., followed in his father's footsteps becoming the sports information director for UCLA. Choc Kelley retired to Glendale, California where he lived into his late 80s, dying in August 1974.

23

Carlisle Captains

In the earliest days of American football, team captains were more akin to modern day head coaches than to current-day captains. Even after head coaches, often called trainers at that time, were introduced to the game, captains still played major roles in running the teams. Many functions associated with modern football coaches were the responsibility of captains around the turn of the last century. Captains played a major role both in running a team and conditioning the players and in field management. Lists of team captains' names were published nationally after elections were held and ownership of a team, in a literary sense, was often attributed to the captain. For example, in the 1880s Harvard played Captain Camp's team [Yale]. Team members played both offense and defense; most stayed on the field the entire game unless they were too seriously injured to continue. Coaches were not allowed to send in plays, not even via substitute players. Instead, a designated player, often the quarterback, called the plays. Pop Warner was sometimes accused of breaking this rule.

Players generally elected their captains, typically at the end of one season for the next. Captains were selected at this time because the outgoing captain was often a graduating senior, and it made more sense to have the same man captaining the team in both the fall and spring practice. Most often it was a single person. Co-captains were not the norm, nor were captains elected for different platoons. The multiple-captain concept came much later.

Captains were not just good players; they were team leaders. Some of the best players, such as Joe Guyon and Frank Mount Pleasant, for instance, were never elected captain. Generally a captain served for just a year, but in the early days of the Carlisle program Bemus Pierce served for three years running. The only others to repeat after that were Martin Wheelock in 1899 and 1901 and Pete Calac, who completed an unfinished term in 1914 before being elected for a full season of his own.

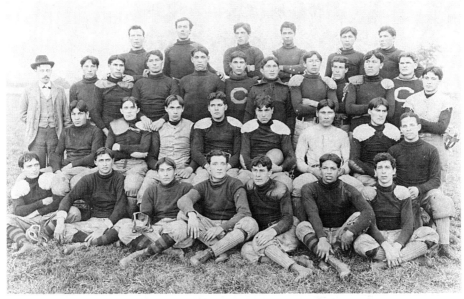

1899 team featured several captains, past, present and future; *Library of Congress*

Captains of Carlisle Indian School Football Team

1894 Benjamin Caswell	1895 Bemus Pierce★	1896 Bemus Pierce★
1897 Bemus Pierce★	1898 Frank Hudson★	1899 Martin Wheelock
1900 Edward Rogers★	1901 Martin Wheelock	1902 Charles Williams
1903 James Johnson★	1904 Arthur Sheldon	1905 Nicholas Bowen
1906 Albert Exendine★	1907 Antonio Lubo	1908 Emil Hauser
1909 Joseph Libby	1910 Peter Hauser	1911 Sampson Bird★
1912 James Thorpe★	1913 Gustavus Welch★	1914 Elmer Busch
1915 Peter Calac†★	1916 George May	1917 George Tibbitts
1918 John B. Flinchum		

†Also served as Captain last half of 1914 season.
★Previously covered in separate chapter.

Several of the captains have earlier chapters in this book devoted to them, so they will not have sections in this chapter. Captains covered in this chapter are presented in chronological order. Each section begins with the captain's name followed by the year or years of captaincy in parentheses.

Benjamin Caswell (1894)

Benjamin Caswell;
*Cumberland County
Historical Society,
Carlisle, PA.*

Name: Benjamin Caswell		**Nickname:**
DOB: February 1869 or 1878		**Height:** 5'6 3/4"
Weight: 150		**Age:** 23
Tribe: Chippewa		**Home:** White Earth Agency, MN
Parents: Father possibly Megazence		
Early Schooling: unknown		
Later Schooling: Dickinson College Preparatory School		
Honors:		

Superintendent Pratt relented and lifted his ban on inter-scholastic football in 1893, allowing Carlisle Indian School students to play a couple of football games against other schools that year. In 1894, Carlisle played its first full schedule of games and, like any self-respecting team of the day, it had to have a captain. It is not known if the first captain was appointed or elected. It could have been either because Benjamin Caswell was exactly the type of student Richard Henry Pratt wanted to produce.

Benjamin Caswell, age 20, arrived at Carlisle on September 9, 1889, from the White Earth Agency in Minnesota. Whether his parents were living or not is a muddle because his 1889 enrollment papers have his father as dead and his mother as living; the 1892 papers are the opposite. Since resurrections are uncommon, it may be safely assumed that the records are not accurate. Megazence was provided as his home address. For many students the home address was the name of the person they lived with on the reservation, often a parent.

Four months after arriving at Carlisle, Benjamin Caswell was elected reporter for the Invincible Debating Society. In May, he went on outing to the White farm near Tulleytown in Bucks County, PA. After his return, he was re-elected reporter for the Invincibles. In January 1891, he argued for the affirmative in a debate whose topic was whether breaking up reservations is not the most important step in progress toward civilization and citizenship. Two weeks later, he reprised his arguments in front of a local judge, physician and Capt. Pratt. After commenting strongly on the merits of the various debaters' arguments, the judge awarded victory to the affirmative. Caswell had one of the more persuasive arguments. Putting his public speaking skills to use, he led afternoon classes in Room No. 12.

That fall, Carlisle boys entered all four of the foot races at the Cumberland County Fair, taking all of the prizes. The stiff competition included H. M. Stephens, winner of the 100-yard dash at that year's Penn Relays. Ben won a gold medal in the 150 yards' race and a special embossed gold medal presented by Niles M. Fissel for the 100 yards' race. However, Stephens was handicapped 5 yards for his specialty.

Benjamin Caswell, then Captain of Company D, graduated on February 24, 1892, and departed for home. On August 27, he returned and re-enrolled at Carlisle but took classes at the Dickinson College Preparatory School. However, he continued to remain active with the Invincibles. In February 1893, his team won a debate arguing for the negative of the proposition that all Indian pupils salute the flag on February 28 in honor of the Dawes Bill. Officially known as the General Allotment Act of 1887, the Dawes Act is generally considered to have had disastrous effects on the native tribes it was supposed to help. Tribal lands were divided among tribe members with excess lands being sold off to non-members. These sales, plus later inheritances, served to distribute much of the remaining native lands to non-natives.

Interscholastic football began in earnest at Carlisle with a nine-game schedule that included a high school, two colleges, two universities, a military academy and three athletic clubs. The only win was over Harrisburg High School; the ties were with Dickinson College and York YMCA. The losses were relatively close games, especially for a first-year team. Caswell, who emerged as a leader, received kudos for his play. At 5' 6 3/4" tall and 150 pounds Ben was small, very small, for a lineman, but he held his position. And he was a very fast runner, reputedly finishing a 100 yard dash in 10 seconds flat. It may have been an inauspicious start, but football had been inaugurated at the Indian school.

At the end of the prep school's spring term, Benjamin Caswell returned home to start a career. The first work he could find was, in his words, "cleaning a house, then working on a farm for $20.00 per month." In the fall he found work as an assistant teacher at Fort Belknap Boarding School near Harlem, Montana. At the school he came into contact with former Carlisle students and sent news of them back to Carlisle along with his best wishes for a successful football season. A former Carlisle student who was then working at Fort Belknap, Lucy Enter Lodge, wrote that the children at the school liked Benjamin. Within a year he was a regular teacher, no longer an assistant.

Ben wrote that he wanted to join the Navy when war broke out with Spain, but his father wouldn't grant his consent. If Ben had been a citizen, he would not have needed permission to join the service due to his age (about 29), but special rules applied to non-citizen Indians that may have required parental or tribal permission.

Leila Cornelius, Oneida, also from Wisconsin got a job at Fort Belknap after graduating from Carlisle in 1896. She and Benjamin were married on May 29, 1899. Mr. and Mrs. Caswell were both on the Fort Belknap faculty for a while.

After teaching at Fort Belknap for 4 ½ years, Benjamin and Leila relocated to Minnesota where he became the Principal Teacher in Charge at the Cass Lake Indian School. They also started their family. Margaret was born in 1900, Robert in 1901, Oliver in 1905 and Helen in 1910. Census records from Cass Lake list the children as having a full-blood father and a Chippewa mother.

During this period, either Benjamin or Leila Caswell received a 160-acre allotment and they bought a second 160-acre tract. The land he bought must have been of better quality than the allotment because, in 1907, he valued the former at $2,600 and the latter at $2,400. Major Mercer had sent him a questionnaire on which he was to value his holdings. Besides the farmland, he owned a house, with electricity and central heating, on two lots worth $2,500 and furniture with a value of $1,500. For recreation and transportation he had a gasoline-powered boat, a bob sleigh and a cutter for which he paid $570. His livestock consisted of pets for the children: a pony ($75), a dog ($15) and a cat (50¢).

After five and a half years as the principal teacher in charge, he took the superintendent's position for a year. After that, he worked for the government as an agent dealing with special disbursements. In 1912, he worked as an "Overseer on Timber Matters." He stayed with government work as least through 1930 when, at age 61, he served as chief of police for the reservation.

When asked about doing anything for the betterment of his people, he wrote, "I have learned to use coffee, tea and tobacco (smoking) since leaving the Carlisle School, otherwise I have lived as near of its teaching as I have been able to do and knowing that actions are louder than words, I have hoped my neighbors, those who would get any benefit of my modes of life, might do otherwise."

Martin Wheelock (1899, 1901)

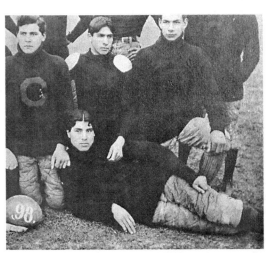

Martin Wheelock (lower right); *U. S. Army*
Military History Institute

Martin Wheelock;
Cumberland County Historical
Society, Carlisle, PA

Name:	Martin Wheelock	**Nickname:**	
DOB:	circa 1874	**Height:**	6'2 1/2"
Weight:	200	**Age:**	25
Tribe:	Oneida	**Home:**	Green Bay Agency
Parents:	Abram Wheelock; mother unknown		
Early Schooling:	unknown		
Later Schooling:			
Honors:			

Martin Frederick Wheelock was probably a cousin of the other Wheelocks, the musicians, who figured so prominently in Carlisle Indian School life. He arrived at Carlisle with a group of Oneidas led by Peter Powlas on September 20, 1890, when he was about 16 years old. Three years later, when Superintendent Pratt relented and allowed the boys to play football against other schools, Martin Wheelock was ready to compete.

By 1896, the team and its players were getting positive press. In *Harper's Weekly*, Caspar Whitney raved, "There is not a stronger nor heavier line in the country than that of the Indians, the centre and guards, Wheelock and B. Pierce, particularly being well-nigh impregnable." By September 1897, the school newspaper considered him one of the team's "big guns" and expressed concern that his ankle sprain was not serious. Apparently it wasn't because in October he received a hero's welcome for playing well in a losing effort against a powerful opponent:

"On Monday morning after breakfast, the football team, who returned the evening before from the Yale game which was played at New York last Saturday, was treated to a free ride across the parade, in the large four horse herdic, drawn by the entire battalion. Capt. Pierce, Frank Cayou, Frank Hudson, and Martin Wheelock occupied the small phaeton drawn by boys, and went in advance of the others. The band played lively marches, as handkerchiefs waved and mouths shouted. The demonstration was a great surprise to all making a unique scene for such an early morning hour. The school is proud of the record made for clean playing, and were gratified that the boys scored."

In November, Martin was injured in a game played in New York City against Brown University. Apparently the idea of taking a then new technology to diagnose an Indian was newsworthy as a press account of the incident was circulated nationally:

USES "X RAY" ON AN INDIAN.
Right Tackle of Carlisle Football Eleven Examined for Injuries.

"Martin Wheelock, right tackle of the Carlisle, football eleven, a big Indian, six feet high, became acquainted with the latest acquisition to the white man's science, the X-ray, in the J. Hood Wright Memorial Hospital at New York City.

During the game with Brown, Wheelock had plunged headlong into a mass play directed against him. He tried to rise, but his right shoulder prevented. It was decided to try the X-ray on Wheelock, to see the exact injury done to his shoulder.

Wheelock was deeply interested in the performance. The bones in his hand were shown him, and he was delighted. Then the ray was turned on his injured shoulder, and it was plainly seen he had suffered a fracture. The physicians declared that the man was the finest specimen of humanity they had ever seen.

The hospital authorities believe that Wheelock will be able to play again during the present season."

With only two weeks left in Carlisle's season, the report was overly optimistic that he would be back in action that year. He was able to continue his studies and complete the school year.

After vacationing at home in Wisconsin that summer, Martin returned, undaunted, to play again in 1898 and again helped to establish Carlisle's reputation. At season's end when Frank Hudson declined re-election as captain, Wheelock accepted the honor. Earlier that month he had been elected President of the Invincible Debating Society, an organization in which he participated actively the rest of his time at Carlisle. He "…maintained the dignity befitting his office, and rendered wise decisions."

In May, Martin accepted another challenge as reported by *The Indian Helper*:

"Captain Martin Wheelock of the football team has been detailed as captain for the small boys' company, and assistant to Mrs. Given. While the football management may try his metal, his position as captain of the small boys will try his manhood, and for that reason is a position to be sought for and to hold if possible. The Man-on-the-band-stand wishes him success."

1899 was Pop Warner's first year at Carlisle. Perhaps it was his idea or maybe it was Captain Wheelock's to hold light practices in cool August evenings to prepare football candidates who happened to be on campus for the season. Whether it was Warner's coaching, the Carlisle players' maturing or, more likely, both, the Indians posted their best season to date. Martin's leadership surely contributed to the team's success. The team's two losses were to Harvard and Princeton. Some thought Carlisle would have defeated Harvard, had Martin been able to play. He was injured in the first half and carried off the field on a stretcher. Examined at the hospital, he was not seriously enough injured to be admitted. Walter Camp placed him on his All America second team for his efforts throughout the season.

In March, Martin Wheelock took on another adult task when he was a pallbearer for Miss Bessie Barclay, a teacher who succumbed to "rheumatic and stomach trouble." He reprised that role in an even sadder situation in May at the funeral for Paul, the ten-month-old son of band director Dennison Wheelock and his wife, Louise. Perhaps needing a break from sadness, he took a short vacation at a resort in the mountains near Pen Mar, Maryland, after which he returned to school ready for action.

Ed Rogers captained the 1900 team, and Martin Wheelock was still fighting in the trenches. He also did most of the punting, kicking off, and goal kicking that year. Initially Hawley Pierce was to captain the 1901 team but complaints regarding eligibility were raised. *The Fort Wayne News* complained, "Hawley Pierce, captain of the Carlisle Indian team, has held that office for several years, there being no limit as to the time a man may play on the team of reformed scalpers." It's not clear if such criticisms, offers to play professionally or injury were the source of complaints against Pierce, but Martin Wheelock was selected to captain the Indians again.

That season had to have been difficult for Wheelock because he and Jimmie Johnson were the only regular starters who returned from the previous year. Big things were expected from Nelson Hare and Charles Dillon because they had had some playing time the previous year. This was Carlisle's last losing season until the decline that began after the 1914 congressional inquiry. But Martin Wheelock still played his hardest and was again rewarded by Walter Camp. As in 1899, he was placed on Camp's All America second team.

At his commencement in February for the Class of 1902, Martin was asked to give one of the addresses. The subject of the talk was "The Indian as an Athlete." In his talk, Wheelock said,

> "The records of colonial times show that he [the Indian] is a born athlete. His very mode of living as a hunter and a warrior, develop his reasoning power, enabling him to plan his campaigns skillfully. The only thing that he lacked for many years has been a knowledge of the real cause of his loss of strength.
>
> "The Indian youth does not differ much from his white brother in his way of displaying energy and spirit. He had games of his own in which he took as much interest as the pale faces do in their modern sports. Since he has been taken away from his favorite hunting grounds and placed in the remote corners of the country called reservations, he seems to have lost his vigorous manhood. Why is this? Because he has been thrust back into the infant's cradle and bound with limits as a child is bound with clothes when put to sleep. It. has caused him to neglect his physical development until he has lost nearly all the energy he displayed before the right of self-guidance was taken from him....
>
> "Since being placed in schools he has been obliged to come into close contact with many classes of people. In recent years, the Indian has been competing with his new friends in sports. When he first played the scientific games his greatest hindrance was his inexperience, yet he went into the contest with the determination to win....
>
> "Four years did he struggle having had very little instruction, but for the last three years a skillful architect [Warner] has helped him to lay out the same kind of plans as his pale faced brothers have for their athletic foundations. Good fortune

befell the Red Man when he secured the services of one who not only presented the usual plans but who improved upon them....

"The Indian is repeating the feats of his ancestors on the race track and has made himself famous as a runner. Not only that but he has made athletic science his warpath thereby making the college world dread him as did their forefathers in old colonial days."

Martin did not return to the reservation after graduating: he stayed at Carlisle for another football season. The 1902 season was difficult for him as he was laid up much of the time with pleurisy. However, when the faintest opportunity to play presented itself, he was out on the field. That he played at all in the Cornell game is a story of valor that is told best in an article by Pop Warner, excerpts of which are included at the end of this chapter. Walter Camp didn't award Wheelock even third team All America honors this year. *The Philadelphia Inquirer*'s Nathan F. Stauffer explained his reasons for downgrading Wheelock when making his picks:

> "There are three strong candidates for centre position, Holt for several years Yale's pivotal man; Wheelock, the Indian chieftain, and McCabe, the Pennsylvanian. Holt, by his steadiness and his great defensive power, has the place, although the Indian pressed him closely for the honor. The Cornell and Harvard teams gave Wheelock a great deal of credit for stopping many of their attacks. His inability to last a whole game, however, places him second."

If Stauffer had had any idea of the condition in which Wheelock was playing, he would have awarded the Indian stalwart something higher than first team accolades.

Now that he was well over a quarter century old, it was time for Martin to put aside the things of childhood and focus on serious pursuits. So, he returned to Wisconsin to farm. On October 18, 1905, he married Lena E. Webster, Oneida, also a former Carlisle student, and they began family life together. They farmed on government land at first and raised Lena's two children, in addition to having four together. Martin also practiced the blacksmith trade he learned at Carlisle and eventually farmed his own land. Family legend has it that he played on the independent teams in Green Bay that preceded the formation of the Packers. Already in his 30s, he probably didn't play semi-pro or independent football for very many years.

In 1916, likely as a reaction to the raids conducted by Pancho Villa across the border into the U. S. and the general suspicion of Mexico at the time, Martin joined other former Carlisle and Haskell students in forming a company of soldiers to defend the country from an invasion through the border with Mexico. Six months later the Zimmerman telegram was intercepted, and Germany's offer to provide Mexico with arms to be used in taking back their former territory was thwarted. So, the offer was not as outlandish as it sounds almost 100 years later.

Martin Wheelock died in May 1937 at age 65. Some years after he had played his last football game, his former coach paid his former lineman a great compliment. In 1913, Pop Warner selected his all-time best Indian players. He chose Wheelock and Wauseka as two members of the team, saying, "Both tackles were magnificent specimens of manhood, and used their brains to advantage." Warner also talked of Wheelock's bravery in a 1924 interview, much of which is included at the end of this chapter.

Charles Williams (1902)

Charles V. Williams;
Fred Wardecker

Name: Charles V. Williams		**Nickname:** Bull	
DOB: 1/26/1880		**Height:** 5'11"	
Weight: 176		**Age:** 20	
Tribe: Stockbridge		**Home:** Shawano County, WI	
Parents: Andrew Williams; Emma Williams			
Early Schooling: unknown			
Later Schooling: Northwestern University; Sherman Institute			
Honors:			

Charles V. Williams and his sister, Priscilla, enrolled at Carlisle Indian Industrial School sometime in the 1890s, after their mother died. Little is known about their early time there.

Charles went out for football in 1900 but received no mention in the school newspaper. He must have been pretty far down the depth chart at that time. The next year, 1901, things changed. The football team was lacking big men for the line that year and Warner was trying everything to put together a winning combination. To illustrate the nearly desperate situation at Carlisle, a single pre-season issue of *The Red Man and Helper* included three mentions of filling holes in the lineup with Charles Williams:

> "Williams, Flores and Lubo are so far the best tackles and their work has been very satisfactory."
>
> "Flores is rather light and inexperienced, but if he continues to play as he has, he will secure a place on the team and allow the removal of Williams to full-back where he will greatly strengthen the team."
>
> "Palmer, who was rather counted upon to fill the position of full-back, has fallen off in his work, and it may be that Williams will be taken from tackle and placed at full-back."

Warner wanted to play Williams at his natural position, fullback, but already by mid-October had injured players and couldn't keep him there:

> "The Indians were slightly weakened in the second half by the retirement of Wheelock, their giant captain, who wrenched his right knee, his place being taken by Williams, Palmer going in as full-back."

Later in the season Warner was able to move Charles back to fullback and was very pleased with his performance:

> "… the gains being made mostly by Phillips and Williams, who tore up the Navy line for gains of from 8 to 15 yards at a time,"
>
> "Williams is proving a good full-back, and is in every play, and a hard man to stop."
>
> "Williams has developed into quite a strong punter since Wheelock's injury, and the team should be fairly strong the remainder of the season in a punting game."
>
> "… Williams put up a star game at full-back, especially on the defense."

The coach wasn't the only one happy with Charles Williams' play. After the season ended, his teammates elected him captain for 1902. That season was a vast improvement over 1901, a rare losing season in the Warner years at Carlisle. The players were more experienced and more filled out, making size less of a problem than in the previous year. Coach Warner and Captain Williams were high on the squad's prospects and weren't disappointed. A press report from Carlisle early in the season shows that Warner expected big things of him: "Captain Charles Williams is from Wisconsin, and he is considered one of the best fullbacks in the country. He weighs 176 pounds, is 5 feet 11 inches tall, 20 years old and has played two seasons." It took some heroics on the parts of several players, including some past and future captains, to upset Cornell, but Carlisle put losing seasons behind them, finishing 8-3.

Charles Williams received accolades for his leadership and play when jubilant students, who met the team at the train after the victory over Penn, picked him up bodily and carried him around in celebration. Although Walter Camp overlooked him at season's end, others did not. *The Philadelphia Inquirer*'s Nathan F. Stauffer placed him on his All America first team:

> "For full-back two men run a close race. They are nearly equal in build and offensive tactics. Both are good kickers, fine line plungers and fast runners, but Williams the Indian is the strongest defensive back in the country to-day, and it is in that department of the game he excels Graydon, the giant player and star of Harvard.
>
> "I have seen Williams stop a three-man tandem tackle coming between guard and tackle so quickly and so hard that it knocked two of the three for a complete loss, and this has happened so often the opposing team gave up trying to break the line. I overheard Williams remark to his coach: 'I liked it to-day because they opened big holes in our line and I could tackle the backs right away.'
>
> "And he tackles just as though he were carrying the ball and trying desperately to make first down. So hard, in fact, that I have seen half-backs perceptibly stop running rather than have Williams tackle them."

Charles Williams was not just a jock; he was also heavily involved in other aspects of school life. As a member of the Invincible Debating Society, he played the title role in a scene from "Banishment of Catiline." In another meeting of the society, he and Horton Elm argued their affirmative position well against Antonio Lubo and Albert Exendine in

"16-1," a debate over the silver standard. In March 1903, the Seniors elected him class critic.

Charley continued to excel at football, but a new player, Wilson Charles, was emerging as yet another great Indian back. Early in the season they split time at fullback but, to get them both on the field at the same time, Warner shifted Wilson to halfback. In his last regular season game (Carlisle made a post-season trip west to play Utah, Reliance Athletic Association of San Francisco and Sherman Institute in Riverside, California) against previously undefeated Northwestern University, Williams shone. According to an AP reporter, "Half-backs Charles and Sheldon, light but fast as the wind, and full-back Williams circled the ends at will," in Carlisle's 28-0 blowout of the Purple.

After commencement for the Class of 1904, *The Red Man and Helper* marked Charles's departure: "Among the graduates who have gone home is Charles Williams of football notoriety. The team will feel the loss of a valuable a man, and his friends at the school will also miss him greatly. Charles is a tower of strength wherever he goes." He may have left Carlisle and the world of big-time football, but it didn't forget him.

According to the *Chicago Daily Tribune,* Northwestern University football manager F. O. Smith visited the Stockbridge Reservation and convinced Charles Williams to enroll at Evanston and wear the purple on Saturdays that fall. The newspaper also claimed that several eastern universities also attempted to recruit him. *The Red Man and Helper* reported: "Ex-Captain Williams, of Carlisle football fame, has entered college at Evanston, Ill. He admonishes all the Carlisle students to try to gain and maintain a good standing. He says: A year of determination is worth just as much to a Carlisle student as to himself at Evanston. 'We should be content wherever we are and work to keep loneliness away.' He sends regards to all and especially to 'Class '04' who are still trying to learn more."

On September 28, after only a warm-up game against Fort Sheridan had been played, the *Tribune* announced that Williams "...did not find the atmosphere of the Evanston institution congenial and preferred to finish his schooling at an Indian school. It is understood he took a train yesterday for Riverside, Cal., where he will enter school. He attended recitations on Thursday, Friday, Monday and Tuesday." The October 20 edition of the *Arrow* reported that Williams was "with Wm. Warner at Riverside, California" – as an assistant coach no doubt. It is believed that Charles played some professional football for three years between 1905 and 1910.

The next that was heard from Williams was that he had joined the Marines. The December 1910 *Red Man* shared that he was, at that time, an officer in the Marine Corps. The following September he wrote from Fort DuPont, Delaware: "I wish the school a continued success in everything, especially football. I am following the work of the team with great interest, and enjoy nothing more than to hear of Carlisle winning from Old Penn or Harvard. "

Charles Williams made a career of the Unites States Army, retiring after 30 years with the rank of master sergeant. He either changed branches of the service before arriving at Fort DuPont or *The Red Man* was mistaken about his being in the Marines because they were never stationed at Fort DuPont. The 1938 Stockbridge roll listed him as being alive, single, 59 years of age and 7/8 blood. After retiring from military service, he lived at Morgan Siding, an unincorporated village near Gresham, Wisconsin, and joined the Old Stockbridge Orthodox Presbyterian Church. In 1946 Charles married Abbie Doxtator at Shawano. Abbie died on October 5, 1970. Charles lived to be 93 years old, dying on September 10, 1973.

Arthur Sheldon (1904)

Arthur Sheldon; *Fred Wardecker*

Name: Arthur Sheldon	**Nickname:** Crow
DOB: 11/27/1881	**Height:**
Weight: 165	**Age:** 18
Tribe: Nez Perce	**Home:** Nez Perce Agency, ID
Parents: possibly Thaddeus Sheldon, a white soldier; Kate Sheldon, Nez Perce	
Early Schooling: unknown	
Later Schooling: Dickinson College Preparatory School	
Honors:	

Arthur Sheldon and his younger brother, Albert, sons of Kate Sheldon, a full-blood Nez Perce woman, and a white man one assumes was named Sheldon, enrolled at Carlisle Indian School, by 1900 after the death of their mother. Arthur's first mention as an athlete came in September 1901 when Coach Warner commented on the new players, saying, "The rest of the material is composed of green men who never handled a football before Of these Saunook, Sheldon, Shinbone, Chatfleld, Tatiyopa and several others have been demonstrating that they only need experience and coaching to make good players." Sheldon received little mention in Carlisle publications until the spring of 1902 when he came in fourth in the 16-pound hammer throw in the inter-class track meet. That fall *The Redman and Helper* observed, "Bowen, White, Shouchuck, Charles and Sheldon all seem to be playing a much harder game than last season, and if they keep up the gait they all will prove valuable players on the first team."

Arthur didn't make the first team but got some valuable playing time as a back up. The press notice of his play in the Gettysburg game stated, "In the second half Dillon, Cornelius, Fisher, W. Charles and Sheldon were substituted, and the team showed up stronger with this combination. Sheldon especially did great work, both in carrying the ball and in defensive playing." It appears that he did not make the traveling squad that went to the major cities to play the big away games: he stayed behind to lead a team from the small boys' quarters called the Westerners. This group played a Thanksgiving Day game against another group who called themselves Easterners when the varsity was in Washington, DC playing Georgetown.

Arthur Sheldon also excelled in extra-curricular activities other than sports. In January 1903, he was elected President of the Standard Debating Society and, in that position, gave "graceful" addresses. He also played Metellus in a performance of "Julius Caesar." As reported in *The Red Man and Helper*, Arthur orated at the January exhibition later that month:

> "The banner speaker of the evening was Arthur Sheldon, No. 13 school room. He had the dignity, the power, the finish and manliness which captured. His personality entered into the splendid words of Senator Hoar's "Political Freedom" and could the Massachusetts statesman have heard his sentiments spoken with the fire and earnestness that we heard them last night from the lips of an Indian he would have been proud of his noble red brother."

After commencement, Arthur became a member of the Senior Class of 1903 but attended classes at the Dickinson College Preparatory School. However, he continued to participate in activities at the Indian school. In May, he played Hamlet in a production of the gravediggers' scene as part of a Shakespeare symposium put on by the Class of 1904. Two weeks later, showing that he had not abandoned athletics, he surprised Penn State in a dual meet by winning the hammer throw event.

For a change of pace that summer, he worked as a waiter at Beacon-by-the-Sea resort in Point Pleasant, New Jersey. The 22 boys in the Carlisle contingent spent their summer just as college students before and after them have done in this Jersey Shore tradition that continues to this day.

That fall, the 1903 football season was to be Arthur Sheldon's breakout year. He played left halfback on the starting team but was overshadowed by his backfield mates, Walter Camp First Team All America quarterback James Johnson, Fritz Hendricks and Wilson Charles. However, his play did not go unnoticed by his teammates because they elected him captain for 1904. Arthur's teammates also gave him the nickname of Crow for reasons unknown. In the spring, he excelled on the track team by setting school records in the hammer throw.

Perhaps Pop Warner's departure had something to do with it or he may have been homesick. Or it simply may have been because he had graduated. Regardless of the reason, he returned home to visit his family that summer and the school newspaper expressed concern that he wouldn't return. But he did. Arthur Sheldon played and led well, helping his team compile a 9-2 record. That season ended with a two-game road trip in which the Indians thumped Ohio State in Columbus on Thanksgiving Day and Haskell Institute at the St. Louis World's Fair the following Saturday. Sheldon had captained the team well. He also became famous, as did many Carlisle stars, because the games were covered in newspapers across the country. His next season was not as glorious.

In 1905, Arthur shared playing time at left halfback with other players. Carlisle had what seemed like an endless supply of good halfbacks wanting to make the varsity every year. It wasn't easy for a player to hold his starting position long. Those who did were phenomenal athletes.

In February 1906, an article with photographs covering teammate Charles Dillon's wedding circulated around the nation. Arthur even received mention in the press coverage of the wedding: "The best man was Arthur Sheldon, famous Indian half back, a polished type of the modern redskin."

Sheldon's polish, honed while participating with the Standards, may have played an important role in his success. In April 1912, *The Red Man* reported, "...he is traveling in the interests of the Overland Auto Company. Last summer he traveled all through the West and the middle States and Canada. Now he is traveling in the Pacific States." Late that year he wrote from Toledo, Ohio, giving Carlisle credit for whatever success he had attained in the business world. He must have been doing pretty well. After this things get fuzzy.

The 1920 census lists an Arthur Sheldon as a garage owner in Spokane, Washington. This may have been our Arthur Sheldon, but the evidence is circumstantial at best. First, he was in the automotive industry. Second, he was living near his home as Spokane is a short distance from the Idaho state line. Third, his father was born in the U. S., his mother in Idaho and he was born in Idaho. Fourth, his children were born in Kansas, Utah, Colorado and Washington, something that could indicate his traveling with Overland. However, his oldest son would have been born in 1904, in Kansas, when Arthur was still attending Carlisle. So, it's not certain by any means that this man was our Arthur Sheldon. This wasn't the last we'd hear of Arthur Sheldon in the automotive industry.

A March 20, 1927 *Modesto News-Herald* article included an interview of an Arthur Sheldon, works manager of the local Willys Overland plant, discussing the problems associated with dusts, gases, fumes and other byproducts created by the automobile manufacturing plant. Sheldon was quoted as saying, "Dust must be collected, shavings conveyed away, gases, odors and fumes driven out if production is not to be hampered and the lives and health of workmen protected. These objectionable dusts and other byproducts result from grinding, polishing and blasting and other operations, and are all handled by air driven at great force by huge blowers and other air-controlled equipment. There is hardly a department for the Willys Overland plant which does not have both intake and exhaust air system for not only proper ventilation but for collecting all these gases and grist. Each system plays a different part but each effectively gives protection and speeds up the manufacturing processes. In the baked enamel shops, where explosive gases are easily formed, air is controlled by machinery to prevent these explosions. It is kept in motion and the gases driven out." The reporter concluded, "Thus, both Sheldon and W. R. Ourand, chief plant engineer for Willys-Overland, are led to believe that practically all the former serious dangers to workmen's health, developed by some of the processes of industrial manufacture, have been eliminated by a sane recognition of the importance of clean, conditioned air and the fact that it can be scientifically controlled." This may not have been the Arthur Sheldon with whom we are concerned but very well could be. Also, working in that environment could have contributed to an early demise.

Both Arthur and his brother, Albert, disappeared from the Nez Perce rolls during the late 1920s. The entries are confusing at times, but it appears that both died before 1930, and at least one was thought to have died of tuberculosis.

Nicholas Bowen (1905)

Nicholas Bowen; *Fred Wardecker*

Nicholas Bowen; *Cumberland County Historical Society, Carlisle, PA*

Name: Nicholas C. Bowen		**Nickname:**	
DOB: 5/10/1881		**Height:** 6'0"	
Weight: 170		**Age:** 24	
Tribe: Seneca		**Home:** Allegany Reservation, NY	
Parents:			
Early Schooling: unknown			
Later Schooling: Syracuse University; Lawrence University			
Honors:			

Because no student file survives for him and census records prior to his arrival haven't been found, we know little about Nicholas C. Bowen before he arrived at Carlisle. Nick tried out for the varsity football team in 1900. Although light for positions on the line, he got a little playing time at guard and center. Bowen slowly but steadily improved throughout 1901 and 1902, playing behind established stars at their positions. An indication that he was growing and improving was that a 1902 press report out of Carlisle devoted an entire paragraph to him: "Nicholas Bowen may play either tackle or guard. He has been substitute for two years, but is playing a hard game this year. He is 6 feet tall, weighs 183, and is 19 years old. He is a Seneca Indian and comes from New York."

By 1903, he must have put on weight because he became Carlisle's starting left tackle. The left tackle carried the ball often enough in the offensive scheme Warner employed at the time to score some touchdowns.

Nick didn't spend all of his time on the football field; he also attended to his studies and participated in the Standard Debating Society. In the spring, he ran the half mile on the track team.

In 1904, Carlisle had a lightweight team, particularly in the middle of the line, prompting the coaches to try out any sizeable new man who appeared on campus. In spite of these efforts to find heavier linemen, Bowen kept his position as a starter. The Indians went through another good season, losing just two games; however, Bowen got little press. This lack of publicity didn't keep his teammates from electing him captain of the 1905 team. The 8-4 record of the 1905 team is a bit misleading because two of the losses were to professional teams: the Canton and Massillon Athletic Clubs were arguably the best independent teams of their day. A highlight of Bowen's year as captain was the 6-5 defeat of Army in the first football game played between the schools. Up to this time, Carlisle had beaten all the nearby colleges, often by large margins. They had even beaten the mighty University of Pennsylvania three times in an almost annual game that had become a rivalry. They had defeated Cornell in 1902. The Indians had not yet beaten Harvard or any other of the Big Four except Penn. They hadn't beaten Navy yet. So, that victory surely was one of the sweetest the Indians ever tasted. Warner later wrote that the Indians got a special satisfaction from beating the "soldiers" for very obvious reasons. Exendine was elected captain for 1906, but Nick had had a very good run during his turn. Perhaps 'quietly competent' was the best way to describe him.

Nicholas Bowen graduated as a member of the class of 1906 but remained at Carlisle while he attended the Dickinson College Preparatory School across town. He played one more season of football for Carlisle. 1906 was a good year for Carlisle as the Indians' speed and deception were of greater value under the new rules. Nick spent most of the season backing up future captains Wauseka and Lubo at the tackle positions. He did start against Cincinnati. Nick's football career was for the most part finished at season's end. He focused on his studies and finished at Conway Hall in 1908.

The fall of 1908 found Bowen and former teammate Antonio Lubo enrolling at Syracuse University. Due to evolving eligibility rules, Nick wasn't allowed to play on the varsity but was eligible to play on Syracuse's freshman team. For reasons unknown to the author, Nick instead enrolled as a freshman at Lawrence University, a frontier school founded in 1847 to afford "gratuitous advantage to Germans and Indians of both sexes" in Appleton, Wisconsin. Coeducational colleges were a rarity at that time, as were institutions of higher education catering to Indians. Lawrence University was unique and continues to flourish. Bowen attended Lawrence through 1910 but did not play on the football team. Nick wrote Carlisle stating that he enjoyed college life in Wisconsin. He wrote Carlisle again in late 1913 or early 1914 from Onoville, New York, where he was doing forestry work. Perhaps that is what he studied at college.

When the U. S. entered WWI and Bowen registered for the draft, he was still living in Onoville, New York, but then had a wife named Esther. He worked as a pipe fitter for American Brake Shoe Company which may have been a subsidiary of General Electric. He died on November 24, 1921, just 40 years old.

Antonio Lubo (1907)

Antonio Lubo; *Cumberland County Historical Society, Carlisle, PA*

Antonio Lubo; *U. S. Army Military History Institute*

Name: Antonio Lubo		**Nickname:** The Wolf	
DOB: 7/7/1876 - 1884		**Height:** 6'	
Weight: 166		**Age:** 24	
Tribe: Cahuilla		**Home:** Tule River Reservation, CA	
Parents: Cornelio Lubo, Cahuilla; Petra Lubo, Cahuilla			
Early Schooling: unknown			
Later Schooling: Conway Hall; Dickinson College; Syracuse University			
Honors:			

Antonio Lubo, the son of Cornelio and Petra Lubo, full-blood Cahuillas who lived on the Tule River Reservation on the rugged foothills of the Sierra Nevada Mountains 20 miles from the nearest town, Porterville, California. By 1900 Antonio was enrolled at Carlisle and trying to make the football squad.

Coach Warner wrote in the *Philadelphia Press*, "Lubo, Thomas Walker, Ben Walker and J. Baine are the new men trying for tackle, and all of them are very light, none of them weighing over 165 pounds. Thomas Walker so far has done the best work, while Lubo and Baine have improved considerably." Antonio most likely spent that year on the second team possibly getting a little playing time on the varsity filling in for injured players but receiving no mention in the press.

Pop Warner had quite a number of holes to fill on the 1901 team, particularly in the line, due to graduations, enrollment completions and injuries. So, Warner looked more closely at the players wanting to make the team. He first tried Lubo at center because, although small for a lineman, he was as large as his predecessor, Smith. In mid-October *The New York Times* interviewed Warner about his team: "Lubo has the mental character-istics of a good football player. Coach Warner thinks that he has very little natural aptitude for the game, but has forced himself to play energetically." When game time rolled around, Lubo played tackle, sometimes left, others right. He played left tackle against Navy in a game considered unnecessarily violent and had his wrist smashed as well as opened. Because Lubo was too injured to play against Penn, Wheelock thought the right side of the line was weak without him. Immediately after the season ended, Antonio went to Baltimore for a while, likely for medical treatment of his injured wrist. He was out of commission athletically speaking for some time. Then a junior, Lubo became active with the Invincible Debating Society.

Antonio spent part of the summer visiting, and likely convalescing, with his family in California. When he returned to school, he doubted if he would play football again but continued his studies. However, the October 3, 1902 *Arrow* announced that Lubo would play against Dickinson College the next day. That game was canceled. The first game that Lubo actually played in was the first half of the Wednesday, October 15 contest against Bloomsburg Normal, which may have been a possible warm-up for the Cornell game which was played four days later. He again played right guard against Cornell. His heroics in that game are documented by Pop Warner and are included at the end of this chapter. Antonio also played against Penn, helping to defeat the Quakers for only the second time in all the games the two teams played to that date. Lubo wasn't fit to play in any more games that season.

After convalescing during the remainder of the school year and spending the sum-mer of 1903 working at the Beacon-by-the-Sea resort in Point Pleasant, New Jersey, Antonio was in better condition for football. He played right tackle early in the season but shifted back to right guard by the Princeton game and stayed there the rest of the season. He didn't receive much notice for his play that year but was probably not back to full strength yet. Antonio graduated in the spring and then enrolled in the Dickinson College Preparatory School. However, he continued to play football for Carlisle. Albert Exendine started the 1904 season convalescing from surgery, necessitating that Lubo be shifted to left tackle while he was out. When Exendine returned, Antonio moved to fullback.

1905 found Lubo playing right end. He stayed at that position until the very end of the season, at which time he subbed at left end. He completed his studies at Dickinson Preparatory School in the spring and enrolled in Dickinson College as a freshman in the fall of 1906. He continued to play football at Carlisle. Lubo was shifted to right tackle. At season's end he was elected captain for the 1907 team and continued his studies at Dickinson College. After his election, the *New York World* wrote:

> "Since 1903 he has played baseball several times in left field. With a view to taking up electrical engineering he is now doing supplemental work at Dickinson College, Carlisle.
> "Lubo is a most polished type of Indian, quiet and reserved in demeanor, and

probably one of the most universally-liked Indians who has ever attended the Carlisle school."

Antonio remained active with the Invincibles and progressed with his studies at Dickinson College. In the fall, he played right tackle and led Carlisle to its best season to that time. The 1907 Indians remain one of the legendary great football teams. The team's on-field demeanor changed with this team. Prior to this, the Indians had been viewed as stoic, seldom saying anything, mostly grunting. That all changed with the Harvard game. *The Arrow* presented a running conversation among Carlisle linemen:

> Capt. Lubo – Who got that last man?
> Hauser – I did, captain.
> Capt. Lubo – Good. Who'll get this man?
> Exendine – I will, captain: I'll get him.
> After the play the conversation began again.
> Exendine – I got my man, captain.
> Capt. Lubo – Good. Gardner, you get this man.
> Gardner – I'll get him. Captain.
> Another play was run off.

Antonio Lubo was not just a good leader; he was a very good player, so good, in fact, that some sports writers thought he deserved All America honors as did teammates Hauser, Exendine and Mount Pleasant. Walter Camp omitted him completely. At season's end, he enrolled at Syracuse University.

The January 5, 1908 edition of *The Syracuse Herald* announced, "The well-meant efforts of Antonio Lubo, captain of last year's Carlisle football team, to secure an athlete for the university, have come to grief. Lubo who to-morrow becomes a student in the engineering course, had persuaded his friend Mount Pleasant, quarterback of the same team, to enter the university some time this month." An unnamed person with Syracuse University wrote Mount Pleasant and Lubo saying that the question of their eligibility to play football at the school would not likely be determined soon. The writer gave them the impression that they weren't really wanted. Both men were indignant because they had planned on entering the engineering program, in addition to playing football. Mount Pleasant went elsewhere. Lubo registered at Syracuse two days later and played football that fall – for a while.

As a special student, Antonio Lubo took courses in the spring and summer sessions. An early August *Herald* headline blared, "Lubo Will Not Play" followed by "Faculty Had Barred Him." Syracuse football supporters had been elated when Lubo's enrollment was announced because they felt the coursework accomplished over the spring and summer would have been enough to make him a sophomore and thus eligible to play. The faculty thought otherwise. The Herald conjectured that Lubo would enter Dartmouth where he would be allowed to play. However, he stayed and played on the freshman team alongside former Carlisle teammate Nicholas Bowen.

With Lubo and Bowen holding up one end of the line, the Syracuse freshmen were formidable. One day in practice, when scrimmaging the varsity, they angered head coach "Tad" Jones by scoring three touchdowns. Disgusted he said, "They are a pretty poor team to let the freshmen score on them. Freshmen ought never to score on a varsity team." Things were looking up for next year's varsity – until a Sunday game was played.

Once the University got wind of Lubo playing for the All Syracuse independent team the previous Sunday, he was barred from further participation in athletics at Syracuse. He continued with his coursework but he played football on Sundays, however.

While at Syracuse, he kept in contact with the Carlisle school. In May 1911, he sent his regrets for missing commencement. He had intended on attending but was involved in a wreck that left him hospitalized just three days prior to his planned departure. He attended Syracuse for three years, but didn't complete his program, reputedly due to illness. When he was able to work, he took a job as a brakeman with the New York Central Railroad, his employer for the rest of his working days. In 1914, he was able to attend Carlisle's commencement and gave talks to the boys' and girls' Holy Name Societies while in town. He also gave a talk in which he said that his success to date had been due to having a fixed purpose. In the fall, the railroad let him take some time off to assist Pop Warner with the team.

Not only did he assist Pop, but he also served as assistant disciplinarian and was involved in campus life. He gave a talk to his old club, the Invincible Debating Society, in which he said, "Carlisle is not a mere school, it is an educational proposition. Most of us have come here with well-made plans. This is a great chance to improve it and come up to the name of Carlisle." When the football season ended, he returned to Syracuse.

It was in Syracuse that his name was changed informally to Anthony or Tony Lubo. His 1918 WWI draft registration listed him has Anthony Joseph Lubo, brakeman on the NYC RR, married to Emma and born in 1880. The next year their son, Cornelius was born. By the late 1920s, Lubo's marriage had become tumultuous. He was paroled for a week in 1928 after pleading not guilty to charges of nonsupport of his wife and two children. A couple of weeks later, he was required to pay $10 a week in support of his family. In 1932, he was jailed again for public drunkenness. Whether his drinking led to problems in the marriage or vice versa is not known, but it appears to have been a problem for some time. However, he remained employed by the railroad for 20 years. He and Emma appear not to have divorced, possibly due to being Catholic.

Antonio was living with his son-in-law, Arthur Meade, daughter and grandson, Kenneth Meade, when he became ill, possibly with tuberculosis. After an eight-month bout, he succumbed at Onondaga Sanatorium on December 7, 1941. When informed of his death, Pop Warner said, "He was one of the most capable and dependable football players Carlisle ever had and one of the finest characters I have ever come in contact with. For his weight he was about the best lineman I ever coached."

Lubo's son, Cornelius, was named after his grandfather, Antonio's father. The younger Lubo followed in his father's footsteps and was a good athlete. "Corn" became a war hero for his exploits fighting the Japanese in the Pacific. He died in 1988 while vacationing at the South Indian River Reservation in Arizona.

Wauseka (1908) and Pete Hauser (1910)

Wauseka (Emil Hauser); *Cumberland County Historical Society, Carlisle, PA*

Pete Hauser; *Cumberland County Historical Society, Carlisle, PA*

Name:	Emil H. Hauser	**Nickname:**	Wauseka
DOB:	11/22/1886	**Height:**	5'9"
Weight:	180	**Age:**	23
Tribe:	Cheyenne	**Home:**	Cheyenne-Arapaho reservation, OK

Parents: Herman Hauser, white army sergeant; Amy Hauser, Cheyenne
Early Schooling: Halstead School; Haskell Institute
Later Schooling: Oregon Agricultural College
Honors: American Indian Athletic Hall of Fame, 1971

Name:	Herman Peter Hauser	**Nickname:**	
DOB:	6/10/1887	**Height:**	5'9"
Weight:	177	**Age:**	21
Tribe:	Cheyenne	**Home:**	Cheyenne-Arapaho reservation, OK

Parents: Herman Hauser, white army sergeant; Amy Hauser, Cheyenne
Early Schooling: Halstead School; Haskell Institute
Later Schooling:
Honors: American Indian Athletic Hall of Fame, 1971

Emil H. Hauser and Herman Peter Hauser were born at Fort Reno on the Cheyenne – Arapaho reservation in Indian Territory (present day Oklahoma) to a white army sergeant father of German extraction, Herman Hauser, and a full-blood Cheyenne mother, Amy Hauser. Herman Hauser, their father, had died and their mother married Waldo Reed in the 1895-97 timeframe. Their mother died before 1908. The boys first attended the Halstead School; then they went to Haskell Institute. It was at Haskell that they really started playing football. In 1904, with Pete at right end and Emil at left tackle, Haskell beat Kansas, Missouri, Texas and Nebraska. Their record and reputation made the match-up against Carlisle at the St. Louis World's Fair a natural, or so it would seem. The Carlisle

Pete Hauser with ball against Chicago, 1907; *Chicago History Museum*

Indians beat Haskell's Fightin' Indians 38-4, providing the Hauser brothers, along with six teammates, ample reason to transfer East as soon as they could.

Emil, almost 20 or 23, depending on the source, arrived at Carlisle without much ado in September of 1906 after his enrollment period at Haskell had expired. At Carlisle, he studied in the business department and didn't work in a trade shop. Soon he became the starting left tackle on the varsity football team and learned Pop Warner's new offense from Bemus Pierce and Frank Hudson. By the fifth game of the season, Emil was using his preferred name, Wauseka. He weighed 173 pounds, large by Carlisle standards, but the Harvard tackle he played opposite, although only 20 years old, weighed 193 pounds. Such weight deficits were expected for the Indians when they played the better teams. Wauseka held up his side of the line and the team had a good season.

In the spring, Wauseka caught for the baseball team and played a little summer ball for the Hagerstown, Maryland team. That summer a Hagerstown paper reported, "Admirers of baseball and particularly those in Hagerstown will learn with regret that Hauser, the big Indian catcher, who has been doing such splendid work for the local team, is going to get out of the game here. He will go to Carlisle school to spend a few days and then go to Oklahoma to take possession of some valuable land he has inherited. He will devote his time to looking after his interests and expects to return to Carlisle in the fall."

After spending some time at home recruiting, he brought back with him his brother, Pete Hauser, and Mike Balenti's brother, John. Pete's reputation preceded him.

A newspaper article citing friends of Arthur Jardine, reputed to have been a star basketball player at Carlisle before Hauser's arrival, as the source, described Pete Hauser's toughness on the basketball court. When Pete was still enrolled at Haskell Institute around the turn of the last century, he played in a game played against Carlisle:

> "…[Hauser] was said to be a lad of only sixteen years, while Jardine was ten years his senior, Hauser guarded Jardine, and as the Indians played an unusually rough game many fouls were called upon them, Hauser being one of the worst offenders. Every time he fouled Jardine the latter scored the point by tossing the ball into the net. Slowly the desire to go on the warpath began to arouse itself within the dusky one.
>
> "'Throw another basket like that and I'll split you open!' hissed Pete into Jardine's ear as the crowd yelled for more gore.
>
> "Jardine didn't see any tommyhawks hanging on Hauser, but he was the least bit scared and told Berggren about it. 'Berggy' laughed and took it as a joke. The

captain decided to do the same, but he missed the first free toss after that, presumably from nervousness. Try as he would to steady himself, Jardine threw only one or two of the remaining fouls because of the hypnotic words which the Indian hissed into his ear."

The Hausers and Balentis were soon out practicing football. Carlisle's 1907 starting line-up boasted two Hausers, Emil at left tackle and Pete at fullback. This team was Carlisle's first to beat Harvard, first to have two wins over Big Four teams, and the first to have a one-loss season. Pete and Emil were significant parts of that.

The last game of the season was against what Amos Alonzo Stagg considered his finest Chicago Maroon team, and Carlisle's big ground gainer and passer, Frank Mt. Pleasant, was out with a broken thumb. So, the passing duties fell to the fullback, Pete Hauser. "Houser [sic] Was The Star," began the section of the article about the game in which Pete's play was discussed. It went on, "Houser, [sic] in fact was a whole team in himself. Backed up by impregnable interference, he carried the ball two-thirds of the time in the Indian attack and seldom failed to gain ground.... Houser's [sic] best work, however, was with his toe. Three times he negotiated goals from placement with Balenti holding the ball. As many more attempts were missed but mainly because Doseff, who was the only Chicago lineman to outplay his opponent, managed to wriggle through in time to hurry the kick."

Carlisle also scored a touchdown on a forward pass. Chicago was double and triple-teaming end Albert Exendine and William Gardner to keep them from going downfield to catch passes, so Ex came up with a plan. Between plays, he told Pete Hauser to hold onto the ball as long as he could to give him time to get downfield. When the play got underway, Ex ran out of bounds and, as expected, the defenders let him go. He ran behind the Chicago bench, downfield along the sidelines, then back onto the field and downfield as fast as he could to intercept the ball that Pete arched his way. With no defender in sight he caught the ball easily and scored a touchdown. Stagg was furious and protested to no avail. (The rules were changed during the offseason to disallow a player from returning to the field of play during a play after leaving it.) This was a victory that Pop Warner savored the rest of his life, and Pete Hauser and Exendine handed it to him on a platter. Wauseka was elected captain for 1908, and Walter Camp named Pete to his All America second team. Not a bad fall for the Hausers.

The 1908 winter wasn't nearly as good. Pete Hauser missed a few weeks of class while he was in the hospital with a wrenched back. He most likely incurred that injury playing basketball. His classmates missed him in the classroom and on the basketball court.

Pete graduated in the spring and enrolled for graduate study in the Commercial Course. That spring, Wauseka played catcher again on the school's baseball team. After a summer away, possibly playing baseball, they returned to Carlisle in September to prepare for the upcoming season. Wauseka showed his leadership abilities while Pete demonstrated his versatility by shifting from fullback to right end. With Exendine and Gardner no longer playing, two huge voids needed to be filled at the end positions. Because there were plenty of talented backfield men at the time, Pete could serve the team better by playing at end. Both brothers got high marks for the season as players but no mention from Walter Camp. The 10-2-1 record during what some might consider a rebuilding year was evidence of Wauseka's leadership.

An incident associated with the Penn game illustrates how the football team's fame had spread. Prior to the game, students and school employees making the trip were taken to Gimbels where the school band gave a short concert before lunch. Gimbels prepared a meal specially for the Carlisle contingent. "The menu consisted of: Vegetable soup, a la Warner; Browned potatoes, touchdown fashion; fried oysters, Mt. Pleasant style; Wauseka pie with ice cream."

Apparently Wauseka had a problem with punctuality because in February *The Arrow* reported, "Emil Hauser, 'Wauseka,' has bought an alarm clock. He intends to follow Franklin's motto: 'Early to bed and early to rise,' etc." Pete became active in extracurricular activities including the Invincible Debating Society. Both played on the basketball team. In the spring Wauseka appears to have sat out the baseball season. Pete pitched and played first base. As a hitter, you could say he was a good pitcher.

Ex-Captain Wauseka was at his usual position, tackle, for 1909 and Hauser was back at fullback. The team's record was only 8-3-1, but the Hauser brothers shone. So potent a weapon was Pete that, prior to the Penn game, *The Carlisle Arrow* ran a limerick about him that also made fun of the way the school's name was spelled:

Advice to Penn in Limerick Style:

Pete Hauser, full back at Carlisle.
Has the power Penn's feelings to risle.
With a stoical grunt,
He can tackle or punt,
And they'll never get next to his stysle.

The *St. Louis Republic* saw it this way: "Pete Hauser and his brother, Wauseka, and Germain, were the stonewall combination of the Indian line. Hauser was also a grizzly, on defense, He tore tremendous holes in the St. Louis line every time he hit the bull's eye. Hauser took nearly all the forward passes handled by Libby."

Wauseka, as captain of the basketball team, gave a short talk at the annual Athletic Association Awards Ceremony in early 1910. He and Fanny Keokuk later won a prize in the dance contest for the two-step. He didn't play on the school baseball team that spring because he, William Garlow and William Newashe played for the Harrisburg League Team that summer. They did, however, find time to attend the occasional Saturday night social at the school. Pete stuck closer to school that spring and participated in a variety of activities, including writing articles for the school paper, reading his essay to the YMCA meeting, holding an office with the YMCA, welcoming guests to the annual athletic banquet, co-authoring an essay on 'Practical Business Training' with Joe Libby and presenting it as part of graduation exercises and, of course, graduating upon completion of his post-graduate course in business.

Pete again pitched for the school's baseball team while Wauseka played baseball for a Harrisburg minor league team. Carlisle won the state interscholastic track and field meet for the third straight year with Hauser's help. According to *The Arrow*, "Hauser sprang a surprise by winning the discus throw and taking fourth place in the shot put." Wauseka got some positive press as well: "Hauser, the Carlisle Indian catcher for Harrisburg, played well in Saturday's game with Scranton. In an account it is said: 'The work of Hauser, the Carlisle Indian, was an interesting feature. His throwing was of the gilt-edge order. His part in a double play was the fastest kind of fielding.'" While Emil played baseball for Harrisburg, Pete spent his vacation at home in Oklahoma. At summer's end he returned to Carlisle, bringing their sister, Anna, with him. It was a matter of opinion as to who were tougher, the Hauser boys or the Hauser girls as both established reputations, at Carlisle.

Warner gave Pete Hauser a prize of dubious value after being elected captain: a 15-game schedule. The Indians did not return to school in fighting form for the season ahead. The entire season was marred by injuries that often result when players are not in top condition. Another contributing factor was that the entire schedule was squeezed into a period lasting only little more than two months. All were regular season games as their schedule ended with the traditional Thanksgiving game against Brown. Players simply had too little time to heal between games. Mercifully, Western Maryland canceled, eliminating one game.

Since they were too injured to play, Warner charged former captain Antonio Lubo and Wauseka with the coaching of the third team and the Reserves, respectively. The second team, usually called the Hotshots, called themselves Wauseka's Braves that year.

Pete shone that year; against Bucknell he kicked a 45-yard field goal and electrified the crowd with a 50-yard touchdown run. He was even hurt for some games, playing either at diminished capacity or not at all. Still he was considered for some All America teams but not by Walter Camp. Pete returned home to Pawhuska, Oklahoma after the season ended.

Wauseka did not confine himself to the football field that school year. He served as President of the Bachelors' Club and entertained the membership by telling a thrilling ghost story at one meeting. He served as toastmaster for the Commercial Department graduation dance. Over the winter, he coached the basketball team and in April assisted Warner with Carlisle's first ever spring football practice. By May, Pete was in Atlanta working with Wahoo at Spalding Brothers. He scored well on a civil service test and looked forward to getting a government job as a clerk. Emil was also in Atlanta as he and Mike Balenti had signed with the Atlanta baseball team for that summer.

The Hauser brothers' careers at Carlisle ended and their enrollments were completed. Emil's returned student report listed both his character and disposition as being very good and recommended him for positions available in government service: disciplinarian, office assistant and athletic director. Pete's work with the new football players paid off in spades the next year. That fall he assisted John Heisman with the Georgia Tech Yellowjackets in Atlanta. Wauseka wrote that he spent the summer on the Pacific Coast and hoped to visit Carlisle in the fall. That visit appears to have not taken place as he wrote in January 1912 that he was visiting his sister, Louisa, in Siletz, Oregon.

In the fall of 1912, Pete Hauser, now 25 or 28, was in Calumet, Oklahoma farming his allotment. Emil enrolled at Oregon Agricultural College (today's Oregon State University) October 1 and went out for football. The next day's *O.A.C. Barometer* had an article about the team and devoted most of a paragraph to Emil, or "Amy," as it said his friends called him. He was to play fullback, although he was 15 pounds overweight. The reporter thought Coach Sam Dolan would have no trouble trimming the fat. The team beat the alumni team and lost to Multnomah Athletic Club, an independent team from Portland. Johnny Bender, head coach of O. A. C.'s next opponent, Washington State College, challenged Emil Hauser's amateur status. A controversy ensued which culminated in a newspaper article that was circulated around the country:

"INDIAN A PROFESSIONAL

"Spokane. Wash, Nov. 8.—The question of the eligibility of Emil Hauser, the big Indian half back of the Oregon Agricultural College, which has excited wide discussion in Northwest conference circles, apparently was settled today by the receipt here of communications from Secretary Farrell of the minor association of baseball leagues, and Manager Baker of the Harrisburg, Pa., team, stating that Hauser had been under contract to and played with the Harrisburg team in 1910 at a salary of $175 a month."

Emil withdrew from college on November 21. In February 1913, he married former Carlisle student Dolly Stone in Tutuilla, Oregon. After a visit with his sister where she worked at the Siletz Reservation, the couple was to engage in farming near El Reno, Oklahoma. However, they were soon back in Oregon, if they ever left, because their children were born there. The January 7, 1916 edition of *The Carlisle Arrow* included a birth announcement in the form of a poem from the E. H. Hausers. Emil Wauseka Hauser was born on December 19, 1915. By 1920, when they were at Salem Indian School (today's Chemawa Indian School), Emil and Dolly also had a daughter, Mary Emily. Emil was employed as a night watchman and coached football at times. In 1923, son Peter Herman Hauser was born.

Pete Hauser remained more active in athletics than did his brother. Pete drew $150 a month umpiring minor league baseball in Oklahoma during the 1920s. For two falls in the early 1920s, he coached the independent Hominy Indians to undefeated seasons, barnstorming across the Midwest and playing other independent football teams in the region.

In 1931, Knute Rockne wrote a syndicated column in which he recalled watching Pete Hauser play nearly a quarter century earlier:

"...I saw this same [Wally] Steffens, who had become one of the greatest quarterbacks and field generals under Stagg of Chicago. In this game he was stopped dead by as great a pair of ends as ever played together on a football team. I refer to the Araphohoe [sic] Gardner and Exendine, who were playing for Pop Warner at Carlisle. What a delight it was to see these two men work. Their down-the-field play under Pete Hauser's punts was as fine as I've ever seen - a thing of beauty. It was so good, in fact, that in the second half Stagg changed his tactics against Pete Hauser's kicking, and put three men on each of the ends to prevent the Indian pair going down to cover the kick. The wiry Hauser was alert. The next time he kicked he stood there with the ball for at least four seconds, while in the meantime Gardner and Exendine had broken loose and streaked down the field with Chief Afraid-of-a-Bear and Lone Star, when Hauser proceeded deliberately to boot the ban his usual sixty yards.

"Deceitful Red Men

"It was in this game I saw Pete Hauser rise up behind center and mop his forehead with a sort of half yawn. The mop was just half finished and the yawn half completed when center snapped the ball and through the line went Hauser for eight yards. The Chicago line had relaxed when they saw Hauser yawning and wiping his forehead.

"Bret Harte tells us about the dark ways and vain tricks of the heathen Chinee [sic], but in football laurels for cunning go to the Indians."

Peter Hauser died on July 7, 1935 while residing at the Osage Agency in Oklahoma. Emil Hauser died on May 19, 1941 of a heart attack in Salem, Oregon, where he had lived for 27 years.

Archie and Joseph Libby (1909)

Archie Libby; *Cumberland County Historical Society, Carlisle, PA*

Joe Libby as a small boy; *Cumberland County Historical Society, Carlisle, PA*

Name: Archie Libby	**Nickname:**
DOB: 1/14/1885	**Height:**
Weight: 146	**Age:** 20
Tribe: Chippewa	**Home:** White Earth Agency, MN
Parents: Mark Libby, white lumberman-farmer; Hannah/Isabelle/Eliza Libby, White Oak Point Chippewa	
Early Schooling: unknown	
Later Schooling:	
Honors:	

Name: Joseph Libby	**Nickname:**
DOB: 2/19/1887	**Height:** 5'10"
Weight: 145	**Age:** 19
Tribe: Chippewa	**Home:** White Earth Agency, MN
Parents: Mark Libby, white lumberman-farmer; Hannah/Isabelle/Eliza Libby, White Oak Point Chippewa	
Early Schooling: unknown	
Later Schooling:	
Honors: American Indian Athletic Hall of Fame, 1971	

Joe Libby, Captain of 1910 team;
U. S. Army Military History Institute

Joe Libby and his older brother, Archie, were enrolled at Carlisle by 1900. Their mother, believed to have been called Hannah or Isabelle or Eliza, and siblings were enrolled in the White Earth Agency as White Oak Point Chippewa. Their father, Mark Libby, apparently a white lumberman from Maine, was not listed on tribal rolls. By 1895, Mark Libby had switched to farming.

The Libby brothers were small but quick. Being older, Archie made his shop team, the Printers, before Joe made a team. In 1903, Archie moved up to the varsity and showed promise. However, he played the same position, quarterback, as did James Johnson, that year's Walter Camp first team All American quarterback. Archie got some playing time mopping up games against the overmatched warm-up teams. Archie received notice for his performance on the track team. In 1904, with the departure of James Johnson, Archie vied with Baker to replace him. Both performed well, but Archie emerged, both as a starter and a star. Meanwhile, younger brother Joe got notice in the school paper for his work with the crew preparing and serving food to the varsity at the training table.

In 1905, Frank Mt. Pleasant emerged and won the starting quarterback position. Archie played well, filling in when Mt. Pleasant was injured or tired or the outcome of the game was already determined. He did get enough playing time to letter, though. Both Libbys were starters on the varsity basketball team that winter. They played the two back positions, guards in current terminology, very likely because they were short. As the season progressed, Joe was moved to the second team on which he played center, a position not normally played by a short man. As the season progressed further, Joe moved up to the first team as center. Archie joined the Standard Debating Society over the winter and participated in debates. Both Libby brothers went out for the school's baseball team in the spring. One of them played first base and batted ninth in several games. One of them did well with the track team. However, it is not clear which Libby participated in either sport. After commencement, Archie was elected Critic of the Senior Class.

When the 1906 football season rolled around, the game was played under the new rules, which created the modern game in which speed and deception increased in value. Mt. Pleasant moved to left halfback, tailback in the single-wingback formation, while Archie started at quarterback and Joe at right halfback. Early in the season Joe moved to the second team where he started at left halfback. On the varsity, Joe backed up Fritz Hendricks at right halfback. However, he did get to start the Cincinnati game; whether it was due to injury to or to Hendricks' fatigue is unknown. Archie lettered again. Several writers and coaches, including Warner, selected him for their All America teams, but Walter Camp did not.

The Libby brothers again played on the varsity basketball team in the winter of 1907. When spring rolled around, Pop Warner, who had just returned from Cornell, compiled a list of school records for the various track and field events from previous years. Archie held the records for both 120 and 220-yard hurdles. Joe played on the baseball team. Both Libbys graduated that spring. Archie returned to Minnesota where he found a good-paying job in the printing industry in St. Paul. In March 1908, Commissioner of the Department of Indian Affairs, Francis Leupp, contacted the Secretary of the Interior to recommend Archie as a check scaler for the logging operations conducted at Leech Lake under the Morris Act. Scalers compute the amount of lumber in trees after they are sawed down to determine how much the tribe should be paid for the lumber. Check scalers spot check the scaling to prevent the tribe from being cheated.

A delegation of Chippewas from the White Earth Reservation traveled to Washington to challenge the appointments of scalers not appointed under the provisions of the Morris Act. This act provided that such appointments shall only be made on the recommendations of the chiefs. One can guess that the tribe was being shorted on the returns from logging on their property and that the tribe did not trust the government's appointees.

Joe may have returned home to farm or may have started the commercial course at Carlisle. Either he didn't play on the 1907 football team or didn't get enough playing time worth mentioning. That year's starting lineup would have been one of the most difficult of all the Carlisle teams to join. However, Joe, then 21, returned in 1908.

The Arrow summed up Joe's contributions to Carlisle football at the end of the 1908 season:

> "Joe, as he is familiarly called by the students, has played on the squad for three years and although he has not been a regular, because of his light weight and the wealth of backfield material, he has played in many big games and his playing has improved so steadily every season that he is sure to be a valuable man for the team next fall and he is capable of playing either half-back, full-back or quarter-back."

On December 18, 1908, *The Carlisle Arrow* reported:

> "Little Boy was elected captain of the team for next year but, as he played in some of the games in 1905 and has been a regular player since that time, the executive committee of the Athletic Association has declared him ineligible to play another year under the rules adopted at the close of the season of 1907, which limit a player to four years of football at Carlisle. Another election will be held after the holidays. Fritz Hendricks will also be prevented from playing again on account of the four-year eligibility rule."

Joe Libby was selected. *The Arrow* discussed the next year's captain: "His experience on the squad in all these positions makes him an all-around player of ability and as he is one of the headiest players on the squad, Carlisle is assured of a capable leader next fall." Joe was the only person elected captain, with the exception of the first team's captain, who had not previously been a starter. Libby was almost always the smallest man on the field when he played, weighing at most 148 pounds.

1909 started off as a very good year for Joe. In the spring, he played left field and generally batted third for the baseball team. He hit over .300 for the season. This success encouraged Jim Thorpe, Jesse Youngdeer, and Joe to run away from Carlisle to play baseball in Rocky Mount, North Carolina. Thorpe managed to stay on the team the entire summer, but the others weren't kept very long due to the high level of competition. Joe was back at Carlisle by September.

Although not as loaded as some other Carlisle teams, the 1909 team was still a potent force. Joe received more press the year he was captain than the rest of his years at Carlisle combined. The coverage he received was very supportive: "Captain Libby showed that he will be a worthy successor to Balenti and the other famous quarter-backs 'the Indians have had. He had the honor of scoring the first touchdown of the season of '09." He had a very good year but his last game, the Thanksgiving Day game against St. Louis University played in the Cincinnati National League baseball park, was his best, very likely the best of his career. The *St. Louis Globe-Democrat* wrote:

> "Little Libby, the cunning quarter of Carlisle, electrified the spectators time and again by his brilliant dashes through the local players. Could he have felt the pulses of the spectators, who were bewildered, affrighted and exalted by turns, he might have divined the warmth that greeted his daring deeds. Misjudging one of Dockery's punts, he allowed the oval to roll to his own goal line, where he regained it, and then dashed through the entire St. Louis team for an 80-yard run, putting the ball on St. Louis' 10-yard line. On other occasions this player, proficient in every department of the game, eluded his opponents and ran 10 and 20 yards through 'broken fields.' Libby was truly the hero of the game."

Possibly to improve his communication skills, Joe wrote some articles for the school newspaper. In December 1909, he wrote "Christmas with the Chippewas" to explain how his people celebrated Christmas. The following April he and fellow business student Pete Hauser co-wrote "Practical Business Education," which discussed reasons for taking the commercial course after graduation. In addition to the usual reasons one would expect to find discussed, they brought up issues very pertinent to Indians:

> "Not only was I taught the art of earning a living, but my practical common-sense was developed, which will enable me to take care of myself out in the shrewd business world after I leave school. And, too, the course has improved my judgment, cultivated my reasoning faculties, made me more confident of myself, and given me that power which is so much needed at home among the Indians, to be more independent of the 'white swindler,' who is there, not to help, but to beat the red man."

Joe, Pete, Morgan Crowsghost and William Nelson completed their post-graduate course and went through commencement. As one of the commencement activities, Joe, Pete and Morgan stood in front of ruled blackboards while Joe read "at a fair speed" three or four sentences about the value of integrity in business. The young men captured the text in shorthand on the blackboards. The text was then read from the shorthand to the "typewriter chorus," which quickly put these words on paper in a finished form.

In September, *The Carlisle Arrow* reported, "The commercial students, Joseph Libby, Peter Houser, Margaret Delorimiere, Marie Lewis, and Morgan Crowsghost, have been assisting with the clerical and stenographic work at the administration building gaining valuable experience. They have all shown great efficiency in their work which speaks well for the training they have received under their business teacher, Mr. Ramsey." One would hope they also made a little money. In mid-October, *The Arrow* reported that Joe, unable to practice because of an injured shoulder, had been assigned to coach the third string.

In January 1911, he was called home because of the death of his brother, George. In April *The Arrow* reported that Joe was working for the government in his hometown, Libby, Minnesota. His days at Carlisle were finally over. Archie married Myrtle McArthur, a young woman from the White Earth Reservation, in 1910. They soon started a family as he had a good job as a salesman with a printing firm. In February 1912, both Archie and Joe wrote to the school to keep in touch. Joe wrote that he was enjoying life in Minnesota and that Archie had become a Justice of the Peace. In 1917, when they registered for the draft, Joe was farming and supporting his mother and Archie was an agent for Webb Publishing. In 1920, Archie, Myrtle and their 10-year-old daughter, Audrey, still lived on the White Earth Reservation where he worked as a salesman for a general store. They had another daughter, Dora, around 1924 and moved to Minneapolis.

In 1930, Joe was listed as divorced, living with his sister, Edith, and working as a presser in a laundry in Duluth, Minnesota. Either he had married and shed a wife since 1920 or the census taker had made an error. By 1932, Joe, now listed as 3/8 blood, had relocated to Portland, Oregon. He worked doing maintenance work at a high school in Milwaukee, Oregon until 1957 when he retired.

Joe had a lot to say when he was interviewed in 1970: "I was the goat when Jim Thorpe got professionalized. We were outfielders. I took him to Rocky Mount, NC, and we both signed up for summer baseball. We didn't get much, just enough to live on. But after the 1912 Olympics the AAU got hold of this engagement, declared Thorpe a pro and took his medals from him. I was the one who got blamed for taking Thorpe to Rocky Mount." He died in December 1981 at age 94.

Elmer Busch (1914)

Elmer Busch; *Fred Wardecker*

Elmer Busch; *Cumberland County Historical Society, Carlisle, PA*

Name:	Elmer Eugene Busch	**Nickname:**	
DOB:	3/14/1890 or 8/17/1892	**Height:**	5'10"
Weight:	192 1/2	**Age:**	20
Tribe:	Pomo	**Home:**	Potter Valley, CA
Parents:	Jack Busch, Pomo; Maggie Busch, Pomo		
Early Schooling:	Potter Valley Indian School; Sherman Institute		
Later Schooling:			
Honors:	American Indian Athletic Hall of Fame, 1973		

Elmer Eugene Busch, son of full-blood Pomo parents, applied to Carlisle and was accepted in 1910. Two adults familiar with him vouched for him as part of the application process. Both of their vouchers give the identical reason for accepting him: "Indian schools near his home do not teach what he desires to learn."

At 5'10" tall and weighing 192 1/2 pounds, Elmer was a large young man for his generation when he arrived at Carlisle in October 1910. At that time, his parents were both in good health, as were his two brothers and one sister. He had no deceased siblings.

His size surely attracted the attention of the Athletic Department. It would be hard to believe that he didn't play on the second team in football his first year at Carlisle because he was the starting right guard on the 1911 team. That is saying something about Elmer's abilities because the 1911 team was arguably Carlisle's finest, and he had only been at the school a relatively short time before making the team. His first newspaper coverage indicated that great things were expected from him in the future: "Busch gave a good account of himself as a guard, and when he develops a little more speed and quickness, will fill a big hole in the line."

Like many of the other football players, Elmer was quite active at Carlisle; he studied tailoring and became active in the Invincible Debating Society where he developed his speaking skills. He spent the summer on outing on George Van Horn's farm in Robbinsville, New Jersey, where, based on his marks for conduct, he appeared to enjoy himself.

It's not clear if it was Pop Warner's training regime or the farm work that did it, but something took a few pounds off Busch as he got into shape for the 1912 football season. Surrounded by established stars in 1911 and '12, Elmer got little press for his work as an interior lineman. Just making the starting lineups on these legendary teams was quite an achievement. In the off season, he developed a reputation as an orator with the Invincibles. He went home for the summer in June 1913.

Elmer Busch wrote Pop Warner on August 12 to tell Warner that he had been unsuccessful in recruiting student athletes: "I can't fine [sic] any big husky Indians here that could play football, all those that I think can play are all married, so I can't get any. Several [sic] want to go with me but they are too light so I don't want bother with it. Before closing I thank you for the offer you have given me for earning out here and returning to the school this fall." The rest of the letter dealt with travel arrangements. Carlisle records indicate that Elmer left Carlisle on May 2 on leave, was dropped on June 7 for not returning, and was readmitted on September 7.

1913 was very likely Elmer Busch's most enjoyable football season for a host of reasons. At the end of Carlisle's third straight one-loss season, Elmer Busch was selected for Walter Camp's All America second team. At season's end, his teammates voted him captain for the 1914 season. In an article in *The Carlisle Arrow* written or at least approved by Pop Warner, Busch was praised:

> "Captain Busch has played right guard on the team the last three seasons and has proven himself to be one of the best guards Carlisle has ever had. He has been an important factor both in the defense and on the offense, being especially valuable as an interferer and in making openings for the backs…. He is one [of] the headiest men on the squad, and his good judgment and knowledge of the game should make him an unusually good leader for the team."

However, a recurring problem Elmer dealt with throughout his career was being fouled in pileups. According to quarterback Gus Welch, Busch's play was lethargic until he was bitten, kicked or punched in a pileup; then the big lineman played like a whirlwind. So, Welch made it his business to "motivate" his right guard when his play was subpar.

About that time, Elmer became more prominent in school life. He read a Bible verse to the joint meeting of the YMCA and YWCA and he started writing news pieces about the tailor shop's activities for the school newspaper. But then a congressional inquiry into the school put things into disarray, particularly in the Athletic Department.

Apparently Elmer, along with Charles Coons and Pete Calac, wrote, or at least signed, a letter to Cato Sells, Commissioner of Indian Affairs, requesting that Warner be retained as football coach, providing that he was not involved in the wrongdoing of which Moses Friedman was accused. Sells responded in a letter to him through Oscar Lipps that his "request would be given as much consideration as may be necessary in the final determination of the policies to be pursued at the school," whatever that meant. Warner was retained but the impact of the letter, if any, is unknown.

On May 9, Elmer left for Eufala, Oklahoma and was reported to be on leave. Exactly what he was to be doing in Oklahoma is unknown, but playing baseball comes quickly to mind. On July 18, Elmer wrote to Oscar Lipps from Kansas City while taking the Missouri Pacific to California. He made reference to correspondence he had had with Coach Warner in which Warner told him that Lipps would probably help Elmer with problems he was having with a certain unnamed school employee. He was apparently asking Lipps to promote him to the junior class, but his writing is difficult to follow. Lipps responded on July 27: "I do not know that I understand exactly what you want. It seems to me that if you would put a greater portion of your time in on your trade and any spare time you have in the library or in taking special work in English Composition, it would be the best thing for you…. I made some inquiry about your work in the tailor shop and I find that you can do good work but that you lack speed. Now, it would seem to me that you could speed up a little and acquire the knack of turning out work rapidly, and that then there would be no trouble next year in getting you an appointment as tailor in some of our good sized schools where they need some one who is also proficient in athletics…. I shall be glad to do anything I can for you but, unless you can make up your mind to stick to one thing until you master it thoroughly, I cannot see where you would be greatly benefited by returning."

The correspondence between Elmer and Oscar Lipps went back and forth with Lipps providing Busch with a listing of his poor grades and Busch wanting a favor to be done. At one point Elmer criticized the training he received at Carlisle, saying that what he got at Sherman Institute was better. On August 22, Elmer informed Lipps that he would not be returning. However, he arrived in Carlisle on September 14 in time for the 1914 football season.

Busch's season started with three wins but by smaller margins than the Indians were used to over these opponents. The next week Lehigh defeated the Indians, something they had not done since 1894, Carlisle's first season of playing football. The loss was attributed to poor tackling and the loss of fighting spirit. Carlisle then lost to Cornell for the first time since 1901. Warner was not pleased. "The worst feature of Carlisle's playing was the lack of that old Carlisle fighting spirit commonly called 'pep' and the want of inspiring leadership. Crane, who gives promise of becoming an inspiring field general, was hurt early in the game and after that the Carlisle machine was without a driver and got nowhere." Elmer resigned his captaincy but remained on the team. The press speculated that Lassaw or Hawk Eagle would be Carlisle's next captain. That honor went to Pete Calac.

The team played better in its 10-3 loss to Pitt and the Indians held Penn to a score of 7-0, still a loss but closer than expected. Elmer played opposite the giant Greek, Dorizas, and more than held his own. Dorizas was a weight lifting champion who, if he found his opponents severely mismatched, let up so as not to hurt them because he valued fairness.

"My being in the game ain't a square deal for those other fellows. I'm so darned strong that I hurt the other fellows, and I don't want to hurt anybody." Dorizas looked Busch over and, believing he was little different from the opponents he had faced earlier that season, let up. After being confused by Dorizas's play for a few minutes, Elmer returned to playing tough football. Syndicated columnist Frank Menke described what he saw after the game: "There was a huge gash on the forehead of this modern Hercules, there were bruises on his body, there were aches and pains in every joint and one knee was so swollen that it made walking a laborious task." Busch had beaten up the strong man.

Most of the remainder of the season was a nightmare. Pop Warner left for Pittsburgh and Elmer did not receive mention on Walter Camp's All America team. However, Athletic Director Harvey Meyer authorized an additional twenty-five dollars in merchandise from Blumenthal's for Elmer as a reward for his play. In mid-April he left for home.

The returning students' form listed Elmer as being 6' tall and weighing 206 pounds. It also indicated that he had completed a tailoring course. Under character and disposition, he was described as, "disgruntled, but nobody seems to know why." His attitude might have been the reason he did not succeed as captain. The October 8, 1915 issue of *The Carlisle Arrow* reported that he had been appointed assistant coach for the Polytechnic High School football squad in Los Angeles. That job couldn't have lasted more than two seasons.

A year and a half later, in January 1917, Elmer wrote the Office of Indian Affairs requesting that he be placed in an automobile factory. He said that, since leaving Carlisle, he had been working in the Boiler Department of the Santa Fe Railroad shops in San Bernardino and that he had also been coaching football in Riverside, at Sherman Institute most likely. Charles E. Dagenette, Supervisor of Indian Employment in the Office of Indian Affairs, requested information about Busch from Carlisle and was informed that he had never worked for Ford. In March, Elmer wrote the Office of Indian Affairs again, this time requesting a coaching position at Carlisle. The Superintendent informed the Commissioner of Indian Affairs that Busch had been an utter failure as captain in 1915 and might succeed at a small school but not at Carlisle.

In June 1917, he registered for the draft in Riverside and listed his occupation as farm laborer. He also listed his date of birth as August 17, 1892. In late September he ordered a subscription of *The Carlisle Arrow* but enclosed only a dime when the price of the subscription was a quarter.

After leaving Carlisle, Elmer led a quiet life outside the interest of the press except for a couple of forays back into football. In 1922 he played for the NFL Oorang Indians and in 1923 for Victor Kelley's Fresno, California American Legion team. When he was with Oorang, assistant postmistress Hazel Haynes got to see him daily when he came in to pick up his mail. "He always seemed to have a scowl on his face," she observed. Little was heard from or about him until 1973 when he was inducted into the American Indian Athletic Hall of Fame. He was thought to be living in California and suffering from arthritis.

George May (1916)

George May; *Fred Wardecker*

Name: George May		**Nickname:**	
DOB: 12/4/1895		**Height:**	
Weight:		**Age:**	
Tribe: Wichita		**Home:** Anadarko, OK	
Parents: father unknown, Wichita; Topsy, Wichita			
Early Schooling: Riverside Indian School			
Later Schooling:			
Honors:			

After previously announcing that they would have no football team in 1916, Carlisle fielded a team late in the season and against opponents of the caliber of their usual early season warm-up game competition. Even at that, the Indians posted only a 1-3-1 record with George May as captain.

George Henry May, full-blood Wichita, was born on December 4, 1895 near Anadarko, Indian Territory (present day Oklahoma). His mother was called Topsy and his father was likely deceased before 1900. About 1906, his mother married Stanley Punlay. George and his sisters, Katie and Margaret, were then listed as stepchildren. George started going to school and attended the Riverside School which was relatively close to his home. He transferred to Carlisle after 1910, where he was immersed in school activities and was elected captain of the 1916 football team.

Like most other Carlisle captains, May was quite active in school life as he participated in the Standard Debating Society, ran track and played football. He worked as a painter at the school. He also participated in the apprenticeship program at Ford Motor Company in Highland Park, Michigan, where he registered for the WWI draft in June 1917. It is not clear if he served in the war as so many Carlisle boys did.

He returned to the reservation in Oklahoma and married Ethel Hunter Edwards, who friends called Nora. They apparently had no children because none were listed on any census. About 1928, Nora's name dropped off the census, perhaps indicating that she died. About 1930, George's name appeared on the Kiowa census as married to Sarah Chaheenah, Commanche. Two years later, his name reappeared on the Wichita census with no wife listed but still classified as married. Perhaps Sarah was listed on the Kiowa census. His listing remained the same through the 1937 census, the last one found for him.

1916 Carlisle backfield; *U. S. Army Military History Institute*

George Tibbets (1917)

George Tibbets; *Fred Wardecker*

Name: George Tibbets		**Nickname:**	
DOB: 1893		**Height:**	
Weight:		**Age:**	
Tribe: Chippewa		**Home:** Consolidated Chippewa Reservation, MN	
Parents: Unknown			
Early Schooling:			
Later Schooling: Ford training program			
Honors:			

1917 was the last year Carlisle fielded a football team, and it played a schedule more or less comparable to those of the past. Carlisle's players were younger, smaller and less experienced than those who played in the school's glory years. As a result, they were overmatched in games against powerful teams like Army, Navy, West Virginia, Georgia Tech and Penn. The dubious honor of leading the team fell to George Tibbetts.

Tibbetts was involved in virtually every aspect of student life. He worked his way up to a lead position in the printing shop, not only putting out the school paper but also writing articles for it. He also was active in the Standard Debating Society, both participating in debates and serving as an officer. He was also involved with the YMCA and served as an assistant scoutmaster in the first ever Indian Boy Scout troop anywhere in the world. He was captain of Company F of the small boys' quarters and won a gold watch in a military drill competition for his troop's performance. He ran track and played football, of course. However, the teams and most, but not all, of the athletes were not of the caliber of Carlisle of just a few years prior.

George, at left halfback, tailback in the single-wing formation, had great games in the 1917 season openers against Albright College and Franklin and Marshall College. The remaining games were losses in which the Indians were shut out in all but one game.

George played left halfback and captained the football team in its last games. He led the team to the school's worst loss in its history, a 98-0 pummeling by one of the greatest teams to ever come out of the South, the Georgia Tech team led by Carlisle alum Joe Guyon. The Indians held a powerful Penn team to 26-0 with a great effort worthy of the school to bring Carlisle's football history to a close, but a captain was elected for 1918.

George Tibbets participated in the Ford training program and stuck, to use Superintendent Pratt's favorite term. George married a Shoshone girl from Wyoming named Effie Agnes. Unfortunately, her family name is not known. George and Effie had a daughter, Grace Katherine, in 1922 and a son, Harold Ralph, in 1926. As of the 1937 census, the last date information was found for Tibbets, the family was living in Detroit and George was working as an electrician at Ford.

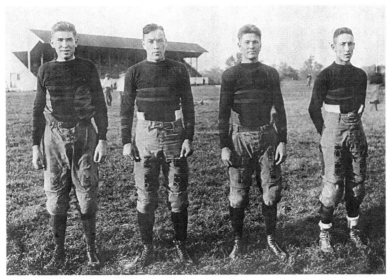

Last Carlisle backfield, 1917: Harman RH, LeRoy FB, Tibbets LH, Miles QB; *Cumberland County Historical Society, Carlisle, PA*

John B. Flinchum (1918)

John Flinchum in school uniform; *Cumberland County Historical Society, Carlisle, PA*

John Flinchum, with ball; *Cumberland County Historical Society, Carlisle, PA*

Name: John B. Flinchum		**Nickname:**	
DOB: 8/7/1897		**Height:**	
Weight:		**Age:**	
Tribe: Choctaw		**Home:** Gerty County, Indian Territory	
Parents: James Samuel Washington Flinchum, white rancher; Julia Turnbull Flinchum, half-blood Choctaw			
Early Schooling: Hughes County, OK public school			
Later Schooling:			
Honors:			

John Benjamin Flinchum was born on August 7, 1897, in Indian Territory near Gerty County, in present day Hughes County, Oklahoma, as the ninth child of James Samuel Washington Flinchum and Julia Turnbull Flinchum. His father, a white man, was a well-known rancher in the area and his mother was half-blood Choctaw. After attending school in Hughes County, John B. Flinchum enrolled in the Carlisle Indian School a year after Jim Thorpe achieved his great fame.

Flinchum, like most Carlisle captains, was not a one-dimensional person. He was active in the Invincible Debating Society and other school affairs. John played football but didn't make the varsity until 1916. After playing left tackle on the 1917 squad, he was elected captain of the 1918 team. Possibly because of this honor, he continued his studies at Carlisle after graduating as a member of the class of 1917. He may have had the experience of leading the team in spring practice but never in an actual game. The school was closed before football season and converted into a hospital to treat soldiers wounded in WWI.

Flinchum returned to Oklahoma where he married and had two children. Beginning in 1927, he was employed by the Indian Territory Illuminating Oil Company (ITIO) until his death, except for 1931 and 1932 when he was a patrolman and scout car officer for the Oklahoma City Police Department.

In February 1936, he was overcome by gas while working in a cellar in the oil fields. His brother, James M. Flinchum, believed that the gas caused pneumonia, which proved fatal. John, only 38, left behind a wife, Emily, a son, John B. Jr., and a daughter, Lorena Katherine. John's life on the oil fields was cut short as had been his football career with the closing of the Carlisle Indian School.

Captain Leadership

In 1924 J. P. Glass and George Byrnes interviewed Pop Warner for a syndicated column that was distributed nationally by the North American Newspaper Alliance (NANA). In this interview, Warner told of the heroic efforts in 1902 of several past, present and future Carlisle captains: Martin Wheelock, Antonio Lubo, Charles Williams, James Johnson and Albert Exendine, in a big game with Warner's alma mater. This is the story in Warner's own words:

"Two men who were dallying with death and should have been in hospital; a third who would have looked well in an invalid's chair; two pieces of leather, which, joined together, closely resembled a puttee; and, finally, a brace of aluminum plate that resembled nothing so much as the rubbing portion of a washboard — these were the chief factors in making possible a strategy that decided one of the most sensational football battles I ever saw.

"It was way back in 1902, during my first term of coaching the famous Carlisle Indian team. In those days our annual game with Cornell was one of the biggest events of the season, notwithstanding that during the course of the hectic schedule which the Indians always played we were apt to engage almost every important team in the country. We set a lot of store on winning from the Ithacans, but this year, as the game approached, it looked as if victory was going to be impossible. In earlier games hard luck gave us a kick that sent us reeling, and Saturday, October 18, the day set for our engagement with Cornell, didn't promise to be an occasion for jubilation.

…"To begin with, my brother Bill had been a big help. Bill was guard at Cornell and one of the best in the game. This year he was captain of the team and mighty anxious to have it make a good showing. Cornell didn't start its training season until September 15 while the Indians got into action on September 1….

"I could picture the rest of my brother's thoughts. He stood over six-feet-one himself and weighed 220 pounds. The Cornell center, Davitt, and the left guard, Hunt, were built in the same proportions. Nobody ever had punctured the Ithacans' lines while those lads were holding forth, but they had done a lot of damage to the other fellows' defense.

"So I knew Bill was going back to Cornell to tell his comrades just what he was thinking then: namely, that the Ithacans must keep possession of the ball when they met us a month later and batter our line to pieces. And I had a hunch that the formation he would have in mind for accomplishing this purpose would be their famous guards-back play. In that, you know, one guard got back of the other to carry the ball, with the whole backfield in tandem formation helping them to plow through the enemy's line….

"Just then everything went wrong. First, after the initial game of the season, Wheelock, our star left tackle, probably the best man in the position that year and the leading drop and place kicker who did all our booting, was taken sick and sent to the school infirmary. He was thought to have pneumonia, but that was averted and then he had a recurrence of pleurisy from which he had suffered the previous year. His pain was so great that he couldn't bear even to have the bedclothes touch him, and the hospital attendants had to rig up a special apparatus that suspended his sheet above him an inch away that they protected him without coming in contact with his body.

"Second, Exendine, our great right end, wrenched his ankle so badly in a succeeding game he could scarcely run.

"Third, Schouchuk, who played at center and was as good as there was in the country, was so badly hurt the week before the Cornell game he had to be placed in the hospital.

"There I was, with the big battle less than a week away, with a line that my brother Bill had called only "pretty good" completely shot to pieces. What could I do? Exendine partly solved my troubles. He insisted he would play despite his bad ankle. It was out of the question for him to take his end assignment. We bound his crippled limb with tape so tightly that he couldn't move his foot and shifted him to right tackle, sending Whitely, who played the position regularly, to fill the left tackle place vacated by Wheelock's illness.

"But I still had no center and no right end. I could throw in a center that might fill Schouchuk's shoes acceptably, but I could not replace Wheelock, whose kicking would be sadly missed. He was my best offensive weapon, having made at least one field goal in every game he played.

"It was at this time that I was given two demonstrations of the red man's courage which fully upheld all the legends of their stoical indifference to suffering ever told. In 1901, when he played the Navy at Annapolis, Lubo, our left tackle, a thin, wiry fellow, who made up in bravery and football brains what he lacked in size—he only weighed 160 pounds — had his left wrist smashed and cut open. The injury was slow to heal. We didn't tell him at the time, but the school physician thought he had a tubercular infection. The superintendent of the academy positively refused to let him play any more football. His arm was placed in a sling and he was instructed to indulge in no exercise except walking, and even then he must conserve his strength.

"Lubo couldn't play, but there was nothing to prevent his watching his team-mates during practice. Throughout my brother Bill's sojourn, he trudged up and down the field, observing everything that was done, listening to everything that was said. He was a true Indian, talking little but retaining every scrap of information that came his way, although in this case it could be of no value to him.

"He was really a pathetic figure. In form, he would have been a tower of strength for us, for despite his size he could hold his own against the huskiest of opponents. But he had been carrying his arm in the sling for a year now and it was shriveled away almost to mere bone.

"All the time, though, he was hoping against hope that luck would turn his way. At the start of the season, he applied for permission to play, but the superintendent's only reply was an order to me.

"'Don't even give him a uniform,' he said. "His health means more to the school than winning a couple of football games."

"Nevertheless he continued his appeals. And when the injury to Schouchuk capped the climax of our troubles he decided to make one more try.

"Four nights preceding the Cornell game a knock brought me to my door. There stood Lubo.

"'Coach,' he said without any preliminary, 'I'd give anything if I could play against Cornell. I know how Schouchuk and Wheelock can't play. I'd like to go up there for you and for Carlisle.'

"I brought him inside and explained as gently as I could that it wasn't possible.

"'Not with that arm,' I said.

"'But that wouldn't make any difference,' he protested.

"'I've been exercising and have kept in good shape in every other way. Besides, coach, I think I can do as much with my right arm as with two arms. I can protect my left so it won't get hurt.'

"I asked where he thought he could play.

"'Tackle, in Wheelock's place.'

"'No. that's out of the question. A tackle must have both arms.'

"'Well, then, center.'

"'No, a center must use both hands to pass the ball.'

"'Well,' he declared. 'I know I could play somewhere on the team.'

"I had to tell him it was impossible, although I appreciated his spirit. But when he left, after two hours of argument, he insisted. 'Somehow, I'm going to play.'

"As to when he saw the superintendent I don't know, for it was half past ten o'clock when he left my house. But the next morning the chief telephoned me to come to his office. Lubo had been to see him again, he said, and had asked to be allowed to face Cornell.

"'I told him, no,' he added, 'but the boy said he must play - he owed it to Carlisle. He's so fine I'm inclined to be lenient, if you and the doctor think it is possible.'

"I didn't because I believed Lubo would be performing merely on his ambition. But when the physician told me that, except for his left arm, the Indian was in fine condition, I began to change my mind. We could at least let him practice a bit. I told him so the next day, which was the Wednesday preceding the date at Ithaca on Saturday.

"He was on hand promptly. It didn't take him long to convince me that, handicapped though he was, he was better than any substitute I could use. If only he hadn't had that withered arm.

"That night he came around to see me again.

"'Coach,' he said, 'there must be some way to fix my arm.'

"I thought hard. I've always been handy at repairing injured players and finally hit on a scheme. I dug up two strips of leather. These I sewed around his bad wrist, extending from the tips of his finger to his elbow. We stuffed the inside with cotton and bound the whole in tape. It seemed to offer adequate protection.

"'Lubo, it looks like you were going to get into that game,' I said.

He just stood there smiling and saying over and over, 'Thank you, Coach, thank you.'

"I don't mind telling you I felt pretty weepy.

"Of course Lubo couldn't play end or tackle. I decided to switch Beaver, the right guard, who had done some playing at end, to Exendine's old position and use Lubo in his place.

"News of this decision soon got me into trouble. All the cripples around the place asked for harness that would enable them to play. But the biggest shock I got came when [Martin] Wheelock showed up at my house. He had been in the infirmary three weeks but in the last few days had been allowed out in the air a bit. Still he was in such pain he couldn't bear to have any one lay a hand on him.

"'Now look here, Coach,' he said, 'if you can fix Lubo you can fix me. There's nothing wrong with my arms or legs; all I've got is pleurisy.'

"I didn't argue with him. Arguments didn't seem to count much with those Indians. We went up to the engineering school and asked for help. Someone dug up two wide sheets of aluminum, resembling, as I said before, the metal portion of a washboard.

"'That's the stuff!' said Wheelock. 'First I'll put on a heavy shirt. Then you can fix these on me, one in front and one in back. Bind them with tape, so they won't slip. Put my jersey on over all and I'll be absolutely all right.'

"There was left but one vacancy on the team. That was center. Fortunately this would be the one position where Wheelock would suffer a minimum of pain, although he was bound to have plenty of it no matter where he was placed. I assigned him to it.

[Warner then discussed some strategy and the events of the game's first half that put Cornell ahead, 6-5.]

"The second half got under way with Cornell rushing us off our feet. And yet, just when it seemed that she was about to score, an Indian would appear from nowhere and throw the man carrying the ball for a loss on third down. Mostly it was Lubo and Wheelock. How Lubo did it with his lame arm I don t know. And time after time Wheelock winced in pain as he came in contact with his opponents. But always they are on the job diving over or under interference and bringing down the man with the ball. Williams backed up both. Johnson was wonderful in running back punts. The lame Exendine, at tackle, more than held his own. Well into the second half we got a break which repaid our cripples for their devotion to the team. Williams, standing on Carlisle's 30-yard line, delivered the best punt of the day. It was a wonderful kick that carried the ball a full 50 yards before it touched on Cornell's 30-yard line.

"Brewster, the Cornell quarter [back], apparently figured that the ball would roll clear to the line. He decided to let it pass, so that it could he brought out again on the 20-yard line. But after one high bound, the ball took a backward instead of forward leap, and struck the leg of Tydeman, right end, who had run back to give Brewster interference. This made a free ball of it and Bradley, Carlisle right end, who had charged down the field, grabbed it.

"It was Carlisle's ball on Cornell's 13-yard line, and Quarterback Johnson immediately proceeded to the most brilliant strategy of the game. This consisted in using the same formation, with variations, four times in succession.

[Warner described an early incarnation of his single-wingback formation which was designed to protect his crippled players. Johnson's brilliant strategy used fakes, deception and speed to confuse the defense as to where the ball was going and who was carrying it. On the fourth play of the series, Willliams dove over the middle of the line for the go ahead touchdown.]

"Lubo was able to continue after this play, but Wheelock's outraged body could endure no more. He fell in an agony of pain and had to be taken from the field. This necessitated the only substitution of the game. We missed the goal after touchdown and the score was Carlisle 10; Cornell, 6.

"But the game was won. Williams played center on defense and we held the Ithacans until the whistle blew.

"Was Lubo happy? Was he! And that reminds me. After the game that night I talked again with Bill, my brother.

"'How did Lubo impress you, Bill?' I asked.

"'Say, Glenn, was that fellow in uniform when I was down at Carlisle?'

"'No, he's the one who followed you around with his arm in a sling watching you at practice.'

"'Well, if that fellow can play like that when he's crippled,' replied Bill, 'I'd hate to tackle him when he was in good condition.'

"In view of the fact that Bill was placed on the All-American that year by Walter Camp and all the other critics, his performance in the Carlisle game being praised particularly, I consider he paid Lubo a fine tribute. But the boy deserved everything good that could be said about him.

"And Wheelock, too. The strategy by which Johnson won the game was fine; but never so wonderful as the splendid feat of these two boys in playing that day. When you get down to facts, it was their devotion to their school and their team that beat Cornell. There's a lesson in it for every lad that aspires to play the game."

Fact or Fiction

A review of the record shows that Warner's memory of a set of extraordinary events that took place over two decades earlier appears to have been fairly accurate. Carlisle played Cornell on Saturday, October 18, 1902 at Ithaca, New York and won 10-6. Game accounts list Exendine, Lubo and Wheelock in the lineup at tackle, guard and center, respectively. However, the *Syracuse Post-Standard* has the Indians at full strength and Cornell crippled. Two days later that paper described Cornell's claims of being crippled as a "lame excuse." The game account discusses Bradley's recovery of the punt that hit Tydeman's leg. On the Wednesday preceding the Cornell game, Carlisle played Bloomsburg Normal (today's Bloomsburg University) at Carlisle. Warner would very likely have viewed the mid-week 50-0 thrashing of a normal school as little more than a scrimmage. Newspaper reports of the game indicate that both Lubo and Wheelock played some of that game. It is probable that Warner tested the protective gear for Lubo and Wheelock in this fortuitously timed scrimmage. He wouldn't have needed his star players to beat a weak opponent, but they provided an opportunity to test and improve the gear if necessary.

A diagram of the special formation Warner used to protect Lubo and Wheelock and which James Johnson used brilliantly to score the winning touchdown was included with the article. This is the earliest known use of a wingback in football, but the development of the single-wing is a story for another time and place.

24

All-Indian Teams

After finishing at Carlisle, many of the football players wanted to continue their on-field participation. Relatively few athletes of any era are good enough at their sport to support themselves playing a boy's game. This was especially true in the years during and immediately following Carlisle's all-too-brief foray into the world of big-time college athletics. However, some of the Indians, as discussed in previous chapters, were talented enough to support themselves by working as athletes. Many who were top-notch athletes and still wanted to play couldn't make enough money at it to consistently put bread on the table for their families. So, some Carlisle alums started teams of their own to give themselves and their former teammates further opportunities to play and, if lucky, to make a few bucks. This chapter covers Carlisle Indian School football players who later played on teams that were comprised of all Indian players, or at least advertised to be so. But first a little background about those teams is needed.

The earliest All-Indian team which was formed to provide a place for former Carlisle students to play was the Detroit Carlisle Indians, or ex-Carlisles or Braves as they were often called. However, the 1915 Altoona Indians and 1916 Pitcairn Quakers could both boast of having many former Carlisle players, the exact number of which may never be known due to the practice of using assumed names, sometimes multiple names, when playing professionally. Current and former Carlisle students working for the Ford Motor Company created the Detroit team in 1916 to give themselves an opportunity to play football on their day off work. Creating an alumni team may not have been an original idea: also operating in Detroit around that time was a team of Harvard alums who, not surprisingly, called itself the Harvards. The Altoona and Pitcairn teams were sponsored by the respective Pennsylvania Railroad operations where many of the players worked during the week.

The Detroit, Altoona and Pitcairn teams played many of the professional teams that later formed the National Football League (NFL). However, not all former Carlisle players still active in professional football played for All-Indian teams. Some, such as Jim Thorpe, Pete Calac and Joe Guyon, played for the Canton Bulldogs alongside All Americans from major universities.

In 1922 an all-Indian NFL team, the Oorang Indians, was formed. Although it listed a number of excellent players on its roster, its primary purpose was to promote and sell Oorang Airedales, a breed of dog sold nationwide by owner Walter Lingo who operated out of that football capital, La Rue, Ohio, the smallest town to ever have an NFL franchise. Lingo loved his dogs more than anything. However, American Indian lore fascinated him. As the story goes, in the winter of 1921, he, Jim Thorpe and Pete Calac were possum hunting on Lingo's expansive farm when the idea struck him to sponsor a professional football team to promote his enterprise. Speculation has it that alcoholic beverages may have played a part in the decision.

It is accurate that Thorpe was an avid sportsman who loved to hunt and fish and kept hunting dogs throughout most of his adult life. It is also accurate that Lingo was a tireless promoter of his Oorang Airedales and often took famous people hunting as a way of getting publicity. It is likely true that he took Thorpe hunting. However, it is unlikely that the team was born at the end of a day's hunting near La Rue, Ohio.

On February 16, 1922, a report came out of Milwaukee that Joe Plunkett and Ambrose Clark of Chicago had acquired an NFL franchise to replace the one in Green Bay that had recently been dropped from the league. Jim Thorpe was reported both to have signed with the team and to have recruited such luminaries as Al Nesser of the Akron Pros, Ed Conley of Valparaiso University, and several players from Notre Dame.

A week or two later, Jim Thorpe announced that he was retiring from football: "I've sung my swan song in football. I have laid aside a tidy sum and feel that it is about time I retired from active football playing. My decision is not influenced by a desire to avoid the hard knocks of the game, for I love it above all others, and am confident I could continue in the game for five years longer without appreciable letdown in my play. It is simply that I feel that I have played long enough and mean to turn my attention to hunting and fishing and less strenuous sports." That didn't sound like a man who had agreed to form a team earlier that winter. Maybe he had something up his sleeve.

On March 18, Walter Lingo and Jim Thorpe announced the formation of a new NFL franchise called Jim Thorpe's Indians of Marion, Ohio, better known as the Oorang Indians, from Thorpe's home in Yale, Oklahoma. Lingo put up the $100 franchise fee which was less than the price of one of his Airedales. Thorpe, as well as a number of other sportsmen, was a shareholder in the Oorang Kennels Company. The primary purpose of the team was to promote Oorang Airedales, not necessarily to win football championships, but a few wins would be nice. And, by the way, almost all the games would be played on the road, a situation Carlisle and Haskell players would find familiar. The team was to be composed entirely of Indians because Lingo had somehow convinced himself that a supernatural bond existed between Airedales and Indians. So Thorpe and Lingo set about recruiting former Carlisle and Haskell stars as well as some others.

The roster included names like: White Cloud, Lone Wolf, Hill, Winnisheik, Busch, Long Time Sleep, Calac, Boutwell, Guyon, Attache, Eagle Feather, Fred and Henry Broker, Sanooke, St. Germain, Downwind, Running Deer, Strong Wind, Thunder, Big Bear, War Eagle and Earth. Some of these names should be familiar from earlier chapters, but others were coined by Walter Lingo to give the players what he thought were more Indian-sounding names. Attache and War Eagle were listed as having attended Sherman Institute and Flandreau Indian School, respectively. The rest were supposed to have attended Carlisle. It's hard to tell exactly who all of these guys were.

Jim Thorpe was paid well – $500 a week to be exact – but his duties were not confined to football. Besides practicing during the week, he and the rest of the team were involved in the daily operations of the kennel. They also had to practice their pre-game stunts. The team required three special train cars to travel to games because they took dogs with them to show off for the crowds. Some credit Walter Lingo with having invented the half-time show. And the dogs didn't perform by themselves; the players were an integral part of the entertainment. Skits included Airedales retrieving targets that

1922 Oorang Indians NFL team included several former Carlisle Indians: Leon Boutwell, Joe Guyon, Stillwell Sanooke, Bill Winneshiek, Bemus Pierce, Nick Lassaw, Elmer Busch, Jim Thorpe, Thomas St. Germain & Pete Calac; *Cumberland County Historical Society, Carlisle, PA*

OORANG INDIANS

No.	Name	Pos.	College	Tribe	Wgt.
30	WHITE CLOUD	L. E.	CARLISLE	TUSCARORA	175
22	LONE WOLF	L. T.	CARLISLE	CHIPPEWAY	190
7	HILL	L. G.	CARLISLE	IROQUOIS	200
3	WINNESHEIK	C.	CARLISLE	TUSCARORA	185
20	BUSCH	R. G.	CARLISLE	MISSION	220
14	LONG TIME SLEEP	R. T.	CARLISLE	FLATHEAD	195
4	COLAC	R. E.	W. VIRGINIA	MISSION	195
8	BONTWELL	Q. B.	CARLISLE	CHIPPEWAY	188
10	GUYON (Capt.)	L. H.	GEORGIA TECH	CHIPPEWAY	190
6	ATTACHE	R. H.	SHERMAN	MISSION	185
32	EAGLE FEATHER	F. B.	CARLISLE	MOHICAN	215
9	F. BROKER	FULLBACK	CARLISLE	CHIPPEWAY	190
11	H. BROKER	QUARTERBACK	CARLISLE	CHIPPEWAY	175
12	SANOOK	END	CARLISLE	CHEROKEE	180
26	WAR EAGLE	GUARD	FLANDEAU	CHIPPEWAY	210
5	EARTH	HALFBACK	`ARLISLE	MISSION	180
2	J. THORPE	HALFBACK	CARLISLE	SAC & FOX	190

Indian marksmen had shot; dogs trailing and treeing a bear; Indian dances; tomahawk, knife and lariat throwing; and Indian scouts demonstrating their war-time exploits with Airedales in WWI, including war veterans delivering first aid in no man's land. Sometimes before a game Nick Lassaw, dubbed Long Time Sleep by his teammates due to the difficulty in getting him up in the morning, wrestled a bear.

The other teams – their owners at least – liked the Oorang Indians because they filled stadiums. Their on-field performance was unfortunately not as good as their theatrics. Most likely they were too tired to play well. Chicago Bears' tackle Ed Healey thought Thorpe was a poor coach, especially with discipline. Healey also thought the players were rough. "I have a vivid recollection of how they used the 'points.' By that I mean the elbows, knees and feet in their blocking and tackling. They'd give you those bones and it hurt. They were tough S. O. B.s but good guys off the field."

However, their off-field antics are the stuff of legends. In one story, a bartender in Chicago wanted to close up shop but some Indians put him in a phone booth and turned it upside down so they could drink until morning. Of course, the Bears killed them on the field the next day. Late at night in St. Louis, several players left a bar to find the trolley they wanted to take going in the opposite direction. Not wanting to wait forever or walk back to the hotel, they picked up the trolley and turned it around to head in the direction they desired. Sometime quarterback Leon Boutwell put it into perspective: "White people had this misconception about Indians. They thought we were all wild men, even though almost all of us had been to college and were generally more civilized than they were. Well, it was a dandy excuse to raise hell and get away with it when the mood struck us. Since we were Indians we could get away with things the whites couldn't. Don't think we didn't take advantage of it."

After two years of seeing his team play uninspired football and coping with shrinking crowds due to having already seen the dog stunts, Walter Lingo mercifully pulled the plug on the Oorang Indians' football team. But he wasn't done with using Indian athletes to promote his dogs. In 1926, the Oorang Indians baseball team, featuring Jim Thorpe, Pete Calac and several of the same players who had formerly played on the football team, barnstormed across Ohio. Although the All-Indian NFL franchise was gone, the concept of all-Indian football teams did not end with the demise of the Oorang Indians.

In the early 1920s, former Carlisle great Pete Hauser coached the Hominy Indians. Based in Hominy, Oklahoma, the Indians criss-crossed the country playing, and beating, most teams that dared to book a game against them. After two successful years, Hauser stepped down. Former Haskell great John Levi took over as player-coach and the team continued to win. The team reached its zenith on the day after Christmas in 1927 in Pawhuska, Oklahoma, the capital of the oil-rich Osage tribe. Their opponents were the new NFL champion New York Giants who featured former Carlisle and Oorang star, Joe Guyon. The Indians won 13-6 and again defeated the Giants two weeks later in San Antonio, Texas. Few Carlislians would have been young enough to have played for Hominy, so it was largely a Haskell outfit. (An early Hominy star was a John Martin who, better known as the Gashouse Gang baseball player Pepper Martin, was eventually discouraged from playing by the St. Louis Cardinal management.) The Great Depression took its toll on such luxuries as barnstorming Indian football teams, causing Hominy to fold its tent in the early 1930s.

Histories of these all-Indian teams are sketchy but Robert L. Whitman wrote a book about the Oorang Indians. One of the biggest problems facing researchers, like Whitman and the author of this book, is determining exactly who played for these teams due to the use of fake names either to disguise players' involvement or to make them sound more colorful. The rest of this chapter is devoted to discussing the lives of those who played on the all-Indian teams. Surely, some will be overlooked for various reasons, the inability to find information on them being the greatest. The author hopes enough information surfaces after publication of this book to make a second, revised edition necessary. In alphabetical order they are:

OFFICIAL PROGRAM 1922
CHICAGO BEARS FOOTBALL CLUB, INC.

CHICAGO
vs
OORANG INDIANS
SUNDAY, NOV. 12, 1922
2:15 P. M.

CUBS PARK
PROGRAM PRICE 10 CENTS

Alex Arcasa

Alex Arcasa running with the
ball; *Cumberland County Historical
Society, Carlisle, PA*

Alex Arcasa; *Cumberland
County Historical Society,
Carlisle, PA*

Name:	Alexander Arcasa	**Nickname:**	
DOB:	3/4/1890	**Height:**	5'9"
Weight:	158	**Age:**	20
Tribe:	Colville	**Home:**	Orient, WA
Parents:	Peter Arcasa, Iroquois-Chinook-white; Margaret "Maggie" Arcasa, Colville		
Early Schooling:	Colville Reservation school		
Later Schooling:			
Honors:	Inland Northwest Sports Hall of Fame, 1963; American Indian Athletic Hall of Fame, 1972		

Alexander Arcasa and his older brother, Joe, enrolled at Carlisle in 1906 at ages 16 and 18, respectively, arriving at the school on October 21. In March 1907, Alex filled out a form on which he indicated that he intended to support himself as a carpenter when he returned home to the Colville Reservation where he had an 80-acre allotment, half of which was wooded and the other half agricultural, 10 acres of which were under cultivation. Alec started out in Room 6 for his academics and moved up steadily, getting good marks for both scholarship and conduct. He spent the rest of his day in the carpentry shop learning that trade. Initially his carpentry instructor, John Nerr, listed Alex's trade as carpentry and football player with only fair ability. Under remarks, Nerr opined that Arcasa was "good at ruff [sic] carpentry."

On November 30, 1908, Alex received a physical examination, possibly because he wanted to play sports. The physician described his condition as "splendid development," but Arcasa was not quite 5'8" tall and weighed less than 165 pounds.

He joined the Invincible Debating Society and gave a select reading in March 1909. The next month he scored 96 in the Sisters of St. Katherine Hall's annual contest but did not win as there were a number of excellent papers submitted by other Catholic students. Later that month he went on outing to Ivyland, New Jersey and quickly gained several pounds.

In October, Alex got his first mention for playing football after getting some playing time as quarterback behind Archie Libby against Bucknell. But most of the time he worked to hone his skills for the time it would be his turn.

In April, he wrote a page and a half long article for *The Carlisle Arrow*, "Practical Training in Agriculture," about his year-long outing at a farm in New Jersey. Besides describing what he learned on that outing, he provided some practical application:

> "In your minds you may be asking how I am going to make use of this knowledge and experience when I return to my reservation home. It will be neither possible or practicable for me to make use of all the experience I have gained under the Outing System, but it adds to my store of knowledge and will better enable me to cope with and overcome the problems I will meet after leaving this institution. The Indians of my tribe have received very little aid from the government besides 80 acres of land each.
>
> "Our reservation, the Colville, is located in Northeastern Washington. My allotment lies like this: About 15 acres is forest the most of which is pine and fir. When I begin farming, it is my intention to leave as much as possible of this timber, as lumber is becoming more and more valuable. However, it may be necessary for me to clear some of this woodland in order to have sufficient tillable land for a profitable farm. I can cut and log the lumber myself from the part I clear thus saving a considerable expense. I do not expect to sell the lumber, but will use it erecting the buildings on my farm.
>
> "The principal crops raised in my locality are wheat, oats, potatoes, timothy and alfalfa. It is also a fine fruit country, and orchards yield enormous profits.
>
> "It is my intention to keep the best breeds of horses, cattle, sheep and hogs and only as many as I can properly care for.
>
> "One of the most important lessons I have learned under the Outing System at Carlisle is that one good horse or cow is worth more than two inferior ones. Also, that not a single head of stock should be kept on the farm that is not constantly bringing in returns."

He delivered the paper as a talk during commencement exercises. After commencement, he went on outing to Williamsport, Pennsylvania, along with Walter Saracino to work with contractor and builder Charles Battorf, who said about them: "I am more than surprised at their ability. While they are doing an entirely different work from that given them at the Carlisle School, they take an interest in it and are very quick at taking hold of new work. The boys are both very obedient, and I always find them willing to do any work I ask of them. They both play baseball and have become favorites among the young people of the town."

In the fall of 1910, Alex Arcasa was elected Secretary of the Freshman Class. He also got some playing time when first-string quarterback Libby went down with an injury. He received praise for his play against Syracuse but went down in pain against Penn. *The

Arrow reported: "The most pathetic incident connected with the game occurred in the first half when Arcasa, quarterback on the Indian eleven, was terribly hurt by being 'kneed' by a Penn player, and forced out of the game because of his injuries. He protested against leaving the field and wanted to play the game, but his dusky brother warriors saw his condition. When leaving the field Arcasa is said to have shed tears because he could not battle against Penn. *He* is one of the Indian stars."

Alex, like most of the others, was not a one-dimensional person with football as his only extra-curricular activity. He continued to be active with the Invincibles and made orations and gave readings at Catholic meetings, including the one Mother Catherine Drexel attended. In the spring, he played 3rd defense on the lacrosse team.

Carpentry Instructor Nerr's opinion of Arcasa's work improved during his time in the program, upgrading his trade to carpentry and cabinet maker and his ability to 'very good.' Because his five-year enrollment was completed in 1911, he was allowed to return home and a Returned Student report was completed for him at the Colville agency. He was down to 150 pounds in weight, but that may have been an estimate. The agency superintendent considered him "… a young man of exceptionally good character and ambitious to become a skilled mechanic. He will return to Carlisle and finish his course."

In the fall of 1911, Alec was elected Critic of the Sophomore class but was a bit late returning from a visit to his home. He played quarterback and both halfback positions at various times, even playing in Jim Thorpe's place in the Penn game because Thorpe had been injured too badly to play. The *Pittsburgh Dispatch* summed up the season in its coverage of the Pitt game: "However, Thorpe wasn't the entire works; there were a few others, white men as well as Indians. Newashe and Arcasa were some stars themselves; so were Powell and Wheelock." Alex Arcasa was an integral part in what was arguably Carlisle's best team ever, and he earned other honors as well.

Shortly after the end of football season, Alex was selected as Secretary of Agriculture in the model republic in which students had an opportunity to learn how to govern themselves. (On Christmas night, Jim Thorpe, disguised as Santa Claus, distributed gifts that included such things as a doll's swing, shin protectors, and trombones to some football players who were included in the group of 275 Catholic students who were assembled in the gymnasium. Exactly which gift Alex received is unknown.)

Captain Arcasa did not wait patiently for lacrosse season to start; he kept busy with the Invincibles and gave a talk to the student body: "Alexander Arcasa's subject was 'Sent to the Bench.' An athlete is often sent to the bench when he is not doing his best in the contest, and so it is with our daily life; we must 'play the-game' in order that it may lead us into a successful life." He also gave an oration for the school's opening exercises.

That fall he was the starting right halfback on another powerful Carlisle team. The 1912 edition was the second of three teams running to lose but one game each. When Gus Welch, the starting quarterback, was injured, Alex filled in at that position. His play-calling completely confused the Brown University players: "The Carlisle attack was bewildering to Brown and the versatile manner in which Arcasa, the Indian quarterback, pulled off his plays had the big Brown bear guessing all the time."

This Christmas he again participated in the Catholic Christmas celebration: "Alexander Arcasa proved a delightful Santa Claus. He had a present and box of candy for each boy and girl." In January he started to work in the Pennsylvania Railroad shops in Altoona, Pennsylvania. He was no longer at Carlisle but his football career was not over.

The October 3, 1913 issue of *The Carlisle Arrow* reported that Joe Bergie, Roy Large and Alex Arcasa, members of the previous year's Carlisle football team, played for an Altoona team on the preceding Saturday. The team was most likely the Altoona Indians, consisting largely of Pennsylvania Railroad employees, many of whom were Carlisle alums. McClellan determined that Arcasa played for that team in the 1915 and 1916 seasons while he worked in the boiler shop. He was a frequent visitor to Carlisle, attending commencement activities and the athletic banquet. Sometime, most likely in 1917, perhaps when the U. S. entered WWI, Alex returned home. When he registered for the draft on June 5, 1917, he was a self-employed carpenter living near Orient, Washington, possibly on his allotment. He wasn't there long.

On April 22, 1918, he enlisted in the Marine Corps and was sent to Mare Island, California. He was transferred to Fort Crockett near Galveston, Texas where he won his Sharpshooter Badge and was promoted to Private First Class (PFC). On November 2 he was arrested and confined to quarters until December 27 when he was court-martialed for "scandalous conduct (associating with public prostitutes)." He remained confined while a decision was being made for his court martial. He was apparently found guilty, was busted down to Private and transferred to Parris Island for incarceration. On March 24, his punishment apparently over, he was promoted to PFC again and stayed on at Parris Island. On June 9 he was promoted to Corporal, the rank he held until he was discharged on August 27 "for the convenience of the government, Character: Excellent." Several others were discharged that month but not all had "excellent" characters; some were only "very good" while still others got BCDs (bad conduct discharges).

From here things get a bit fuzzy because tribal rolls list him continuously but do not indicate where he lived. Around 1921, he married Jeanette Whitelaw, a half-blood Colville. (Note that half-blood on Colville rolls means half Colville blood not half white blood.) Alex and Jeanette had a son, Alexander Jr. on June 21, 1922, who died of unknown causes on September 16, 1925. Some time after returning to the Colville Reservation, he took a job with the Bureau of Indian Affairs Forestry Department at Colville. In 1935 at 44 years of age, Alex was divorced from Jeanette. Later that year he married Louise, a Sioux woman. A December 1943 Bureau of Indian Affairs photograph of part of the Colville forestry staff lists Alex Arcasa as a scaler. He died on September 1, 1962.

Joe Bergie

Joe Bergie; *Cumberland
County Historical Society,
Carlisle, PA*

Name: Joseph Bergie	**Nickname:**
DOB: 7/18/1889 or 1891	**Height:** 5'10"
Weight: 168	**Age:** 19
Tribe: Chippewa	**Home:** Warwick, ND

Parents: Bernard "Barney" Bergie (AKA Bonnar Bonzie), mixed blood;
Celine (or Clarina) Bergie, half-blood Sioux

Early Schooling: Catholic Mission School near Fort Totten;
Fort Totten Indian Industrial School

Later Schooling:

Honors: American Indian Athletic Hall of Fame, 1971

Joseph Bergie was the son of Bernard "Barney" Bergie (AKA Bonnar Bonzie), mixed-blood, and Celina (AKA Clarina) Bergie, both of whom were thought to be largely of Chippewa blood. The Bergies moved to the Fort Totten Reservation in 1899 where Celine became half-blood Sioux by adoption into the Devils Lake (today's Spirit Lake) Band. Either or both parents may have been born mixed-blood Chippewa because Joe's Carlisle records indicate that he was considered to be half-blood Chippewa by that institution. The 1930 census listed him as Cree-Sioux.

Joe transferred from Fort Totten Indian Industrial School to Carlisle on February 6, 1910, to start a three-year enrollment. At Carlisle he learned the masonry trade in addition to attending academic classes. His conduct started off as 'good to excellent' but dropped to 'fair to bad' when he returned to, or was returned to, school after running away in August of 1910. A year later his conduct improved, returning to the good to excellent range.

After returning to Carlisle, Bergie joined the football team and played on the scrubs for a year. For the 1911 season, he was moved up to the varsity and was soon the starting center on what Warner expected would be a great team. Early in the season, *The Washington Post* reported, "Garlow in this week's practice has been shifted from center to left guard, and Bergie, a player upon the scrub team last year, is being used as the varsity center. He is a lightweight, but is aggressive and fast, his defensive playing being a feature of last Saturday's game." He also started getting coverage in the school newspaper:

> "Joe Bergie was a power on the defense and he made many Lafayette players think they had run into a stone wall." – November 3

> "Bergie's defensive playing was a feature. He made more tackles than any man on the team." – November 24

After football season was over, Joe received a couple of honors. Santa Claus, played by Jim Thorpe, gave special presents to eight athletes one of whom was Bergie. He was awarded his first letter "C" at the annual athletic banquet for his fine work in football.

In the spring, *The Arrow* praised him for his play in lacrosse, a sport new to him: "Bergie, at point, knew his position well. Guyon, at cover-point, loped away with the ball whenever it threatened to score for Hopkins. Both of these men are new this season and deserve much credit for their performances." But students' lives at Carlisle were not just extra-curricular activities; they had trades to learn.

"Joseph Bergie and James Crane, members of our football team, are not only 'star' players but they are 'star', brick-layers as well. They are now putting up a diamond-bond wall for the commencement exhibition." H. B. Lamason, the masonry instructor, had improved his opinion of Joe's work from 'fair to good' and remarked that Joe was 'good in cement.' After the school year was over, Joe spent the summer in Altoona, Pennsylvania, a railroad town, working for E. D. Worthington, possibly repairing boilers.

The 1912 Carlisle team was another powerhouse. Three starters departed from the 11-1-0 1911 team but were replaced by rising stars. Joe Bergie returned as starting center and got generally good reviews from the press, but the *Syracuse Herald* was less flattering: "Bergie at center is an aggressive man, who is especially valuable upon the defense but his passes [center snaps] have been rather careless and erratic thus far, causing numerous fumbles in the back-field." Just three days later, the same paper ran a piece describing Joe's performance in a scrimmage against Dickinson College in preparation for the upcoming game against Syracuse: "The aborigine center, Bergie, proved the star of the afternoon, time and again breaking through the line and nailing the runner for a loss. He also out-distanced the ends and tackles in running down the field under punts. 'Warner and followers of the game here declare that Bergie is the greatest center to ever don a Carlisle uniform.'"

The Arrow was also positive about his performance: "Joseph Bergie; center, is 5 ft. 9 in. tall, weighs 168 pounds, and his age is 20. He is a Chippewa, and his home is in North

Dakota. Joe was promoted last year from the scrubs to the first team, where he made a great record as center. This year he continued to improve, and his playing entitled him to a very high rank among the best centers of the country. Many critics placed him next to Ketchum, the greatest center of the year. Joe played fullback in several games and proved to be as effective in that position as he was at center. He was the greatest defensive player on the team." Walter Camp, not surprisingly, was not as impressed and omitted any mention of Bergie when it came time to name his All America teams.

In January 1913, Joe returned to Altoona to again work for E. D. Worthington, but he did not assimilate completely nor isolate himself from his heritage. Later that month he began a process to claim an allotment. He tried over a two-year period to get one from the Turtle Mountain Agency but was unsuccessful because he wasn't listed on their tribal roll. Apparently his father wasn't listed, a missing detail that made it impossible for Joe to receive an allotment. He wasn't eligible for one from the Devils Lake Reservation because that band had only adopted his mother and not her children.

Bergie's name appeared in *The Carlisle Arrow* several times in the 1913-14 school year, sometimes to announce that he had visited the school for special functions such as the athletic banquet and commencement, or that he had a special work assignment, such as the time he and Alex Arcasa were dispatched to Atlantic City, New Jersey, to repair telephone lines and poles along the Pennsylvania Railroad's right-of-way. It appears that Joe and Alex worked and played football together at that time.

Joe played football again in 1913 but not for Carlisle. The October 3, 1913 issue of *The Carlisle Arrow* reported, "Bergie, [Alex] Arcasa, and [Roy] Large, who were on the team last year, played with an Altoona team last Saturday, defeating a high-school team by a small score." Most likely, Joe was playing for the independent or semi-pro Altoona Indians alongside some of his former Carlisle teammates. He probably also played for other independent teams when they needed help for a particular game. In *The Sunday Game*, Keith McClellan documented part of Bergie's professional career. Bergie continued playing for Altoona; in 1915 he played center for Altoona and, on occasion, fullback for Massillon. In 1916, when the Altoona team was supported by the Pennsylvania Railroad to the extent of getting free transportation to games and wearing the PRR logo on their jerseys, he coached the team while playing center. That year he also played fullback for the Pitcairn Quakers and coached the team along with his old Carlisle teammate, George Vedernack. On his spare Sundays that fall, he filled in at fullback for the Massillon Tigers. In 1917, he left Altoona and returned to North Dakota where, on June 4, he registered for the draft while working on a farm near Warwick, North Dakota. In the fall, he was in Pittsburgh where he played center for Pitcairn. The October 25 *Fort Wayne Journal-Gazette* included his full-length photo as the coach and center of the Pitcairn Quakers, that week's opponent of the Fort Wayne Friars. At season's end *The Fort Wayne Sentinel* selected Bergie as an easy choice for best pro or military team center for 1917.

On June 27, 1918, Joe Bergie was inducted into the army at Minnewauken, North Dakota, and was shortly sent to Camp Dodge, Iowa, where he served in the 163rd Depot Brigade until July 13. He was then transferred to Battery D of the 337th Field Artillery, his unit for the remainder of his tour of duty. He was shipped overseas with his brigade on August 17. Joe was promoted to PFC on September 20, but less than a month later was demoted to Private. He remained in Europe until January 20, 1919, at which time he was shipped back to Camp Dodge and discharged on January 31, still as a Private.

After the war, Bergie returned to athletics briefly. A hand injury cut short his careers as a professional football player and professional wrestler, a sideline he began after returning from Europe.

On June 10, 1920, Joe married Rosalie Bercier, mixed-blood Chippewa, in Minnewaukan, North Dakota, the same town in which he had been inducted into the army. The Bergies had five children on the Fort Totten Reservation before moving to Poplar, Montana in 1930 where they lived the remainder of their lives. Joe worked on local farms and enlarged his family: four sons, Bernard, Thomas, Franklin and Ronald, as well as four daughters, Genevieve, June, Helen and Eleanor. Joe must have had a hand in building the first football field in Poplar because his old friend, Jim Thorpe, took part in the dedication ceremonies and stayed with the Bergies during that visit.

Later life brought some sadness and loss for Joe. His wife, Rose, died in 1965; his daughter, Eleanor, died at age 38 in 1969; and son Ronald, a WWII veteran, was confined to in a state hospital. Joe died on March 10, 1970, after a long illness of "complications of diabetes and infirmities of old age." Newspaper reports believed him to be the last survivor of the 1911-12 Carlisle teams as Gus Welch had died two months earlier.

Leon Boutwell

Boutwell, Guyon and Peter Jordan canoeing;

Leon Boutwell in baseball uniform;

Leon Boutwell with Joe Guyon, dressed as Chinese for a movie made in Florida; *Jay Garvie*

Name:	Leon Adelbert Boutwell	**Nickname:**	Little Cyclone
DOB:	10/3/1892 or 1893	**Height:**	5'7"
Weight:	155	**Age:**	29
Tribe:	Chippewa	**Home:**	Cass Lake, MN
Parents:	Rodney C. Boutwell, mixed-Chippewa; Isabelle Porter Boutwell, Chippewa		
Early Schooling:	Pipestone Indian School; White Earth Reservation school		
Later Schooling:	Keewatin Academy		
Honors:	American Indian Sports Hall of Fame, 1971		

When he was still a small child, Leon Adelbert "Lou" Boutwell moved from Orr, North Dakota, where he was born, to the White Earth Combined Chippewa Agency near Cass Lake, Minnesota. Around 1910 Leon's name began appearing on the Carlisle Indian School census. His name became a permanent fixture in the school newspaper shortly after that, but seldom in the Athletic Department. Although a fine athlete, Leon wasn't of the same caliber as his famous teammates.

Oddly, Leon's father received mention at Carlisle before he did. According to the March 10, 1911 issue of *The Carlisle Arrow*, Rodney C. Boutwell had been promoted from laborer and acting interpreter at the White Earth Agency to interpreter. Leon got some press for operating a press – the Miehle printing press – in the January 5, 1912 edition. He and William Palin had charge of the presswork in printing Superintendent Friedman's annual report. This was quite a responsibility because the report was distributed through-out Congress and throughout the government bureaucracy as well as to interested indi-viduals. Before the end of March, he spent part of his day working at the Cornman printing office in town. The September 6, 1912 issue of *The Arrow* started the new school year off by announcing that Leon was then employed as a job pressman in the *Evening Sentinel's* job department. As usual, the Indian School administration was very supportive of such endeavors, stating, "We heartily predict his success." At that time Carlisle's print-ing office formed a self-governing office called "The Chapel" modeled on those found in private enterprise. Actually, it formed two chapels, one for each shift. Leon was elected Chairman of "The Gutenberg Chapel," the afternoon shift. He was also learning about philanthropy as he donated a small part of his earnings made as a printer to the YMCA.

Leon Boutwell was probably mentioned in the school paper for a broader variety of activities than any other Carlisle student in school history. He participated in debates and gave extemporaneous speeches and recitations at meetings of the Invincibles. He also gave a declamation at chapel exercises and recited "The Man Who Wins" "in an excellent manner," as it was reported. Leon played cornet in the school band and played solos for the Invincibles until they formed their own band for which he was elected leader. He also conducted the school band at an outdoor concert. Apparently light on his feet and popular with the ladies, he and Elizabeth LaVatta won first prize in a waltz contest at the band reception. Not long after that, he and Leila Waterman won second prize in the two-step contest at the Mercers' reception. The next school year he and Ada Curtis won second prize in the waltz contest at the Invincibles' reception. He was the tenor in a quartet that sang "We Shall Meet Him Face to Face" for a YMCA meeting and was appointed leader of the tenors in Miss Dunagan's choir.

Despite his heavy involvement in extra-curricular activities, Leon Boutwell did not neglect his printing trade. He spent part of the summer of 1913 working as a pressman for a company in Lancaster, Pennsylvania and could have stayed with that job indefinitely. After returning to school from a vacation in Minnesota, Leon rejoined the school print-ing shop as a job compositor setting type for jobs that others would print. At times he assisted George Tibbits on the cylinder press. At commencement, he was awarded his industrial certificate in printing. However, that was late in the school year and many football games had yet to be played.

According to *The Arrow*, Philadelphia newspapers "…pronounced Leon Boutwell as invincible on the gridiron during the game last Saturday between the 'Easterners' and the 'Westerners.'" This was only one of two times he received mention for having played football at Carlisle. It seems unlikely that he would have been a major player for either of those teams, had he not been playing on a school team. He wasn't playing on the varsity, at least not enough to letter, but may have played on the second team or scrubs. As an aside, it was a tribute to the quality of the Carlisle Indian School football program that the "Easterners" vs. "Westerners" games received coverage in big city newspapers. The second mention was about him starring in a game between the Band and the Specials. His name appeared just one more time in *The Arrow* with regard to sports, and that was for placing third in the 120-yard hurdles in the annual class track and field meet held in May 1914.

In his last year at Carlisle, the 1914-15 school year, after receiving his printing certificate, Leon continued his previous extra-curricular activities and broadened himself in some areas. Previously, his name had often been in print and, as part of his work, he had actually printed the papers. But this year he was writing copy for *The Arrow* as he reported on the activities of the Band. Toward the end of the previous year, he had warmed up a bit for this task by writing a few columns on the Invincibles' activities. However, one of those columns carried the byline of L. Adelbert Boutwell. That byline was surely the handiwork of one of his buddies in the print shop, a typesetter in this case, having a little fun at Leon's expense. Perhaps he chose to write the Band column that year because there was so much to write about and much of the news involved him.

Early in the school year, he, his good friend and roommate, James Garvie, and some others formed the "Mahogany Orchestra" in which Boutwell played clarinet. The small size of the group and the fact that Garvie played trap drum imply that the combo may have been a dance band. However, in February, the "Mahogany Orchestra" furnished the music for a vaudeville show at the school that raised $100.15 for the YMCA.

In early 1914, Boutwell and Garvie started taking piano lessons. It is well-known that James Garvie was quite an accomplished musician, but Lou Boutwell must have had significant talent in that line as well. In December, school band members elected Garvie as Principal Musician and Boutwell as Chief Musician. In January, Leon, as solo clarinetist, practiced an unspecified Mozart piece for an upcoming concert. In February, *The Arrow* reported that Leon had resigned as Principal Musician and was immediately elected 1st Lieutenant of the Band Troop. That was probably a typo as he was Chief Musician; Garvie was Principal Musician. A week later, after Kenneth King, Ponca, resigned, Leon was elected Captain. In March, the Band boys gave Boutwell a fruit basket in honor of his birthday on March 13. That date varies considerably from October 3, the date he provided when he registered for the drafts for both world wars. He may have learned more about his heritage as he got older. His last mention in the Carlisle school publications was on March 19, 1915, when it was announced that he, James Garvie and two others accompanied the Carlisle Eighth Regiment Band to play in a Sunday school temperance parade.

After leaving Carlisle, Leon Boutwell enrolled at Keewatin Academy in Prairie du Chien, Wisconsin for a year. It's not clear what he studied there or in which extra-curricular activities he participated, but it's fair to expect that he continued the work he had begun at Carlisle. One known fact is that he and Joe Guyon played Chinese characters in a movie that was shot in Florida, most likely during Keewatin Academy's winter session. A second photo – this one of Boutwell, Guyon and Peter Jordan canoeing – puts the three at the same place at the same time, most likely spring of 1915, given their clothing. Jordan had coached football at Keewatin Academy in the fall of 1914 in exchange for free tuition and was probably still there when Leon arrived.

After a year, he returned to the White Earth Reservation. However, he may have spent a summer or two playing minor league baseball. James Garvie's grandson, Jay Garvie, recalls his grandfather discussing his old Carlisle roommate and mentioning that Leon played some minor league ball. Jay's mother has a photograph of Boutwell in a baseball uniform. When he registered for the WWI draft on June 5, 1917, he was living near Ogema, Minnesota, with his sister, Emma, and her husband, Antoine Bisson, for whom he worked as a chauffer.

Soon after registering for the draft, Leon enlisted in the army where he served as a corporal in the 14th Field Artillery Band at Fort Sill, Oklahoma. After receiving an honorable discharge, he returned to Ogema where he again lived with his sister and brother-in-law but this time worked on a farm. His tilling the land would be interrupted by the siren song of professional football.

1922 was the first year for the Oorang Indians' NFL franchise, and they needed a quarterback. Carlisle stars such as Gus Welch and Mike Balenti were otherwise occupied, but Leon Boutwell was available. Thorpe, Guyon and Calac would have known him from Carlisle, and Guyon probably played alongside him at Keewatin Academy. The person in LaRue, Ohio who remembered the Indians best was assistant postmistress Hazel Haynes. She got to know the players a bit from talking with them each day when they came in to pick up their mail. Of Boutwell she said, "He was as bright as shiny silver dollars. He was very genteel, reserved, and friendly." His Oorang name was Little Cyclone. Leon played and trained dogs for Oorang for two years and stayed in Ohio after the franchise folded.

An opening for a linotype operator opened up at the Mechanicsburg, Ohio newspaper, *The Daily Telegram*, in 1924 and Leon took it. Some time in the 1920s he married Euphemia MacLaren, originally from New Jersey and the daughter of Scottish parents. Leon had the opportunity to buy the paper in May 1930 and took it. From then on he and Phemie, as his bride was called, edited and published *The Daily Telegram*. Significant was the fact that Mechanicsburg, Ohio population 1,752 in the mid-1940s, was the smallest town in America to support a daily newspaper.

Leon, or Lou as he was often called, and Phemie settled in to small town life, becoming active with a number of local organizations. He was a member of the American Legion, the F. & A. M. 32nd Degree Scottish Rite Masons, the Lions Club and the London Country Club. He even organized and directed an old fashioned brass band, perhaps not so out-of-date when he started it. In the mid-1940s, he lectured on Indian topics throughout the state of Ohio. In 1938, he was asked by a Mr. Carlisle of Columbus, Ohio to compare the pioneers' taking of America from the Indians with Hitler's move into Czechoslovakia. He responded, "Indians were called savages, but I don't know what you call those on the other side," referring to the Germans.

In 1947, Lou began his second term as Senior Warden of the Church of Our Saviour, having already been licensed as a lay reader in the Episcopal Church, Diocese of Southern Ohio. His interest in religion came honestly as his paternal grandfather was Rev. William Thurston Boutwell, a missionary who served in Minnesota. Rev. Boutwell married Hester Crooks, the daughter of Ramsay Crooks, John Jacob Astor's headman in the fur trade, and his wife, a woman from Mackinac of French and Indian heritage. People who knew Leon's grandmother described her as having the brains of her brilliant Scottish father and the soft eyes of her mother. His grandfather, who was also a Latin scholar, is perhaps best remembered for naming the headwaters of the Mississippi River. On seeing it, he formed a name for it from the middle syllables of *veritas caput*, Latin for 'true head,' or 'Itasca.'

As Leon got older and business concerns occupied more of his time, he continued his athletic pursuits as best he could, given his other obligations. For a while he was golf pro at the country club and shot a hole in one. He coached a football team for young boys that was quickly called Boutwell's Little Indians by the townspeople. By 1927, he was coaching the high school team, and that team took on the Indians moniker. After buying the newspaper, he was probably too busy to coach the team and, over time, the credentials needed to teach and coach public school students changed. In 1943, he was granted special permission from the state of Ohio to coach the Mechanicsburg High School football team.

In 1948, after running the newspaper for 18 years, he and Phemie sold it. Two years later he purchased a printing concern in Bellefontaine and operated that until 1958. He spent the last decade of his life working in Robert Schetter's printing business in Mechanicsburg. Leon "The Chief," then 76 or 77, was taken ill suddenly on the morning of October 3, 1969, and died at 11:30 a.m. in Mt. Carmel Hospital in Columbus after being transferred there from Madison County Hospital. He was buried at Maple Grove Cemetery. Leon was survived by his wife, a brother, Sydney of Detroit Lakes, Minnesota and sisters Hester Horsely of Mesa, Arizona and Jean Bolis of San Francisco. Signs of Leon Boutwell live on in the Buckeye state. The Mechanicsburg High School football team continues to be called the Indians and his maroon and orange Oorang uniform is in the Professional Football Hall of Fame.

Frederick Charles and Joseph Henry Broker

Fred and Henry
Broker; *Fred Wardecker*

Fred Broker; *Cumberland County
Historical Society, Carlisle, PA*

Henry Broker; *Cumberland
County Historical Society,
Carlisle, PA*

Name:	Frederick Charles Broker	**Nickname:**	Hippo
DOB:	3/17/1893	**Height:**	5'9"
Weight:	190	**Age:**	29
Tribe:	Chippewa	**Home:**	White Earth Reservation

Parents: Eric Broker, white; Charlotte Broker, 3/4 blood Chippewa
of the Otter Tail band

Early Schooling: Pine Point Elementary School; Morris Industrial School

Later Schooling: Conway Hall

Honors:

Name:	Joseph Henry Broker	**Nickname:**	
DOB:	9/10/1891	**Height:**	
Weight:	175	**Age:**	31
Tribe:	Chippewa	**Home:**	White Earth Reservation

Parents: Eric Broker, white; Charlotte Broker, 3/4 blood Chippewa
of the Otter Tail band

Early Schooling: Pine Point Elementary School; Morris Industrial School

Later Schooling:

Honors:

Henry Broker appeared to have already been at Carlisle when his brother, Fred, made his appearance on Christmas Day 1909. Their father had died of heart failure some time before Fred arrived, possibly before Henry enrolled. They had two living brothers and four sisters in good health. Another brother had previously died of pneumonia and a sister had died of unknown causes. Fred had survived typhoid in 1905. The Broker boys soon received much press coverage for their accomplishments. The May 27, 1910 edition of *The Carlisle Arrow* announced, "Henry Broker, a Chippewa, has joined the force of apprentices at the printing department." Meanwhile, Fred had been learning to be a harness maker but, with the advent of the Model T, may have seen little future for that trade and switched quickly to blacksmithing. References of the Broker brothers in Carlisle publications were often ambiguous because often only the last name was provided. The reader was expected to know in which activities each brother was involved and which positions they played. Please forgive any errors of interpretation on the part of the author. The first issue of *The Arrow* for the 1910-11 school year included an account of a baseball game played by boys present at the Indian school over the summer against a local team, the Salad Birds, "'Pete' Houser [sic], the celebrated football player of the Indians, was on the mound for the redskin team and [Fred] Broker was behind the bat. Peter is a former Kansas league pitcher and pitched great ball at Haskell, where he has a fine record. He was speed 'to burn.'"

Fred was soon elected to the office of Critic of the Freshman Class and actively participated in class meetings. Both boys joined the Invincible Debating Society and became quite active, making extemporaneous speeches and participating in debates. In April 1911, *The Arrow* reported that Fred was happy in his new surroundings at his outing home in Lancaster County. Perhaps his contentment was exaggerated because school records reflect that he ran away in May. Fred returned in July and was elected Vice-President of the Sophomore Class in September.

According to a game report, Broker's kick was blocked and returned for a touchdown in a game played by the Reserves against Middletown Athletic Club in November. This first mention of a Broker playing football for Carlisle must have been referring to Henry because he was older and Fred was listed as being 5'9" tall and weighing 148 pounds when he was readmitted in July. In December, on the other hand, *The Arrow* mentioned that the Junior Class was glad to have Henry back with them because he had been ill for some time, something that argues against his playing football six weeks earlier. However, the December 20, 1912 *Arrow* may have settled this because it mentioned Henry's getting some playing time with the varsity.

In January 1912, Henry started working for Cornman Printing Company in the Borough of Carlisle. In May, *The Arrow* commented on his brother's progress: "Fred Broker is doing good work at his-trade in the blacksmith shop. His instructor, Mr. Shambaugh, thinks he is thorough enough to command first-class wages in any blacksmith shop in the country."

Henry – or Joseph H. Broker to be precise – graduated in April 1913. He gave a talk and demonstrated homebuilding as part of the commencement activities. After Henry served as a groomsman in Alfred Lamont and Margaret Mantell's wedding at St. Patrick's Church, a beautiful building that still stands in Carlisle, the Brokers vacationed in Minnesota. Upon their return, Henry took courses across town at Conway Hall but remained involved in life at the Indian school. In April, Fred C. Broker, "of baseball and football fame," spoke on "Citizenship" as part of his class's graduation exercises. He also co-wrote a class history for publication in *The Carlisle Arrow*. After commencement, he worked as a blacksmith at Federal Dam near Leech Lake, Minnesota, with expectations of coming back to Pennsylvania to attend Lebanon Valley College. Henry spent a profitable summer working at a resort in Atlantic City with Gus Welch.

Fred returned to Carlisle in September, "… looking bigger and broader and altogether fit for college preparatory work and athletics." He enrolled in Conway Hall with no reason suggested for his not having enrolled at Lebanon Valley College. It may have been at this time that he picked up the nickname of Hippo. Both Brokers got playing time that fall, including some starts, generally in backfield positions. In March 1915, Henry made the opening remarks at Pop Warner's final farewell reception.

Fred and Henry spent the summer of 1915 working as apprentices at the Ford Motor Company in Detroit, making good wages for the time. Henry received kudos for the unusual progress he made in his student course at Ford. Both returned to Carlisle in September to play football. They also worked in the new Mechanic Arts course established at Carlisle that year. Both played on this weak Carlisle team that got little positive press, but Fred got some of it for being an effective line plunger. Two weeks after the season came to a merciful end, Fred, Henry and several other football players returned to Detroit to continue their work for Ford.

In addition to working at the Highland Park Ford plant, Carlisle students attended classes to improve their job-related skills. They also played basketball at the "Y" to keep in shape. In the fall, they formed their own football team with Henry Broker as quarterback. Fred was back in Minnesota, having taken sick in August. His letter to Oscar Lipps indicated that his stomach troubles weren't being solved at his local hospital and that he was going to Minneapolis for treatment. That could explain why Henry earned $833.80 working for Ford during the year ending June 30 and Fred made just $175.00. Regardless of health, the Brokers' careers at Ford were to be short-lived as war intervened.

The U. S. entered WWI in 1917 and the Brokers entered the service. Henry left his job as an inspector at Ford to enlist in the army; Fred joined the Navy. In December 1917, *The Carlisle Arrow and Red Man* reported that Henry was at home on leave from Fort Snelling and that Fred was on the *U. S. S. Roe* and that he could be written care of the New York Postmaster. Little is known about the Brokers after that point. Both Fred and Henry Broker were listed on the Oorang Indians' roster for the 1922 game with the Chicago Bears at Cubs Park, but neither is believed to have played. Tribal rolls provide little information about them except that Fred was living at Lame Deer Village near Rosebud, Montana. He is believed to have married a woman from that tribe and to have had a son named Charles. Henry is believed to have married a woman from the Lac du Flambeau band and to have had a son named Henry. Both are thought to have lived on or near their wives' reservations.

Nick Lassaw

Nick Lassaw, 1915;
Fred Wardecker

Nick Lassaw; *Cumberland County
Historical Society, Carlisle, PA*

Name:	Nicholas Anthony Lassaw	**Nickname:**	Long Time Sleep
DOB:	7/11/1898	**Height:**	5'10"
Weight:	205	**Age:**	25
Tribe:	Flathead	**Home:**	Flathead Reservation, MT
Parents:	? Lassaw; Mary Lassaw Paul Sawsaw Deere		
Early Schooling:	unknown		
Later Schooling:	Haskell Institute		
Honors:			

Nicholas Anthony Lassaw was enrolled at Carlisle Indian Industrial School by 1911. Nothing is known about his father and little about his mother, but there is a good chance one or both were Bitterroot Salish who lived on the Flathead Reservation in Montana. Lassaw's daughters believe that he was full-blood Pend d'Oreille from Camas Prairie. At age 11 he was captured and sent to the Jesuit school in St. Ignatius, Montana. Although Nick shared little about his early life with his parents, he did tell his daughters that his family name was Quinta until the missionaries changed it. About all else he told them was that he had a sister, Mary, his aunt, Susette Hamintso, grew up in Camas Prairie, and they had relatives in Worley, Idaho. Eventually, he was enrolled at Carlisle.

In September 1913, young Nick was elected captain of the newly organized small boys' football team. It does take some imagination to think of this 5'10", 210 pound lineman as ever being a small boy, but he was only 15 at the time. The following spring, he received a certificate in shoemaking at commencement but remained at Carlisle to continue his education. Nick excelled in sports at Carlisle. He most likely played on shop, junior varsity or second teams until fall 1915. Prior to that, he heartily cheered for those who were representing the school. His support was so good that *The Carlisle Arrow* reported, in January 1915, that Nick was "a capable leader of cheers" at an intramural basketball game between Easterners and Westerners. And in September, he led cheers at a football rally in the auditorium. Later incidences in Nick's life suggest that he would have been quite effective as a cheerleader.

1915 was the year that Nick broke into the varsity lineup in more than one sport. He must really have enjoyed athletics because *The Arrow* reported that he "…enjoys training so much that every evening after practice he has a cross country run by himself." In the spring he emerged as the shot putter for the track team just before leaving for his outing on a New Jersey farm for the summer. When he returned in the fall, he won a starting guard position on the Carlisle line. However, Lassaw came to age football-wise at an inopportune time. Carlisle's 1915-17 teams were the worst in the school's proud history, and in 1916 a team was barely fielded amidst newspaper articles saying the school had dropped the sport.

Lassaw contributed what he could to the school's teams but that wasn't enough to make them competitive. His talents caused a new play to be put in the playbook. "Lassaw Back" may have been a modernized version of the old "guards back" play that Penn used so successfully decades before. One guard was stationed behind the other in the backfield to increase the force at the point of attack before seven men had to be on the line of scrimmage. Nick's non-athletic extracurricular activity was the Invincible Debating Society for which he served as treasurer in 1917. He was 20 when Carlisle closed in 1918, but he wasn't through with his education so he headed west.

Nick Lassaw enrolled at Haskell Institute in Lawrence, Kansas where he carried the mantle of Indian college football leadership from Carlisle. He played for the Fightin' Indians through the 1921 season. After seven years of varsity football, Lassaw was 24 years old and ready to begin supporting himself. Also, the opportunity to play on another all-Indian team presented itself. Nick heard the call of the Oorang Indians and joined them.

Nick played for Oorang both seasons of its existence, using his size and strength to play all the interior line positions. His name wasn't exotic enough for the team's owner, so the players gave him the nickname of Long Time Sleep because of the difficulty in arousing him in the morning. He was the only player to start every game Oorang played. However, Nick's on-field performances, at least playing football, weren't what made him legendary. It was largely his off-field antics that made his reputation. He would sometimes wrestle the bear Walt Lingo used in training his dogs as part of the pre-game or halftime entertainment. That might count as on-field activity but definitely wasn't football.

Nick was one of the few players to live in LaRue, Ohio year-round during the team's existence and the only one to remain there after its demise. Long Time Sleep is generally remembered by townspeople as a kind, generous man who loved children but was mischievous when drunk on moonshine. Even during, or especially in, the days of Prohibition, anyone wanting to imbibe could easily find alcoholic beverages to drink providing he or she wasn't too picky. One of Lassaw's favorite tricks was to scare the telephone operators. He would pull his coal-black hair down over his eyes and peer into the window of the telephone office at night. The women working there didn't appreciate his sense of humor. Nick's escapades would sometimes land him in the town jail where he would sleep it off and be fine the next day.

A local farmer named William Guthery told a story about Jim Thorpe, Pete Calac and Nick Lassaw helping him and his father castrate some boars. They came out to his farm on a hot Sunday morning to do a job that normally required four men and some rope. But the three football players jumped into the pen and threw the 350 pound boars to the ground, using nothing but their considerable strength and the knowledge of how to best apply leverage. After the job was finished, the three jumped into a 2,000 gallon concrete holding tank to wash off while everyone else left (there were surely some curious spectators watching these Indians in action). Three hours later when Guthery returned, Thorpe, Calac and Lassaw were lying on top of the tank, stark naked, still drying out.

Nick Lassaw made LaRue, Ohio his home after the Oorang franchise folded, staying at least through 1930. He supported himself by working for the telephone company and doing odd jobs.

Bob Greenwood got to know Nick quite well because his older brother, Ike, was Nick's manager when he wrestled professionally. He recalled that Nick lived in an apartment above Cook's Meat Market, which provided a convenient home base in the center of town for his exploits, a favorite of which was walking down the middle of the street naked except for his shoes.

When he wasn't creating a ruckus in LaRue by wrestling Walt Lingo's bear for fun, Nick would often wrestle for money in the nearby towns, making two or three dollars for each bout – if he won. Nick's favorite was to lie on the mat stretched on his stomach while his opponent tried in vain to turn him over for a pin. In the middle of one such "match" Nick told young Greenwood, "This is the easiest money I ever made!" Greenwood also recalled another of his antics: "Nick liked to draw attention and could draw a crowd. In the summer, he'd go to Charlie Allen's restaurant where Charlie had an old gas-heater corn popper that cranked by hand. He'd take it outside on the sidewalk in front of the store and pop corn. The people really flocked around. Sometimes he would dress in his Indian garb."

Bob Greenwood also told of the time Walter Lingo had him go with Lassaw out by the old training camp to get a boat out of the frozen lake. Nick chopped the ice from around the boat but couldn't pull it out. So, he chopped a hole in the ice at the stern of the boat, then took off his clothes and jumped it. He got under the boat and pushed it free. After the boat was ashore, Nick reached up asking for help getting out of the freezing water. "As soon as he clasped my hand, he deliberately pulled me into the water. I darn near froze!"

Marie and Gene English were also friends of Nick and would have him out to their house: "He was a nice person to sit down and talk to. After we'd get through eating, Gene and Nick would go into the front room and have a good time talking. He wasn't lazy, either. He could put in a good day's work." She also recalled a good deed he had done for her: "At that time, there were a lot of bank robberies, especially in smaller towns. I had to work alone in the bank at noon, but Nick didn't like to see me do that. He asked my husband if he could watch over me. So Nick would sit out in the lobby and read the paper during the noon hour." That surely discouraged most bank robbers.

Some time in the 1930s, Nick returned to the reservation. The most probable reason was that it was the depth of the Depression and jobs were hard to find. He likely lived on his allotment, and it is believed that he found employment as an Indian agent. On February 7, 1937 he married Rose Cecille Sorrell who was 14 years his junior and had a small child from a previous relationship. Nick wrote in his Bible that they were married at the St. Ignatius Mission and that Father Louis Talman, S.J. performed the ceremony. On October 15, 1937, the Lassaws became the parents of twin girls, Marian and Marie. The girls, now known as Marie "Buzzie" Wheeler and Marian "Skee" Pichette, celebrated their 70th birthday in 2007 and were interviewed by Maggie Plummer, reporter for *Char-Koosta News*. Buzzie lives in the old family home up the hill from Camas Prairie School while Skee lives in St. Ignatius. They were joined by a brother, Nick, Jr., in 1946, but he died in 1992. Nick and Rose also adopted a cousin from Idaho, Zella M. Lassaw, when she was seven months old.

The girls recalled their father having a number of different jobs when they were growing up. He was Tribal Chief of Police when they were infants. Later he worked in the mines near Wallace, Idaho and still later, herded sheep. He also worked in the Dupuis mills at Dog Lake, Polson and Kerr Dam. Buzzie also remembered him working at a railroad tie plant she called "the sawdust shack." In addition to supporting his family, he took leadership positions in the tribe, serving on Tribal Council from 1935 to 1939 and again from 1948 to 1951. In the early 1960s, Nick and three others from the Flathead Reservation drove to Washington, DC to inquire into a government land issue. The took a small detour to visit LaRue, Ohio, but by then only the old-timers would recognize the large man in the black car that sported steer horns on its hood as the Oorang star.

When Nick got married, he settled down. His daughters remember him as strict but not stern and laughing a lot: "He insisted that we listen. We had to have respect. He loved to fish. And we would go visiting in Idaho, around Worley." He also participated in powwows and became an area legend. Buzzie recalled, "At the powwows they used to call him 'Walking Mouse' as a joke. Nick loved to play stickgame at powwows. He would pull a burning stick out of the fire and put it in his mouth without ever burning his hands or mouth. Some thought he could eat fire.

He used to scare the kids when he was dancing, just goofing around with his hatchet." Their father also spoke Salish fluently and told ancient stories in that language. However, he would not allow the girls to be present because he was afraid the language would be taken away from him if he taught it to his daughters. They did learn it from Susette, though. He sometimes emceed powwows. Buzzie remembered him making a speech at the dedication of the Hot Springs Tribal bathhouse dedication in 1954. She said he had a loud booming voice. She also remembered Jim Thorpe coming to visit in his huge, fancy car right after the dedication.

In his later years, Nick worked on his autobiography and had typed up a two-inch stack of papers by the time he died of lung cancer at St. Patrick's Hospital in September 1964. His wife then burned his papers and his buffalo outfit that he wore at powwows. His memory lives in the hearts of his family

William Newashe

William Newashe;
*Cumberland County
Historical Society,
Carlisle, PA*

William Newashe tackling
Possum Powell; *U. S. Army
Military History Institute*

William Newashe,
1911; *Fred Wardecker*

Name:	William Newashe	**Nickname:**	
DOB:	10/5/1889	**Height:**	5'10"
Weight:	187	**Age:**	21
Tribe:	Sac & Fox, Shawnee	**Home:**	Shawnee, OK
Parents:	Naw-Haw-She - father, Ko-Lay-Pah-Way-Se - mother, AKA John and Susan Newashe		
Early Schooling:	Sac and Fox Indian Agency school		
Later Schooling:			
Honors:			

No sooner had Carlisle's football team become successful than it began to be criticized as being professional. Those claims were not based on the players getting paid to play football, at least initially, because there was limited opportunity to play independent or professional football for pay at that time. However, athletes could get paid for playing baseball, even if their pay just covered living expenses. Newspapers began running articles that criticized Carlisle for allowing boys who played baseball for pay to then play football. They ignored the fact that some of the college boys against whom the Indians played football also played summer ball but were more sophisticated and used fictitious names. William Newashe was one of the better baseball players to enroll at Carlisle but, ironically, his success in summer ball contributed significantly to the demise of baseball at the Indian school and gave ammunition to Carlisle's critics.

Bill and his younger sister, Emma, arrived at Carlisle in July 1905 from the Sac and Fox Reservation in Oklahoma. They were the orphaned children of a Sac and Fox father, John, and Shawnee mother, Susan, Newashe (sometimes written as Nawashe). Their father is believed to have died of tuberculosis and their mother of pneumonia. Emma soon received considerable press coverage at the school for a variety of activities, including her writing. William got very little mention in his first years at the school and, when he did, it was almost entirely related to athletics. His first time in the limelight was a very short March 1907 piece. The reporter said he was trying to move up from the junior varsity baseball team to the varsity and wished him luck because he and Frank LeRoy were the j. v.'s best players.

Bill did make the varsity team. We know that because he was listed among the players who were off for a big road trip to Atlantic City. He reported back to his friends at Carlisle that he was having a good time on the early-season road trips. He soon broke into the starting line-up, playing first base and batting fifth or sixth. Game summaries showed that he was stealing bases, turning double plays, getting hits and scoring runs. In May, after Wauseka departed, Newashe demonstrated his versatility by shifting to Wauseka's old position, catcher.

Bill quickly found out that playing baseball for Carlisle wasn't all fun and games, especially those long road trips. *The Arrow* reported on something that happened on the team's May road trip to play Syracuse: "At the hotel in Elmira, N. Y., Wm. Newashie[sic] was barred from his room by Wm. Garlow who was his room-mate. Newashie stayed out too late and consequently Garlow locked the door and went to bed. The next morning one of the boys found him sleeping out in the hall."

Being on the diamond was no piece of cake for him either. In July, when he was away playing summer baseball in Maryland, *The Arrow* reprinted an article about a serious incident: "Newashee [sic], an Indian playing with Hagerstown, was struck in the mouth with a foul tip off his own bat on Wednesday and had to retire from the game. He was attended by two physicians who were on the grandstand." Ouch! Two weeks later *The Arrow* had something more positive to report, "William Newashe, who is playing with the Hagerstown nine, is making good and looks forward to the time when he can sign B. L. after his name (Big League)." It was clear to him that wasn't going to happen any time soon, so after the season was over Bill returned to Carlisle. In September, he wrote about his experiences for *The Arrow*:

> "Last Spring when I went away from here I thought I would play only two or three games a week. But I soon found out that we had to play every day.
> "I got used to it and the first game I played seemed funny to play in a strange place, and besides it was my first time out in playing ball. I enjoyed it very much. Garlow pitched the first game against Shippensburg, and shut them out 7-0.
> "The first week went pretty fast for Garlow and I and we both enjoyed playing.
> "The team would play with Martinsburg, W. Va., Winchester, Va; Berkeley Spring, W. Va., Frederick, Md., Hanover, Pa., Carlisle, Pa., Sparrows Point, Md.

"The crowds in Virginia and West Virginia were not as good as the crowds in Maryland and in Pennsylvania, and there is usually some betting done on the game nearly every day.

"We played in Hanover where Mike Balenti joined us and soon some more new players came and we played ball in regular style.

"There were only four members of the team that played all the season, and the rest were released, the players were Hawks, Garlow, Peaster of Baltimore, and myself, who stuck to the team from start to the finish.

"I made two home runs for our team, center fielder, two home runs. Balenti one. Finnell of Baltimore one."

The Arrow also included a letter from J. Frank Ridenour praising Bill's performance both as a player and as a person. That letter was previously included in the chapter on William Garlow.

Football season had already begun when he returned to school. The 1907 team was one of Carlisle's finest, and William Newashe wasn't ready for the varsity yet, so he played on a shop team. He was so badly injured in a game between the Printers and the Tailors that he had to be replaced by little Ray Hitchcock. The same week he told an *Arrow* reporter that "…he would take us all to Philadelphia if he had his way." Bill was referring to the special train to take students, faculty and staff to the Penn game. But he didn't have the resources to get his way, and many Carlisle students couldn't afford the trainfare to the game and the tour of the art museum earlier in the day. In November, an anonymous reporter, who called himself Pigskin, reported that Newashe was coaching the junior varsity team. Apparently he was a player-coach and had healed enough to play again, because he kicked a field goal for the j. v. against the Soldiers' Orphans School team from nearby Scotland, PA.

A bit of sibling rivalry was reported shortly after that: "Emma Newashe, who is out in the country, expects to get ahead of her brother, William, in her studies, but William is bracing up, too." Carlisle students were sometimes able to attend public schools all day when on outing. Some students thus progressed more quickly than those at Carlisle who attended academic classes half days only.

In January of 1908, Bill organized a basketball team for the small boys and wanted to take on the freshman boys. Shortly after that he was mentioned in *The Arrow*, one of the few times for a non-athletic activity, when he visited a meeting of the Susan Longstreth Society. He then took sick and was hospitalized for a few days. However, the Susans likely played no role in his hospitalization.

In February at the Football Banquet, Bill received his letter "C" for baseball. He received nothing for football nor mention in any other sport. A month later *The Arrow* published "Our Base Ball Team of '07," some prose found in the mail and signed J. W. T. (Joseph W. Twin who also wrote under the byline of Walter Camp) which described each player. Of Bill it said, "Newashe is our first sacker; a thrown ball can't get through 'Willie.'" The school paper again mentioned him later that month, this time for a rare vocal performance: "William Newashe favored the Dickson Society with a melodious song at the last meeting."

In the spring, William Newashe was again playing first base but was moved up to batting third in the order. Batting third probably indicated that he was becoming a better hitter, both in slugging and consistency. Bill spent the summer in Oklahoma where he most likely played baseball, as was his habit. At summer's end, he and fellow Sac and Fox football player, Jim Thorpe, returned to Carlisle. That fall he was a member of the Freshman Class.

Bill probably played football on the Second Team in 1908, but there was no mention of it in *The Arrow*. In late January 1909, it reported, "William Newashe, a member of the Freshman Class left last Monday morning for Hershey, Pa., where he will spend the rest of the winter. William, being a basketball player, will be missed immensely by his teammates as well as by all of his classmates and friends." Captain of the freshman basketball team was Bill's classmate, Jim Thorpe.

William Newashe started the 1909 baseball season behind the plate where he had finished the previous season but was now batting cleanup. The decision to shift him down one spot in the batting order was a good one because, in addition to leading the team by hitting .417, he was belting home runs. That is exactly the kind of hitter a manager wants batting clean up. Part way through the season, Bill was moved to second base and Hayes took over the catching responsibilities, likely reducing the frequency of Newashe's injuries. After a successful spring, including a win over the Hagerstown team for which he had previously played, he headed to Atlantic City to play ball that summer, probably for a hotel team that provided him room, board and tips.

That fall, in 1909, for the first time, the varsity football line up included Newashe at left end. He played well, even scoring a touchdown after catching a forward pass at his own 15 yard line. The Freshman Class chose him as captain of its basketball team. To close out his great year in December, he and Anona Crow won second prize in the twostep at the Mercers' reception.

Spring 1910 must have been an odd one for Bill; it was the first time in years that he wasn't playing baseball. That was because Carlisle dropped baseball as a sport. So Newashe joined the track team and started competing in the hammer throw. In April after commencement, he, Bill Garlow and Wauseka started playing for the Harrisburg baseball team. The proximity of Harrisburg to Carlisle made frequent visits to the school easy for the ballplayers. The *Patriot* reported Newashe's first try at a new position:

> "Newashee [sic], the Carlisle Indian, made his debut at Harrisburg Wednesday in the role of pitcher, after two of his teammates were knocked from the box, and pulled the game out of the fire. The Lancaster pitchers were found for thirteen hits. Score, Harrisburg, 10; Lancaster, 5."

The *Sentinel* told the story of his debut this way:

> "He took hold of things at a bad time and pulled through in fine style and after the third inning was over but one more run was scored off his delivery. The youngster was like both the other pitchers, wild, but he kept his bases on balls scattered. The run in the fifth inning was secured by a single, base on balls, sacrifice and the squeeze play. While he kept things safe through his pitching he caused trouble for the visiting pitcher for he was the one that started things moving in the fifth inning with a two-bagger. Again in the sixth he was first up and singled safely to left field."

Bill returned to Carlisle in time to start practicing for the 1910 football season. For a while he was shifted to fullback where he was an effective ballcarrier. However, Warner needed a tackle, so Newashe became the left tackle. But his talents carrying the pigskin weren't wasted. Against Penn, Pop Warner dusted off an old play – a concealed double pass – in which the back who received the snap would head toward Newashe's end of the line, he would pull out of the line, take a hidden handoff and race around the opposite end of the line for sizeable gains. He filled in at fullback for Hauser the next game and performed well. If nothing else, Bill Newashe was as versatile on the gridiron as on the diamond.

After football season was over, he went on outing to his usual location, Hershey, Pennsylvania, where something unusual happened: he and Louis Island played for the Hershey YMCA team in a basketball game against Carlisle's Varsity.

For the summer of 1911, he signed with a baseball team located in Jackson, Michigan, a town best known for the prison located there. Bill wasn't lonely that summer as Bill Garlow also played on the Jackson team. Newashe showed unusual talent: "'Chief' William Newashe, the star performer of the Carlisle Indians on the gridiron, is one of the stars of the Jackson, Mich. State League baseball team. During the past season he filled every position on the team in an acceptable manner. Michigan League sport writers predict that he will break into the big league next season."

Back at Carlisle in the fall, Newashe was again out on the football practice field. The 1911 team is considered by many to be Carlisle's best, so making the starting line up was no mean feat. He played left tackle that year and was a major ground gainer, teaming with his counterpart on the right side of the line, Lone Star Dietz, on the tackle-through-tackle play. Down with pneumonia, he missed the game with Lafayette but bounced back into his starring role when he recovered. Bill Newashe was a major cog in a legendary team, one of few that ever beat two of the Big Four in the same season.

At season's end, he apparently left the school because, in January 1912, *The Carlisle Arrow* implied that he was no longer a student: "William Newashe was in Carlisle calling on his friends last Monday afternoon." In February, Emma visited him in his home in Harrisburg which suggests that he was living and working in the area. In late February, he wrote Friedman that he was starting work at a packing company and that he intended to work there until April 25th, at which time he would start to play summer ball again. In May, a short piece in *The Arrow* confirmed that he was no longer a student but raised some other questions: "From the Hotel Ruhl, in Jackson, Michigan, comes a 'happy' message from Emma Newashe, Class '12, who is there with her brother William and his wife. She says: 'I am enjoying life immensely and my sincere wishes are that you and other friends at Carlisle find life as happy as I see it now.'" Who had he married? How was he supporting her? Was he still playing baseball? Why wasn't he in the majors? Later correspondence in his student file revealed that she was the daughter of J. B. and Anna Stambaugh. The Stambaughs lived in Derry Township (Hershey, Pennsylvania) in 1910 and in Carlisle by 1915. Neither censuses nor city directories list their daughter. It is quite possible that she was living on her own when she met Bill.

In November 1912, Mrs. Newashe was the luncheon guest of Angel DeCora, wife of Lone Star Dietz. Somehow, the two women had become acquainted or possibly knew each other before the Newashes married. There is just too little information to know anything with any measure of certainty. Because they were spending the off-season in Paxtang, a suburb of Harrisburg, it is reasonable to assume that Bill had a job there, possibly at the nearby Hershey chocolate plant. In March, Angel visited the Newashes in Paxtang, and later that month Bill visited Carlisle briefly. In April, Gus Welch visited them in Hershey, and they visited Carlisle during commencement week. While the school said nothing officially about Mrs. Newashe, it appears that she was known to and accepted by the Carlisle community.

Bill must have been doing well financially at this time because he bought some real estate, probably in Paxtang, that included a house and a lot with a carpenter shop on it. Emma put up some of the money and William was to repay her $50 from each of his semiannual lease payments from his allotment in Oklahoma. Things weren't going so well for him physically because his sister wrote Superintendent Friedman that, after he underwent an undisclosed operation, he would be much better. His life soon took a sharp turn downward.

In early 1914, Horace Johnson, Superintendent of the Sac and Fox Indian School wrote Oscar Lipps about Bill's situation. Johnson was concerned about Bill's financial condition: "Mr. Newashe has had something like six thousand dollars during the past two years some of which, if not much, has been spent in riotous living." He detailed some of Newashe's spending which included living several weeks in one of Oklahoma City's best hotels and mortgaging his property. In a later letter, he described Mrs. Newashe as a white woman and "somewhat of an adventuress." In February 1914, Newashe visited the Indian school, perhaps to get money. That summer he played some minor league baseball in Peru, Indiana for a time, but a major league contract was never to be.

In late 1915, Mrs. Newashe was living with her parents at 420 North Street in Carlisle and was in dire straits, both financially and physically. She wrote Superintendent Lipps at the Indian school in an attempt to get some money from her husband to replace winter clothing that he sold to buy liquor. He was in Michigan but was trying to get money from Lipps to use to come to Carlisle. Apparently the government had some of the lease money from his allotment. She supported the idea: "…which I think would be a good thing as he can't buy liquor here." She also wrote that she was preparing to go to the Mont Alto Sanitarium and that her physician, Dr. Plank, thought she should have gone six months ago. She didn't say why she needed to go to the sanitarium but it was most likely to treat tuberculosis because the Mont Alto institution had had some success in that regard. In her case, it was too late.

The remaining correspondence in Newashe's file, of which there were several, had to do with Anna Stambaugh's request for reimbursement of the $150 cost of her daughter's funeral. Some of the letters dealt with partial payments whereas others were attempts to determine where he was. He was found to have been playing for the Carlisle Indian Base Ball Team for part of the summer of 1916. That team, or at least its booking manager, Nat C. Strong, owner of the Brooklyn Royal Giants and powerful figure in black baseball, operated out of the Pulitzer Building in New York City.

Starting around 1915, Newashe began playing professional football in the fall. That year and the part of the next, "Chief" Newashe played guard for the Detroit Heralds. He also played tackle for the Pitcairn Quakers in 1916. Shifting from team to team, even during the season, was common in those days. Some players stayed with one team an entire season but played for other teams only on Sundays their team had nothing scheduled.

When William Newashe registered for the WWI draft in June 1917, he was a professional baseball player, living in Oklahoma City, and single. His gravestone reflects that during WWI he served in the Military Police as a corporal.

He remarried, probably after the war. About all that is known about his wife is that, according to the 1920 census, her name was Myrtle Cowan, she was the niece of Louis F. Cowan, a mine operator from Miami, Oklahoma, and she had been born in Arkansas around 1897. Sac and Fox rolls listed her as a white woman, but the 1930 federal census classified her as being of mixed blood. Grandniece Donna Newashe McAllister recalls that Myrtle was a white woman who was bedridden in later years and that William, a very quiet man, cared for her.

He played baseball professionally in the Western League in 1920. He and Myrtle, spent the off-season in Miami, Oklahoma with her uncle. Around 1921, a son, William Jr., was born and his sister Susan was born three years later.

Bill's last known competitive athletic endeavor was to play for the Oorang Indians in 1923 when he was about 34 years old. He played five games at tackle for them in the latter half of the season. In 1930 he was living with Myrtle and the children in Vinita, Oklahoma and working as a machinist on an oil derrick, a pretty good job to have during the Great Depression. In 1947 William Newashe appeared as a representative of the Sac and Fox nation in a lawsuit against the Federal government. Which William Newashe, Jr. or Sr., was involved is not clear. He also raised his granddaughter, Emma Rosanne, to adolescence.

Bill's sister Emma married Fred McAllister around 1913 in Oklahoma City. Not long after that they moved to a farm in Luther, Oklahoma that is still owned by the family. Emma, an accomplished writer and musician, died young while giving birth to her tenth child.

About the time the Jim Thorpe biopic was playing, William was interviewed by *The Oklahoman*. When asked about Carlisle's grueling schedule, he responded, "We used to play two or three home warmup games at home then we'd travel most of the rest of the season." When asked which was the toughest opponent, he replied, "They were all tough. Our greatest rival was Pennsylvania. When we played them we'd run a special train from Carlisle and take our band along" He explained that the big eastern schools did not exactly enjoy getting beaten by small schools such as Carlisle, something that created several interesting rivalries.

When questioned about his friend, Jim Thorpe, he said, "A lot of people think Jim was all out for himself. At Carlisle he was strictly a team man. Not exactly a leader but he was always encouraging the players and was good for the morale of the team. He was a marked man at all times but he had tremendous stamina and could take it. He never did want to hog the limelight." As to their coach, Newashe said, "Warner had no pets and played no favorites. A truly fine coach."

The interview turned to then modern football, Bill opined, "We had no reserves. Every player wanted to play the full 60 minutes. There were no huddles and we wasted no time. I think the free substitution of today kills football from the spectator viewpoint but it does give more boys a chance to play."

He was a member of the Christian Church, served on the Sac and Fox Tribal Claims Council, and helped establish the service club for Sac and Fox Indians. Bill served as a pallbearer in 1953 for his former teammate and fellow Sac and Fox, Jim Thorpe. He lived until February 8, 1962 and died in Luther, Oklahoma at 72 years of age. He is buried in the Luther Cemetery Expansion.

Stancil Powell

Powell playing lacrosse; *U. S. Army Military History Institute*

Chief Powell at the Wigwam; *U. S. Army Military History Institute*

Stancil Powell, 1912; *Fred Wardecker*

Name: Stancil Powell		**Nickname:** Possum; Steamroller; Wrinklemeat	
DOB: February 1890		**Height:** 5'10"	
Weight: 176		**Age:** 21	
Tribe: Cherokee		**Home:** Ocona Lufty Township, Swain County, NC	

Parents: John Powell, mixed-blood Eastern Cherokee; Tooka (Dooka, Duke) Powell, full-blood Eastern Cherokee

Early Schooling: unknown

Later Schooling: Haskell Institute

Honors: American Indian Sports Hall of Fame, 1971

That both Moses and his younger brother, Stancil (Stansill), Powell were enrolled at Carlisle by 1900 may indicate that their father was ill and no longer able to support the family. Although Stancil enrolled for five years in 1899, he was discharged in 1902 as "Undesirable." Something must have changed because he was allowed to re-enroll in 1906. His father was dead by that time and his guardian was Wesley Bigjim. It's not clear where the younger Powell picked up 'Possum' as a nickname, but it stuck with him at the Carlisle Indian School where he studied carriagemaking and participated in athletics. After several years at the school, Possum started getting a little press. The November 20, 1908 issue of *The Carlisle Arrow* described a game played by Carlisle's second team, The Hustlers, as a punting contest between Powell and Serber of Walbrook Athletic Club.

In January 1909, he was named as one of six players to participate in Carlisle's first ever inter-collegiate basketball game. Powell figured prominently in reports of this game against Penn: "The Indians did not have a single foul called on them during the first half, and those called on Powell in the second half were for holding, an offense to which the redman was driven by utter exhaustion."

In May, Powell returned to the school to devote more time to his trade after working on a nearby farm for some time. Later that month at the Annual Class Meet, he placed behind Jim Thorpe and George Thomas in both the high jump and the shot put events. He placed 12th in total points for the meet. At the Fourth of July celebration, he teamed with Pierce Ute and Peter Jordan to come in 2nd in the wheelbarrow race. Soon he was involved in more serious competitions.

In the fall of 1909, Possum Powell made the varsity football team but didn't start. He was the first substitute to be put in at the end position and, as such, got some playing time, limited though it was. In the spring of 1910, he participated in track again. In that fall's football season, he got more playing time and press coverage. In the winter, he played on Wauseka's basketball team that showed "promise to become stars of the first magnitude." In the spring 1911 track season, Stancil earned his first Carlisle letter by winning the high jump and discus events in the dual meet with Dickinson College. He also placed first in the shot put against Lafayette. Powell contributed to Carlisle's winning the Pennsylvania Intercollegiate Track and Field Championship by winning the high jump and coming in second in the 16-pound shot put. After that, he left for a vacation at home in North Carolina.

The fall of 1911 was his best season at Carlisle. With Pete Hauser gone, Possum Powell was the starting fullback, and he made the most of his opportunity by being a consistent ground gainer and pretty good place kicker. He got a fair amount of press, considering that he was playing in Jim Thorpe's shadow on what many consider was Carlisle's finest team. *The North American* wrote, "Powell scattered the Penn forwards when making his plunges much in the manner that a rearing and plunging horse forces a crowd out of his way." After the Harvard game, the *The Boston Globe* commented, "On the direct passes from center, Powell, the fullback, in particular, found it no trouble to plough ahead for 5 and 10-yard gains." *The Boston Journal* credited the coach: "Glen Warner has molded together a wonderful team this year, and Thorpe and Powell are two of the greatest all-around football players ever seen on Soldiers Field, and that is saying a good deal." After the last game of the season against Brown, *The Providence Journal* raved, "Powell was also constantly in the limelight, the big fullback hitting Brown's line like a catapult."

Placing Jim Thorpe on his All-America First Team was all the mention Walter Camp granted the 1911 Indians. Fortunately, others saw things more clearly. *Outing Magazine*'s annual poll of coaches listed Powell at fullback in its "Football Honor List for 1911."

Back at school, Possum Powell received positive mention for cutting down all the Christmas trees used to decorate the campus that year. In February, he built a fine under-cut surrey to be used in the commencement exhibition and in March left for Mascot, Pennsylvania to work in a carriage shop. He returned from that outing in time to compete with the track team, coming in second in both the high jump and shot put in the state championship meet.

At 5'10" and 176 pounds, he played fullback for the Indians again in 1912. Although the team did well again, his performance was off from its 1911 level. The press described him as "not as effective as last year."

He spent some time at home in North Carolina and returned with a batch of new students. But he didn't stay long as he headed west to Haskell Institute in Lawrence, Kansas. Besides stating that he had no special musical ability, his Returned Student record described his character and disposition as "good, only." It deemed him suitable to work as a wagon wood worker or laborer, but "Should be under strict supervision to get good results." His instructor, Martin L. Law, saw things differently. He considered Possum's ability and conduct both to be very good and thought he "will make a first class mechanic."

The 1913 football season found Stancil Powell playing fullback once again, this time for the Fightin' Indians. Perhaps thinking his chapeau clashed with his purple and gold Haskell uniform, *The Lincoln Daily Star* commented on his attire: "Powell wore no head gear and covered his head with a red cap, recalling to the minds of the old timers, Indian [Charles] Guyon the speedy end of years ago. He is a fearless player and appeared dangerous at all times."

The fact that Powell and a teammate or two had previously played some football was not lost on *The Star*: "For the Indians, Powell an ex-Carlisle player who had the distinction of playing by the side of the famous Jim Thorpe, was head and shoulders above his teammates in both the offense and defense. In the latter part of the contest, when Nebraska was charging through the enormous gaps opened by Ross, this flashy player took the place of his opposing guard and succeeded in choking up the holes."

The former Carlisle players found themselves at the center of a controversy as opponents were objecting to their having previously played on the Carlisle varsity. Just before the Haskell-Nebraska game, *The Star* wrote, "The men were neither overconfident nor gloomy over the coming contest, preferring to retain their verdict until the Aborigines have been met. Reports continue to filter through that Coach 'Snapper' Kennedy has more than the two Carlisle players upon his squad which he has reported. In fact it is said and from reliable sources too that this Stover person who is evidently in the Haskell lineup is none other than the famous Ogallala, who played with the eastern redskins when they so merciless massacred the Huskers in 1908."

Carlisle did beat Nebraska 31-6 in 1908, but the records do not list anyone named Ogallala ever playing for Carlisle. Almost immediately, a reader countered the accusations:

Fort Hall, Idaho, Oct 27.—Sport Editor of *The Daily Star.*

Dear Sir:

I note in The Star of Saturday, October 25, you intimate that Stover, the center on the Haskell Indian football team, is none other than 'Ogalalla,' who helped Carlisle defeat the 'Huskers way back in 1908. As one who is in a position to know, I want to say that nothing could be further from the truth.

I lived at Haskell Institute for a number of years, though not directly connected with the school, and I know both of these Indians well. Ogalalla, whose real name is Nekifer Shoushuck, is an Alaskan; Stover is an Oklahoma Indian. Ogalalla is married and at present working in a bake shop in Lawrence. Stover entered Haskell in 1910 and I might say a 'greener' Indian never tried for the team. Kennedy, who is known for his clean sportsmanship throughout the Missouri valley, has developed Stover into one of the best centers ever at the school. Stover has never seen Carlisle, and I might add that since he is a member of what is known as the five civilized tribes, he is not eligible for enrollment at Carlisle.

The only two players on the 1913 Haskell football team who ever attended Carlisle are Powell and Charles Williams. The former entered Haskell last spring, paying his own transportation to the school. He goes to school and is learning a trade. Charles Williams is a brother of 'Bill' Williams, the captain of the Haskell team. His term of enrollment at Carlisle expired last spring and he enrolled at Haskell this fall, desiring to be with his brother. In this connection, I might say that the whole Haskell team is composed of a group of young Indian men who for manliness and cleanness can not be surpassed by any football team in the country. Most of them are active Christian workers, and have few, if any bad habits. Much of this is due to the teaching of Coach Kennedy and Captain Williams, the latter having just been elected to the presidency of the Haskell Young Men's Christian Association, an organization with about 200 members.

In closing, I, who am not an Indian, wish to say that if some of the Indian football teams of the past have had unsavory reputations, through the bringing in of 'ringers' and ineligible players, it has been because of the white men who have handled the teams and not through any desire of the Indians themselves. The newspapers ought by this time to know Coach Kennedy well enough to discredit any rumors that would in any way reflect upon his integrity or true sportsmanship. He is by long odds one of the cleanest and best sportsmen in the middle west, and The Star knows it. I left Lawrence October 1, am well acquainted with all the members of the Haskell football team, and know whereof I speak.

C. E. McBride of the *Kansas City Star* or any of the Kansas university authorities can easily certify to the truthfulness of this statement.

Very truly,

MILTON M THORNES.

The Carlisle Indian School file for Nekifer Shouchuk, to use the spelling he used himself, includes an article about the 1909 Haskell-Denver game. The Haskell lineup included O'Galla at center, Deloria at right end and Island at quarterback. Someone at Carlisle made some annotations in the right margin. "N. Shouchuk, ex-stu" alongside O'Galla, "John, ex-stu" next to Deloria and "Louis, '1908'" next to Island. The open question is why would anyone have an Aleut try to pass as Irish?

The *Salina Union* chimed in:

A good many sport followers are greatly excited over the recrudescence of the Haskell football team. They ascribe the success of that aggregation of pigskin chasers to the 'marvelous work' of the coach. The real truth is that all Indians on the Haskell team who can play football above the high school class are graduates or former students of Carlisle, who for one reason or another are no longer eligible to play on the eastern team and have been brought to Lawrence to continue their work as professional sportsmen. The Haskell coach is a very clever imitator of other people's good work. He has taken the veteran material secured from the east and by using the plays and tactics of Coaches Moses and Frank of the University of Kansas, has developed a fairly effective football team. There never was a successful Indian football team, either at Carlisle or Haskell, that was not rotten to the core with the worst form of professionalism.

From the editor of *The Star*:

This was written by W. C Lansdon, who was athletic manager at Kansas university while Kennedy was the coach. Evidently he has something sticking in his throat concerning the 'Snapper' which does not taste very palatable.

Stancil Powell stayed at Haskell for the 1914 season, playing fullback again and filling in when necessary at center and tackle. After leaving Haskell, he found work at an oil refinery in Tulsa, Oklahoma. When the U. S. entered WWI, Ben, as he was called in later years, enlisted in the army. He served with distinction in the 358th Infantry of the 90th Division. He was wounded once in the fighting at St. Mihiel and twice in the Argonne. After the war was over, he returned to Oklahoma where he coached the Tahlequah State Teachers College football team for a couple of years. Then he got a call from his old teammate, Jim Thorpe.

In 1923, the Oorang Indians needed help on their line, and Possum Powell was young enough and big enough – barely (5'10", 185 pounds at 32 years old) – to fill in where needed. He liked getting paid $100 a week, which was a lot of money in those days. He was dubbed "Wrinklemeat" as a more colorful name. Apparently "Steamroller" didn't sound Indian enough. Hazel Hynes, the assistant postmistress, remembered Wrinklemeat from coming in to pick up his mail: "He was a lot younger than the other Indians. He looked like a kid right out of high school, especially when he stood beside the other Indians." In a 1934 interview he said, "Football was fine in the days when I could run 10 miles without stopping for breath." Unable to do that any longer, he returned to North Carolina to farm. He married a full-blood Cherokee and in 1929 had a daughter, Dorothy. The three of them lived on the 20-acre farm until 1937 when, a few days before Christmas, his wife, Kina S. Powell, died. He continued farming until his death at age 67 on October 15, 1957 in an automobile accident.

Thomas St. Germain

Thomas St. Germain (top center), University of Wisconsin
1905 water polo team, goalkeeper; *University of Wisconsin*

Name: Thomas Leo St. Germain	**Nickname:**	
DOB: circa 1879	**Height:** 6'1"	
Weight: 224	**Age:** 26	
Tribe: Chippewa	**Home:** Lac du Flambeau Reservation, WI	
Parents: Joseph St. Germain, Chippewa & French Canadian; Mary St. Germain, Chippewa		
Early Schooling: Haskell Institute; Harlem Park College; University of Wisconsin		
Later Schooling: Yale Law School		
Honors:		

The September 17, 1909 issue of *The Carlisle Arrow* contained an unusual report: "Another visitor, who is also more or less of a football enthusiast, is Mr. Thomas St. Germain who paid a visit to friends at Carlisle, while enroute to Washington, this week. Mr. St. Germain played on the teams of Harlem Park at Des Moines and at the University of Wisconsin. He is now engaged in the practice of law at Ashland, Wisconsin." Mention of this visit was peculiar because the visitor was neither a dignitary nor an alumnus. Given the number of students from Wisconsin, it would not be difficult to believe that he had friends at Carlisle. Perhaps more peculiar was that Thomas St. Germain enrolled in the commercial course. Why would someone engaged in a law practice enroll at Carlisle?

A review of his enrollment records from the University of Wisconsin showed that St. Germain had already completed a three-year law course at Highland Park College in Des Moines, Iowa and had been admitted to the Iowa bar. In August 1904, he applied for admission to the University of Wisconsin Law School and was admitted on the weight of his transcript from Highland Park College. St. Germain attended Wisconsin for one year where he played football and was goalie on the water polo team. He apparently returned to practicing law in Iowa after that. Why would school officials encourage him to enroll? Perhaps he knew one of the administrators or was a star athlete. The fact that he was 26 years of age, being 6'1" tall and weighing 224-1/2 pounds may have had something to do with it. Soon his name started appearing regularly in the school publications.

On September 25, he started at center against Villanova. No one ever moved into Carlisle's starting lineup that quickly. The next week, against Bucknell, he played one of the guard positions. Later in October, he sang bass in a 32-member co-educational choir organized by the band director. The YMCA boasted a new member: "Thomas St. Germaine [sic] read a story on the 'Criminal Neglect of Duty' and followed his reading with words of advice and counsel." On Thanksgiving, the Indians pounded St. Louis University in a game played in Cincinnati: "Pete Hauser and his brother, Wauseka, and [St.] Germain were the stonewall combination of the Indian line."

In December, Thomas attended the Susan Longstreth Literary Society's annual reception at which dancers competed for prize cakes and didn't go home empty-handed: "The booby prize was awarded, amid much applause, to Thomas St. Germaine [sic] and Miss Gaither, who lead [sic] the grand march."

In February, St. Germain read a short passage at a service of the Second Presbyterian Church during which a special offering was collected for Indian missions. In April, he was elected reporter for the Invincibles and gave "a brief but inspiring talk" to the YMCA boys. At term's end, he departed to take a government job in Washington, DC as a clerk at the Land Office. On June 1, he wrote Superintendent Friedman, "I am able to say to you, in confidence, that while 'my official title' is that of Asst. Messenger I am assigned the duties of a stenographer. It is my plan to prepare for the regular examination for clerk & stenographer to be held some time this summer here." Friedman responded, "I take this opportunity because I am a friend of yours, to urge that you pay close attention to your work in the office with a view of pleasing your superiors, and winning their confidence. I would also strongly counsel you to so shape your life outside of the office and so choose your companions as to reflect credit upon yourself and win you the approbation of the people with whom you come in contact." Did Friedman know something about him that wasn't widely known? The October 21, 1910 *Arrow* informed readers that St. Germain, then about 31 years old, had enrolled as a member of the Senior Class at the Yale Law School. Oh, and he also joined the Yale football team and played on the scrubs!

After spending the summer of 1911 working at the Sac and Fox Agency in Cushing, Oklahoma, St. Germain returned to Yale to continue his study of the law. He reputedly assisted with the coaching of the football team as well. On September 13, 1913, in response to a query from Superintendent Friedman, possibly prompted by a visit from St. Germain, John W. Edgerton wrote, "I beg to say that Thomas St. Germaine [sic] graduated with the degree of Bachelor of Laws in June 1913. He was not a brilliant student but by hard work managed to get through. – He was faithful and diligent." Yale listed Thomas as having been a member of the Yale Senate, Kent Club, University Wrestling Association and University Water Polo Team. He was quite active in extra-curricular activities, particularly for a law student. In September, he visited Carlisle, renewing old ties and spoke briefly to the Catholic meeting on Sunday evening. Then he headed east again.

The fall of 1913 found Thomas St. Germain holding down the position of head football coach at Villanova University. Perhaps Tom's being there had something to do with Carlisle and Villanova not scheduling an early season game that had become a tradition. He went 4-2-1, which was an improvement over the vast majority of his predecessors.

St. Germain attended Carlisle's 1914 commencement and advised the students: "Faith in yourself, no matter what the world thinks, will win. Be a useful citizen is my motto." *The Arrow* reported that he also impressed the fact that to be a Carlisle student meant something.

He was looking for a job in the fall of 1914. Perhaps factors other than his coaching prowess were involved. He wrote Oscar Lipps stating, "Because of Villanova's unwillingness to re-engage me with my terms, the State College at Jonesboro, Arkansas' final decision to get a Newbraska [sic] man instead of hiring me to act as their Athletic Coach the year round, I find myself out of a coaching position for this fall." He then asked Lipps to hire him as an assistant and specified the terms of his proposed employment. He went on to say, "This is not much, but it will enable me to get on my feet nicely when I return to Oklahoma where I am arranging to go into a prominent law firm after the football season is over." He was in New Haven, Connecticut at that time, where he had been tutoring a professor's son for the past month. Lipps replied, "'Economy' is now the watch word throughout all the Departments of the Government, and I am sorry that I am unable to make you any offer whatever."

Thomas needed a job and in the worst way. He had quietly married a white woman and they had a child on the way. Thomas Jr. was born on October 8 and Thomas Sr. needed a way to support his wife and child. He reputedly coached Princeton Township High School football in Illinois and practiced law in Iowa and may have been in the real estate business in Wisconsin. He and his wife were soon divorced. The exact chronology of events is not clear. After being out of the public's eye for a few years, his name adorned newspapers nationwide in January 1917.

Miss Jeanette Black, daughter of a wealthy Philadelphia realtor, appeared before Judge Stelk in the Court of Domestic relations in Chicago holding her two-year-old son. She told the judge her story of meeting Thomas St. Germain at Villanova and that he had promised repeatedly to marry her. But, on January 8 of the previous year, 1916, the day set for their marriage, he instead made Miss Janet Wilkins of Crown Point, Indiana his second wife. Miss Black said, "After my baby came, my father was going to prosecute St. Germain under the Mann Act and I prevented it because he had promised to marry me." Thomas told the judge that her parents objected to the marriage because he was an Indian. As the *Chicago Herald* put it: "Thomas St. Germain, Indian athletic and lawyer, winner of many football games and women, was released by Judge Stelk in the Court of Domestic Relations yesterday on his promise to pay $100 within a few days to Miss Jeanette Black of Philadelphia, mother of his two-year-old boy." The judge ordered him to pay Miss Black $100 plus nine annual payments of $50 each. He claimed to have already paid more than the judge required.

It appears that Thomas St. Germain lived and worked as a lawyer in Iowa, at least to 1920 when the Federal Census listed him as being a roomer with the Thomas Trissel family in Mason City, Iowa. Lac du Flambeau rolls list a second son, Joseph, as having been born in 1918. Janet and Joseph were living with her parents in Davenport, Iowa at that time. In the fall of 1922, at an age considered to be too old to be playing football – 37 according to some sources, but 43 according to others - St. Germain came out of retirement and played the interior line positions for the Oorang Indians, at least for the first half of the season. He was the starting center in the Oorang's first game. Assistant Postmistress Hazel Haynes remembered him well: "He was a lug! He filled up that whole, great big, old window. He was nice. 'Well good morning to you, and have a nice day,' he would say to me each day he came to the post office." For whichever reason, injury or the threat of divorce, prevailed, he again retired from the game. This time it appears to have been permanent.

A third son, John, arrived in 1922 and daughter Margaret A. St. Germain was born in 1923. It's not clear where, or even if, wife Janet, was living at this time. The 1930 Federal Census listed the two children's mothers as Chippewa. It also listed an Emma St. Germain as Thomas's white wife from Delaware. Either the census is wrong (a distinct possibility) or Thomas's two youngest children came from a marriage or liaison with an unknown Chippewa woman. For all we know, they may have been from Janet Wilkins.

According to Yale's obituary, St. Germain was the first Indian lawyer to be admitted to the Wisconsin bar. His areas of practice were Federal and Indian law. He served with the U. S. Indian Service, with Lac du Flambeau School and Agency, as a justice of the peace, and on the Objiwa Tribal Council. His Ojibwa name is believed to have been *Mi-ni-si-no-wi-jig*. He died on October 4, 1947 at about 69 years of age of coronary thrombosis and was buried in the Protestant Cemetery in Lac du Flambeau.

St. Germain's oldest son became known as Thomas St. Germain Whitecloud II. He received his medical training at Tulane University and was also known as a writer. Whitecloud II's son, the late Thomas St. Germain Whitecloud III, followed in his father's footsteps and became the head of the Orthopaedic Surgery Department at Tulane. He also turned down Vince Lombardi's offer of a contract to play football for the Green Bay Packers. His son, Jacques, followed in his footsteps and is now Assistant Professor of Orthopaedic Surgery at Tulane.

George Vedernack

George "Cotton" Vedernack;
Cumberland County Historical Society,
Carlisle, PA

George Vedernack
catching a pass;
Cumberland County
Historical Society,
Carlisle, PA

Name: George Vedernack		**Nickname:** Cotton	
DOB: 4/16/1890 or 4/16/1892		**Height:** 5'6"	
Weight: 140		**Age:** 21	
Tribe: Chippewa		**Home:** Lac du Flambeau Reservation, WI	
Parents: Joe Vedernack, possibly German; Mary Vedernack, 3/4 blood Chippewa			
Early Schooling: Lac du Flambeau Reservation Boarding School			
Later Schooling:			
Honors:			

George Vedernack came to Carlisle from the Lac du Flambeau Reservation in September 1909. His younger brother, Frank, also attended Carlisle about the same time. George started off in Room 8 and worked in the tailor shop. A year later he was promoted to Room 9 and shifted to working in the stables. Six months later he began his training as a painter. At first his ability was deemed only 'fair,' but it soon improved. A couple of months later George Vedernack's name, spelled various ways, started showing up in Carlisle Indian School publications.

He apparently went out for track because he placed 3rd in the pole vault at the

Annual Class Track Meet in April, 1911. If he weren't already on the track team, Warner would surely have tried to recruit him. Pole vaulters tend to be wiry and George's physical dimensions imply that he was. After spending the summer in Martin's Creek, Pennsylvania, working for Henry McEwen, George returned to school in time for football season.

After playing on the scrubs in 1910 and possibly 1909, George forced Warner to put him on the varsity squad. He was very small but the quality and intensity of his play demanded that he be promoted, although he was only a substitute. In what many consider Carlisle's greatest victory, Vedernack stood strong. The *Philadelphia Ledger* raved, "Carlisle's defeat of the Harvard team strengthens the conviction that not only has Glenn Warner developed one of the greatest of Indian elevens, but that this 1911 team is about the best among the Eastern colleges." It went on to report that a major cog was missing: "Carlisle was without the services of Captain Burd, [sic] who is considered as having few equals as an end. He was so seriously injured, in the Penn game that he could not play against Harvard." *The Arrow* reported, "Vedernack, who played in Captain Burd's [sic] place, was in the game every minute and very few gains were made around his end." Not bad at all for a first-year man. His contributions were significant enough that Santa Claus, in the person of Jim Thorpe, selected George as only one of nine athletes to receive special gifts at the Catholic reception on Christmas night.

George didn't spend all of his fall on the football field. He was active in the Invincible Debating Society, made extemporaneous speeches, was elected Sergeant-at-arms and visited a girls' debating society meeting. He was also elected mayor of his classroom's model city, Oglala.

Putting his training as a painter to work in January 1912, George made a sign puzzle that students had difficulty solving. About that time, he teamed with Peter Jordan to argue the negative of, "That the divorce laws of all the states should be made uniform" at an Invincibles meeting. Ovilla Azure and Andrew Dunbar, arguing the affirmative, won. In the spring George placed third in the high jump at the Annual Handicap Track and Field Meet, then headed home, his enrollment commitment fulfilled.

George Vedernack, now 22 years old, returned to Carlisle on September 6, 1912, and enrolled for another year on October 3. Perhaps he waited to see if he was going to make the starting line-up before he committed. *The Carlisle Arrow* summarized his play: "George Vetternack, [sic] right end, is 5 ft. 6 in. tall, weighs 140 pounds, and 21 years- old. He is a Chippewa from Wisconsin. 'Cotton,' as he is called, forced his way up from a scrub to a substitute on the team last year, and won his place as a regular by his hard work and his aggressiveness. He was about the smallest player on any first-class team this year, and his success in winning a place on the team shows what fighting spirit and 'pep' can do."

Gus Welch often told a story about that year's Carlisle-Army game:

> "I remember the game well. Jim [Thorpe] took the opening kickoff and ran through the Army team for a touchdown but we drew a penalty and the touchdown was nullified. Thorpe was our captain and went to the referee to ask what the penalty was for. The referee said our little end Vedernack, who weighed only 130 pounds, was holding. 'Thorpe told Vedernack to go to the sideline on the next kickoff and keep out of the way. The kickoff rolled into the end zone. Jim loafed a little, as if he was going to down the ball for a touchback, then suddenly picked up the ball and ran more than 100 yards for a touchdown."

Joe Guyon told another story about that game in which Vedernack was a key ingredient:

> "Cotton Vedernack, a Chippewa weighing 137 pounds, played end. He was the best tackle on our team but lacked the blocking equipment. Consequently, the tackles and ends switched positions on offense. Thorpe and I were detailed to block Army Captain All-American [tackle] Devore."

George spent the summer at home in Wisconsin. Apparently, Superintendent Friedman requested that he recruit students for the school. On August 15, Vedernack wrote Friedman: "Received your letter some time ago and was out trying my best to get students for Carlisle. I have about seven so far that want to go for three [years] and not any longer. Otherwise they won't go." Friedman responded promptly, "A three year term of enrollment will be allowed those students who are eighteen or more years of age, but those who have not reached the age of eighteen should be enrolled for the longer period of five years. If there are any exceptions, however, that should be made, Superintendent Everest will recommend to me what action should be taken." On September 18, P. S. Everest, Superintendent of the LaPointe Agency, wrote Friedman to inform him that Vedernack was bringing Frank Holmes, Jr., Arnold Holliday, Francis Obern and Eliza Denomie to Carlisle with him.

Cotton returned for the 1913 season and, though not much larger, had improved. After the opening game against Albright College, *The Arrow* noticed his improvement: "Pratt, Vedernack, Kelsey, and Wallette showed up well enough on the ends to show that Carlisle will be stronger in those positions than last year." After defeating the tougher Penn team, the reporter observed, "Pratt and Vedernack on the ends did not allow a single gain around them and they spoiled every trick play Penn attempted. They also got down the field better than did the Penn's ends on Guyon's long punts." The *Washington Star* noticed his fine play against Georgetown:

> "Vedernack stands out as one of the best ends in the East, and that despite his rather small stature. He is short and stocky, and seems small to be playing the position, but there is no doubt that he delivers the goods. He gets around and through the interference in a way that is astonishing. It seems to be almost impossible to eliminate him from the play. It is seldom that he fails to get his man, and yesterday he went through four or five Georgetown men time after time and dropped the man with the ball. He uses splendid judgment in going in to help out on plays through the line and off-tackle, and seems to know just when not to get in fast in order to prevent an opposing back from slipping around him. He would compare favorably with much larger and heavier men who are playing end positions in the big universities."

Two weeks later, early in the Dartmouth game, Vedernack suffered a wrenched elbow and was through for the day. Fortunately, his elbow had recovered enough for him to play part of the game against Syracuse the following week. Back at full strength, he played the entire game against Brown a week later to end the season and his football career at Carlisle. George Vedernack had been a significant cog in the legendary Carlisle teams of 1911-1913 that had lost but one game each year and ranked highly among the best teams in the country each year. However, his athletic career at the Indian school wasn't over.

In December 1913, George was promoted from Private to 1st Sergeant of Troop E, a position that brought considerable responsibility. For instance, in March 1914, he supervised the oiling of the floors in the Large Boys' Quarters. Earlier that month, football lettermen, "C" men, drew for game balls from the previous season's victories. He won the ball from the Syracuse game. Cotton kept in shape that winter and early spring playing – practicing mostly – lacrosse until commencement. After receiving his certificate in painting, he was off to Altoona to work in a railroad shop, but not before withdrawing his money from agency and school accounts.

Although no longer at Carlisle, George kept in touch with old friends there and occasionally visited them. He played for the ex-Carlisles football team which was also called the Altoona Indians - that is, when he wasn't playing for someone else. In 1915, he became one of a handful of players ever to play for three professional teams in the same year: Altoona Indians, Pitcairn Quakers and Youngstown Patricians. At Pitcairn he was joined by his younger brother, Frank, another Carlisle alum who worked as an expert painter of passenger railcars. Frank received $4 to $5 a day for his work. Compared to this, $50 a game playing football looked great. In 1916, George just played for Pitcairn and Youngstown and in 1917 just for Youngstown. That was probably because he had moved to Youngstown where he was working as a shipping clerk. Although these were the ragtag days of professional football, the better teams often included All-Americans, against whom Cotton more than held his own.

He was in Wisconsin, probably visiting, when he enlisted in the National Army on June 29, 1918 at Eagle River. He listed 22 New Court Street in Youngstown as his residence. Private Vedernack spent the war at the Machine Gun Training Center at Camp Hancock, Georgia and was honorably discharged on March 26, 1919.

After the war, the Patricians attempted to reform a team and signed George Vedernack. Reeling from a 27-0 thrashing by Massillon on October 5, 1919, the team disbanded. After this, things get fuzzy due to lack of information. A 1929 census lists George as married and living in Columbus, Ohio. However, he was likely married some time prior to that and had at least one child, a daughter, Carol. He died on July 14, 1936, of "Lob. Pneumonia and Pyloric obstruction" while living in Youngstown, Ohio. Carol's wedding announcement described her late father as a "professional football star," so it is likely that his football career continued after the demise of the Youngstown Patricians.

Hugh and Joel Wheelock

Joel Wheelock in track
uniform; *Cumberland County
Historical Society, Carlisle, PA*

Joel Wheelock,
1912; *Fred
Wardecker*

Hugh Wheelock,
1911; *U. S. Army
Military History
Institute*

Name: Joel Wheelock   **Nickname:**
DOB: 3/2/1891   **Height:** 5'9"
Weight: 160   **Age:** 22
Tribe: Oneida   **Home:** West DePere, WI
Parents: James Wheelock, Oneida; Sophia Wheelock, Oneida
Early Schooling: unknown
Later Schooling: Lebanon Valley College preparatory school
Honors: American Indian Sports Hall of Fame, 1971

Name: Hugh Wheelock   **Nickname:** Huge
DOB: 3/2/1891   **Height:** 5'10"
Weight: 172   **Age:** 19
Tribe: Oneida   **Home:** West DePere, WI
Parents: James Wheelock, Oneida; Sophia Wheelock, Oneida
Early Schooling: unknown
Later Schooling:
Honors:

If the Carlisle Indian School had a first family, it would have been the Wheelocks. Brothers Dennison and James Wheelock were students who, at different times, later held the bandmaster position and made the Carlisle Indian School Band famous. Among other things, Dennison composed two marches named after the Carlisle school. Both Dennison and James attended the Dickinson College Preparatory School after completing their Carlisle studies. After leaving government service, they formed Indian bands of their own and traveled around the country. Dennison set aside his baton and took up the law, spending much time in Washington, DC. Laurence M. Hauptman relates that many Oneidas today regard Dennison as "an 'apple,' red on the outside and white on the inside." Sister Ida was quite active in school organizations such as the Susan Longstreth Literary Society. Several other Wheelocks were mentioned prominently in Carlisle publications but were probably cousins. Martin Wheelock comes quickly to mind. But there were also Wheelocks who played football as well as making music with the band – on Carlisle's vaunted varsity. For example, musician James Wheelock led a shop team, but that team didn't play against other schools. However, his younger brothers did.

Joel and Hugh Wheelock were younger brothers of Dennison, James and Ida, children of James A. Wheelock. The May 1, 1896 edition of *The Indian Helper* reported that Sophia Metoxen Wheelock had died recently, leaving James Sr. with several small children to raise. Wheelock Sr. was known to Superintendent Pratt because he had visited Dennison, James and Ida during commencement. Sophia, however, probably wasn't their mother, because she was only eight years older than Dennison. Also, there was a seven-year gap between Ida and Louisa. The older children, Dennison through Ida, must have been from a first wife. He must have remarried and had the younger ones with Sophia. Hugh's enrollment papers list James A. Wheelock as his father and Sophia as his mother. However, Joel's papers list his father as deceased due to old age and his mother as having died in childbirth. The boys' guardian was their older half-brother, Dennison. At the time they came to Carlisle, each had four living brothers and five living sisters in good health. One brother had died of alcoholism and a sister had died of tuberculosis. Hugh, called Hughie J. on the census, and Joel enrolled at Carlisle in 1905 and, at times, had an older sibling on campus, sometimes as bandmaster.

Like most children attending Carlisle, their names did not start showing up in school publications immediately upon arrival. Joel's name first appeared in the fall of 1908; Hugh's came later. Most of Joel's early mentions were for athletics, such as leading the "Devils" to victory in a football game played between his shop, the printers, and the blacksmiths. The following January, he played on the school's first inter-scholastic basketball team. In the spring, he earned his letter "C" in track by placing 4th in the 120-yard hurdles at the state intercollegiate track meet held in Harrisburg. He even raked in prizes at the 4th of July track meet held at the school as part of the festivities. Joel won a pair of running shoes for winning the 120-yard high hurdles for boys over 15 years old. He also won two dozen oranges for winning the 220-yard dash and another dozen for his share of the prize for placing 2nd in the 100-yard three-legged race with partner Joseph Loudbear. Lastly, he won a pair of tennis shoes for winning the 220-yard wheelbarrow race with teammates John Goslin and Levi Williams. Joel made quite a haul.

In late September 1909, Hugh Wheelock returned from outing and joined the football squad. Apparently, Joel had been on the squad previously because he ran for a long touchdown a week before in the Hotshots' game against Steelton. That fall Joel got considerable playing time as a halfback, generally at right halfback, and "showed up well" until he twisted his knee in the Bucknell game. He recovered and got into the game with Syracuse and made the trip to St. Louis and played in that game. A post-season description said that, at 18, he was the youngest man on the team.

Joel wrote a piece entitled "My Trip to Washington" for *The Carlisle Arrow* about traveling to the nation's capitol to play George Washington University. He also was credited as being part of the force that printed *The Arrow* and *The Indian Craftsman* and later for doing part of the composition on the program for that Athletic Banquet program. He played a clarinet solo for his class meeting and was elected captain of the Sophomores' basketball team. He was an all-around man about campus.

To further that image, in early January 1910, Joel won first prize in the two-step dance contest with Sara Hoxie as his partner at the Carlisle Indian Band reception. In the spring he continued to compete in several track events, gaining an occasionally 1st place. At commencement, he was awarded his industrial certificate as a compositor, but he remained in school. If anything, he expanded his range of extra-curricular activities to include the Invincible Debating Society without dropping any existing activities. He was made an officer both for his Junior Class (after commencement) and by the Invincibles. He even recited "The American Flag" as a Saturday evening school social.

The following autumn the Wheelock boys were back out on the gridiron; Hugh didn't yet get significant playing time, but Joel did. The *Philadelphia Public Ledger* was quite impressed with his play: "In [Pete] Hauser and [Joel] Wheelock they found backs of the heavy, slashing, plunging type that are as good as any playing in the East today." Although Carlisle failed to win any of its big games in 1910, Joel received frequent kudos for his play. One that stands out was from the *Philadelphia Press*: "Wheelock was another Indian who played a spectacular game. He was able to gain through the line many times, and was strong on defensive play. Wheelock shone particularly at recovering Hauser's lone forward passes, standing directly beyond center with his back toward the opponent's goal and by superhuman strength, keeping off Penn men until he had the ball safe in his arms."

In 1911, Joel took time out from his responsibilities as captain of the track team to play in the band, to give clarinet solos to class meetings, to serve as an officer of the Invincibles and of his class, to serve as Lt. Governor of the Model Government afternoon session, and, in the spring, to give his first speech as a Senior, "The Price of Success."

In February, for an assembly of the entire school, Hugh Wheelock performed in, "Brahmin, Jackal and Tiger, a three-act comedy with a good moral, artistic and up to the jungle standard of acting." After spending his summer at home, Hugh returned to school in September, when *The Arrow* reported, "The Seniors are rejoicing over the return of Joel Wheelock, who spent a most profitable vacation in Canada." It failed to mention exactly what he did during that vacation.

Both boys excelled in extra-curricular activities, but neither impressed his vocational instructor. E. K. Miller rated Joel's ability as a compositor as "Fair – Slow" although he considered him a willing worker with excellent behavior. Hugh's instructor was less kind, rating his ability as "not much good as a carpenter."

Hugh and Joel both made the varsity for 1911, arguably Carlisle's strongest team. However, with the return of Jim Thorpe and the maturation of some younger players, neither became a regular starter. Injuries to regulars gave them both opportunities to start, and they made the most of these opportunities. Joel stood out as right halfback, wingback in Warner's scheme, against Georgetown: "Wheelock was especially strong in helping to block opponents upon plays around his end of the line." Both got into the games and played well against the two Big Four teams the Indians defeated that year, Penn and Harvard. *The Carlisle Arrow* bragged, "The Carlisle line out-charged and out-played Harvard in every spot, and it was the Indian forwards who made it possible for the backs to gain. Carlisle was without the service of Captain Burd [sic], our star end, and Newashe was in such condition that he only played a short time, but the Wheelock brothers, Joel and 'Huge,' filled their positions so well that there was no apparent weakness anywhere in the line." Hugh played left tackle in both games, but Joel was needed at right end to stop the Crimson. The *Pittsburg Dispatch* summed up the season in its coverage of the Pitt game: "However, Thorpe wasn't the entire works; there were a few others white men as well as Indians. Newashe and Arcasa were some stars themselves, so were Powell and Wheelock." Both Wheelock brothers got into enough games and played well enough to letter that year.

Hugh must have joined the Standard Debating Society at some time because he and Cora Bresette won a prize, most likely for dancing, at the New Year's Mercer-Standard reception. "Huge" was also active with the YMCA, giving a talk at the April volunteer meeting. Hugh, along with several others, spent the summer of 1912 working at a large brickworks in Mt. Union, Pennsylvania and improving the quality of the town band. Known today for being the home of the biggest Easter grass factory in the U. S., at that time, Mt. Union, located 45 miles southeast of Altoona, claimed to be the world's largest manufactory of silica bricks. Hugh didn't return to his studies that fall. Instead, he got married and continued to work at the brickworks and play in the town band. He may have also played on or coached the town's football team. *The Arrow* did not give any information about his bride. It did report that he visited the school and attended a game at Franklin Field in Philadelphia. Perhaps he married a Carlisle girl.

Joel was even more heavily involved in extra-curricular activities in 1912 than he had been in previous years. He started the new year as the "star" of the Easterners vs. Westerners football game and was elected captain for 1912. A week or so later, he sang "Silent Night" in a quartet accompanied by a lantern light show for a YMCA – YWCA Union meeting. A week after that, he and Joseph Saracino debated successfully the proposition, "That Richard III was a worse monarch than Charles II," at a meeting of the Invincibles. The following week, also with the Invincibles, he delivered the declamation, "The Boss Sees You." And, of course, he competed in track again.

At commencement, Joel Wheelock's name was listed alongside those of other star athletes in the class of 1912, his class, that included future College Football Hall-of-Famers Gus Welch and Jim Thorpe. The Commencement Issue of *The Arrow* include a short poem he wrote:

Music is the art of prophets
> When J. W. hath forgot his notes,
> he makes as though a crumb were in
> his throat.

Joel again played football in the fall of 1912 but didn't get as much playing time as before on what was another powerhouse Carlisle team. *The Arrow* summarized his season: "Joel Wheelock is 5 ft. 9 in. tall, weighs 160 pounds, and is 22 years old. He is an Oneida from Wisconsin. Joel won his C by his work in the backfield when he relieved some regulars in important games. All he lacked to make a first-class back was fighting spirit and he showed considerable of this in the latter part of the—season."

Even though he had graduated and was now taking a commercial course, Joel continued his usual dizzying array of extra-curricular activities throughout the school year and gained an additional responsibility when he was promoted to captain of a set of troops. *The Arrow* commented a couple of times on his leadership. First: "It seems that everybody takes notice of Captain Wheelock's troop as they march over to the Dining Room." Then later: "If they keep up their good work, Captain Wheelock and his troop will receive some notice at the inaugural parade."

After completing the commercial course at Carlisle, Joel enrolled at the preparatory school for Lebanon Valley College (LVC) in Annville, Pennsylvania where he – big surprise – also played football and ran track for the Dutchmen. Down 10-0 against the Carlisle reserves, he donned a uniform, and according to the *1915 Bizarre*, "His presence fired the entire team with enthusiasm and for the first time during the game they showed what they were capable of doing." He quickly scored two touchdowns to snatch a victory from the Indian second team. Shortly after that the *Manitoba Free Press* (Canadian papers often ran article about Carlisle sports) ran a short critique: "Joe [sic] Wheelock, the famous Carlisle star of other years, is playing end [sic] for Lebanon Valley. Evidently Lebanon Valley plays them to a ripe old age." In a losing effort against Bucknell, he made a gutsy performance. LVC's newspaper, *College News*, reported, "Wheelock, although playing with a twisted ankle, a knee in not any too good shape, and a nose very nearly broken, stuck to his place and played his hardest during the whole time." He not only ran the ball for touchdowns and up the middle for tough yardage, but he was also their kicker.

In the winter and spring, he played basketball and ran track in their respective seasons. Joel visited Carlisle several times during the school year. Could he have left a girlfriend behind? In August, he wrote Superintendent Lipps asking for trainfare from Mt. Union, where he had been working, to Carlisle to assist Pop Warner with the football team. Lipps did not receive the request well: "Athletics are being conducted differently at Carlisle than has been the custom and no inducements whatever can be held out to students who desire to be enrolled or to former students who desire to return to school for the purpose outlined in your letter." He would not be coaching at Carlisle so returned to Annville to play for LVC.

In October 1914, Lebanon Valley College beat Gettysburg for the first time in 20 years due, in great part, to halfback Wheelock's efforts both in smashing through the line and skirting its ends. Joel was named to the All-Pennsylvania backfield at the end of the season. In December, *College News* included Henry L. Wilder's selections for the "All-Time-All-Lebanon Valley team." After just two seasons with the Dutchmen, Joel was named left halfback on the first team of LVC's all-time greats. A couple of months later, he was appointed assistant coach for the Blue and White for the upcoming year.

Joel Wheelock's weekends were filled with football in 1915, assisting with the coaching for Lebanon Valley College on Saturdays and playing for the Altoona Indians on Sundays. He was joined in Altoona by his brother, Hugh. Due to the close proximity between Mt. Union and Altoona, it may have been Hugh that arranged for the two to play alongside several of their old Carlisle teammates. Joel and Hugh played for Altoona again in 1916.

By June 1917, when they registered for the WWI draft, both Joel and Hugh had found gainful employment, if only for the summer. Joel worked as a tool and die maker at the Bethlehem Steel plant in Lebanon, Pennsylvania and Hugh was a deputy sheriff in Mt. Union but was then single. Either his wife died or his 1912 marriage didn't work out.

Joel served in the army during WWI but, before joining up, served as head football coach at LVC for the 1917 season. This was quite a feat for a student still in the prep school. According to the *The Quittapahilla 1919*: "The success of the season depended on 'Chief' and he did his best which was excellent. He was unbiased in picking men for their respective positions. He gave them new plays which were very effective, also new tactics on the defence that helped a great deal. 'Chief' had the faculty of bawling you out when you didn't do the right thing, but that only made you fight the harder. On the whole he was a good coach and deserves praise for developing such a fine squad out of so many raw recruits, for we must remember that only a few of our last year's Varsity men came back this year." The school's yearbook recorded 1917 as a 3-4 season but *cfbdatawarehouse.com* includes two more games, a forfeit by Temple and a 73-0 thrashing of Millersburg, giving Wheelock a 5-4 record for his only year as a head coach.

It is not known what Hugh did during that time period, although he did likely serve because he was later a member of the VFW. After the war, Joel organized an All-Indian band which toured widely. Musicians in his large band included former Carlisle students, one of whom was James Garvie. His grandson, Jay Garvie, has a large photograph in which his grandfather is sitting in the front row. Wheelock is dressed in Oneida regalia including a war bonnet.

The 1920 census lists Hugh as divorced, living in Lewistown, Pennsylvania and working as a helper in an ice plant. The 1925 Oneida rolls listed both brothers as being married. In 1930, Hugh, 36, was still living in Lewistown but was then working as a laborer at the steel works. His then wife, Annie Halbert, 49, was a white woman originally from Virginia. He was 19 when first married and she had been 22. If these ages were within a few years of being correct, Annie would not have been Hugh's first wife.

Joel died in Oneida, New York on February 18, 1932. It is not clear if he was visiting family or on a concert tour with a band. He was survived by his wife.

"Chief" Wheelock, Hugh, was well-known in western Pennsylvania for playing bass and tenor drums in various bands including the Tyrone Division (of the Pennsylvania Railroad) band and his brother Joel's all-Indian band, the Veterans Of Foreign Wars Band and the Methodist Church orchestra. He traveled with the J. E. Eshchew Rodeo Indian Band during the 1939-40 season. He worked as a bricklayer's helper at the Standard Steel Works in Burnham for his day job.

Hugh Wheelock died in November 1943, in Lewistown, Pennsylvania, a week after having a gangrenous appendix removed. He was recovering well and was expected to be discharged from the hospital when he was stricken fatally. His cause of death was listed as coronary occlusion.

The Wheelocks were the family who arguably best represented the things that made the Carlisle Indian School famous: its band and its football team. Other band members, such as James Garvie, played football on shop or band teams but didn't make the varsity starting line-up. The Wheelocks were unique in that regard.

They Also Played

The lives of three other Carlisle football players, who don't neatly fit any of the groupings, deserve to be included, and the story would not be complete without them. This chapter presents Carlisle's first Walter Camp First Team All-American, a moderately famous quarterback who later became a physician and the player whose injury almost prevented the story from happening.

Boston Post, November 29, 1912

25

Isaac Seneca

Isaac Seneca; *U. S. Army*
Military History Institute

Isaac Seneca; *Cumberland County*
Historical Society, Carlisle, PA

Name: Isaac Seneca	**Nickname:**
DOB: 10/7/1875	**Height:** 5'9"
Weight: 155	**Age:** 23
Tribe: Seneca	**Home:** Cattaraugus Reservation, NY
Parents: Isaac Seneca, Seneca; unknown, Seneca	
Early Schooling: unknown	
Later Schooling:	
Honors:	

Carlisle's First Walter Camp All-American

Isaac Seneca, Jr. was not alone at Carlisle as his brother, Victor, and sister, Nancy, attended at the same time he did. That their mother had died some years before and his father, Chief of the Senecas on the Cattaraugus Reservation, had remarried may have had something to do with the decision to send these children to the Carlisle Indian School.

Isaac spent much of his first year at Carlisle away from school on outing with a W. German in Newtown, Pennsylvania, possibly learning the blacksmith trade. He was gone from school nearly a year from mid-June 1894 to mid-May 1895. Two weeks later, he returned to his outing home and stayed there until mid-September. When actually at Carlisle and not on outing, Isaac immersed himself in the school routine and played football for his shop team, the Blacksmiths. After commencement, he returned to the country for the summer, his last summer outing.

1896 was Isaac Seneca's first year on the varsity and he got enough playing time to be included in the team photo, an honor extended to only 14 players. The *New York World* reported on a major incident in the Yale game in which he played a major role:

"Cayou had retired in favor of Seneca, and the big chief ripped things, while the crowd howled in glee. The second half was nearing its close. There had been a tremendous scrimmage. The interference of the Indians was marvelous. Big Seneca was plunging through the line, going like a steam-engine, when he was tackled. As he fell Jamison grabbed the ball. Chauncey made a grab for him and missed. Instantly three of his mates were at Jamison's side. They galloped wildly down the field, making a touchdown.

"Now, it was as fair a play as could have been. But it was not allowed. Hickok had sounded his whistle, indicating that the ball was down, that is, on the ground and not in play. The error was made by Hickok, as he himself admitted, because the ball was not dead. But inasmuch as he had sounded the whistle there was nothing to do but to bring the ball back. The crowd howled and hissed at the decision for five minutes.

"The Indians were furious, not so much so as their teachers, however, and Hickok was so unhappy that he didn't know what to do. The professors wanted to take the Indians from the field, but they preferred to play on.

"They returned to the game. They played more determinedly than ever. You could see them standing calm, and perfectly motionless and at the word springing forward with tremendous intensity and fighting with everything in them.

"They never panted as did the Yale men; they never trembled with eagerness.

"It looked as if they must carry things before them and win another touchdown, so tremendous was their struggle. But the whistle sounded and the game was over."

The Indian Helper discussed the reaction to the Yale game: "Rarely has a contest excited such widespread attention and voluminous comment in all of the best papers of the land. Dr. Lyman Abbott in his pulpit on the following Sunday evening referred to the unfair treatment of the Indians and spoke of their noble manhood. Much of the comment was owing to what is conceded by the best football experts to be an unjust decision of the referee, which ruled out a touch-down by the Indians." A sad irony was that the referee, William O. Hickok, was also the Indians' coach. Not lost on journalists was that he was also a Yale man, having been an All-American guard in 1893 and 1894 for the Elis. He admitted that he had blown his whistle too early. Some likened him to a corrupt Indian agent.

Isaac wasn't as involved with extra-curricular activities as were many other football players, so he didn't receive much mention in the school's publications. He did receive notice in March 1897, however, for throwing a surprise party for his sister when she left for Medico-Chirurgical Hospital in Philadelphia where she had enrolled in a nursing program.

Seneca spent the summer of 1897 at home and returned to Carlisle in time for football season. He continued to improve his skills but played in the shadows of such players as Frank Cayou, Martin Wheelock and Bemus Pierce. The most tragic accident in Carlisle Indian School history happened on November 6, 1897, when the team was returning home from the Penn game in Philadelphia. Newspapers across the country reported on the sad event. *The Indian Helper* provided more detail:

"On the way back from Philadelphia last Saturday night, when a little way out of the city Victor Seneca put his head out of the car window and was hit by something which cut a great gash in his head causing concussion of the brain, from the effects of which he died the next day. Victor came in 1895 and had reached the third grade. He was a good, quiet, steady young man of 18 years, well esteemed by his classmates and all with whom he associated. The sad accident cast an abiding gloom over the school. On Monday night his teacher, Miss Carter, and brother Isaac Seneca, went with the remains to Versailles, N. Y., the home of the deceased. Nancy Seneca, class '97, who is at the Madico Chirurgical Institute of Philadelphia, was summoned to the death bed of her brother who she had seen and talked with but a few hours before in Philadelphia. It was a great shock to her."

The school administration often made special arrangements for the students to be able to attend the Penn game because it was a major rivalry and, of the big games, it was played closest to home. Victor had probably gone to see his brother play. One cannot imagine how this freak accident impacted Isaac, his sister and the other students.

Isaac learned the blacksmithing trade well and was soon leading the other boys. In August 1898, he took charge over summer vacation as *The Indian Helper* reported:

"One of the most interesting places on the grounds to visit is the blacksmith shop, especially when the anvil is ringing to the tune of busy Indian boys working without an instructor, as now, when Mr. Harris is off on his vacation. Isaac Seneca is in charge and has two or three boys under him. The deftness with which they hammer bolts, braces, clevises and what-not into shape handling red hot iron with the ease that putty is manipulated in the fingers, speaks volumes for the instruction they received and would be a revelation to those who think that Indians can never learn to work skillfully."

The 1898 football season was the last one Isaac Seneca played in the shadows of more famous teammates. Perhaps it had to do with Pop Warner arriving at Carlisle in 1899; perhaps not. Regardless, Isaac Seneca came into his own that year. These year-end notes put it into perspective:

"At a meeting of the Carlisle Indian football players, Isaac L. Seneca was elected captain of the team for the season of 1900 to succeed Martin L. Wheelock. He was the unanimous choice of the players. Seneca has played three years on the team. He belongs to the Seneca tribe of New York. He is twenty-one years old is 5 feet 10 inches in height and weighs 150 pounds. He is a fierce player and one of the best punters in the team. His position is right halfback ... he made a number of brilliant runs, twice carrying three men over the goal line. The Indians are much pleased with their successful season on the gridiron. The season was a big success in a financial way also, the Indians clearing about $10,000."

Walter Camp was so impressed with Isaac's play that he took the unprecedented step of naming an Indian to his All-America First Team. Prior to that, only six schools (Harvard, Princeton, Yale, Penn, Cornell and Chicago) had had their players named to Camp's All-America First Team. Seneca brought the total to seven, with the addition of Carlisle to this elite list. Some thought Seneca to be faster and stronger than Jim Thorpe and that is quite a comparison. A description in a 1909 edition of *The Indian Craftsman* tolled his virtues: "Seneca, Hendricks and Thorpe were great halfbacks. Seneca was a fast running back, full of fire and when not carrying the ball for good distances was always interfering for the runner. He was also a great defensive man."

Isaac graduated with his class in the spring of 1900 but, although elected captain, did not return to lead the team that fall. However, he was not done playing football. The Greensburg, Pennsylvania independent team, as part of a move to improve chances for a championship, hired Seneca for the 1900 season. On paper the team looked like a world-beater, but some losses caused it to suffer financially. PFRA Research provided an anecdote that summed up their season:

"The Greenies' season turned on the games with Latrobe. Three had been scheduled, with the first at Greensburg on October 27. A disappointing but spirited crowd of a little over 2,000 showed. When a fight broke out between Greensburg's Isaac Seneca and Latrobe's Al Kennedy, the crowd joined in to produce a general donnybrook. That was most of the excitement for Greensburg fans, as Latrobe handed their heroes a third straight loss, 6-0."

The Greenies ceased operation near the end of the season. That may also have been the end of Isaac's football career because no documentation of him playing for other teams has been found to date.

By the next summer, Isaac Seneca's name started appearing on rolls of government employees. In 1901 he was working as a blacksmith at the Cheyenne and Arapahoe Agency in Oklahoma. A November issue of *The Red Man and Helper* wrote that he was "enjoying Western life, particularly the hunting of quails and ducks." Whether he was hunting for it or not, he found something else while working there - a wife.

Rosa Frass was the orphaned daughter of a Cheyenne woman and a white man, probably from Germany. Rosa had attended Haskell Institute so she knew English. Otherwise, she and Isaac would not have had a common language.

In 1904, *The Arrow* reported on him: "Isaac Seneca class 1900, now employed at Chilocco in ordering the *Arrow* says: 'Be sure and shoot or aim one shot at Chilocco Indian School, and you'll hit me there.' Isaac was transferred from blacksmithing in the service to engineering." Some time prior to January 1907, he was married, living in Darlington, Oklahoma, and working as an instructor in blacksmithing at Chilocco Indian School. He and Bloss Jaloma, his assistant, also operated a blacksmith and wagon shop to meet the demands of the school for all repairs of iron work.

Either he, Rosa or the two of them had been investing their money because, at that time they owned a quarter section in Texas, a quarter section in Oklahoma, property of indeterminate size in old Mexico and building lots in Oklahoma City. He said that he had but $200 in savings at that time.

Their son, Russell, was born in 1906, so Isaac and Rosa were probably married some time before that date. Isaac received a $100 raise from $680 to $780 in 1910, a significant increase at that time. The timing was good because their daughter, Maurine Vivian Seneca, was born that year. In 1914, *The Arkansas City Traveler* reported, "Seneca is a cracking good mechanic and has been a very efficient blacksmith at Chilocco for some time. He is a fine specimen of the athletic Indian and is a handsome fellow to boot."

In 1930, he was still working as a blacksmith but was widowed and living in Ponca City, Oklahoma. Later in the 1930s, it appears that he and Maurine moved back to the Cattaraugus Reservation, perhaps to be near his aging father. They were living near Irving, New York in 1937.

Louis A. Island

Louis Island; *Cumberland County Historical Society, Carlisle, PA*

Sgt. Louis Island; *Iris Davis*

Name: Louis A. Island	**Nickname:**
DOB: 7/12/1890 or 7/12/1893	**Height:** 5'5"
Weight: 137	**Age:** 21
Tribe: Oneida	**Home:** Green Bay, WI
Parents: Louis Island, Oneida; unknown, Oneida	
Early Schooling: Oneida Boarding School likely	
Later Schooling: Haskell Institute	
Honors:	

Drugless Physician

Louis Abraham Island was first enrolled in 1898. However, the records of that enrollment have been lost as has documentation of his birth, believed by family members to have been in Canada, if such paperwork ever existed. Island was somewhere between five and eight years old when he first came to Carlisle. His father, also named Louis, was alive in 1905 to re-enroll his son for a second term, but his mother was deceased by that time. Like most small boys at Carlisle, he received little mention in the school newspaper during his early years at the school. Louis Island's first mention in *The Red Man and Helper* listed him as one of the students returning from summer outing for the new school term in September 1900. His next mention was over two years later when he scored a touchdown for the Blacksmiths in the shop championship game against the Printers.

Island became a freshman in the fall of 1903, at which time he was elected president of the Class of 1907. Louis was very active in school affairs. He joined the Invincible Debating Society where he frequently spoke, participated in debates and became an officer. In December 1906, the Invincibles elected him president. Sometime in his Carlisle career, Island shifted from blacksmithing to printing.

Though only 5' 5-1/4" tall and weighing 148 pounds, Louis went out for football and made the varsity in 1906, playing quarterback behind Archie Libby. He got into the early games and onto the scoreboard by kicking a 30-yard field goal against Albright College. After that, his major playing time came with the second team. He drop-kicked a field goal against Dickinson Seminary in Williamsport, Pennsylvania but missed the kick after Theodore Owl's touchdown.

In the winter, Louis Island played left forward on the basketball team that represented Carlisle well against Franklin and Marshall College. In the spring, he played baseball on the school team. Somehow, he also found time to run track. He showed another side of his athletic prowess and chivalry at the Senior outing when he quickly donned a bathing suit to retrieve a purse a damsel dropped into the lake. A week later, he spoke at the local Methodist church he regularly attended. Staying at Carlisle over the summer, he pitched for the Printer's Devils against the Velvet Treaders, a team made of faculty and staff members, trouncing the elders 21-7.

Frank Mt. Pleasant was shifted back to quarterback in 1907, keeping Mike Balenti and Louis Island from moving up on the depth charts. Island and Balenti got into the early-season games and received good reviews. After the Villanova game, *The Arrow* reported, "His [Mt. Pleasant's] successor, Island, worked very creditably." *The Sentinel* echoed those sentiments: "Mt. Pleasant is better than ever in running with the ball and he handles the team well, although Island does as well in the latter respect as he." A couple of weeks later against Bucknell, the reports weren't as positive: "Mt. Pleasant was not in the game and Island filled his position most of the time, until replaced by Balenti. The former ran the team fairly well, but was poor on running back punts and was responsible for some heavy losses. Balenti was also weak in handling the ball. Both seemed to be anxious to get in the lime-light by kicking drop-kicks, and Island did succeed in scoring in this manner." He also kicked a goal after touchdown. Filling in for a player who many thought should have received first team All-America honors is never easy, especially for players who would have been starters for most other teams. Because Mt. Pleasant was injured so badly in the Minnesota game, he had to sit out the big game with Chicago. Student reporter William Yankee Joe observed, "Every student thought that it was up to Island who has been backing up Mt. Pleasant during the season. But when we heard the line-up and with Balenti at quarter back some of the students were a little shaky." *The Arrow* reported that those fears were unfounded: "Balenti and Island ran the play without a hitch, and the accurate kicking of Hauser, coupled with his slashing runs and line plunging, made up for the ground-gaining and scoring abilities of the regular quarterback."

After football season, Louis focused his attention on his numerous other activities until graduation in April 1908. In addition to his diploma, he received an industrial certificate in Printing, Two-Thirds. Apparently there was another third to the printing program. However, graduation from Carlisle didn't end his education.

In the fall of 1908, Louis Island enrolled at Haskell Institute. He also joined the football team. The purple and gold Fightin' Indians played such teams as Missouri, Texas, Nebraska, Texas A & M, LSU and Alabama. After two years in Kansas, 18-year-old Island returned to the reservation but thought of the Cumberland Valley.

From West DePere, Wisconsin, Andrew Doxtator wrote Carlisle, "Louis Island is returned student and he wishes to go back to Carlisle again. This is all puples [sic] I could get." Island re-enrolled at Carlisle, this time in the commercial course, on September 10, 1910, and played football again. Again a solid player but not a star, Louis completed his career at the Indian school but remained nearby.

Island took a job at the Hershey Chocolate Company, which made visits to campus practical. On March 17, 1911, *The Arrow* reported that Louis and William Newashe, also employed at Hershey, played on the Hershey YMCA basketball team against their old school. Their old classmates applauded their play loudly. In May the *Harrisburg Telegraph* announced that Louis had registered as a student at Lebanon Valley College in Annville, Pennsylvania.

In the fall of 1913, Louis Island started his professional football career. He played end for the Jackson, Michigan All-Stars or Independents, as they were sometimes called. Made up largely of University of Michigan players no longer eligible because of grades or other infractions, the Independents were a competitive team. In fact, they claimed the southern Michigan championship until defeated by the Fort Wayne Friars in a game played in a snowstorm on the Friars' home field, League Park, in Fort Wayne, Indiana. The Friars were so impressed by Island that they hired him for the 1914 season. He played well enough in 1914 to be brought back in 1915. The Friars went 7-1-1 with him playing right end and quarterback. He would have likely been back for another season, but an off-field accident ended his playing days.

At some point, Louis located in Fort Wayne and took a job as a punch-press operator at the local General Electric plant. In his spare time, he officiated whatever game was in season for area teams. In early May 1916, his playing career ended as the result of a punch-press accident in which his left thumb was crushed. Island lost the best part of a month's work due to the injury but returned to the same job in late May.

That fall, Louis began his coaching career by taking charge of the West End junior team. Because the West End of Fort Wayne, now a historic district, was populated by many of the movers and shakers of the town, Island very likely coached the scions of important families and made contacts that would serve him well in the future. At the beginning of the season, pundits considered it the strongest team West End had ever fielded. Louis's team played well most of the season but lost their last regular-season game to the rival Badgers, throwing the city junior championship into turmoil with three teams making claims to it. Once football season ended, he began officiating basketball games. Island continued officiating through the winter. He had arranged a nice life for a bachelor: he had a job that covered his living expenses and in his free time he participated in his first love – sports. This idyllic life was rudely interrupted by events thousands of miles away across the Atlantic.

The June 27, 1917 edition of *The Fort Wayne Sentinel* crowed, "When Battery D [sic] leaves here the latter part of this week or the first of next week its roll will include the name of one of the best athletes of the city, Louis Island. Louis went to headquarters last night and signed up, ready to do his bit as a true American wherever the unit may be ordered…. When he leaves the city it will be with the best wishes of a host of friends and admirers." That day's *Fort Wayne Journal-Gazette* gave him a send off: "Believing that he, a true American, should 'do his bit,' Louis Island, the well-known football player, appeared at battery B recruiting headquarters last night and signed up for service with the artil-lery…. Island should make good with the battery as he had four years' infantry training at

Carlisle. It is a sure thing that if he plays the artillery game as hard as he did the gridiron game there are bound to be some German lines smashed and a few plays broken up. Here's to you, Louis, and success."

Three days later, *The Fort Wayne Daily News* reported that Pvt. Island was given the honor of carrying the unit's flag. The flag was purchased with funds raised by contributions collected by Mrs. F. H. Banks. "Lieutenant L. F. Woods received the flag and then handed it to Private Louis Island, saying that he knew of no one in the battery more worthy to carry the colors." About six weeks later, *The Journal-Gazette* covered a parade: "When Battery B paraded yesterday as United States regulars, Fred Fosmire, of German and Irish parentage, and Louis Island, a full-blooded Indian, carried the Stars and Stripes and artillery guidon. Thus does Americanism unite all under the flag in common service to the nation." On August 16, Louis A. Island was promoted to the rank of sergeant. It isn't known if the fact that 18 men failed to pass the physical examination affected his promotion.

Battery B shipped over to France, arriving in November 1917, as a component of the 150th United States Field Artillery of the Rainbow Division. He was engaged in fighting at Chateau Thierry, Verdun, second battle of the Marne, St. Mihiel and the Argonne, where he was on the firing line when the armistice was signed. He accompanied the army of occupation into Germany and was stationed at Coblenz until sent home. In April 1919, Sgt. Island and seven others, one of whom was dead, were cited for "especial bravery" for serving the guns while under fire during the American drive at Chateau Thierry. The May 11 *Journal-Gazette* praised him with the headline, "Friar Grid Star Is Welcomed Home With Batteries B and D." A photo of him accompanied the article. "Loie, we greet you. May you live long and prosper."

And that was exactly what he intended to do. Soon Louis Island's name was showing up again on the sports page for coaching football. He continued his life of working at mundane jobs while coaching and officiating on the side until the late 1920s. His employment history during this time included working as a gardener and as a meter man. But in 1928, he had no occupation. This likely means that he was attending a professional school to better his position in life because the next year he was listed on the Fort Wayne city directory as being a chiropractor. The 1930 census listed his occupation as drugless physician, which was likely another term for chiropractor at that time. Indiana didn't license chiropractors until 1955, so he may have been practicing under some other title. In some states, chiropractors practiced as drugless physicians to avoid going to jail for practicing medicine without a license, which happened to some of those who called themselves chiropractors.

Dr. Island, as he was now called, had made a major life change in the early 1920s. He married a white woman named Phebe Harsh from Mentone, Indiana. Phebe was a farm girl who had four sisters but no brothers. So, Louis was the only young male at family gatherings for a while. Niece Iris Davis and nephew Dick Boganwright knew him only as small children but recall that he was "a nice, friendly guy" who liked children. Outgoing without being loud, Louis was soon well thought of by Phebe's family. He and Phebe had a son, Harsh Louis Island. Just as Louis had settled into a career and family life, the unexpected struck. In September 1933, Dr. Island died of tuberculosis. Phebe lived 22 years more. Their son, who was also known as Louis, died young as had his father, but of muscular dystrophy thought to be the result of an infection acquired in the Korean War.

Stacy Matlock

Stacy Matlock, Pawnee Chief;
Fred Wardecker

Name: Stacy Matlock	**Nickname:** Young Chief
DOB: circa 1865	**Height:**
Weight:	**Age:**
Tribe: Pawnee	**Home:** Pawnee Reservation, OK
Parents: Stacy Matlock, white; unknown, Pawnee	
Early Schooling: Pawnee Reservation School	
Later Schooling: Lincoln Institute, possibly	
Honors:	

Lone Chief

"Stacy Matlock like most other Indians of his age knows very little about the time and place of his birth. He was born, probably in Nebraska before the removal of the tribe [Pawnee] to this reservation [Oklahoma]. When a school was started, he was a pupil under the tutelage of Mary L. Burgess. He attended school at the agency until the year 1883 when he was taken to Carlisle, Pa." *The Arrow's* account of Stacy Matlock's life is accurate as far as it goes. Various census records place his birth in the 1866-1868 timeframe, which would most likely mean that he was born in Nebraska. He likely participated, to the extent that a small child can, in the 1873-1875 migration from what remained of Pawnee lands in Nebraska to Oklahoma. This removal was not due to war with the United States as the Pawnee never fought U. S. soldiers. In fact, they served as scouts during various Indian wars. The reasons for relocating were a depleted food supply and war with the Sioux.

Stacy's original name is lost to posterity because his first teacher, a white woman, found the Pawnee names difficult to pronounce and assigned English names to the students. Young Stacy was probably named in honor of a white man who had been working to build respect between the whites and Indians in Nebraska, Kansas and Oklahoma. Both men's last names were often spelled Matlack. Stacy's father was an important man in the tribe because young Stacy was in line to be a hereditary chief. Nothing is known about his mother.

Coming to Carlisle in 1883 after his father died, Stacy Matlock was very active in school activities and a favorite of the Man-on-the-band-stand. In December 1885, he was promoted to Sergeant of Company A and by 1890 he was in charge of several class rooms. Matlock was quite active in the YMCA both on campus and in regional events. He was active in the Standard Debating Society and was one of the students chosen to debate the merits of the Dawes Act at his commencement in 1890. His trade was harness making. He chose to go on outing after graduation and earn some money rather than to return home.

He returned to school in the fall as assistant disciplinarian but was called home in September to see his sick mother. When he returned in November, he brought a new student back with him. According to *The Indian Helper*, "Stacy reports the Pawnees as having improved since he was home last. They have better homes and better farms. He speaks well of nearly all the returned Pawnee boys and girls. There are one or two exceptions."

Later that month, he was involved in an incident that influenced the development of organized sports in the U. S. Football at Carlisle up to this time was of the intra-mural variety. Occasionally students played pick-up games with students at other local institutions, but nothing was formalized. Stacy participated in one of those games with far-ranging complications. An article in the school newspaper, likely written by the superintendent, explained what had happened:

> "One of the most serious accidents that has ever happened at our school occurred last Saturday afternoon during the foot-ball game on the Dickinson College athletic grounds between a college team and one composed of our Indian boys. The game had only begun when in the rush Stacy Matlack fell, was trampled upon and received what the doctors call a comminuted fracture of the tibia. In plain English the large bone of the leg was broken in two places. One break is transverse and about 3 ½ inches above the ankle; the other is oblique and about the middle of the bone. He has suffered intensely at times, but everything possible is being done to make him comfortable. That Stacy is a man of strong constitution is greatly in his favor, and he will no doubt be out on crutches before long and will in time completely recover the use of his leg."

Pratt later wrote about his dislike for what he considered a brutal game and why he banned students from playing football with other schools. He considered Stacy one of his best students and did not want additional injuries. Stacy recovered and was soon involved in school activities again.

In July 1891, Stacy Matlock was one of four Carlislians who attended Moody's School for Bible Study in Northfield, Massachusetts. Stacy was selected to give a talk about missionary work in Indian Territory. He said, "In the olden times the white people did not dare to go to church without being armed for fear of being killed by Indians. Now it is reversed. The Indian does not dare to go without being armed for fear of being killed by the white men, what are called cowboys. They are trying to make the Indians quiet by shooting. Instead of the gun take the Bible to him."

That fall Stacy was appointed disciplinarian of the Fort Totten Indian School located near Devils Lake, North Dakota. This was Matlock's first position in the Indian Service. However, it didn't last long because, at about 25 years of age he was back at Carlisle as a student in March 1892. After a short period, he returned to the Pawnee Agency. In August 1893, he informed his friends at Carlisle that he and fellow Carlisle alum William Morgan had become district government farmers. Within a couple of years he married Ella, about whom little is known other than she was born in Oklahoma Territory in 1874 and was carried on the Pawnee rolls. In 1895, they had a daughter named Cecelia.

Stacy may have gotten more education, possibly at Lincoln Institute in Philadelphia, because in 1900 he worked as a bank clerk at the Arkansas Valley Bank near Tulsa. In 1901 he was appointed to the position of issue clerk at the Ute Agency in Utah by the Commissioner of Indian Affairs. However, he must have been keeping in touch with Carlisle through this time. The December 15, 1904 issue of *The Arrow* brought the news that Stacy had returned to Carlisle as Assistant Disciplinarian and brought Ellie and five new students with him. The Matlocks set up housekeeping in the cottage formerly occupied by a Mr. Weber. A month later Stacy made a trip to Washington, DC to conduct some business with the government on behalf of his tribe. He stayed in the city a couple of weeks and brought three influential Pawnee chiefs back with him to visit Carlisle. Stacy immersed himself in the busy routine that came with his position. One of his more pleasant duties was to visit the meetings of the student organizations. In December 1906, he gave a talk to the Standard Debating Society about its membership of 20 years prior when he was a student. After over two years of working at Carlisle, the Matlocks returned to Oklahoma where he worked at the Pawnee County Bank. But their comfortable life there did not last long.

Tragedy struck in October 1907 when Ellie contracted typhoid fever and died within two weeks. Stacy, now 41, and Cecelia, 13, were left without a wife and mother. Stacy was not about to remain a widower for long.

In early 1908, Eagle Chief, the principal chief of the Pawnees, passed away, leaving a leadership void. Stacy, grandson of Pipe Chief, was selected to fill that position and took the title of Young Chief. Soon after that he brought a delegation from his tribe to Washington. On that trip, he visited Carlisle. There he met or, more likely, became reacquainted with Blanche Bill, a 21-year-old Pawnee student. A handwritten note in Stacy's student file recorded the event: "Married Blanche Bill, who was next in relative line when his wife died. Married at Friedman's." Pawnee customs dictated who would replace young wives who died. This was often an unmarried sister of the deceased. They were soon married and returned to Oklahoma. No mention of their wedding was found in *The Carlisle Arrow*, possibly because of the age difference.

This union was blessed with two children: Chauncey F. in 1909 and Bessie V. four years later. During this period, Stacy made annual trips to Washington to conduct business for the tribe and visited Carlisle while in the East. He had multiple reasons for these visits because his oldest daughter, Cecelia, was enrolled at Carlisle. After a rocky start, she was soon in the middle of school activities as her father had been.

Stacy received a report that Cecelia had demonstrated poor industry in her work in the laundry, causing him to intercede on her behalf. He wrote Friedman, asking him to "go slow with her, please do not punish her right away, go slow with her, or else send her home for her punishment. She never work[ed] in her life, but she can learn as she grows older. Now Mr. Friedman take the matter up for me as a brother in Mason." Friedman responded, "I have also investigated the matter and have given instructions for those in charge of the girls to be patient with her. She is large for her age and rather slow in her movements, but the girl seems willing enough to learn how to work and I am sure that there will be a decided improvement in her report on industry if a sufficient amount of patience and tact is exercised in her behalf." Based on later reports, things worked out for Cecelia.

A 1912 *Philadelphia Record* article described Matlock as being a prime example of a new type of Indian chief:

> "This up-to-date aborigine is of massive build and in his immobile countenance one may-read the stoicism of his nature. Here his resemblance to the old-style Indian chief ends, however. Matlock dresses in the most modern kind of clothes and does not have to be led around by an interpreter. He was graduated from the [Carlisle] school in 1890, having been one of the early students here....
>
> "'Young Chief' is a match mentally for the most astute of Indian agents, and is fortunate in being able to deal in person with the Interior Department and the Federal Senators and Representatives with whom he has relations. He is now in Washington, arranging to have the Government compensate his tribe under an old treaty in an amount of money that will run into several millions of dollars."

Back in Oklahoma, he continued to work as a bank clerk and interpreter.

In the 1920s, Young Chief allowed ethnomusicologist Frances Denmore to observe some of the Pawnee rituals:

> "The ceremony of Painting the Buffalo Skull is held every spring by the Chaui Band of Pawnee and is in [the] charge of Mr. Stacy Matlock, a prominent member of that band. The closing events of the ceremony are the Buffalo and Lance dances, which were witnessed by the writer through the courtesy of Mr. Matlock, no other white person being present. The ceremony and dances were held in a large earth lodge, several miles south of the town of Pawnee. The opening of the lodge was toward the east. At some distance was a framework, probably that of a sweat lodge. Only members of the Buffalo Society were admitted to the painting of the skull, but during the Buffalo dance the skull painted a few days previously, lay on a folded blanket in front of the 'altar' which was opposite the entrance. This occasion and the Lance dance held a few days later afforded exceptional opportunities to listen to Pawnee songs, but the semidarkness of the lodge and the solemnity of the occasion precluded the taking of notes upon either the music or the details of the ceremonial dances."

Note: Pawnees' culture differed significantly from that of their neighbors. For example, the sun dance was not an important ritual for them.

By 1925, Matlock was known as Lone Chief as he was the sole surviving Pawnee principal chieftain. In October 1925, Pawnee and Sioux chiefs smoked the peace pipe to signify the making an end to historic hostilities. According to Marie Herrin of *The Lincoln Star*, the sticking point in arranging the peace-making ceremony was that some survivors of Massacre Canon, where 156 Pawnee men, women and children were slaughtered after Sioux scouts surprised their hunting party near present-day Trenton, Nebraska, felt the 52-year-old wounds to be too fresh to be forgotten. Herrin wrote, "Of the Pawnees, Chief Ruling Hisson, who is 105 years old, John Haymond, and Chiefs Walking Son and

Leading Fox were all survivors, while among the Sioux, Chiefs Spotted Weasel and Flies Above were the only ones who had actually taken part in the battle. The others of the two parties were younger men and women, sons and daughters of survivors who have now answered the call to the Happy Hunting Ground. But these younger Pawnees and Sioux had inherited their elders' hatred for each other." When the time came to actually smoke the pipe, Ruling Hisson could not do it because the memory of his wife and three children being murdered senselessly still haunted him. "'You smoke if you want to. I can't. Sioux kill my wife – my children.' And he raised his hand palm outward to the Great Spirit Terahwah, calling down once more the Pawnee curse on the Sioux." The others smoked and made peace.

Herrin's article also mentioned that, in addition to being a Carlisle graduate, Stacy Matlock was a Knight Templar and a Shriner. Other newspaper articles remarked that he had taken on all outward aspects of modern civilization.

In 1931, Lone Chief played a key role in initiating John Philip Sousa into the Pawnee tribe. Sousa was dubbed Chief Singer of the Pawnees. Stacy stood next to Sousa in a photo of the event in which the inductee wore his bandleader's uniform.

In 1934, the U. P. reported that Stacy had changed his position on drinking from one of abstinence: "'Before prohibition it was illegal to give or sell Indians whisky. Since we were denied the right to drink intoxicants, we couldn't see why the white men should, so we were for prohibition.' The ban against selling wine and beer to Indians died with [the introduction of] prohibition." It appears that his positions were based on equal rights as opposed to the merits of drinking alcoholic beverages.

Stacy Matlock lived to be about 74 years old, a ripe old age for a man of his generation, dying on July 7, 1939, after suffering a stroke some time previous to that. He was survived by his second wife, Blanche, who died in 1970.

The book has now come full circle. The story of the player whose injury almost prevented Carlisle from ever fielding a football team has been told. Perhaps his broken leg and the ban against football helped build the resolve that Carlisle students showed in convincing Pratt to change his mind in 1893 and in their play on the gridiron. The author hopes that this is a beginning, not an ending, because so many Carlisle students' life stories remain to be researched, and so many other interesting ones wait to be told.

Appendices

Carlisle Indians Inducted into
the College Football Hall of Fame

Player*	Position	Year Inducted
Albert Exendine	End	1970
Joe Guyon	Halfback/Tackle	1971
James Johnson	Quarterback	1969
Ed Rogers	End	1968
Jim Thorpe	Halfback	1951†
Gus Welch	Quarterback	1975
Glenn S. "Pop" Warner	Coach	1951†

Carlisle Indians Inducted into
the Professional Football Hall of Fame

Player	Position	Year Inducted
Joe Guyon	Halfback	1966
Jim Thorpe	Halfback	1963†

Citizens Savings (originally Helms)
Athletic Foundation

Player	Position	Year Inducted
Lone Star Dietz	Coach	1976
Jim Thorpe	Halfback	1950
Glenn S. "Pop" Warner	Coach	1951

*Lone Star Dietz on 2008 ballot as coach.
†Charter member.

Selected Bibliography

Carlisle Indian Industrial School publications

The Indian Helper, weekly newspaper, 1885-1900.

The Red Man, weekly magazine, 1888-1900.

The Red Man and Helper, weekly combined newspaper and magazine, 1900-1904.

The Arrow, weekly newspaper, 1904-1908.

The Carlisle Arrow, weekly newspaper, 1908-1917.

The Indian Craftsman, monthly literary journal, 1909-1910.

The Red Man, monthly literary journal, 1910-1917.

The Carlisle Arrow and Red Man, monthly combined newspaper and magazine, 1917-1918.

Other School Publications

Alumni Record. Dickinson College, Carlisle, Pa.

Anadarko Yearbook. Anadarko High School, Anadarko, Ok.

Aucola. American University, Washington, D. C.

The Badger. University of Wisconsin, Madison, Wi.

Bizarre. Lebanon Valley College, Annville, Pa.

The Calendar. Hutchinson Central High School, Buffalo, NY.

Catalog. Dickinson College, Carlisle, Pa.

College News. Lebanon Valley College, Annville, Pa.

The Dickinsonian. Dickinson College, Carlisle, Pa.

The Evergreen. Washington State University, Pullman, Wa.

The Franklin and Marshall Weekly. Franklin and Marshall College, Lancaster, Pa.

Georgetown College Journal. Georgetown University, Washington, D. C.

The Hatchet. Washington University, St. Louis, Mo.

HailToPurple.com. Northwestern University, Evanston, Il.

The Hoya. Georgetown University, Washington, D. C.

The Indiana Daily Student. Indiana University, Bloomington, In.

Instano. Indiana University of Pennsylvania.

The Microcosm. Dickinson College, Carlisle, Pa.

Murmurmonte. West Virginia Wesleyan College, Buckhannon, WV.

O. A. C. Barometer. Oregon Agricultural College, Corvallis, Or.

Oriflamme. Franklin and Marshall College, Lancaster, Pa.

The Pharos. West Virginia Wesleyan College, Buckhannon, WV.

The Pow Wow. Washington State University, Pullman, Wa.

The Quittapahilla. Lebanon Valley College, Annville, Pa.

The Rotunda. Southern Methodist University, Dallas, Tx.

The Sophist. Indiana University of Pennsylvania, Indiana, Pa.

The Tiger. Clemson University, Clemson, SC.

Taps. Clemson University, Clemson, SC.

Ye Doomesday Booke. Georgetown University, Washington, D. C.

Books

Alft, E. C. *Elgin: an American history*. Elgin, Il.: Crossword Communications, 1984.

Boren, Lyle H., and Boren, Dale. *Who Is Who In Oklahoma (a biographical history of men and women in Oklahoma life today.)* Guthrie: The Co-Operative Publishing Company, 1935.

Braunwart, Bob, and Carroll, Bob. *The Journey to Camp: the origins of American football*. Huntingdon, Pa.: P. F. R. A., 1997.

Bynum, Mike, ed. *Pop Warner Football's Greatest Teacher: the epic autobiography of major college football's winningest coach, Glenn S. (Pop) Warner*. Football Gridiron Properties Corp., 1993.

Carroll, Bob. *The Tigers Roar: professional football in Ohio: 1903-1909*. Huntingdon, Pa.: P. F. R. A., 1990.

Carroll, Bob, and Braunwart, Bob. *Pro Football: From AAA to '03: the origin and development of professional football in Western Pennsylvania, 1890-1903*. Huntingdon, Pa.: P. F. R. A., 1991.

Carroll, Bob, and Gill, Bob. *Bulldogs on Sunday 1919: twilight of the Ohio League*. Huntingdon, Pa.: P. F. R. A., 1991.

Carroll, Bob, and PFRA Research. *The Ohio League: 1910-1919*. Huntingdon, Pa.: P. F. R. A., 1997.

Cope, Myron. *The Game That Was: the early days of pro football*. Cleveland: The World Publishing Company, 1970.

Crawford, Bill. *All American: the rise and fall of Jim Thorpe*. Hoboken: John Wiley & Sons, Inc., 2005.

Curran, Bob. *Pro Football's Rag Days*. New York: Bonanza Books, 1964.

Danzig, Allison. *Oh, How They Played the Game: the early days of football and the heroes who made it great*. New York: The Macmillan Company, 1971.

Finoli, David, and Aikens, Tom. *The Birthplace of Professional Football: Southwestern Pennsylvania*. Charleston, SC: Arcadia Publishing, 2004.

Fry, Richard B. *The Crimson and the Gray: 100 years with the WSU Cougars*. Pullman: Washington State University Press, 1989.

Gridley, Marion E. *Indians of Today*. Crawfordsville, In.: Lakeside Press, 1936.

Gridley, Marion E. *Indians of Today*. Chicago: Millar Publishing Company, 1947.

Gridley, Marion E. *Indians of Today*. 3rd ed. Chicago: Towertown Press, 1960.

Groshans, Lorraine. *The Complete Borzoi*. New York: Howell Book House, 1981.

Hart, Charles. *Memories of a Forty-Niner (1896-1945)*. Philadelphia: Dunlap Printing Company, 1946.

Heimel, Paul W. *Eliot Ness: the real story*. Nashville: Cumberland House, 2000.

King, C. Richard, ed. *Native Americans in Sports*. Armonk, NY: Sharpe Reference, 2004.

Lester, Robin. *Stagg's University: the rise, decline, and fall of big-time football at Chicago*. Urbana and Chicago: University of Illinois Press, 1995.

Marsh, Scott; Hope Stout, and Debbie Moore, comps. *Here's to the High School on the Hill: a scrapbook of 105 years of Mechanicsburg Indian football*. Mechanicsburg, Oh., 2004.

McCallum, John D., and Pearson, Charles H. *College Football U. S. A. 1869-1971: official book of the National Football Foundation*. Greenwich, Conn.: Hall of Fame Publishing, Inc., 1971.

McClellan, Keith. *The Sunday Game: at the dawn of professional football*. Akron: The University of Akron Press, 1998.

McDaniel, Mike. *Stand Up and Cheer: the official history of du Pont Manual High School, Louisville, Kentucky*. Louisville: Butler Books, 2005.

Newcomb, Jack. *The Best of the Athletic Boys: the white man's impact on Jim Thorpe*. Garden City: Doubleday & Company, 1975.

O'Conner, Candace. *Beginning a Great Work: Washington University in St. Louis*. St. Louis: Washington University in St. Louis, 2003.

Ohio, State of. *The Official Roster of Ohio Soldiers, Sailors and Marines in the World War 1917-1918*. Columbus: The F. J. Herr Printing Co., 1926.

Oriard, Michael. *King Football: sport & spectacle in the golden age of radio & newsreels, movies & magazines, the weekly & the daily press*. Chapel Hill, The University of North Carolina Press, 2001.

Pratt, Richard H. *Battlefield and Classroom: four decades with the American Indian, 1867-1904*. New Haven and London: Yale University Press, 1964.

Ratliff, Harold V. *The Power and the Glory: the story of Southwest Conference football*. Lubbock: Texas Tech Press, 1957.

Roster of the men and women who served in the army or naval service (including the Marine Corps) of the United States or its allies from the state of North Dakota in the World war, 1917-1918. Bismarck: The Bismarck Tribune Company, 1931.

Samuelsen, Rube. *The Rose Bowl Game*. Garden City: Doubleday & Company, 1951.

Smith, Ronald A. *Sports & Freedom: the rise of big-time college athletics*. New York: Oxford Press, 1988.

Steckbeck, John S. *Fabulous Redmen: the Carlisle Indians and their famous football teams*. Harrisburg, Pa.: J. Horace McFarland Company, 1951.

Thisted, Moses N. *Pershing's Pioneer Infantry of World War I*. Hemet, Ca.: Alphabet Printers, 1982.

U. S. Army, Special Staff. *Order of Battle of the United States Land Forces in the World War (1917-19): Zone of the Interior*. Washington: U. S. Government Printing Office, 1931.

Warner, Glenn Scobey. *A Course in Football for Players and Coaches*. Carlisle, Pa.: Warner, 1912.

Warner, Glenn Scobey. *Football for Coaches and Players*. Stanford University: Warner, 1927.

Weyand, Alexander M. *The Saga of American Football*. New York: The Macmillan Company, 1955.

Wheeler, Robert W. *Jim Thorpe: world's greatest athlete*. Norman: University of Oklahoma Press, 1975.

Whitman, Robert L. *Jim Thorpe and the Oorang Indians: N. F. L.'s most colorful franchise*. Defiance, Oh.: The Marion County Historical Society, 1984.

Whittingham, Richard. *Sunday Mayhem: a celebration of pro football in America*. Dallas: Taylor Publishing Company, 1987.

Williams, E. I. F. *Heidelberg, democratic Christian college 1850-1950*. Menasha, Wi.: The George Banta Publishing Company, 1952.

Williams, Eustace. *That Old Rivalry: Manual vs. High School 1893-1940*. Louisville: John P. Morton & Co., 1940.

Winchester, Shirley Phillips, Jones, Saundra Phillips, and Hall, Helen Phillips. *The Heritage of Caldwell County North Carolina Volume I*. Winston-Salem: Hunter Publishing Company, 1983.

Witmer, Linda F. *The Indian Industrial School: Carlisle, Pennsylvania 1879-1918*. Carlisle, Pa.: Cumberland County Historical Society, 1993.

Periodicals

Baine, William. "Key to Shorthand Notes," *The Stenographer*, 8 no. 7 (1898: 186.

Becker, Carl M. "Jim Thorpe and the Oorang Tribe," *Timeline*, 20, no. 5 (2003): 2-17.

Braunwart, Bob; Bob Carrol and Joe Harrigan. "Going to the Dogs," *The Coffin Corner*, 3 (1981).

Grange, Red. "The College Game is Easier," *The Coffin Corner*, 25 no. 6 (2003): 3-8.

Kish, Bernie. "Sideline Chatter," *Journal of the College Football Historical Society*, 21 no. 2 (2008).

Phelon, William A. "On the Home Stretch of the Great 1912 Pennant Races," *Baseball Magazine*, 9 no. 6 (1912): 15-24.

Prescott, Archie. "Time Tunnel," *College Football Historical Society Newsletter*, 3 no. 3 (1990): 11-12.

Plummer, Maggie. "Long Time Sleep: the stuff legends are made of," *Char-Koosta News*, October 25, 2007.

Santorum, Rick. Senate resolution 91, *Congressional Record – Senate*, S4607, 1999.

Scott, Hugh. "The Oklahoma Athletic Hall of Fame," *Oklahoma Today*, 22 no. 2 (1972): 13-17.

Shoemaker, Arthur. "Hominy Indians," *Oklahoma Today*, 17 no. 4 (1967): 7-9.

Tanner, Virginia ed. "B&O's Indian Engineers," *B&O Magazine*, 38 no. 10 (1952): 1-3, 46.

Wells, Fred. "Foot Ball Season Brings Memories of Mt. Pleasant," *The Arrow*, 3 no. 11 (1920): 12.

Ephemera

Minnesota, University of. *Souvenir Program, Minnesota vs. Wisconsin*, November 15, 1902.

Minnesota, University of. *Souvenir Program, Dedication of Northrop Field*, September 19, 1903.

Minnesota, University of. *Souvenir Program, Michigan vs. Minnesota*, October 31, 1903.

Southern Methodist University. *Texas Aggies -6 vs. S. M. U. -17 Official Program*, November 11, 1922.

Index

Printed in the United States
206182BV00003B/88-261/P

9 780977 448678